a Headpress Book

Hollywood Haunts The World

An investigation into the cinema of occulted taboos

Robert Guffey

A HEADPRESS BOOK
First published by Headpress in 2025, Oxford, UK
headoffice@headpress.com

HOLLYWOOD HAUNTS THE WORLD
An Investigation into the Cinema of Occulted Taboos

Book layout: G. FOLEY
Cover design: MARK CRITCHELL mark.critchell@gmail.com
With thanks to Gareth Wilson and Jennifer Wallis

10 9 8 7 6 5 4 3 2 1

A CIP catalogue record for this book is available from the British Library

ISBN 978-1-915316-37-0 paperback
ISBN 978-1-915316-38-7 ebook
ISBN NO-ISBN hardback

Hollywood Haunts The World

An investigation into the cinema of occulted taboos

Dedicated to J.E. Liebenau

Contents

"Artists have always been the real purveyors of news."

—John Dewey, *The Public and Its Problems*, 1927

"By its nature, esoteric thought looks for the hidden aspects of the universe, assuming that nature is composed of multiple connections not easily recovered by natural science's usual means of investigation. Esotericism was like a counterforce to the emerging mechanistic view of the world fostered by science in the early modern period, espousing an organic view of nature, seeing the world as a complex whole with many intricate parts interacting in marvelous ways. The purpose of life for the esotericist was to decode these interactions, called 'correspondences,' unraveling the wisdom found in symbolic and natural associations. The elements of nature corresponded to parts of the body and to the planets. Understanding these relationships meant that the esotericist could unlock the mysteries of reality. Also, biblical and other ancient texts were assumed to have hidden meanings that could be revealed through careful esoteric study showing the correlation of scriptural details with the natural world.

"Once these secrets were unveiled, esotericists were led into yet deeper meanings. The world would never yield all of its secrets, but the persistent investigator could find more and more truth, like peeling the layers of an onion that has no core. This great knowledge was a precious, even sacred possession, and esotericists felt that only the mature in mind and heart should have access to it. Their secrecy, then, was also a matter of the elite or initiated protecting wisdom from people who were not trained to appreciate that wisdom."

—W. Michael Ashcraft, *The Dawn of the New Cycle*, 2002

"Artists to my mind are the real architects of change, and not the political legislators who implement change after the fact."

—William S. Burroughs, *William S. Burroughs: A Man Within*, 2010

Foreword

By Gary D. Rhodes

DIFFICULT, IF NOT impossible to believe, but it's true. In the early years of the twentieth century, when nickelodeon film theaters spread like wildfire across the United States, many feared that American cinema was fated to become French cinema. There were far too many American nickelodeons and viewers for far too few American films. Importing so much French product from the likes of Pathé Frères resulted in what Richard Abel has called the "Red Rooster Scare,"[1] the bird in question being Pathé's logo.

But then American companies sweetly caught up to the demand for indigenous eye candy, in part because they relocated to California where the wonderful weather allowed them to shoot year round, and in part because producers like Thomas H. Ince merged their screen art with the assembly line, creating veritable and verifiable dream factories. They manufactured unforgettable cinema.

Did their process rely on repetition? Absolutely, and not only with story types (the word "genre" being discussed in *Moving Picture World* as early as 1910[2]), but also of structure, leading one critic in 1911 to complain that American films too often had "happy endings."[3] No roosters allowed; just winner, winner, chicken dinner.

It was during this period, incidentally, that Americans coined the slang word "movie," a corruption of the industry term "moving picture."[4] And how important that slang became. As Sam Shepard explains in *True West* (1980), "In America we make movies. Leave the films to the French." And as François Truffaut admitted, "in the final analysis, we loved American cinema because the films all resembled one another."[5] Incidentally, the subtitle of Richard Abel's book reads, "Making Cinema American."

But more must be said, given that American cinema essentially became Hollywood cinema, a place beyond time and space, a land beyond land. Maybe that's why the Hollywood sign no longer needs to read "Hollywoodland." For that matter, most studios and production companies haven't actually been located in the Hollywood city limits.

And the viewers of Hollywood film are truly global. Consider the wonderfully strange logo that Universal Pictures used during the early 1930s: a stratospheric plane circles our planet, a visual sign of the company name "Universal." Forget red roosters: Hollywood became the cock of the walk, a position it has retained for over a century.

More than once I have been outside of America and have heard people from various countries in the same conversation speak about their love of filmmakers ranging from Frank Capra to Steven Spielberg. All Hollywood films are universal pictures, even if that's spelled with a lower case "u." Hollywood cinema is Earthen cinema.

And Hollywood has indeed haunted the world. Time after time, decade after decade, Hollywood has haunted a world that desperately needed and wanted to be haunted by it.

Which brings us to Robert Guffey's magnus opus. Given that Guffey's name is on the cover of this book, it would be easy to make the mistake of believing that he writes about film, but that isn't the case. I have admired Guffey's work for many years, and I have said more than once in print that he and Cormac McCarthy are my two favorite living American novelists. (And with McCarthy deceased, alas, Guffey is the last man standing.)

But when it comes to the cinema, I would repeat, Robert Guffey does not write about it. That would wrongly suggest he's apart from his subject, like a journalist covering the moon landing or a historian writing about the Peloponnesian wars.

By contrast, Guffey is forever in dialogue with the cinema, a conversation between him and, well, never, ever just a single film, but Hollywood and American tradition, history, and context. As much as anyone, Guffey reminds us of the maximus of all maxims when it comes to art: there is no text without context. Eat a Madeleine at Guffey's café, and he'll remind you of the ghosts of cinema past.

To our great benefit, however aged these cinematic ghosts are, however much we believe we know them, they are paradoxically new to us in these pages. As Guffey explains, they represent a "secret history of the world," one that he has finally decoded for us.

Hollywood Haunts the World is necessarily a film history, driven not by pure chronology or dry data, but rather a well-mapped cartography that lets us sail amongst phantom ships, those unmoored by their filmmakers and harboring at theatrical shores across the globe.

Herein Guffey is the adventurous archeologist who excavates a forgotten tomb as well as the learned scholar who translates its hieroglyphs for us.

Herein Guffey is the explorer who rediscovers precious scrolls as well as the gnostic who interprets them.

In his Introduction, Guffey informs us that "the truth, often by accident, will shine through." It does, time and again in this volume, not by accident, but by Guffey's wonderfully kabbalistic conversation with Hollywood cinema.

Put another way, Robert Guffey not only serves up the Madeleines, but also provides the requisite lime blossom tea.

Hollywood has truly haunted the world. So too should this book, one of the best ever written on American cinema.

Gary D. Rhodes, Ph.D.
Oklahoma City, Oklahoma
2024

Introduction

Hollywood Haunts the World

THE SECRET HISTORY of the world can be decoded through film. More so than any other medium, perhaps due to its populist roots, film records the cultural taboos of the day in such a way that any future sociologist/psychologist/archaeologist/anthropologist can easily view a random film from generations before and gain important insights into the unique mores of the society that produced it. That film does this unintentionally, more often than not, is an added bonus to the future scholar. After all, the primary concern of any filmmaker, even those with hidden agendas, is to tell an *entertaining* story that will be embraced by the masses. This is why studying films can tell us more about history than poring over the minutiae of a thousand presidential speeches. When one is most concerned with telling an entertaining story rather than fashioning a persuasive speech or an opaque legal document that will resist the scrutiny of a battery of attorneys, one tends to relax and let one's guard down. And the truth, often by accident, will shine through.

Paleontologists are always pleased to discover a new prehistoric insect preserved in amber. Celluloid is a medium tantamount to amber, but instead of preserving ancient insects it preserves taboos. The true shape, the true shadow, of any culture can best be defined by knowing—and, hopefully, *understanding*—what that culture deems to be unacceptable to discuss or even think about in polite society. Taboos have always been dark mirrors that reflect the hidden face of society, the Dorian Gray monstrosity lurking just beneath the surface.

What you refuse to face defines you; it can even destroy you. This is why popular art so often functions as a safety valve, creating temporary autonomous zones in which taboos can be contemplated within an acceptable context—a context that's so seemingly innocuous that even the most staid, church-going senior citizen wouldn't even realize (at a conscious level) that potentially mind-shattering taboos are being broached. Film allows one to have a brief dance with taboos without needing to feel the lingering shame of having wallowed in the filth of the forbidden.

Some "primitive" cultures believe that the spirits of the dead surround us all the time, influencing our paths through life, the decisions that we make, our attitudes toward the nature of existence itself. Since we don't consider ourselves to be "primitive" or "superstitious," however, such beliefs have never been popular in Western culture. And yet we most certainly are influenced by insubstantial phantoms that co-exist with us on a daily basis, and these phantoms are called films: poltergeists produced by the off-kilter minds and wild talents of modern day druids living in a sacred grove called "Hollywood," angelic thought forms and demonic ghosts that are projected out into the ether of the real world to wreak havoc—or bring psychic balance—to a spiritually starved culture. In the early 1900s, movie palaces replaced churches and cathedrals as the spiritual centers of the world. For a long time now Hollywood has functioned as the Vatican of the twentieth and twenty-first centuries. Just as a papal decree could influence the thoughts of millions in the medieval world, the ghosts of Hollywood often slip into the neural pathways of the masses and slowly—imperceptibly—alter human consciousness itself.

In the twenty-first century, Hollywood haunts the world; it has done so ever since its inception. The ghosts that Hollywood produces on a daily basis are undoubtedly the most important exports produced by the United States. Why? Because, unlike drugs and guns and bombs, they don't seem subversive or dangerous in any way. Because they are welcomed with open arms even by fanatically religious regimes in the Middle East who don't admit to indulging in such evil Western decadence—in public, that is. Because they are time-released thought-bombs that are eagerly *sought out* by their intended targets. After all, one needn't waste millions of black budget dollars on covertly smoking out one's enemies when the enemies themselves insist on inviting the fatal bombs into the back rooms of their own opulent palaces where said infernal devices are detonated within the context of their own lavish entertainment systems. Why do any work when the enemy can do it for you and even more enthusiastically than *you* can?

Hollywood Haunts the World

Cultural landscapes are shifting all around the globe, but this process is happening so gradually that most people are unaware of it and often see no hope for a better future in certain authoritarian areas of the world. But the future is only brought about by dreams. Dreams can change the attitudes of a culture far more effectively than official sanctions or "uffish thoughts" (as Lewis Carroll might have said) or orders-from-on-high. People change only if they want to change. And sometimes only the military-industrial-*entertainment* complex can spark that desire for change. One might call this process cultural osmosis, or mass thought control, or one might be so bold as to see it from the perspective of "primitive" man: In the long run, invisible entities guide our destinies. The ghosts decide. Dreams point the way.

This book is a map by which one can trace these cultural shifts throughout the twentieth century—as well as the beginning of the twenty-first century—via the etheric medium of film. Each chapter explores a different cultural taboo and how society's collective attitude toward that taboo is reflected in the frozen amber known as celluloid—sometimes through only a single film, sometimes through multiple films over the course of many years or decades.

Chapter One, "What's at the End of Main Street?," analyzes the increasing ascendency of "Gnostic cinema" in both American and foreign films beginning as far back as the silent movies of the 1920s, such as Buster Keaton's *Sherlock Jr.*, and progressing all the way to the final years of the twentieth century (e.g., Alex Proyas' *Dark City*, Peter Weir's *The Truman Show*, Gary Ross's *Pleasantville*, the Wachowskis' *The Matrix*, David Cronenberg's *eXistenZ*, Josef Rusnak's *The Thirteenth Floor*, Tom Tykwer's *Run Lola Run*, Stanley Kubrick's *Eyes Wide Shut*) and the first years of the twenty-first century (e.g., Cameron Crowe's *Vanilla Sky*, Mark Pellington's *The Mothman Prophecies*, Francisco Athié's *Vera*, M. Night Shyamalan's *The Village*, Christopher Nolan's *Inception,* Jennifer Kent's *The Babadook,* Scott Derrickson's *Doctor Strange*, Steven Spielberg's *Ready Player One,* Anthony and Joe Russo's *Avengers: Infinity War,* Matt Shakman's *WandaVision,* Larry Wade Carrell's *Girl Next,* and Guillermo del Toro's *Nightmare Alley*).

In Chapter Two, "The Box in the Desert: Budd Boetticher, *Breaking Bad,* and the Twenty-first-century Western," I unveil the highest hopes of the past and the worst fears of the present by juxtaposing Budd Boetticher's subtly subversive Westerns of the 1950s with Vince Gilligan's iconoclastic television series, *Breaking Bad.*

Chapter Three, "The Brain(s) that Killed Kennedy," digs deep into the world of interconnected conspiracy theories with a comprehensive analysis of the John F. Kennedy assassination (as well as the related subject of illicit US government mind control programs) as seen through a series of disparate American films, some of which predict the assassination, many of which comment retroactively on the crime. The films under discussion include Edward L. Cahn's *The Creature with the Atom Brain,* John Gillig's *The Gamma People,* John Frankenheimer's *The Manchurian Candidate,* Alan J. Pakula's *The Parallax View,* William Richert's *Winter Kills,* John Carpenter's *They Live,* Oliver Stone's *JFK,* and Jonathan Demme's reimagined version of *The Manchurian Candidate.* This analysis begins in the 1950s and takes us all the way forward to the first decade of the twenty-first century.

In Chapter Four, "One Chants Out Between Two Worlds: *It Came from Outer Space, Twin Peaks,* and the Legacy of Jack Parsons," we examine the considerable—though little known—influence rocket scientist/ceremonial magician Jack Whiteside Parsons exerted upon the books and films of writers and directors such as Jack Arnold, Ray Bradbury, Mark Frost, and David Lynch.

In Chapter Five, "The Man from Planet X," we examine a cultural taboo that's alive and well today (that of the subject of Unidentified Flying Objects and extraterrestrial visitors) in the form of Edgar G. Ulmer's groundbreaking 1951 science fiction film, *The Man from Planet X.* Sometimes, taboos disguise themselves in seemingly innocuous forms. To the comfortable, to the privileged, taboos can be utterly invisible. It's very easy—from the perspective of the present—to look back at the nineteenth century and understand that one of the most controversial cultural taboos at that time was, just as an example, the women's suffrage movement; however, it's far more difficult to identify the most sensitive taboos of the society in which you yourself live.

Back in 2002–03, while ensconced in the MFA program at CSU Long Beach, one of my fellow creative writing students turned to me one day and said, "You know, I'd like to write some cutting edge stuff, but all the big taboos have already been broken. All the important fights were fought and won in the sixties. There's nowhere else to go." My tongue and eyeballs almost tumbled out of my skull. My colleague's naivety was charming but mindboggling. Needless to say, the idea that there are no more taboos in the world is laughable, and yet my colleague's bizarre lament is evidence that this does indeed *need* to be said. If there were truly no more cultural taboos, if all the barriers of pure rational thought had been obliterated by the cultural revolution of the 1960s, then I certainly wouldn't get into quite as much trouble as I tend to do with my own writing.

Media theorist Marshall McLuhan once said, "We don't know who discovered water, but we know it wasn't a fish. A pervasive medium, a pervasive *environment*, is always beyond perception."[6] Because fish are surrounded by water all the time, they are not even aware of its existence. Similarly, we are surrounded by the effects of a thousand cultural taboos every single day, but those of us who are unaware of our surroundings tend to assume that the major strictures limiting freedom of expression somehow magically disappeared after the advent of the civil rights movement in the 1960s. Taboos, however, are not only political in nature. They don't begin and end with the admittedly serious issue of human rights (violations of which still occur on a daily basis in this and many other countries, despite the utopian world view of my colleague).

The fact is that the most important taboos today are *exopolitical* in nature, and UFOs represent a perfect example of this. Just because UFOs are a common topic of endless cable documentaries, some people might suggest that the issue is not in any way taboo. They would be incorrect. Just bring up the topic of UFOs at a cocktail party, or at an academic conference, or at a random business meeting, and watch almost everyone in the room grow increasingly uncomfortable, as if one had insulted the recently deceased grandmothers of every individual within hearing range.

If, on the other hand, you bring up the subject on a metropolitan bus, you might very well find several average people who are more than willing to discuss the subject of UFOs without any qualms whatsoever. Is this because people who ride buses are subnormal? No, it's because people who ride buses aren't quite as invested in the official narrative of how the world is supposed to operate and function. I've noticed, for example, that the people most ill-equipped to deal with genuinely taboo subjects are those whose lives are most dependent on the perpetuation of the American university system, i.e, college professors.

A story: One day, in the midst of a conversation about cultural taboos, I brought up the topic of UFOs in a literature class during my final semester in the MFA program at CSU Long Beach. Within seconds the professor was clearly writhing in discomfort and wished to either a) teleport out of the room, or b) move on to a whole new topic. Unbidden, a fellow student chose this moment as an opportunity to ask everybody in the class how many of them believed that UFOs existed and might be vehicles from another planet. Slowly, somewhat reluctantly (as if trained to keep this belief to themselves their entire lives), almost every single student in that classroom raised his or her hand. The professor was nonplussed, to say the least. The thought balloon floating above the learned professor's head was self-evident: *Can such things be? In a college classroom such as* this? *Are these the dark depths to which American culture has sunk?* It was quite fascinating watching an entire world view crash down around someone's head within a matter of seconds. Such ruptures of the solipsistic thought patterns instilled in academicians will occur more and more frequently as we move further and further into the twenty-first century, as technology advances to the point where *we ourselves* become the very extraterrestrials we're so concerned about. Chapter Five of this book, "The Man from Planet X," documents the very beginnings of the paradigm shift that so traumatized the professor on that spring day over twenty years ago.

In Chapter Six, "Golden the Film Was—Oh! Oh! Oh! Cinema and the Art of Perception Management," we investigate the documented links between Hollywood and a plethora of American intelligence agencies going at least as far back as World War II.

In Chapter Seven, "Invisible Ghosts," we examine the intangible (and yet very real) impact that André Breton's revolutionary theories of Surrealism and Dadaism had on the twentieth century thanks to Breton's innumerable unwitting accomplices—i.e., screenwriters, directors, cinematographers, actors, etc.—toiling on the fringes of the Hollywood mainstream at the same time that the central tenets of Surrealism were also impacting the culture of America through far more respectable venues. This chapter focuses in particular on a disconnected series of accidentally avant-garde B-films starring the Hungarian actor Bela Lugosi throughout the 1930s, forties and fifties.

It should be noted that Bela Lugosi casts a powerful shadow over this peripatetic investigation. The film historian Dr Gary D. Rhodes once suggested that the history of Lugosi represents the history of Hollywood itself:

> If Francis Ford Coppola once likened Bram Stoker's novel *Dracula* (1897) to the history of cinema, I believe much the same could be said of Lugosi. An investigation into his career yields insight into early nar-

> rative film, Germany's Weimar period, and the transition the cinema made from the stage. Lugosi represents the genre-specific nature of the classical Hollywood paradigm, as well as the fickle qualities of the public that consumes it. The tragic aspects of his life and career highlight the inevitability of the star system: the dark spaces of silence between the frames.[7]

The more I've studied Hollywood, and the career of Lugosi, the more I'm convinced that this is true. If any film icon encompasses the bipolar extremes of success and failure, artistic triumph and public humiliation, pathetic desperation and unearthly perseverance so interwoven in the enduring myth that is Hollywood, it is Lugosi. Over the course of this investigation, Lugosi emerged as my familiar—the otherworldly guide leading me on to deeper insights into the cinematic world of the occulted taboo. Since Lugosi's most famous role was that of a Faustian, demonic prince who hypnotically led the naïve and the curious into a web from which they could never escape, it seemed appropriate somehow that he became my Virgil, pointing me in the direction of the amorphous cobwebs and shadows lurking in the hidden corners of Hollywood history and thus bringing further occulted taboos to my attention. It turns out that some webs are not necessarily traps, but labyrinths that require careful navigation on the part of the explorer. (Bela, therefore, deserves thanks for not leading me astray as he has so many other unwary victims.)

In Chapter Eight, "The Suppressed Science of Dr. Mirakle," we trace the public's incrementally shifting attitudes towards Charles Darwin's theory of evolution through an analysis of wildly diverse horror films—ranging from highbrow German Expressionism to bottom-of-the-barrel giant monster flicks—beginning in the 1920s and culminating in the early 1960s.

Chapter Nine, "Here Among the Dead," focuses on the 1920s when the medium of film began to crawl out of its infant stage. The dream I've chosen to conclude our journey is Victor Sjöström's little known—but extremely influential—film from 1921 titled *The Phantom Carriage*. Masquerading as a Christian parable, this film dares to explore the ultimate taboo—the question of what awaits us after death—through the transgressive metaphysics of Theosophy and related fringe philosophies that took advantage of Victorian millennialism to begin challenging the Judeo-Christian ethos that had dominated the Western mind for so long. This challenge was still progressing in the early 1920s, and the nascent medium of film was the perfect vehicle by which to deliver an alternative message of Theosophical universalism over autocratic monotheism. These metaphysical, Gnostic quandaries lead us all the way to our present time…

…A time in which the secret history of the world is at last decodable through film. Anyone with eyes and ears and a working medulla oblongata can easily see through the opaque veil Hollywood casts over its sacred grove to protect its magicians from the merely *curious* who wish to gawk in awe and fear at the strange nature of the rituals performed within. But rest assured, folks, there's nothing to be afraid of here. These illusionists are Wizard-of-Oz-like mountebanks, and their ghosts aren't real at all. But that doesn't mean these cleverly constructed phantoms will not have an effect on you, your life, or your future.

Perhaps it's not a bad thing that these celluloid spirits carry such a heavy burden on their insubstantial shoulders—the Promethean/Herculean burden of remaking the world, of softening the blow of successive paradigm shifts, of reordering the cultural landscape in this dimension and the next.

After all, somebody has to do the dirty work. No living being wants the job. So the magicians conjure up their little ghosts to float out into the night and work their magic on the slumbering hordes.

Let's just hope these ghosts are friendly and wise. Let's hope they know what they're doing when they take it upon themselves to haunt the subconscious of the world.

And if not… well, then, perhaps it's time we make some ghosts of our own.

After all, this whole magician-business is open to anybody with the proper tools.

The proper wand.

The proper dreams.

Welcome, initiates, to the sacred grove that lies behind the flickering, silver veil… and the beginning of our investigation into a century (or more) of occulted taboos…

The Phantom Carriage is black and silent, drawn by a skeletal horse that sometimes seems transparent in the pale moonlight. The driver is an old man with a gaunt face and a long beard. He has haunted eyes, filled with the memories of a million corpses (and a million more beyond that). The Phantom Carriage is not bound by time or space. It rolls through the centuries in what would seem to you or me to be mere seconds. One moment the Carriage is trundling through the ancient, dilapidated cemeteries of Sweden; the next it's in Paris, France in 1845, retrieving the beaten remains of a prostitute from the bottom of a dark river that's kind and soft and rocks one to sleep gently and asks no pay from its numerous young victims; the next moment the Carriage and its helpless driver are in World-War-II-era, small town America, collecting its murdered wards from a large house—where anything can happen (and usually does)—owned by a tortured old man who can't move past the death of his disloyal wife; the next it's in the moors of Scotland in the early 1950s, picking up the diminutive corpse of what might be the Carriage's most unusual passenger of all: a dead extraterrestrial who has crash landed on Earth and has been met with nothing except distrust and greed and cruelty; the next it's on Millionaire Row in Pasadena, California where a man who's half-scientist and half-magician has just transformed himself into a pillar of iridescent flame; the next it's in Dallas, Texas in November of 1963 on a gray, rainy afternoon—within the dead end curves of a parade route that goes nowhere at all—to scoop up the shattered, red-and-white skull fragments of a ritually sacrificed leader more akin to a king than a president; the next it's in the barren deserts of the Old West, piling up corpses of cowboys and Indians alike until the desiccated flesh melts into a single, shapeless mass under the harsh and unforgiving rays of the Western sun; the next it's rolling off the edge of Main Street and floating in the depths of what appears to be the infinite blackness of deep space. Still, the Carriage continues its journey despite the fact that the driver no longer knows if he's steering his vehicle through the reality in which he began his journey oh so long ago. The driver shrugs. "No matter," he seems to say. In whichever reality he and his spectral horse find themselves, death exists. Death is the one constant throughout the known (and unknown) multiverse. The one immutable truth. The ultimate taboo that can be shattered by no man, dead or alive or in between.

The driver snaps the reins of his undead steed and quickens the pace, despite the fact that he knows speed alone will not draw him any closer to the end of a task that has no real conclusion.

Not in this universe.

Or the next.

Or the next…

Chapter 1

What's at the End of Main Street?

The Struggle between the Artificial and the Real in Recent Gnostic Cinema

1. Precursors of the Non-real

SINCE THE RELEASE of Alex Proyas' *Dark City* in February of 1998, there have been an unusual amount of "reality-bending" films in which the world as we know it turns out to be a clever fraud perpetuated on the main character(s), usually for nefarious reasons. In fact, there have been so many of these films lately that one could almost call it a subgenre in itself, as vital to the cultural zeitgeist of the twenty-first century as zombie flicks and superhero extravaganzas. One might call this subgenre "Gnostic cinema," since many of these films reflect the core aspects of Gnostic mythology.

According to Rev. Stephan Hoeller, author of *Gnosticism: New Light on the Ancient Tradition of Inner Knowing*:

> Gnosticism holds that human beings are essentially not the product of the material world [...]. [The first Gnostics] believed that the human body originates on earth but the human spirit has come from afar, from the realm of the Fullness, where the true Godhead dwells. A human being consists of physical and psychic components, which are perishable, as well as a spiritual component, which is a fragment of

> the divine essence, sometimes called the divine spark [...]. People are generally ignorant of the divine spark residing within them [...]. Modern esoteric teachers (notably G. Gurdjieff) have capitalized on this Gnostic theme, representing humanity as a throng of sleepwalkers. Awakening from this sleep is the combined result of our desire for liberation and the supernal help extended to us [...] [by] divine men, or messengers of Light.[1]

What human beings perceive as "reality," according to the Gnostic model, is a clever illusion orchestrated by the Archons, "inferior cosmic being[s] ruling over and imposing limitations on creation."[2] Hoeller writes, "Anything that causes us to remain attached to earthly things, including the mental concepts we hold, keeps us in enslavement to these lesser cosmic rulers."[3] These Archons are, in turn, ruled over by the Demiurge, an imperfect architect "of limited wisdom" who built the flawed material world in which humans are forced to exist.[4]

Marshall McLuhan, the author of *Understanding Media* and numerous other books analyzing the detritus of popular culture, often liked to quote this line from James Joyce's 1939 novel *Finnegans Wake*: "Pastimes are past times."[5] In other words, that which is popular usually reflects the trends of the past, not the present. For example, this Gnostic-tinged "reality-bending" theme so prevalent in popular cinema today was a favorite of science fiction novelist Philip K. Dick throughout the 1950s, sixties, seventies, and early eighties, but it took about seventeen years after Dick's death in 1982 for Hollywood to wholeheartedly pick up on the idea. (We can extend the implications of this even further: If one wants to know what types of films Hollywood will be making in the future, read the most outré and obscure novelists of today. I suspect that the works of Steve Aylett and Jack Womack, to name just two examples, are representative of the cinema's future.)

There are precursors to this theme in the cinema, of course. One could go all the way back to the classic 1924 comedy, *Sherlock Jr.*, in which a young projectionist (Buster Keaton) merges with the virtual world of the cinema by willingly stepping through the screen and becoming a part of the film in progress. As early as the 1920s, the film community was already aware that the line between the real and the non-real was beginning to blur; however, one would have to fast forward over forty years to find a more sophisticated example. During the late 1960s, various episodes of Patrick McGoohan's cutting edge

Joseph M. Schenck presents
BUSTER KEATON
in SHERLOCK, Jr.
A METRO PICTURE

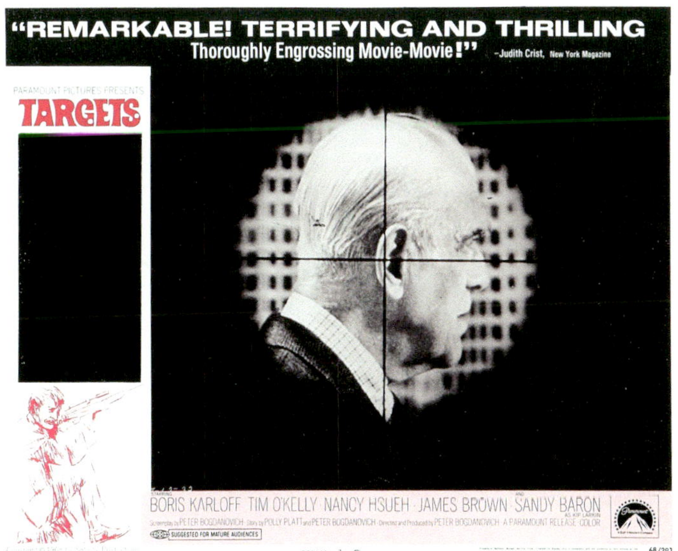
"REMARKABLE! TERRIFYING AND THRILLING
Thoroughly Engrossing Movie-Movie!" -Judith Crist, New York Magazine
PARAMOUNT PICTURES PRESENTS
TARGETS
BORIS KARLOFF · TIM O'KELLY · NANCY HSUEH · JAMES BROWN · SANDY BARON
SUGGESTED FOR MATURE AUDIENCES
68/291

television series, *The Prisoner*, involve the protagonist, Number Six (McGoohan), being trapped in elaborate virtual reality environments (though of course they are not referred to by that name) without his knowledge. See, for example, the episodes titled "A, B and C" and "Living in Harmony" (produced in 1967).

Only a year later, in 1968, Peter Bogdanovich's first film, *Targets*, contains one of the most postmodern cinematic moments up to that point. Crazed Vietnam vet, Bobby Thompson (Tim O'Kelly), assaults a drive-in theater in Reseda, CA with a high-powered rifle during the premier of a B-flick called *The Terror* starring Byron Orlok (Boris Karloff), an aging horror star who's making a swan song public appearance at the theater in order to promote his final film on the night before his retirement. Thompson begins picking off moviegoers from a sniper's nest near the top of the screen. The massacre stops only after Thompson accidentally drops his ammunition from his nest. He crawls down the screen and onto the ground in order to retrieve the ammo. Before he can begin reloading the rifle, however, he sees an enraged Orlok limping toward him from a nearby limousine. Enraged by the sniper's actions, Orlok throws caution aside and begins marching feebly towards the sniper armed with nothing more than a cane. Thompson glances up at the massive screen and sees Orlok's celluloid image mirrored there (in a scene from *The Terror*). Both Orlok the cinematic character and Orlok the human being are wearing tuxedoes and walking with a cane. Thompson grows confused. Suddenly, he can't tell the difference between the actual and the virtual. He reloads his weapon and begins shooting at the on-screen Orlok, leaving the real Orlok unharmed. The real Orlok snatches the gun away from Thompson and slaps him across the face, like a stern father disciplining a naughty child. Thompson, a mass murderer (first in Vietnam, and now again at home), crumples into a pathetic ball and begins weeping like an infant. "Is *that* what I was afraid of?" Orlok asks no one in particular, the actor's penultimate line in the film.

This scene not only prefigures the mass shootings so prevalent today, but also the confusion between the virtual and the real so often exhibited by such shooters before finally giving up and committing suicide. This theme becomes more prevalent in the early eighties, with such diverse films as *The Ninth Configuration* (1980), *Videodrome* (1983), *Brainstorm* (1983) and *Dreamscape* (1984), but there were far too few of these appearing on the screen at the time to claim that any of them were part of a genuine pattern.

Not until 1998 does that pattern become obvious.

2. Dark City

AS IS THE case with any trend in Hollywood, the film that kicks off the wave is usually the best. I think it could be successfully argued that this is the case with *Dark City*.

A financial disappointment when it was first released at the beginning of 1998, *Dark City* is a multifaceted, black jewel of a film that offers up deeper insights upon each viewing. It's possible that *Dark City* was released just a few months before the culture was ready to accept the unsettling implications of such a philosophical story. Unlike almost every other film under discussion in this chapter, *Dark City* does not stop short of exploring the outermost edge of its most disturbing—and enlightening—implications. Many of the films that fall into this "reality-bending" pattern will conclude on an ambiguous question mark. The main characters, having woken up to the realization that they're trapped in an artificial environment, will often end up in a state of confusion. Are they *still* trapped in an artificial reality or aren't they? They haven't progressed far beyond the state of ignorance at which they began their journey, and therefore the audience hasn't progressed far as well. We emerge from the journey wondering why we even began in the first place.

Dark City, however, is not content to leave its protagonist in a perpetual state of bewilderment. By the end of the film, our hero has woken up to the most paradigm-dissolving revelation that a human being could possibly hope to comprehend: With the knowledge that the physical world is malleable, one should not withdraw into fearful or ambivalent confusion, but should instead realize that reality is merely a canvas that can be altered according to the whims of the painter, and *each* of us can be that painter.

In *Dark City*, the protagonist, John Murdoch (Rufus Sewell), wakes up naked in a bathtub, uncertain as to who he is or how he got there. His quest to retrieve his memories uncovers a vast conspiracy perpetuated by a secret society of extraterrestrials known only as the "Strangers" who can inhabit the bodies of dead humans. In order to study the exact nature of the human soul, these hive-minded aliens (to whom the concept of individuality is a tantalizing mystery) are performing a complicated experiment on a group of abducted humans by shifting their personalities from body to body. Murdoch prematurely wakes in the middle of one of these body-shifts, causing the experiment to go awry. Unlike his fellow abductees, Murdoch has buried within him the same latent psychic powers utilized by the aliens to alter the reality around them. After coming to grips with this, Murdoch is able to use these abilities to overwhelm his extraterrestrial abductors and wrest away control of the artificial satellite upon which he and his fellow humans have been imprisoned. Murdoch journeys from complete ignorance to torturous confusion to ultimate illumination; the painful revelation that the world around him is a fake is by no means a curse, but instead a blessing, for Murdoch can take control of his personal reality and reshape it into whatever form he prefers. This secret society of "Strangers," therefore, emerges as a metaphor for the faceless authoritarian forces that attempt to control all of us on a daily basis by extinguishing—or slowing down—our imaginations. As Jon Rappoport, a painter and investigative journalist, writes in his *sui generis* book *The Secret Behind Secret Societies* (synchronistically released the same year as *Dark City*):

> The secret behind secret societies and cults and hierarchical religions is the artistic creation of a universe which is then frozen for mass consumption.
>
> The pressure of major elites, in government, in war, in power-struggles, involves the slowing down of the imagination so that a central mural about reality can be set in concrete. From it, an agenda can be spun off. The agenda inevitably involves control of large numbers of people.[6]

In an interview published near the end of his book, Rappoport comments on this idea further:

> The Formula of the Secret Society [is] to make a world out of art and convince us that it's the best one, the only one [...] to live in. And then there is the far-ranging use of our own imaginations, and what we can do with that [...]. I know beyond a shadow of a doubt that we can each create many, many realities, and I have seen the result of that on many fronts. [...] I'm basically an artist who got involved in politics and found that art was the trick of the ages. That's what they have used to ensnare us, and we have the creative power to invent our way out of that, and we need to do it. That's really the bottom line [...]. I'm trying to move ahead and put more muscle in the imagination, I'm trying to extend the range and the power and show [...] that we can make our own worlds.[7]

Though not widely praised upon its initial release, in retrospect *Dark City* emerges as the perfect cinematic metaphor for the vital process of conjuring new worlds though the power of the untethered imagination, a uniquely *human* quality that's rapidly being stamped out beneath the collective boot of philistines and social engineers who want nothing more than to impose institutionalized helplessness on the spirit of the human race while themselves unaware of—and, paradoxically, frustrated by—their own utter lack of originality and creativity. As Diane di Prima once wrote in her poem "Rant," "THE ONLY WAR THAT MATTERS IS THE WAR AGAINST/THE IMAGINATION." Combine this declaration with Charles Bukowski's following one-sentence poem titled "Art": "As/the/spirit/wanes/the/form/appears." The "Strangers" are Bukowski's dreaded and oppressive "form" manifested into reality—the dystopian and yet ultimately optimistic reality of Proyas' *Dark City*.

3. The Truman Show

ABOUT FOUR MONTHS after the release of *Dark City* came *The Truman Show*, written by Andrew Niccol and directed by Peter Weir. Perhaps its deft mixture of comedy and drama made it more palatable for mainstream audiences than the unrelenting neo-noir strains of *Dark City*. In *The Truman Show*, Jim Carrey plays Truman Burbank, a twenty-nine-year-old insurance salesman who doesn't realize he's the star of a popular reality TV show conceived by a monomaniacal producer named Christof (Ed Harris). The first orphaned child to be adopted by a corporation, Truman has no conception that the world he's inhabited since birth is the largest sound stage ever constructed for a television show. After various anomalies alert him to the reality of his predicament, Truman tries to escape his prison by taking a sea voyage. His suspicions concerning the fakeness of the world around him are confirmed when the bow of his boat rams into the horizon which is revealed to be nothing more than a painted backdrop. Truman runs his hands wonderingly along the surface of the canvas, at which point Christof at last elects to confront his creation and gives him the choice to lead an unpredictable life of individuality beyond the painted backdrop or remain in the ordered paradise of Truman's manufactured hometown. Ultimately, Truman chooses freedom and steps through a door in the canvas that leads to the outside world.

After the final credits have begun to roll, one can't help but wonder about Truman's fate in the real world. Imagine the mother of all post-traumatic stress disorders experienced by this now terminally paranoid man who would be wondering if every subsequent friend or acquaintance is actually an actor in disguise. Does he get a job doing exactly the same thing he was doing in his home town? I can't help but recall a story I heard my psychology teacher tell one day during my first semester in college: Horses that grow up walking the same circle within a fence their entire lives, when moved from a smaller track to a bigger one, invariably walk the same exact circle despite having the ostensible freedom to graze farther. This doesn't bode well for Truman's final fate.

Andrew Niccol and Peter Weir, like Christof himself, take their creation to the edge of the canvas, but don't bother to give him the skills to survive in the real world. Unlike with John Murdoch, we never see Truman awaken fully to the ultimate implications of his revelation. Is Truman now an illuminated human being or just a slave who has traded in one prison for another?

4. Pleasantville

ALMOST ALL OF the films under discussion here are obsessed with the geographical contours of reality. The protagonists of each of these stories eventually meet up against the physical edge of their individual prisons. Often it is this moment of physical contact with "The Edge" that marks the character's illumination, his or her moment of *gnosis*. One is reminded of the famous nineteenth century wood engraving (known as the "Flammarion Engraving") in which a robed traveler is pushing his way headfirst through a domed barrier of stars into an otherworldly realm of spinning wheels and glowing orbs and endless clouds and blazing light. In *Dark City*, when John Murdoch finally reaches the edge of his artificial prison, he responds by slamming his way through a brick wall with a sledgehammer. Beyond lies nothing except the perpetual blackness of outer space. In *The Truman Show*, the outermost edge of the protagonist's world turns out to be a painted canvas-horizon depicting the point where the sea meets the sky. In 1998's other "reality-bending" offering, the edge of the world lies at the very end of Main Street.

Gary Ross's *Pleasantville* was released four months after *The Truman Show*. As with *The Truman Show*, *Pleasantville* was a tremendous

What's at the End of Main Street?

financial and critical success, perhaps due to its mixture of social satire and straightforward melodrama. In this film two teenagers from the 1990s, David (Tobey Maguire) and his sister Jennifer (Reese Witherspoon), are transported into a fictional 1950s television show by a supernal helper (angel?) played by Don Knotts. The show is called *Pleasantville* and is an object of obsession for the main character, David. He prides himself on the obscure details he knows about the show and thinks that his less-than-ideal existence in present day America is far inferior to the orderly life depicted in this long defunct sitcom. These assumptions are challenged when David is forced to deal with the authoritarian strictures imposed upon Pleasantville. Unlike a fascist society that exists within the real world, however, Pleasantville boasts a certain advantage (or disadvantage, depending on your point of view) in that the inhabitants of the town were never aware of their potential freedoms in the first place. From the very moment of conception, the consciousness of each individual has been limited by the standards and practices of 1950s American television.

David and Jennifer adjust gradually to life in Pleasantville. While doing so, both attempt to understand the rules that govern this new world. One day Jennifer is in class listening to a geography lesson delivered by her high school teacher. The extent of the geography lesson consists of a description of Main Street and Elm Street and nothing else. At one point, clearly frustrated and bewildered, Jennifer raises her hand and asks her teacher a key question: "What's at the end of Main Street?"

The teacher responds that nothing lies at the end of Main Street. It simply loops back upon itself. All of her classmates seem satisfied with this absurd answer. Jennifer is not. Of course, her classmates are not aware that the answer is absurd. They've never known anything other than Main and Elm.

Unlike in the other movies of this subgenre, it is not the protagonists of *Pleasantville* who are unaware that they're trapped in an artificial environment, but all the characters who *surround* them. David and Jennifer's presence in the town introduces the concept of free will to the sleepwalking inhabitants, changing Pleasantville for the better... Or, perhaps, for the worst? It's possible that some might walk away from the film thinking that the presence of David and Jennifer has polluted Pleasantville's precious bodily fluids forever. Indeed, it's this very dissatisfaction with the seemingly chaotic trends of modern life that have pushed the mass mind deeper and deeper into itself—into a solipsistic bubble impervious (at least temporarily) to the mutations the outside world continues to undergo on a minute to minute basis.

5. The Matrix, The X-Files and eXistenZ

SIGNIFICANT SIMILARITIES ARE shared by the films that inhabit this subgenre, one of which is the disturbing notion that one must commit suicide or murder someone else in order to a) prove that one is living within an artificial environment, or b) escape the artificial environment forever.

In 1993 I heard a radio interview with Robert Dobbs, a scholar of the works of media theorist Marshall McLuhan, in which he casually predicted that in the near future many people (particularly teenagers) would have to kill other people in order to distinguish whether or not these other individuals are real. I couldn't help but recall this prediction when, on April 20, 1999, only twenty days after the release of the Wachowskis' "reality-bending" film, *The Matrix* (a hyperkinetic hybrid of 1980s cyberpunk tropes and the highly stylized aesthetics of ultraviolent Japanese martial arts movies), video game aficionados Eric Harris (aged eighteen) and Dylan Klebold (aged seventeen), while dressed in black trench coats reminiscent of the ones worn by hacker-revolutionaries Neo (Keanu Reeves), Morpheus (Laurence Fishburne) and Trinity (Carrie-Anne Moss) in *The Matrix*, staged their own bloody "action-adventure" film on the campus of Columbine High School in Littleton, Colorado, resulting in the shooting deaths of twelve students and one teacher and the double suicide of Harris and Klebold.

Nineteen days after the Columbine High School massacre occurred, on May 9, the popular television show *The X-Files* aired an episode titled "Field Trip" written by John Shiban, Vince Gilligan and Frank Spotnitz, and directed by Kim Manners, in which the protagonists, Fox Mulder (David Duchovny) and Dana Scully (Gillian Anderson), are trapped in separate hallucinations induced by spores released from a patch of strange psychedelic mushrooms that are, unbeknownst to Mulder and Scully, slowly digesting the pair alive. When Mulder begins to doubt the nature of his reality, his method of testing its veracity is to shoot his boss, Frank Skinner (Mitch Pileggi), in the chest. This unexpected murderous assault causes the artificial reality to recede and enables Mulder and Scully to escape their paralysis. One wonders, however, what Mulder would have done if his peculiar assumption had been wrong. Perhaps the same thing that Harris and Klebold, and Jacob Tyler Roberts (the Clackamas, Oregon shooter of December 11, 2012), and Adam Lanza (who perpetuated the Newtown, Connecticut elementary school massacre of December 14, 2012) and so many other recent mass shooters have done: commit suicide.

Like hallucinogenic spores released by cryptozoological mushrooms, something was definitely in the air at the end of the twentieth century. As a significant portion of the Earth's population held its breath in anticipation of a computer-generated apocalypse called "Y2K" (i.e., the dire prediction that computer systems dependent on two-digit, date-related processing would go haywire at the moment the year '99 rolled over to '00, thus causing computers all around the world to shut down just past midnight on January 1, 2000), the human race decided that it could no longer trust its own senses, that its traditional assumptions about reality were no longer valid, that the world was not at all what it appeared to be. And the only way to bust out of this future dystopia known as the present was to kill others or kill ourselves.

If these movies are to be believed, once human beings are unencumbered by reality, the first thing they want to do is learn how to kill more efficiently. This is certainly true in *The Matrix* as well as in David Cronenberg's *eXistenZ*, coincidentally released twenty-three days after *The Matrix* and only three days after the Columbine massacre. More complex than its far more popular counterpart, *The Matrix*, *eXistenZ* presents several artificial realities embedded within each other. It's also the only "reality-bending" film I'm aware of that blatantly advertises its debt to Philip K. Dick within the story itself via a brief reference to "Perky Pat," a character in Dick's 1965 novel, *The Three Stigmata of Palmer Eldritch*.

At the end of the film, after having tumbled from one chimerical scenario to another, anti-virtual-reality terrorists, Allegra Geller (Jennifer Jason Leigh) and Ted Pikul (Jude Law), assassinate a famous game designer named Yevgeny Nourish (Don McKellar) for his crimes against reality. In the last moments of the film, as Geller and Pikul point their guns at one of Nourish's obsessive fans (Oscar Hsu), the nonplussed devotee asks them if they're still engaged in Nourish's virtual reality scenario. The confused expressions on the faces of Geller and Pikul suggest that they themselves aren't certain of the answer. As with *The Thirteenth Floor* and Christopher Nolan's 2010 film *Inception* (about which, more later) we end where we began: adrift in limbo.

6. The Thirteenth Floor

IN MAY 1999'S *The Thirteenth Floor*, directed by Josef Rusnak and co-written by Rusnak and Ravel Centeno-Rodriguez (based on Daniel F. Galouye's 1964 novel, *Simulacron-3*), a computer scientist named Douglas Hall (Craig Bierko) discovers that the Earth, or what he thinks is the Earth, is nothing more than a computer simulation. This is revealed to him when he drives to the very edge of the modern metropolis in which he lives to discover that his world is surrounded by a tremendous green wall composed of zeros and ones. At the conclusion of the film, Hall believes he's made his way into the primary Earth that created his simulated realm, though the entire film ends on yet another question mark when this final idyllic scene blinks out like a computer screen that's been suddenly switched off by an unseen programmer.

Oddly enough, in 2012 a team of physicists at the University of Washington published a peer-reviewed scientific paper titled "Constraints on the Universe as a Numerical Simulation" that takes Daniel Galouye's premise quite seriously indeed. What follows is an excerpt from a December 16, 2012 Discovery.com article titled "Are We Living in a Computer Simulation?" in which science reporter Ray Villard writes about this theory extensively:

> In 2003, British philosopher Nick Bostrom published a paper that proposed the universe we live in might in fact really be a numerical computer simulation. To give this a bizarre *Twilight Zone* twist, he suggested that our far-evolved distant descendants might construct such a program to simulate the past and recreate how their remote ancestors lived.
>
> He felt that such an experiment was inevitable for a supercivilization. If it didn't happen by now, then it meant that humanity never evolved that far and we're doomed to a short lifespan as a species, he argued.
>
> To extrapolate further, I'd suggest that artificial intelligent entities descended from us would be curious about looking back in time by simulating the universe of their biological ancestors.

"DAZZLING! PLAYFULLY PROFOUND! HOT, FAST AND POST-HUMAN!"
-Janet Maslin, THE NEW YORK TIMES
RUN
LOLA
RUN
arte
SONY PICTURES CLASSICS

> As off-the-wall as this sounds, a team of physicists at the University of Washington (UW) [headed by Prof. Martin Savage] recently announced that there is a potential test to see if we actually live in [a computer-generated environment]. Ironically, it would be the first such observation for *scientifically hypothesized* evidence of intelligent design behind the cosmos.[8]

I suppose it shouldn't be surprising that such science fictional speculations have escaped the printed page and silver screen and have now invaded the minds of respected physicists in the real (?) world. As is so often the case with science, fiction (and art in general) often point the way.

If the notion that the world we inhabit is the product of an advanced computer program strikes one as disturbing, perhaps one can take an uneasy form of solace in this supposition from biologist J.B.S. Haldane: "[M]y own suspicion is that the Universe is not only queerer than we suppose, but queerer than we *can* suppose,"[9] which suggests that if a team of physicists at UW dreamed up the theory then it's probably safe to assume it's not an accurate representation of reality.

From Haldane's perspective, at least, the human imagination does have certain limits.

7. Run Lola Run

THOUGH NOT ALL of the films under discussion here are science fiction, the vast majority of them could be classified as a type of storytelling that definitely falls within the general parameters of the genre. But there are other films, decidedly *non*-science-fictional, released in the United States since *Dark City*, that could be included within this survey. On June 18, 1999, only a few weeks after the debut of *The Thirteenth Floor*, we saw the US premiere of Tom Tykwer's *Run Lola Run* starring Franka Potente, a film that's definitely about alternate realities, albeit in a metaphorical way.

Lola, a young woman living in Berlin, is forced to raise 100,000 marks within twenty minutes in order to prevent the murder of her boyfriend by disgruntled drug dealers. We see the same suspenseful scenario play out, with slight variations, three times in a row. The first two scenarios end with the death of the boyfriend as well as

Lola. Each time she fails, Lola (much like John Murdoch in *Dark City*) wills herself into a new reality in order to make the attempt all over again. With the third try, Lola finally manages to align disparate synchronistic events in such a way that what was once chaos becomes order.

Like an ancient alchemist experimenting with different chemical combinations, Lola uses nothing more than her will and indefatigable spirit to experiment with various combinations of events, people, and places until reality aligns in rough accordance with her wishes. Though no alien "Strangers" stalk the edge of Lola's consciousness, this is still a story about the malleability of reality just as valid—indeed, if not more so—than almost any strictly science fictional exploration of the idea heretofore seen in film.

8. Eyes Wide Shut

ONLY A MONTH later, in that banner year of "artificial reality" films, on July 16, 1999, Warner Brothers released Stanley Kubrick's final film, *Eyes Wide Shut*. Co-written by Kubrick and Frederick Rafael, based on a 1926 novella titled *Traumnovelle* by Arthur Schnitzler, the film explores the overwhelming power of dreams, as evidenced by the title itself. New York physician Bill Harford (Tom Cruise) meanders in a very *Alice-in-Wonderland*-like way (despite the preponderance of *Wizard of Oz* references that permeate the film) through a metaphorical labyrinth of mirrored corridors that constantly force him to confront his own previously unexplored sexuality and repressed carnal desires. Thanks to a synchronistic meeting with an old college friend, Harford is given a once-in-a-lifetime chance to infiltrate an exclusive party thrown by a powerful secret society who engage in ancient occult sex rituals. Harford's presence at the bacchanal is discovered by the masked occultists who proceed to threaten his life, as well as the lives of his family, if he reveals what he has seen. The problem is this: Harford himself is not sure of what he's seen. Throughout the film Harford and his wife, Alice (Nicole Kidman), wrestle with the thin line between fantasy and actuality, temptation and satiation, in the form of both dream and reality, though it's not clear to the solipsistic Harford how much of what he experiences is genuine or simply staged for his benefit alone.

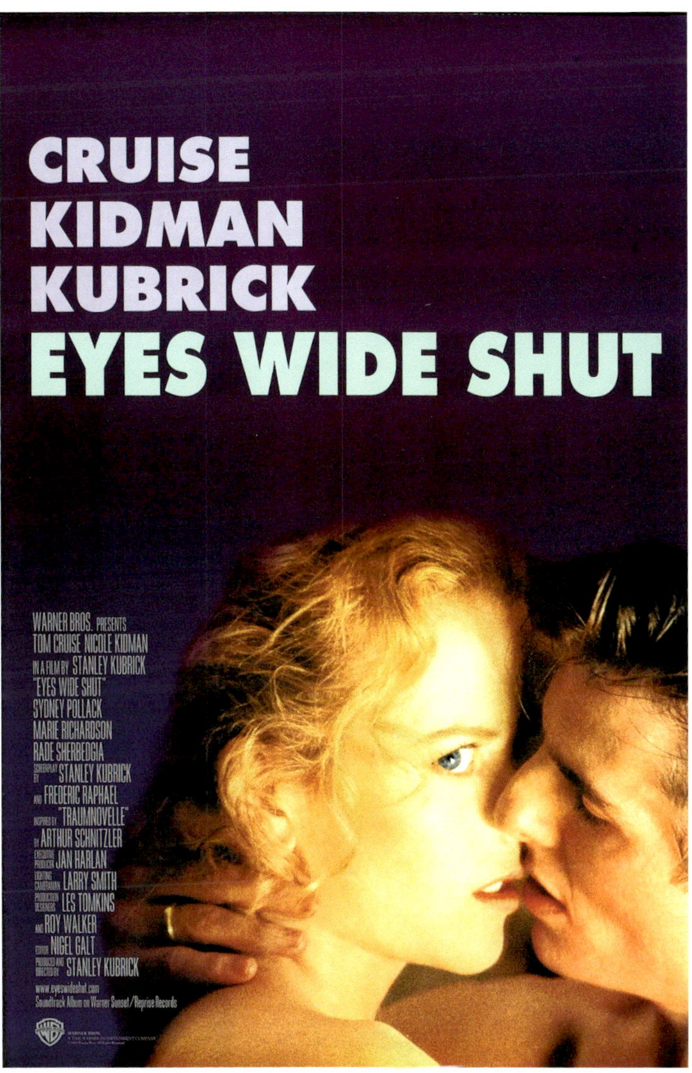
CRUISE
KIDMAN
KUBRICK
EYES WIDE SHUT
WARNER BROS. PRESENTS
TOM CRUISE NICOLE KIDMAN
IN A FILM BY STANLEY KUBRICK
"EYES WIDE SHUT"
SYDNEY POLLACK
MARIE RICHARDSON
RADE SHERBEDGIA
SCREENPLAY BY STANLEY KUBRICK
AND FREDERIC RAPHAEL
INSPIRED BY "TRAUMNOVELLE"
BY ARTHUR SCHNITZLER
EXECUTIVE PRODUCER JAN HARLAN
LIGHTING CAMERAMAN LARRY SMITH
PRODUCTION DESIGNERS LES TOMKINS
AND ROY WALKER
EDITOR NIGEL GALT
PRODUCED AND DIRECTED BY STANLEY KUBRICK
www.eyeswideshut.com
Soundtrack Album on Warner Sunset/Reprise Records
WARNER BROS.
A TIME WARNER ENTERTAINMENT COMPANY

Though by no means a "virtual reality" film à la *The Matrix* and *The Thirteenth Floor*, Kubrick's film follows a pattern of cinematic tales about individuals forced to navigate a confusing maze of fantasies disguised as reality (and vice versa).

9. Vanilla Sky

THAT MOST OF these "reality-bending" films are blood-spattered, ultraviolent narratives is telling. The body count in *The Matrix* series, *eXistenZ* and *Inception* is astronomical; however, the assumption that freedom from the basic laws of reality would inevitably lead to the desire (and/or the necessity) to kill or commit suicide is, perhaps, not too far off-base. After all, the first virtual reality shooter games were designed by the military to teach soldiers how to end lives more effectively.[10]

In Cameron Crowe's 2001 film *Vanilla Sky*, Tom Cruise is David Aames, a handsome young playboy who has inherited his late father's lucrative publishing firm. Disfigured in a car accident, Aames opts out of his unbearable existence and uses his tremendous wealth to place himself in cryogenic suspension until technology advances to the point where his disfigurements can be fixed. This state of suspended animation induces extremely complex lucid dreams that, in Aames' case, soon devolve into nightmares. In this *faux* reality constructed by his own subconscious, his feelings of inadequacy and self-loathing drive him into madness, causing him to suffocate the only woman he ever loved, Sofia (Penélope Cruz), a name that might be a nod to the "Sophia" of Gnostic mythology, the goddess who represents divine reality in a corrupt world of fakery.

Within the dream, a representative of Life Extension, the cryogenic company, explains to Aames that the only way to break out of his limbo state is to kill himself. He chooses to do so by jumping off the roof of a skyscraper. The last scene is an extreme close-up of Aames opening his eyes and viewing unaltered reality for the first time in 150 years, though the audience itself is restricted from seeing the exact nature of this reality.

As with Truman Burbank, David Aames' final fate in this brave new world remains in doubt.

10. The Mothman Prophecies

IN JANUARY OF 2002, forty-two days after the release of *Vanilla Sky*, Mark Pellington released his peculiar horror film, *The Mothman Prophecies*, scripted by Richard Hatem based on the 1975 nonfiction book of the same name by John A. Keel. At first glance this film may not seem to belong in this discussion, but if one looks closely enough one will find that this film is riddled with references to reality being akin to a dream world that can be distorted and re-ordered by higher powers—both malignant and benign—unknown to us in our daily mundane lives. The blurring of the line between dream and reality begins early on when we're told that the film is based on true events.

The source material of the film, Keel's book *The Mothman Prophecies*, is considered by many to be one of the classic works of UFOlogy. Upon encountering it for the first time, one feels the exhilarating thrill of unexpectedly tumbling down a strange rabbit hole and ending up in a topsy-turvy world parallel to our own. Far more than just a standard recitation of saucer sightings by dubious witnesses, Keel's book is in fact a postmodern, metaphysical detective story that prefigures—and, indeed, perhaps even *influences*—the small town surrealism of Mark Frost and David Lynch's genre-warping television series *Twin Peaks* (1990–91) and its sequel, *Twin Peaks: The Return* (2017). Pellington's film could in no way ever approach the level of high strangeness found within the book; however, the film does offer up its own charms, if taken on its own terms. Though by no means a cinematic classic of the *fantastique*, when one takes into consideration the unusual restraint the film exhibits, one could legitimately claim that this particular twenty-first-century horror film is probably the most comparable to the style of quiet horror pioneered by Val Lewton in the 1940s. (Lewton admirers will no doubt consider this to be a blasphemous statement, but keep in mind that this observation says more about the dearth of quality horror films released in the first decade of the twenty-first century than it says about the relative worth of Pellington's film.)

Ultimately, this film deals with loss. After losing his wife to a seemingly random car accident, investigative journalist John Klein (Richard Gere) is drawn by supernatural forces to a small town called Point Pleasant in West Virginia which happens to be experiencing a sudden upsurge of paranormal events including UFO sightings, precognitive dreams, mysterious phone calls, ominous doppelgangers, and the relentless onslaught of a weird beastie called "Mothman" (or at least "that's what the Ukrainians called him," as Alexander Leek, played by Alan Bates, says at one point in the film).

It turns out that the Mothman is a harbinger of death. His appearances foretell great tragedies. Gordon Smallwood (Will Patton), a "contactee" who encounters the creature several times, eventually kills himself in part because he can no longer tell the difference between dream and reality. "I've been lyin' awake at night," the confused witness tells Klein not long before his suicide. "I feel like I'm sleeping, but I'm awake."

The Mothman, or forces aligned with it/controlling it, seem to be trying to warn the small town of what will soon occur: that thirty-six people will die during the collapse of a bridge on Christmas Eve. Kline's presence in the town prevents the taking of one more victim, a small town sheriff named Connie (Laura Linney). As in most "reality-bending" films, one's fate seems to be controlled by an outside force. In *The Mothman Prophecies*, however, we're never quite certain of the exact nature of that force. But perhaps that's appropriate, since in the original book John Keel makes no definite conclusions about it either. How do you explain something that's been specifically designed from the beginning—by someone or something beyond our ken—to be an eternal mystery?

The events in Point Pleasant vexed Keel for years. They so disturbed him that it took him seven years to actually sit down and write the book based on the extensive notes he had taken at the time. As Keel wrote in August of 2001, the filmmakers "managed to squeeze the basic truths into their film. Not an easy task. But the truth is always the most difficult thing to sell."[11] In a January 24, 2002 interview with *Coast to Coast* AM radio host Art Bell, Keel commented that the film was at its best—and most accurate—when portraying the mental dissolution of an average human being driven slowly insane by forces beyond his comprehension. Though the film's protagonist starts out as a man who's confident he understands the nature of reality, he soon transforms into an unhinged seeker after truth who's not even certain the world exists as we understand it.

Keel claimed this central dissolution was the core of his own personal experiences in West Virginia, and these emotional upheavals were successfully carried over onto the silver screen.

11. Vera

SOMETIMES IN THESE films, death itself creates the artificial reality as opposed to dissolving it. In 2003's *Vera*, a beautifully phantasmagoric film written and directed by Francisco Athié, an unnamed miner (Marco Antonio Arzate) accidentally causes a cave-in while working alone deep in an isolated tunnel beneath Mexico. Cut off from the rest of the human race, the old man spends his final seconds undergoing a series of spectacular transformations that force him to confront various symbols of the transcendent from cultures far-flung. Like the late mythologist Joseph Campbell, author of *The Hero with a Thousand Faces*, Athié seems intimately familiar—and equally respectful—of myths and legends from a variety of different religions and nationalities: Mayan, Egyptian, Christian, Japanese, Greek, Russian, Italian, Spanish, etc. The title itself, *Vera*, is representative of all these cultures. According to Athié, *Vera* "means trust and faith in Cyrillic (Russian), the truth in Italian, the side of the road in Spanish, and it is a very beautiful feminine name. Therefore, in a way, it points to the faith and trust you need to follow a path that is true to your own perception of the otherworldly."[12] Though each individual consciousness interprets the reality of death in its own way, the miner in *Vera* is a true Everyman who experiences all of them at the same time. He is an unconscious and accidental shaman who undergoes the ultimate journey for the benefit of those of us not yet ready for the final (?) transformation. *Vera* is a visually poetic guide, attempting to prepare all of us for our inevitable confrontation with "the otherworldly." Athié, like Alejandro Jodorowsky and Jean Cocteau before him, is an unusually sensitive and ambitious director who doesn't seem to recognize the unnecessary boundaries most artists (not just filmmakers) seem compelled to impose upon their individual visions. Many artists are content to merely replicate works that have come before them with only slight variations added to the final product. Almost every film released these days is a sequel, remake, or mutant progeny of some better film originally produced decades ago. Not so with Athié's *Vera*.

It's very clear that Athié's main inspirations are not other films, but a long literary tradition of metaphysical odysseys that include Dante's *Inferno*, Lewis Carroll's *Alice in Wonderland*, George MacDonald's *Lilith*, H.P. Lovecraft's *The Dream-Quest of Unknown Kadath*, and Flann O'Brien's *The Third Policeman*. Athié's substantial palette draws upon images that invoke genetic memories of ceremonies performed by high priests in the dark to ease the transition between worlds while also utilizing more postmodern images reminiscent of new myths and legends like science fictional aliens that grace the covers of supermarket tabloids. This collision of the old and new, while playing out against such breathtaking backdrops as the real life caverns of Yucatan, is both disorientating and comforting at the same time, thus mirroring the confusing and yet ecstatic sensation of surrendering to Death itself. *Vera*, almost totally ignored in the United States, is worth more than a thousand tent-pole summer blockbusters. Even though Athié's film deserves much wider success, perhaps its subtle treasures were only meant to be seen by the few, just as the ancient rituals that transmitted faltering souls across the river Styx were also performed only for those who desperately needed them.

12. The Village

THE GEOGRAPHICAL BOUNDARIES of consensus reality inform the story structure of M. Night Shyamalan's 2004 release, *The Village*. In this film, what seems to be a nineteenth-century small town community is in reality a careful recreation established in the 1970s by an American History professor named Edward Walker (William Hurt). Fed up by the social chaos of the post-Vietnam era, Walker concludes that it would be best to create a mini-utopia based on the values of an earlier, simpler time. The Village has been built within a wildlife preserve beneath a no-fly zone that will never be disturbed by the outside world. Only the Elders of the town are aware of the true nature of the Village and manufacture folklore about monsters who live in the surrounding woods in order to discourage the rest of the town from ever venturing into the outside world. The protagonist of the film, a young blind woman named Ivy (Bryce Dallas Howard), uncovers the counterfeit nature of the Village after she manages to escape, encounters a high wall outside the woods, climbs over, and is abruptly thrust into "the future" when we, the audience, see that she's surrounded by a modern highway populated by cars. Temporarily, at least, Ivy manages to break out of the artificial contours of her own personal Main Street.

Unlike *Pleasantville* and all the other movies on this list, *The Village* ends on a peculiar note; it seems to suggest that remaining within the womb of the Village is preferable to interacting with the real world, that willful ignorance is sometimes better than truth. In many ways *The Village* is a reactionary version of *The Truman Show*, the Edward Walker character being portrayed as a wiser and more benevolent Christof.

13. Inception

IN CHRISTOPHER NOLAN'S blockbuster 2010 heist flick/science fiction mash-up, *Inception*, "dream architect" Dominick Cobb (Leonardo DiCaprio) must win his freedom by invading the dreams of a wealthy businessman's heir, Robert Michael Fischer (Cillian Murphy), and implanting the self-destructive idea to disintegrate the conglomerate founded by Maurice, Robert's father. Saito (Ken Watanabe), Fischer's arch business rival, has hired Cobb to carry out this unusual form of industrial espionage with the promise that he will use his substantial political influence to lift a false murder charge against Cobb that has, until now, prevented him from returning to the United States and his two children.

At one point Cobb explains that, in the past, he and his wife, Mal (Marion Cotillard), took their explorations of the dream realms too far, resulting in them no longer being able to tell the difference between dream and reality. Because time moves more slowly in the dream worlds, they end up spending an entire lifetime there. It's only when they choose to commit suicide, by lying down on a stretch of railroad track and allowing themselves to be run over by a high-speed train, that they're able to escape the endless limbo realm of the dream. Unfortunately, upon returning to the real world, Mal's sanity begins to disintegrate. She's convinced that she and Cobb never escaped the dream at all. She becomes so convinced of this disturbing notion that she leaps to her death from a hotel window in order to return to "real" reality. Instead, she ends up dead.

Later in the film, Cobb is by necessity drawn back down to limbo. His new partner, a talented young dream architect named Ariadne (Elliot Page)—a symbolic name no doubt chosen to evoke the Greek myth in which the goddess Ariadne helps the hero, Theseus, navigate a labyrinth inhabited by a savage Minotaur—follows Cobb deep into the dream in order to help him escape. He convinces Ariadne that he'll be able to find his own way out and encourages her to return

LEONARDO DICAPRIO
KEN WATANABE JOSEPH GORDON-LEVITT MARION COTILLARD ELLEN PAGE TOM HARDY CILLIAN MURPHY TOM BERENGER AND MICHAEL CAINE
YOUR MIND IS THE SCENE OF THE CRIME.
A FILM BY CHRISTOPHER NOLAN
INCEPTION
FROM THE DIRECTOR OF THE DARK KNIGHT
WARNER BROS. PICTURES PRESENTS
IN ASSOCIATION WITH LEGENDARY PICTURES A SYNCOPY PRODUCTION A FILM BY CHRISTOPHER NOLAN LEONARDO DiCAPRIO "INCEPTION" KEN WATANABE
JOSEPH GORDON-LEVITT MARION COTILLARD ELLEN PAGE TOM HARDY CILLIAN MURPHY TOM BERENGER AND MICHAEL CAINE MUSIC BY HANS ZIMMER EDITED BY LEE SMITH, A.C.E.
PRODUCTION DESIGNER GUY HENDRIX DYAS DIRECTOR OF PHOTOGRAPHY WALLY PFISTER, A.S.C. EXECUTIVE PRODUCERS CHRIS BRIGHAM THOMAS TULL PRODUCED BY EMMA THOMAS CHRISTOPHER NOLAN
LEGENDARY PICTURES
WRITTEN AND DIRECTED BY CHRISTOPHER NOLAN
inceptionmovie.com
WARNER BROS. PICTURES
EXPERIENCE IT IN IMAX

to the real world before it's too late. She does this by leaping to her death from a skyscraper. Cobb spends a lifetime wandering through the dream until yet another mortal injury, this time a fatal gunshot, releases him from purgatory one last time.

Though this film is a heady and ambitious conglomeration of all the "reality-bending" films already examined here, combining the previously mentioned geographical boundaries of the dream realms with the notion that only suicide or death can break one from the restraints of the non-real, *Inception* never really manages to transcend its own self-imposed limitations. Like *eXistenZ* and *The Thirteenth Floor*, *Inception* ends on a question mark, leaving the audience to decide whether or not Cobb has successfully broken free of limbo by the final scene. From a thematic perspective, no progress has been made. Ultimately, the arc of the film ends up being nothing more than an inward spiral into indeterminacy.

Here to Go

EVEN MORE RECENT films than *Inception*—ranging from the relatively obscure to the undeniably popular—continue this theme, this Gnostic hell/limbo of recurring nightmares regarding sentient beings trapped in artificial environments. One can detect the theme, in an obliquitous way, throughout the Academy-Award-winning film, *The Social Network* (released only a few months after *Inception*), a darkly absurd drama that—if sent back in time only a few decades—would no doubt be interpreted by twentieth-century filmgoers as a satirical, Kurt-Vonnegut-esque cautionary tale about technology run amok in a futuristic dystopia where vacuous, ego-driven citizens are addicted to spying on themselves (and others) via a peculiar invention with the rather unlikely moniker of "Facebook" while wasting the majority of their lives enmeshed in an artificial world in which perfect mediocrity is the only goal venerated—or even deemed reachable—by a generation of imagination-starved organic robotoids who deal with the emptiness of their quasi-lives by sitting in front of glowing computer screens, interacting with phantoms, and pretending to be characters they've seen only on TV. One can detect it throughout *Summer Wars* (released in the United States in December of 2010), a Japanese animated film about an eleventh grade computer whiz named Kenji Koiso who must use his advanced math skills to escape a digital world called "Oz" and defeat a misanthropic Artificial Intelligence program known as "Love Machine"; one can detect it throughout Disney's "fun-for-the-whole-family" 2012 blockbuster *Wreck-It Ralph*, the story of preprogrammed video game characters who rebel against the arbitrary limits imposed upon them by their nameless, faceless creator—and yet, despite this individualistic streak, decide in the end that a virtual life in a virtual world is the best of all possible existences.

Perhaps most significant is Phil Lord and Christopher Miller's *The Lego Movie* (2014), which appears on the surface to be nothing more than a facile children's movie designed to generate sales for a multi-million dollar toy line; it turns out, however, that it's also one of the most purely Gnostic parables produced within the confines of recent American cinema. The plot of the film revolves around a toy named Emmet (Chris Pratt) who experiences a moment of *gnosis* during which he catches a glimpse of "the Man Upstairs," the Demiurge-like deity who originally constructed the flawed world that has kept Emmet and his friends imprisoned all their lives. Only by transcending the artificial and penetrating the outer dimensions of the actual does Emmet ("Emet," by the way, is the Hebrew word for "Truth") succeed in saving his world from the myopic, authoritarian deity that controls its fate. Like the protagonist in *Wreck-It-Ralph*, at the conclusion of the film Emmet chooses to remain a slave in the virtual world despite having undergone this genuine moment of *gnosis*.

In Jennifer Kent's *The Babadook* (2014), we find ourselves immersed in a dark, claustrophobic parable about how the human mind can deceive itself without even intending to do so. This is a fictional illustration, in metaphorical terms, of what Gnostics call "the generation of error."[13] In his 2006 book *Not In His Image: Gnostic Vision, Sacred Ecology, and the Future of Belief*, John Lamb Lash writes:

> In the Sophia mythos the Archons emerge because of Sophia's plunge into elemental matter, before the Goddess morphs into the earth and continues her Dreaming as Gaia [...]. This unforeseen event is called "the generation of error" because the anomaly triggered by Sophia's plunge introduces a subliminal effect in the human mind, exaggerating our natural tendency to err and shifting it beyond the scale of correction. The presence of the Archons in the solar system *dangerously widens the margin of human error*, thus impacting the way we learn and evolve. At the very least, the Archons can be taken for a brilliant parapsychological metaphor that explains how

THEY COME IN PIECES
THE LEGO MOVIE 2
THE SECOND PART
ONLY IN THEATERS
FEBRUARY 2019
SEE IT IN REAL D 3D

> humans can think and act out of scale, inhumanely [...].
>
> No matter what one makes of the Archons in a literal sense, the Gnostic theory of error is certainly one of the supreme achievements of human reasoning. The Gnostic seers insisted that Archons cannot control or manipulate us unless we give them power to do so. This happens when we do not optimize nous, our endowment of divine intelligence. Our omission is *their* salvation. Gnostic error theory states three simple, interlocking truths: (1) humans are creatures who learn by making mistakes; (2) to learn from our mistakes we must detect and correct them (hence our collaborative role in Gaian evolution and Sophia's "correction"); and (3) when we fail to detect and correct our mistakes they can extrapolate wildly and spin us beyond human limits. The Archons intrude at just that point where we let our errors go uncorrected, and lend their deviant force to what is already going off course, taking us with them in a wayward spiral. Without our cosmic cousins in the picture we would still commit errors, but we would always be able to stand back and correct our course before we go too far out of alignment with Gaia and our own potential.[14]

In *The Babadook*, this spiritual conflict between unconscious self-deception and divine revelation is dramatized by the precarious psychological state of our protagonist, Amelia Vannick (Essie Davis), who's struggling to raise her six-year-old son, Samuel (Noah Wiseman), as a widowed single mother. Years before, on the very same night Samuel was born, Amelia's husband perished in a car accident. It's clear that Amelia associates Samuel with the tragic loss of her husband. Unconsciously, she blames Samuel for her husband's sudden, violent death.

As Samuel becomes more and more difficult to raise due to his abnormal behavior at school and at home, both Amelia and her son begin to be haunted by a malicious entity called the Babadook, a character that appears to have emerged from the pages of a mysterious children's book Samuel finds on his shelf one evening. Significant details about Amelia's past (e.g., the casual revelation that Amelia once had the ambition to be a professional illustrator of children's books) suggest that Amelia herself is the unknowing creator of the weird storybook. The audience begins to wonder if the Babadook is real or merely a product of Amelia's troubled mind. As the film progresses, it's clear that's the truth of the situation is not an either/or proposition. The monster is indeed a sentient being that exists in objective reality; however, it's *also* a product of Amelia's mind. The Babadook is a *tulpa*, a physical manifestation of her own worst nightmares. Amelia is literally haunting herself.

This scenario clearly parallels Gnostic beliefs. As Lash writes:

> The Dialogue of the Savior says, "Anyone who does not know how fire came into existence will be burned by it, because he does not know the root of it." With typical Gnostic flair, the revealer adds, "Whoever does not know the root of evil is no stranger to it" [...]. Zoroastrian single-source duality asserts an autonomous force of evil in the cosmos, but Gnostics refuted this view. The root of evil is human error, the mind mistaking itself. To defeat evil, we must unmask it by seeing its origin in the erring operations of our own minds.[15]

This is precisely what Amelia must do in order to defeat the Babadook—or rather, more accurately, to keep the creature under some semblance of control. Due to a critical moment of *gnosis* in which Amelia becomes aware of her own unconscious "generation of error" (i.e., her misplaced feelings of hostility for her own son and the resultant creation of the Babadook), she is able to "detect and correct" her mistakes, choosing the safety of her child over the false reality created by her own flawed senses. In a very real sense, she makes a deal with the devil (in this case her own mind), allowing the Babadook to continue existing only as long as it remains confined within the darkness beneath her home. In other words, Amelia chooses to enter into a détente with the monster rather than destroy it completely.

This theme, the willful comingling of darkness and light for the greater good, continues in Scott Derrickson's superhero extravaganza, *Doctor Strange* (2016). This film represents a very peculiar but compelling paradox. Though the film successfully captures the psychedelic, four-color surrealism and Gnostic-themed preoccupation with multiple layers of reality so integral to the original 1960s Steve Ditko comic books from which this blockbuster was adapted, its thematic core would no doubt be considered anathema to the creator of Doctor Strange. (Those of you who believe that Marvel Comics frontman Stan Lee is the creator of Doctor Strange would be demonstrably wrong. In his own words, published as far back as February of 1963 in a magazine called *The Comic Reader*, Lee admitted that Doctor Strange was Ditko's idea alone. For evidence of this, see p. 95 of Florentino Floresco's comprehensive 2016 book, *Ditko Unleashed: An American Hero*, as well as p. 69 of Blake Bell's

2008 biography, *Strange and Stranger: The World of Steve Ditko*.)

Hardcore comic book fans are already well familiar with the fact that Ditko has long been a devotee of Ayn Rand and her objectivist philosophy as laid out in such classic novels as *The Fountainhead* and *Atlas Shrugged*. The main tenet of Rand's philosophy is that "justice is objectively identifying a thing for what it is and treating it accordingly. No one gets the unearned. The innocent is not penalized, the guilty is not rewarded."[16] Ditko's most passionate exploration of objectivism can be found in his *Mr. A.* stories. Mr. A. is an objectivist vigilante whose unbending, Aristotelian attitude toward justice is represented by a calling card that is painted half-black and half-white. As Ditko explains:

> Mr. A.'s black and white card symbolizes the Law of Identity. It identifies the two moral potentials possible: the good and the evil, and by one's chosen actions the best or the worst potential can be actualized [...]. The card is a refusal to violate the root of justice, the Law of Identity, by a grey compromise, a refusal to sacrifice the good to the evil or to accept any part of the evil as a greater good.[17]

This is the exact opposite of the theme that drives the main plot of Derrickson's *Doctor Strange*, which was scripted by the team of C. Robert Cargill, Scott Derrickson and Jon Spaihts. As in the original comic book, Dr Stephen Strange (Benedict Cumberbatch) is an arrogant, rationalist surgeon who—through an uneasy combination of desperation and inner resolve—eventually evolves into the Master of the Mystic Arts; however, the more this cinematic iteration of Doctor Strange learns about the true nature of reality (i.e., that there is no "true" nature of reality), the more he adopts a relativist view of morality and ethics. Strange's mentor, the Ancient One (Tilda Swinton), teaches him that the universe cannot be perceived in strictly black-and-white terms, that only by adopting the tenets of moral relativism—by devoting oneself to a life colored in shades of grey—can the metaphysical forces of chaos and order be balanced. Therefore, in this twenty-first-century version of *Doctor Strange*, the deeper the Master of the Mystic Arts descends into the Gnostic levels of inner reality, the deeper he descends into the solipsistic sphere of the self, into an indeterminate world of the "grey compromise," as Ditko would say. Again, as in so many Gnostic films, the journey within ultimately spirals down into a state of murky indeterminacy.

In Steven Spielberg's *Ready Player One* (2018), adapted from Ernest

Cline's bestselling 2011 novel of the same name, Our Hero (Wade Watts, played by Tye Sheridan) is not a reality-bending magician but a teenage boy who lives—or, rather, *survives*—in a dystopian 2045 in which America's economy has collapsed to such an extent that the only way for people to deal with their unbearable existences is to retreat into a complex virtual reality program called the OASIS. In the opening narration, we are told that anything is possible in the OASIS and the only limit is one's imagination; the limit of the imagination, however, is actually the main theme of this film, though I'm not at all certain the director or the screenwriters (Zak Penn and Ernest Cline) are aware of this.

The OASIS has nothing to do with liberating one's imagination. It's clear that the OASIS is merely a preprogrammed script composed of *other people's* dreams and nightmares—a patchwork quilt of pop culture dross composed of snippets torn here and there from films, TV shows, and video games created by other people, most of them long dead by 2045. In other words, the OASIS appears to consist entirely of the dreams of dead men. Imagine being granted the power to create any reality you wish and instead you use it to wander around inside old episodes of *I Love Lucy*, or mix-and-match random elements of low grade B-films made years before you were born.

The main conflict of *Ready Player One* is a struggle between Wade Watts and his adolescent friends to wrest control of the OASIS from a cadre of Evil Guys In Neckties who wish to place limits on the virtual reality program in order to make a fortune off the OASIS's innumerable users. We are supposed to feel a sense of triumph when Wade succeeds in this quest, and yet we feel very little because nothing of any real consequence has been accomplished. We've spent two hours and twenty minutes watching a film about two warring dystopias: one dystopia in which humans are forced to pay premium prices in order to enslave themselves to other people's dreams, and another dystopia in which humans are allowed to enslave themselves to other people's dreams for a semi-reasonable price—except, that is, on Tuesdays and Thursdays, the only two days of the week when Wade demands that the OASIS be shut down so the sheeple can reacquaint themselves, at least briefly, with the joys of reality.

2018 saw the release of two separate films that revolve around the self-imposed, artificial limits of the imagination. In Anthony and Joe Russo's *Avengers: Infinity War*, the Evil Dark Lord, Thanos, gains control of a magic talisman called the Reality Stone that allows its wearer to manipulate reality any way he sees fit. Because Thanos is a Malthusian (i.e., one who believes a significant amount of the population must be killed off because there aren't enough resources to go around), he uses the magic powers of the Reality Stone to destroy half the population of the universe. Since no limits have been placed on what this talisman can accomplish, Thanos could easily use the powers of the Stone to double the size and resources of the universe, thus solving the perceived problem. Thanos does not do this because his imagination is limited, fixed on a single, obsessive goal he believes can be accomplished only through destruction. Before you judge Thanos too quickly, however, consider this: If you yourself were given the key to control reality, what would *you* do with it?

The fact is, every person alive has access to such a key right now, but they either refuse to use it to benefit themselves or they don't even know they have it in their possession.

Some people use the key of reality to commit slow suicide.

Others use it to emulate the mistakes of their parents.

Others use it to create bloody conflicts where none previously existed.

Others use it to create vapid, multibillion dollar blockbuster films for the consumption of the masses.

Matt Shakman's nine-part television series, *WandaVision*, which premiered on Disney Plus in January of 2021, combines elements from many of the films previously discussed in this chapter. Like Bobby Thompson in *Targets*, Wanda Maximoff (Elizabeth Olsen) can no longer tell the difference between the objective universe and the simulated realities of Hollywood fiction. Being a witch, possessed of supernatural powers even she does not understand, Wanda's confusion spills over into the world around her, causing widespread chaos. The town of Westview, New Jersey is transformed to fit Wanda's limited reality tunnel—a fragile epistemology built from childhood traumas and even more recent tragedies such as the death of her beloved Vision (Paul Bettany), an android capable of exhibiting deep human emotions, including love. From a hermetic perspective, the Vision that appears here is unique; he's a golem twice over: an artificial human, recently destroyed, who has been reconstructed entirely through Wanda's subconscious desires. He is, therefore, a golem and a tulpa at once. His existence is dependent on Wanda's subjective view of reality, just as the Babadook's reign of horror is dependent on Amelia Vannick's "generation of error."

What's at the End of Main Street?

Wanda's magic has fashioned a picture-perfect, solipsistic, suburban oasis—a Garden of Eden—that serves as an escape from her complete inability to deal with the mounting tragedies in her life. In Westview, Wanda and Vision lead a pre-scripted existence based on the clichés of American sitcoms. As in Gnostic mythology, however, this Garden of Eden turns out to be a "Black Iron Prison" (to steal a phrase from Philip K. Dick's 1981 Gnostic science fiction novel, *Valis*) from which there appears to be no escape—unless, of course, the Sophia in this scenario (Wanda) manages to wake herself up from her self-imposed dream.

Just like in *Pleasantville*, Westview contains a street beyond which the residents are not meant to travel. In the town of Pleasantville, nothing appeared to exist beyond Main Street; in Westview, Vision is cautioned by Wanda not to "go past Ellis Avenue." In every golem story ever imagined, the creation invariably rebels against his creator; for this reason, it should be no surprise that Vision disobeys Wanda and decides to chart out the exact parameters of his beatific prison. As a result, he comes upon a camouflaged barrier not unlike the green wall discovered by Douglas Hall in *The Thirteenth Floor*. Like the robed traveler in the aforementioned "Flammarion Engraving," Vision manages to push his way through Wanda's magically generated dome and emerge on the other side of reality.

Meanwhile, back in Westview, we learn that a rival witch, Agatha Harkness (Kathryn Hahn), has taken up residence inside the artificial town in order to study Wanda's magic with the hopes of harvesting it for herself. Agatha has been creating illusions in Westview (dreams within dreams, à la *Inception*) for the express purpose of ferreting out Wanda's true motivations for creating this Black Iron Prison in the first place. Like Number Six in Patrick McGoohan's *The Prisoner*, Wanda finds herself trapped inside a jail she herself created and tortured at the hands of a power mad martinet who wants to drain Wanda of vital information (or "IN-FOR-MA-TION," as the word is so memorably pronounced in *The Prisoner*). In a Gnostic sense, Agatha is the archon summoned by the "generation of error" committed by Sophia during her descent into elemental matter.

It's interesting to note that Westview, New Jersey is a wholly fictional town. One can only wonder if the writers of *WandaVision* chose the name based on its esoteric significance. After all, in any Masonic Lodge, the west side of the Temple (where the Senior Warden sits) is always associated with the setting sun, and thus represents a realm of ignorance and darkness, a place presided over by pure illusion. Some Freemasons consider the view in the West to be obscured by self-imposed lies. Alas for poor Wanda, once one has willingly taken up residence in a Black Iron Prison constructed of such lies, it's difficult to find your way out again. What appears to be an EXIT sign might just lead deeper into the illusion's thrall.

Synchronistically, "West" is the name of the protagonist in our next film. Larry Wade Carrell's *Girl Next* (2021) is about a beautiful young woman named Lorian West (Lacey Cofran) who's abducted from a supermarket parking lot and forced into a human trafficking ring funded by a secret government agency. Lorian is soon imprisoned in a remote Texas ranch, home to a trauma-based mind control program that tortures women, breaks them down both physically and psychologically, and remakes them into "dolls" (or "SOPHIAs") who essentially sleepwalk through what's left of their lives as obedient sex workers; however, Lorian's function is not only to please people sexually. At one point we see Lorian being trained to shoot a rifle; later, she's deployed as a remote controlled assassin to murder a necrophiliac on command. Her main programmer is a German scientist named Heinrich (Marcus Jean Pirae) whose mind control operation is assisted by his sadomasochistic wife, Misha (Paula Marcenaro Solinger).

By the end of the film, it's revealed that the true purpose of the sex trafficking ring is to conduct human experiments involving an otherworldly, hallucinogenic "Quantum drug" nicknamed Aqua Velva. This drug has the potential to break down reality and open portals to other dimensions. Not only is Heinrich injecting copious amounts of this substance into his kidnapped victims, he's experimenting with it himself. When used in combination with other drugs such as DMT and steroids, its purpose is to make his subjects docile, but when Heinrich experiments with Aqua Velva in extremely high doses, his hope is to transform himself into something more than human.

Though the plot of this film is open to interpretation, Lorian's ultimate fate reminds me of the wise words of consciousness researcher David E. Worcester: "When Pavlov went to the Russian hierarchy to report on his last findings before his death, he warned them that when you condition people… you condition them to receive something in exchange for that conditioning, and if that is not given to them they cannot be conditioned again. He warned them,

'You may develop the first cosmically aware people, people who have been taken to the point where they cannot be conditioned by mass media.'"[18] In other words, it appears that Lorian has been conditioned, manipulated, and brainwashed to such an extreme degree that she's gone through the wall and out the other side; she's been subjected to so much control that she's become almost immune to it. Heinrich and his wife have programmed her to such an extent that she's became *unprogrammed*, so much so that she appears to have evolved into a unique, "cosmically aware" being. As a result, she makes contact with what appears to be an ultradimensional entity that manifests in the form of a giant floating clown head. The ultraterrestrial whispers to her, "*There are two worlds*." She now understands that her entire reality has always been a simulacrum.

"Everything is fake," Lorian says. "A box within a box within a box. A game." She believes that "they programmed me before they took me." Later in the film, she states flatly, "The world is a simulation [...]. I know everything now." By the conclusion, we see that she's using her newfound awareness, her own innate abilities, to help protect other women from being inducted into these self-same mind control programs. Despite this ostensible note of optimism, the film's final image is a grid of thirty-five television screens on which we see Lorian's image replicated over and over again. This is soon replaced by thirty-five images of the floating clown head we saw earlier in the film. The camera zooms in on a single screen until all we can see is the clown overlaid with grating sounds of maniacal laughter. A second later, we hear the ultraterrestrial entity speak: "*You have eaten from the tree/Now you will be as we*." Fade to black. This enigmatic epilogue seems to suggest that the ultraterrestrial is a false god/archon/trickster figure who has some sort of hold over Lorian, and that her newfound "awareness" comes with invisible strings attached. Perhaps Lorian isn't quite as free as she thinks.

It's worth noting that *Girl Next* was written and produced by Zeph E. Daniel, formerly known as Woody Keith, whose first feature length film was the psychotronic classic, *Society* (1989), co-written by Rick Fry and directed by Brian Yuzna. *Society* is a truly bizarre hybrid of body horror and social satire that seems more and more prescient with each passing year. It's about a teenage boy, Bill Whitney (Billy Warlock), who begins to suspect that his wealthy parents are members of a murderous secret society who have been grooming Bill since birth to be the featured sacrifice at an elite, Beverly Hills party that revolves around an orgiastic ritual known only as "The Shunting." It soon becomes clear that Billy's entire life is a fake, a false front that hides the systemic corruption that has always been the source of Billy's ostensibly privileged life. The tagline for the movie poster reads, "THE RICH HAVE ALWAYS FED OFF THE POOR. THIS TIME IT'S FOR REAL." These two sentences come across more like a simple statement of fact than a gimmicky come-on for a low budget horror flick. This tagline frames the image of a young blonde woman wearing a spaghetti strap baby blue satin dress with white, over-the-elbow gloves that evoke the glamor of Marilyn Monroe and other unattainable starlets; significantly, the woman is ripping her own face off, rendering the subversive intent even more transparent.

Perhaps far more disturbing than any gory images that appear in *Society* is the fact that the primary screenwriter, Zeph E. Daniel, claims the film is semi-autobiographical and based on his own experiences being raised by "a powerful and influential Hollywood family" who subjected him to "satanic ritual abuse [...] from a very early age."[19] As a testament to the film's enduring power, the socialist journal, *Jacobin*, published an insightful article about *Society* on Halloween of 2021. The article's author, Branko Marcetic, alludes to the real life basis for the film: "Daniel had come from a well-off Beverly Hills family similar to Billy's, and has said that the movie is 'about things in our society that shouldn't be there but are.'" Marcetic focuses on the film's relevancy in the twenty-first century: "[T]he movie's indictment of the rich and portrayal of class antagonism [make it] feel far more from this era than [the 1980s]." Marcetic goes on to describe the film as "one of the more fantastically deranged cinematic artifacts from [...] the decade of Ronald Reagan [...]. *Society* stands out not just for the sensational physical effects that solidified it as a cult classic for horror fans, but the directness and savagery of its class critique. For all the pastel colors, poofy hair, and teen sex antics that date it firmly to the 1980s, *Society* oddly feels like it was meant for our era of Jeffrey Epstein, QAnon, and oligarchic scheming."[20]

Despite the fact that *Society* came out thirty-years before *Girl Next*, the two films share similar themes—particularly the notion that the lives built for us from birth are little more than artificial prisons—and would make for a very disturbing midnight double feature on any theater's marquee.

Manufacturing fake realities in order to harm others is also a major theme in our final film, Guillermo del Toro's *Nightmare Alley*

(2021). The main character, Stan Carlisle, is not only a master of the con, he's also a masterful psychologist. In the twenty-first century, he would no doubt be working as an internet influencer or a propagandist for one of the many smiling political candidates eager to pretend to improve your life while working overtime for the sole purpose of elevating their own societal status and wealth. Today, Stan Carlisle might establish a Washington, D.C. think tank and rent out his services to a panoply of political operatives on both sides of the skullduggery spectrum. In the early twentieth century, Carlisle decided to set himself up as a fake psychic with a direct link to the afterlife and a penchant for lending his mediumistic talents to the wealthiest of grieving widows (for a substantial fee, of course).

Carlisle's main strategy in his mission to attain more and more power is laid out in Chapter Four of William Lindsay Gresham's classic 1946 crime noir novel that served as the basis for del Toro's film: "[You can] control anybody, by finding out what he's afraid of [...]. Fear. Find out what they are afraid of and sell it back to them. That's the key. The key!"[21]

In his 1969 book, *The Satanic Bible*, Church of Satan founder Anton LaVey wrote, "So long as man knows the meaning of fear, he will need the ways and means to defend himself against his fears."[22] Perhaps LaVey was channeling Gresham's spirit when he wrote that line. According to the late psychological warfare officer and former Church of Satan devotee, Col. Michael Aquino, the original cinematic adaptation of *Nightmare Alley* (released in 1947 and directed by Edmund Goulding) was an essential source of inspiration for LaVey.[23] In fact, LaVey went so far as to name one of his daughters "Zeena," an important character in Gresham's novel and both film adaptations. Is it possible that LaVey identified with the charismatic showman who figures out how to transform Fear into Gold with nothing more than a talent for clever carny patter? According to Aquino, that possibility is not only likely but "undeniable."[24]

Alas, Aquino never mentioned if LaVey also drew inspiration from Tod Browning's little known silent film, *The Mystic* (1925), the plot of which revolves around a cast of characters similar to Stan Carlisle and his carny accomplices. In *The Mystic*, a con artist named Michael Nash cheats gullible Wall Streeters out of their fortunes with the help of a beautiful young Hungarian trance medium named Zara and her thuggish partner, a former circus knife-thrower. During Zara's socialite séances, the knife-thrower's main function is to create a variety of otherwordly illusions while dressed in black from head to toe in order to blend in with the darkness of the séance room. This illusionist's name is Anton. Anton, of course, is the moniker the Chicago-born Howard Stanton Levey adopted when he chose to rebrand himself as San Francisco's High Priest of Satan under the far more colorful name "Anton Szandor LaVey."

It's not unlikely that William Lindsay Gresham drew some of his inspiration from the work of Tod Browning as well. Gresham would have been a teenager in the 1920s when Browning was busy producing one cinematic masterpiece after another in collaboration with screenwriter Waldemar Young. Browning specialized in psychologically intense dramas such as *The Unholy Three* (1925), the aforementioned *The Mystic*, *The Show* (1927), *The Unknown* (1927), *West of Zanzibar* (1928), *The Thirteenth Chair* (1929), *Freaks* (1932), and the surprisingly lighthearted—and perennially underrated—murder mystery, *Miracles for Sale* (1939). All of these films explored the thin line between positive lies (what Kurt Vonnegut called "foma" in his 1963 novel, *Cat's Cradle*) and negative lies. In Browning's films, most of which either take place at carnivals or feature carnival performers as the main characters, we often see the carny's deft talent for lying used to heal as much as harm. Browning was obsessed with the power of lies to build as well as destroy. It's clear that Browning felt a responsibility to use the popular medium of film in order to expose the purveyors of these negative lies (e.g., fake mediums such as Gresham's fictional anti-hero, Stan Carlisle).

Gresham's—and, by extension, del Toro's—imperative seems to be somewhat different than Browning's. Unlike magician-cum-skeptics like the late James Randi (who assisted in the research of Gresham's 1959 nonfiction book, *Houdini: The Man Who Walked Through Walls*), Gresham and del Toro do not reject the profound significance of the supernatural out of hand. In every other film del Toro has made, he has embraced the power of the magical. In Gresham's original novel, much attention is given to the divination capabilities of the Tarot. Indeed, Gresham used the Major Arcana of the Tarot to structure the twenty-two chapters of the novel. In his personal life, Gresham respected the power of the Tarot a great deal and claimed he used them for "spiritual quests," transgressive endeavors that contributed to his ultimate abandonment of Christianity, the basic doctrines of which he could no longer "understand" or "accept."[25] In an odd twist of literary history, these "spiritual quests" helped drive his wife, Joy, into the arms of Christian theologian, C.S. Lewis, best known as the author of the fantasy series, *The Chronicles of Narnia* (1950–56). Joy divorced Gresham in 1954 and married Lewis in 1956. She and Lewis remained married until Joy's unexpected death from bone cancer in 1960. Lewis ended up raising Gresham's two sons. In 1962, Gresham took his own life after checking into the Dixie, the very same rundown Manhattan hotel he had frequented while writing *Nightmare Alley* back in the late 1940s.

Unlike the protagonists of Browning's films, the main character of Gresham and del Toro's narrative is brought down not merely because he's a shifty con man. He's brought down for cheapening the genuinely numinous, for not according the proper amount of respect to the unbridled power of the supernatural. Carlisle is a master of illusion, a skilled creator of fake realities. But unlike the *faux* realities fashioned by artists and storytellers and poets, Carlisle's lies are hollow, as precarious and fragile as a house of trick cards. Carlisle creates fake realities not to illuminate but to *confuse*. His fictions are not positive. They do not attempt to heal. They only destroy. And like a black magic spell that boomerangs back on the practitioner, Carlisle meets the same end as any archon who arrogantly believes he has total control over the constructed realities he has elected to conjure forth.

Nightmare Alley is about what happens when a simulated reality crashes down on the flawed architect who built it out of little more than bent playing cards, tattered cheesecloth, and faulty wires. *Nightmare Alley* is a long and narrow corridor that leads to a tiny pinpoint of light—the divine spark—which can never be reached by the pitiful seeker who chases it out of desperation and fear rather than a genuine desire to know the truth.

The main reason *Dark City* is superior to the other recent films in this "reality-bending" subgenre is because its central theme is one of ultimate liberation as opposed to ultimate enslavement. Not only is it about overcoming the artificial, but it's also about overcoming the world that lies beyond the artificial. The special power that John Murdoch accesses at the conclusion of *Dark City*, the power to remake the world around him, is the power that we all have. More importantly, it's the power that very few *want* you to have.

In ancient Egypt, the high priests were the only ones who knew the "occult" secrets of reading and writing. These skills were highly guarded by the priest caste. Not even the pharaoh was allowed to know how to read and write. (No doubt, it was far easier to manipulate him this way.) Those who were not priests considered the ability to read and write a form of magic that was inaccessible to the average person. This is why T.S. Eliot said in 1936, "You have to consider that any esoteric occult ritual is today socially acted out by the daily publishing and consuming of newspapers."

The same situation exists at this very moment, only slightly altered. Like the alien "Strangers" in *Dark City*, there are control-crazy authoritarians running the world today who don't want us to know how much power each of us actually possesses. A reality in which each of us has total mastery over our own destinies is far too dangerous for an incestuous elite who wish us to believe that the ability to remake the world is as inaccessible to us as the power of the hieroglyphic alphabet was to the most lowly Egyptian slave breaking his back every day dragging ten-ton blocks of limestone to help build the tomb of an illiterate pharaoh. But such abilities are far from impossible, and it's this call to power—both metaphorically *and* literally—that lifts *Dark City* above its contemporaries.

The original *Matrix Trilogy* (specifically 2003's *The Matrix Revolutions*) ends with an ostensible reconciliation of opposites: the merging of the artificial with the real world, though it's strongly implied that this reconciliation is little more than a temporary measure. A step above such reactionary fare as *The Village*, the first three films in *The Matrix* series represents a *half*-surrender to the artificial. Such films as *The Truman Show*, *Pleasantville* and *Vanilla Sky* (though all extremely intelligent and innovative in their own way) take us to the very edge of *gnosis*, but ultimately turn back at the very last second. Other films like *eXistenZ*, *The Thirteenth Floor* and *Inception* all end on ephemeral question marks, abandoning our protagonists—and the films themselves—in unresolved limbos. The audience may walk away from these films feeling stimulated, but not empowered.

What lies at the end of Main Street appears to be a simple choice: either the surrender to the artificial or the mastery over reality itself. *Dark City* refuses to surrender to what the mass mind believes is the inevitable.

Other films need to become equally pertinacious. Cinematic science fiction in particular must now evolve to a higher level if it wishes to have any relevance in the coming decades. Filmmakers attracted to science fiction should study the unique trajectory that these genre films have followed since the end of the 1950s.

What's at the End of Main Street?

In the 1950s science fiction films trumpeted the exploration of the unknown. Time and time again, they celebrated the initiation of humanity into the mysteries of outer space. Examples are numerous: *Rocket Ship X-M* (1950), *Destination Moon* (1950), *Cat Women of the Moon* (1953), *Riders to the Stars* (1954), *This Island Earth* (1955), *Forbidden Planet* (1956), *It! The Terror from Beyond Space* (1958), *From the Earth to the Moon* (1958), *First Man into Space* (1959), *Angry Red Planet* (1959), etc. The good, the bad, the sublime, and the just plain weird are all represented on this list. All were outward journeys, extensions of America's expansion to the West and the Edge of the World. Where do you go after you've reached the Edge of the World? You go up and *out*. There was a sense in those days, before the death of John F. Kennedy and the invasion of Vietnam, that anything was possible in America.

The trauma of successive tragedies—i.e., the assassination of a popular president, the escalation of the war in Vietnam, the Watergate conspiracy, the revelations surrounding the Iran-Contra scandal of the 1980s, etc.—evicted us from our bodies and turned our attentions inward. This is perfectly natural. An extended period of self-discovery followed, and it was reflected in our science fiction films. That's why science fiction cinema is no longer about journeying outward, but about journeying *inward*: a never-ending tumble into the center of the mind. The center of the ego. The center of the "I" of individual consciousness. But what began as a spiritual journey of self-reflection has now devolved into a solipsistic obsession with the self and little more. Like Cobb and Mal in *Inception*, our playful explorations of our inner worlds has led to a self-imposed trap in purgatory. Hopefully, it won't take an act of suicide to break us out of that trap.

Film writers and directors must unchain themselves from the artificial either/or dichotomy of choosing between the "physical/material" science fiction of the 1950s on one hand and the "nonphysical/astral" science fiction of the late 1990s and early twenty-first century on the other. If they can take what they've learned from their decades-long sojourn in the non-physical realms, and apply that knowledge to the physical-world-template of the 1950s, they just might emerge with a whole new form of science fiction, one that has its roots planted firmly in both the material as well as the astral at the same time: a genre that perfectly synthesizes the inner and outer worlds for a brand new century in desperate need of genuine psychic balance.

In Victor Sjöström's influential 1921 dark fantasy film *The Phantom*

Carriage, the main character, David Holm, is evicted from his physical body by Death's Servant, and Holm's astral body is taken on a metaphysical journey of self-discovery. Once this journey is complete, however, Death's Servant returns Holm to this body so he can complete his odyssey in the real world.

We, as a society, have not yet reached that stage. Our astral bodies are still evicted from the physical, and we're desperately trying to find our way back. The films under discussion here are subconscious manifestations of that struggle to find the frayed string in the labyrinth in order to guide us back home again.

Buoyed by this new knowledge of the inner worlds, perhaps it's time to return to the physical. The science fiction films we haven't yet made can help us do that. Art is a reflection of ourselves, but we are also a reflection of our art. Perhaps a slew of well-made, clever, optimistic science fiction films that celebrate the marriage of the physical and the astral, the outward-journey conjoined with the inward-descent, would help us navigate the confusing maze back into our bodies. Perhaps a retrieval of the aesthetics of the past, reshaped to the unique sensibilities of the present day, would fill the hole in our spirits. Perhaps what we need is the phoenix-like resurrection of the outward journey transmogrified into a strange new beast heretofore unseen by human eyes.

William S. Burroughs, one of the most innovative American novelists of the twentieth century, often liked to quote the poet Brion Gysin: "[W]e are here to go. The future, if there is a future, is in space. The only thing that could unite the planet is to turn the planet into a space station." However, Burroughs also adds this important caveat that science fiction writers—and scientists—should keep in mind: "Space travel may be a spiritual rather than a technical achievement. If you want to move a human creature, alter his basic perceptions."[26]

Now that our perceptions have indeed been effectively altered by decades of inner travel in the virtual worlds of the silver screen, perhaps we can now realize that we have indeed been placed here to travel *outward* in the physical worlds of noumenal space. To fly. Transmigrate. Leave the planet and confront the unknowns of the infinite worlds that surround us.

We're not here to reflect endlessly on our own inner dream lives, accomplishing nothing until our physical selves dissolve into dust, but to sculpt reality to match our noblest dreams. As William Burroughs wrote in his 1983 novel, *The Place of Dead Roads*, an imaginative exploration of America's reshaping of the West in the latter half of the nineteenth century, "*Happiness is a by-product of function.*"[27]

Human beings can't function for long as insubstantial astral forms untethered to the physical. Inward self-reflection is necessary for the human spirit to thrive, but it can't be the end-all of existence. In the first half of the twenty-first century, David Holm—*The Phantom Carriage's* ghostly protagonist—and his fetterless spiritual descendants are still adrift. They need to return home. They need a meaningful purpose. Will the cinema—specifically science fiction cinema—help them attain this? Or will it continue to enable their exile in limbo?

The answer lies in William Burroughs' favorite dictum.

Since H.G. Wells, and even earlier, the function of science fiction has always been to point the way *forward*, not to reinforce our worst tendencies toward entropy.

We're here to go, Burroughs' spirit reminds us.

We're here to go.

Chapter 2

The Box in the Desert

Budd Boetticher, Breaking Bad, and the Twenty-first-century Western

I ONCE HAD a girlfriend whose stepfather lived in Riverside, California. My girlfriend had lived there until her early twenties when she moved to the coastal city of Redondo Beach, California. Once she had experienced the laidback atmosphere of Southern California, she never wanted to return to that forsaken desert city known as Riverside.

The first time I visited Riverside was in my girlfriend's company. As we passed the city limits, I saw scrawled on the side of the freeway the following piece of graffiti:

HOMICIDE
SUICIDE
MATRICIDE
PATRICIDE
INFANTICIDE
RIVERCIDE

When I met my girlfriend, she was twenty-five. The high school friends she had left behind in Riverside were roughly the same age. It seemed as if every single one of them desperately wished to escape the confines of their native city and move to fabled Los Angeles which was only about an hour away but, for some reason, very few of them could figure out how to accomplish this simple task. They seemed to be trapped there as if by some siren's spell outsiders could not hear. My girlfriend was one of the few who had (somehow... through sheer force of will?) made it out alive. Perhaps owing to Riverside's freefalling economy, everyone from the age of sixteen to twenty-nine had little to do except smoke methamphetamine; it seemed as if almost every one of them was either addicted to meth or recovering from it.

Given my personal experiences with this city, it did not surprise me when, in the latter months of 2013, I happened to stumble across an interview with television writer/director/producer Vince Gilligan in which he offhandedly mentioned that his hit television series, *Breaking Bad* (2008–2013), a five-season crime drama about a chemistry teacher named Walter White (Bryan Cranston) who resorts to cooking meth in order to pay for his cancer treatments, had been set in Riverside, California in the first draft of the pilot episode.[1] Upon selling the series to AMC, Gilligan intended to film all five seasons in Riverside. The only reason this did not occur was a financial one; these days, the cost of filming a television series in California is far too high. After scouting around for different locations that might match the soul-deadening desolation of Riverside, Gilligan discovered that New Mexico would offer the show a substantial tax break if he chose to relocate the plot to Albuquerque.

In several different interviews, Gilligan has stated that this major alteration was ultimately to the show's benefit because the state of New Mexico became another character in the show.[2] What did Gilligan mean by this? At the beginning of season three's final episode, "Full Measure," Walter is about to have a meeting in the middle of the desert with his employer, Gustavo Fring (Giancarlo Esposito), a ruthless drug lord. As Walter strides through the sparse New Mexico landscape, the background music redolent of Ennio Morricone's scores for such Sergio Leone Westerns as *A Fistful of Dollars* (1964) and *The Good, the Bad and the Ugly* (1966), one cannot help but realize that the writers of the show are drawing a parallel between the blood-drenched plains of the Old West and America's current state of affairs at the beginning of the twenty-first century.

Unlike Riverside, New Mexico is a land steeped in the mythic history (and historical myths) of the Old West: the Battle of Blazer's Mill of 1878, the Variety Hall Shootout of 1880, the Frisco Shootout of 1884, the legendary exploits of lawmen such as Elfego Baca, James W. Bell, Sam Bernard, Mariano Barela, "Longhair" Jim Courtright, Pat

Garrett, Dave Mather, Herbert James McGrath, Bob Ollinger, and John Joshua Webb. These were the men whose real life adventures spilled over into the pulp exaggerations of a thousand fictional gunslingers whose "rugged individualism" continues to resonate in the shrinking frontier known as the twenty-first century.

Only a few generations ago, the twenty-first century was the traditional setting for a slew of optimistic science fiction epics such as *2001: A Space Odyssey* (1968) in which the human race has gotten its act together and launched out of the nest to begin a bold exploration of other worlds, other galaxies, pushing the frontier of the Old West into the furthest reaches of space. Instead, when the real 2001 arrived, we were still so ensconced in tribal warfare that 2,977 people died in New York in a single day, mainly due to religious superstitions that date back 1,400 years. Rather than wielding spears and clubs and flaming arrows, we choose instead to use flaming missiles made of metal. We launch them into buildings far taller than Mount Olympus and watch the final fate of tiny, frightened gods falling from a sky choked with fire. And we mourn and strike back in anger and thousands of innocents die. And sometimes, to get our minds off the madness, we put our feet up and watch television, perhaps an old "Cowboys 'n' Indians" flick in which massacre piles upon massacre and the love of land and money almost always overshadows all the supposed civilized traits of Western man. And we make no connection to recent events, to Mexican standoffs in the US Congress, to dozens of influential bankers taking their own lives under mysterious circumstances, to zombie banks bilking their customers out of fortunes, and to whole countries being bombed into dust in a futile attempt to search for nonexistent weapons of mass destruction in order to rake in substantial profits for American munitions manufacturers. Though we love to think of the human race as a constantly evolving species that learns from its many mistakes, the truth is that we are still living in the nineteenth century. The dead myth of the Old West was never a myth, and it never even died. In fact, we're all living the myth right now.

In the middle of watching all five seasons of *Breaking Bad*, it just so happened that I also began revisiting the films of Budd Boetticher, with a special emphasis on the now famous Westerns he made in collaboration with Randolph Scott in the late 1950s and early 1960s. Halfway through this cycle, while also in the middle of season three of *Breaking Bad*, I suddenly realized that Vince Gilligan's contemporary crime drama was—at its core—a twenty-first-century Western.

It did not surprise me later when I found an online interview with Gilligan in which he commented that, for him, *Breaking Bad* had always been "a modern Western."[3] I think we can be a little more specific and state unequivocally that *Breaking Bad* is a modern *Budd Boetticher* Western.

Though obscure when they were first released, since the late 1960s Budd Boetticher's films have acquired greater and greater critical acclaim. His most highly regarded movies are those that have become to be known as the "Ranown Cycle"—named after the production company that made the majority of these films. (The name "Ranown" was a mixture of Randolph Scott's first name as well as the last name of Harry Joe Brown, the producer.) *Breaking Bad's* substantial debt to Boetticher's sixty-year-old films is a testament to their impressive staying power in a society that often discards the artifacts of popular culture like dross.

The most significant quality that both Boetticher's best films and *Breaking Bad* share is the refusal to insult the intelligence of the audience. Each allows the viewers to experience a wide array of emotions that are often contradictory. The common conception of a "good guy" and a "bad guy" is far more nuanced in both the Old West of Budd Boetticher and the New West of Vince Gilligan. The loyalties of the audience shift as the respective stories unfold. I suspect this is a valuable lesson Gilligan learned from watching Boetticher's Ranown Westerns.

The Ranown Westerns include *Seven Men from Now* (1956), *The Tall T* (1957), *Decision at Sundown* (1957), *Buchanan Rides Alone* (1959), *Ride Lonesome* (1959), *Westbound* (1959), and *Comanche Station* (1960). In almost all of these films, the supposed "bad guys" are by no means cardboard cutouts as they so often are in the traditional Western narrative. In Boetticher's films, which benefited from strong scripts by Charles Lang and Burt Kennedy (who later went on to direct his own Westerns such as 1969's *Support Your Local Sheriff!*), the characters—even the supporting players—are all driven by motivations with which all of us can sympathize. In *Ride Lonesome*, for example, Sam Boone (Pernell Roberts) and his friend Whit (James Coburn) intend to murder the protagonist, Ben Brigade (Randolph Scott), in order to win amnesty, to be free. These two characters are so finely drawn, so utterly *human*, that the audience understands and likes them, even if they might deplore the act the duo are preparing to commit. Even the far less likable Frank (Lee Van Cleef), the central antagonist of the film, wins our sympathy with the palpable expression of pain and worry on his face as he watches the hero threatening to snap his little brother's neck from the dead branches of a hanging tree.

The detestable Ben Lane (Claude Atkins), the antagonist of *Comanche Station*, also challenges our expectations of the traditional Western narrative when he goes out of his way to save the protagonist, Jefferson Cody (Randolph Scott), from an attacking band of Comanches. By letting Cody die, Lane could kidnap the woman Cody has saved from the Comanches in order to claim the $5,000 reward that has been offered for her return. Despite this, Lane will not allow Cody—a man he respects—to die in such a savage manner. As Lane says to Cody, "I never could've enjoyed spending that $5,000 if I done you that way." This line is mirrored in *Ride Lonesome* when Sam Boone saves Ben Brigade from being killed under similar circumstances. Boone tells Brigade, "Never would've enjoyed being a free man if I done you that way." This echoes an even earlier line of dialogue in the very first of the Ranown Westerns, *Seven Men from Now*. Near the conclusion of the film the antagonist, Bill Masters, explains why he didn't kill the protagonist, Ben Stride (Randolph Scott), when he had the chance: "I never could enjoy spending this twenty thousand if I done you that way, Sheriff." These little moments of humanity set the antagonists in Boetticher's films far apart from the one-dimensional villains that populate most of the Western fiction that emerged from the pulp landscape of America in the late 1800s. As film director Taylor Hackford has commented, "Budd Boetticher introduced the sympathetic bad man in American film."[4]

Vince Gilligan's *sui generis* television drama, *Breaking Bad*, similarly warps the traditional notions of hero and villain. Over the course of five seasons, our protagonist, Walter White (an average Joe just trying to make ends meet), gradually morphs into the antagonist. Though at the beginning of season one, the emotions of the audience are firmly invested in seeing Walter succeed in his extralegal schemes, ever so slowly, we begin to back away from him as his actions become more and more questionable.

Characters who at first appear to be mercenary, possessed of very few positive qualities, win our sympathies due to the slow unveiling of their true natures. Mike Ehrmantraut (Jonathan Banks), a hired thug, is a perfect example. In season three, Mike is cast in the role of an antagonist whose job is to eliminate the ostensible "hero" of the show, Walter, but our expectations and emotions are turned upside down

THE ONE-MAN WAR AGAINST THE COMANCHEROS!
$5000
REWARD
R THE RETURN OF MY WIFE
ALIVE
COLUMBIA PICTURES
Presents
RANDOLPH SCOTT in
COMANCHE STATION
co-starring
NANCY GATES
with CLAUDE AKINS · SKIP HOMEIER · RICHARD RUST
Written by BURT KENNEDY · Produced and Directed by BUDD BOETTICHER
Executive Producer, HARRY JOE BROWN · A RANOWN PRODUCTION
CINEMASCOPE · EASTMAN COLOR

as this dynamic is reversed suddenly and quite unexpectedly later in the series. Gustavo Fring, the kingpin of a vast drug empire, appears to be devoid of all emotions. Later, however, as the layers of his back story are peeled away, we begin to understand his motivations and even root for him to succeed in a decades-long revenge scheme.

Hank Schrader (Dean Norris), Walter's brother-in-law, is a DEA (Drug Enforcement Administration) agent whose ultimate goal is to arrest the manufacturer of the powerful new brand of methamphetamine now poisoning the Four Corners of the Southwest. Throughout *Breaking Bad's* five seasons the audience knows that, at some point, Hank will realize that the man he is looking for is his seemingly meek brother-in-law, Walter. This notion of the relentless pursuit is a tried and true aspect of popular television narratives that can be traced at least as far back as *The Fugitive* (1963–67). Distillations of this well-worn theme can be found, to varying degrees of success, in later television shows such as *The Invaders* (1967–68), *The Man from Atlantis* (1977–78), *The Incredible Hulk* (1977–82), and *Werewolf* (1987–88). What makes this aspect of *Breaking Bad* infinitely more than just another television cliché, however, is the point of view from which the tale is told. Thirty years ago, the protagonist of *Breaking Bad* would have been Hank. The audience would have been expected to root for him and him alone. Any deviation from this norm would have been considered perverse, but because this particular tale is told from Walter's perspective—because we have been riding around inside his mind every step of the way and have experienced how much hardship he has gone through in order to reach his seemingly impossible goal—we root instead for what would otherwise have been considered the antagonist in almost any other television narrative.

Budd Boetticher and his screenwriter, Charles Lang, brilliantly executed upsetting the traditional expectations of the viewers in regard to the motivations and likeability of the protagonist in *Decision at Sundown*. Of all of Boetticher's Westerns, this is the one that most resembles the central themes of *Breaking Bad* though perhaps not in a way that would be obvious to the casual viewer. The plot of *Decision at Sundown* involves a pair of gunslingers, Bart Allison (Randolph Scott) and his friend Sam (Noah Beery), who assault the frontier village of Sundown in order to kill a single man: town boss Tate Kimbrough (John Carroll). Allison seeks revenge against Kimbrough for having an affair with his wife. (As one movie poster puts it, "Now he was face-to-face with the killers who had *dishonored* his wife!") Alli-

RANDOLPH SCOTT
BRINGS A NEW KIND OF ADVENTURER TO THE SCREEN!
DECISION AT SUNDOWN
A COLUMBIA PICTURE
"SOMEBODY WILL DIE FOR THIS!"
JOHN CARROLL
KAREN STEELE · VALERIE FRENCH
NOAH BEERY · JOHN ARCHER · ANDREW DUGGAN · JAMES WESTERFIELD · Screen Play by CHARLES LANG, Jr.
A SCOTT-BROWN PRODUCTION · Produced by HARRY JOE BROWN · Directed by BUDD BOETTICHER
TECHNICOLOR

IN THE ERA WHEN THE MOB-RATS RAN WILD HE WAS THE WILDEST!
"THE RISE AND FALL OF 'LEGS' DIAMOND"
They said he couldn't be killed!
One by one he rubbed out the underworld big shots of the '20s!
There's never been anyone like him before... or since!
Always a hideout —always a girl!
Presented by WARNER BROS. STARRING
RAY DANTON · KAREN STEELE · ELAINE STEWART · Written by JOSEPH LANDON
A UNITED STATES PRODUCTIONS PICTURE · Produced by MILTON SPERLING · Directed by BUDD BOETTICHER

son's wife, Mary, has recently committed suicide, and Allison blames Kimbrough for this.

This appears at first to be a straightforward Western movie plot: intrepid gunfighter seeks justice for the death of his wife. This ten-word sentence could just as easily describe the aforementioned *Seven Men from Now* and *Ride Lonesome*. *Decision at Sundown*, however, differs from almost every other Western in this sense: Our sympathies change throughout the film, at last dissolving into utter uncertainty.

At the beginning of the film, we are led to believe that Bart Allison is in the right. His wife has been "dishonored" and vengeance is a must. There is no doubt in the minds of the viewers that Kimbrough will be dead by the end of the last reel. But that is not what happens. As the story unfolds, the other characters begin to question Allison's motivations. Even his best friend, Sam, tries to talk Allison out of this suicide mission. Bit by bit, we learn more about Allison's late wife or, rather, we learn more about how others *perceive* her. Like a B-grade version of Akira Kurosawa's *Rashomon* (1950), no objective reality exists in *Decision at Sundown*. All we have to measure the truth of the situation are conflicting points of view. According to Allison, his late wife was a saint of a woman whose honor was stolen from her by Kimbrough. According to others, Allison's wife was the exact opposite. Even Allison's best friend, Sam, implies that he himself had had an affair with the late Mrs Allison, and further suggests that Allison's wife was the aggressor in the situation. Unlike in *Rashomon*, we are never privy to the perspective of the dead. What would Mary have to say on her own behalf? The audience is not limited to only two options: saint or whore. There's another possibility: that Allison's wife was simply independent minded and far ahead of her times, a quality that would no doubt brand her as a "no-good whore" in the late nineteenth century. Even by the end of the film, we are not quite certain about the truth of the situation. Neither is Allison. He begins the film absolutely certain of the righteousness of his violent actions. By the end of this film, he's so confused that he agrees to let Tate Kimbrough ride out of town… with Kimbrough's new girlfriend in tow.

I cannot think of any other Western in which the inevitable final showdown never occurs and the "bad guy" simply leaves town at the end. The title of the film is no doubt meant to be ironic. The film could just as easily be called *Indecision at Sundown*. The central theme of the film concerns itself with the dissolving of what psychologist Timothy Leary once referred to as "reality tunnels," those shaky frameworks of perception that guide our daily journeys through the illusory social construct we think of as the objective universe. When we allow this framework to collapse, even for a moment, the subjective and ephemeral notions that have controlled the consciousness of Western humanity for so long begin to soften and melt away. Suddenly, our normal justifications for violence no longer seem quite as important; we are left, like Bart Allison at the end of the film, confused and liberated at the same time, uncertain about not only our future but everything that has occurred in the past as well. In America, uncertainty has always been a dangerous taboo. You *must* be certain of reality—and your place in it—at all times. If not, you'll risk being accused of mental instability, sedition, or blasphemy. One can only wonder what the typical moviegoer, expecting just another shoot-'em-up starring Randolph Scott, thought about the "anti-climactic" ending of *Decision at Sundown*. Did it frustrate them to have their God-given expectations of righteous violence stripped away from them at the last minute?

Like Bart Allison, the main character of *Breaking Bad* is a man who appears to be certain of his goals at the very beginning of his journey. After learning he is dying of lung cancer, high school chemistry teacher Walter White decides to develop the purest form of methamphetamine in existence (we are told that his unique product is 99.9% pure) in order to make as much money as possible within the meager time left to him so he can leave a nest egg for his family once he's passed on. As in a crime noir novel of the 1950s and 1960s, such as those written by Jim Thompson, David Goodis, and Frederic Brown, this criminal plan quickly spirals far out of Walter's control. Within three episodes Walter is forced to commit murder (twice) in order to cover his tracks. By the end of the final season, a train of corpses has been left in Walter's wake. Some of these deaths are unintentional. Some of them are not. As Walter's ambition grows more and more grandiose, the sympathies of the audience become less and less certain. Vince Gilligan and his writing team do not allow the audience to feel at all comfortable in rooting for a man whose moral compass grows further and further askew. Gilligan has stated that his goal was to "see how many viewers he could shake off" and repulse.[5] Having built up a substantial audience out of nothing, the trick now was to see how many of these viewers would stick by Walter's side as the "hero's" actions grew more depraved.

This is a practice that would not be recommended or encouraged by many Madison Avenue advertising executives. The main goal of any advertiser is to grow the viewership, not frustrate them to such an extent that the viewers will be frightened away. Ironically, Gilligan did not manage to shake off anyone or, if he did, new viewers rapidly replaced such deserters. The show kept attracting more and more of an audience, so much so that DreamWorks CEO Jeffrey Katzenberg offered Gilligan $75m to produce three additional episodes beyond the finale.[6] Gilligan turned down this offer. After all, Walter's story had been told.

One could either explain this exponential growth of the viewership on the general perverseness of modern society or on the fact that—despite what the gatekeepers believe—the audience will often flock to the novel and the controversial and the ambiguous over the tired and the comfortable and the staid. It is common for the gatekeepers to push potential audience members away by refusing to take creative risks.

It takes iconoclasts like Budd Boetticher and Vince Gilligan to take such risks. Despite the fact that Boetticher died in November of 2001, eight years before the premiere of *Breaking Bad*, his effect on the show is substantial. There are small but significant clues embedded throughout *Breaking Bad* that Boetticher's maverick spirit had a direct influence on the show's approach to unconventional storytelling. The ways in which Boetticher and Gilligan deal with ambiguity are demonstrably similar. Both allow the audience to reach their own conclusions about certain unanswered questions involving the motivations of their main characters. In *Breaking Bad*, one of Walter's major motivations for launching his drug empire is a sense of mounting frustration over having been denied the fruits of the research he conducted during his college years. Walter feels that this research was hijacked and exploited by his former college friends, Elliot and Gretchen Schwartz. Despite the fact that he helped launch the Schwartzs' company, Gray Matter Technologies, now worth billions, Walter never made a penny off his early work. We know that Walter and Gretchen dated in college. We know that, when the relationship ended, Gretchen began dating Walter's best friend, Elliot. Walter then detached himself from the company, and the Schwartzs moved on to fame and fortune.

Early on in season one, the Schwartzs offer to pay all of Walter's healthcare expenses in order to help him fight his cancer. His extreme pride compels him to reject this offer. Later, we see Gretchen call Walter on the phone and ask him if his refusal had "anything to do with us," meaning her and Walter. Walter hesitates at first, then avoids answering the question. To get her off the phone, he lies and insists that his health insurance came through for him after all. He no longer needs their financial assistance, he claims.

Given Walter's seemingly passive nature, we at first assume that Gretchen left *him*, prompting his withdrawal from Gray Matter Technologies; during season two, however, Gretchen uncovers Walter's lie and demands to know the true reason for refusing her initial offer. The truth, suppressed for so long, erupts out of Walter in a paroxysm of anger. He feels ripped off by both Elliot and Gretchen and insists they made their billions off his hard labor. Gretchen seems stunned by this accusation. "That can't possibly be how you see it," she says. "*You* left *me*." This new revelation upends our initial impression of the dynamic between Walter and Gretchen. Over the course of the show's five seasons, we are never definitely told the true story of Gray Matter Technologies. In the penultimate episode, both Gretchen and Elliot insist that Walter had nothing to do with the founding of the company except for coming up with the name. What's the truth of the situation? The answer could go either way. We know that Walter has a strong capacity for self-delusion which seems to indicate that Elliot and Gretchen's version of reality is the correct one. On the other hand, we have also seen an equal amount of evidence that Walter is a highly intelligent and self-reliant man capable of dreaming up never-before-seen ideas and seeing them through to fruition. Therefore, this could indicate that Walter's version of reality is correct. By the end of the series, Gilligan and his writing team do not give us a definitive answer. It is entirely up to the viewer to decide which version is the right one.

In *Decision at Sundown* we are not certain who is telling the truth about Allison's wife. We're never definitively told what led to Mary's suicide or who's really to blame—indeed, if anyone is to blame at all. We're given the subjective impressions of several different players—including Allison, Sam, and Kimbrough—but any sort of objective answer is veiled from us, just as *Breaking Bad* relies on the viewers to exercise their imaginations and reach their own conclusions about the reality that lies behind the actions of the characters.

Another clue pointing to Boetticher's influence on Gilligan is the visual style of *Breaking Bad*. As noted earlier, Gilligan has stated he was pleased that the show's setting was diverted from Riverside to Albuquerque because New Mexico became an essential character on the show. According to *New York Times* reporter Emily Brennan, "Only after he arrived in Albuquerque and saw the desert stretching to the horizon [...] did [Gilligan] realize that the show, in that landscape, could be a modern-day Western."[7]

Perhaps better than any other Western director, Boetticher knew how to use the vast desert landscapes in his films as visual poetry, not merely as a tired signifier to establish the exact nature of the film's genre. Boetticher himself once said:

> What I would do that other directors didn't do—*I* know every inch of Lone Pine [a picturesque area in Inyo County, California, characterized by a high desert climate that has served many different film productions going as far back as George Melford's *The Roundup* in 1920 and as recently as Gareth Edwards' *Godzilla* in 2014] on horseback, 'cause I went where [other directors] never went.[8]

Having an intimate knowledge of such remote environments no doubt invested Boetticher's films with a unique visual style. When Boetticher began shooting his films in CinemaScope, he took full advantage of this much wider canvas to establish important character beats with nothing more than a single image. For example, at the very beginning of *Ride Lonesome*, the emotional state of our protagonist is subliminally laid bare for the audience when we see a beautiful—and yet paradoxically barren—desert landscape that threatens to overwhelm the tiny black dot off in the distance which at last emerges as our hero, Ben Brigade. With a rich tableau like this unfolding before our eyes, the audience doesn't need to be explicitly told anything about Brigade's tragic past, at least not yet. Instead, the breathtaking images subtly reveal the emptiness at the center of Brigade's soul.

Gilligan makes similar use of the desert landscape in *Breaking Bad*, often contrasting its vastness—the primal sense of freedom it instills in the human mind—with the increasing sense of confinement felt by Walter as his ambitions of economic freedom lead only to a further sense of entrapment brought down on him by rival drug lords and encroaching law enforcement officers. As with the very best directors, such as Alfred Hitchcock and Orson Welles, both Boetticher and Gilligan know how to compress an array of complex emotions within a single image. Gilligan once gave this piece of advice to young screenwriters:

> Show your story, don't tell it. Try not to depend too much on dialogue. Try to remember that it's very much a visual medium and that sometimes more can be said with a look between characters [or perhaps a tracking shot of a desolate desert landscape] than a whole spat of words.[9]

Further connections can be drawn between Boetticher and Gilligan. Whether intentional or not, one theme that so often winds its way through Western fiction is that of the primal brutality of social Darwinism, the dog-eat-dog harshness of a capitalistic system run amok. Whether it's Joseph H. Lewis' *Terror in a Texas Town* (1958), Nicholas Ray's *Johnny Guitar* (1954), or even a simple farce such as Edward Buzzell's *Go West* (1940), starring the Marx Brothers, the plots often revolve around the destructive consequences of greed. In his October 2013 interview with Karen Herman, vice-president of the Archive of American Television, Gilligan has gone on record as stating that his original intention behind *Breaking Bad* was to explore complex characters rather than make any overt moral or political statements about the United States, and yet one cannot help but see an implicit critique of the crumbling American empire in the image of a beaten-down Walter White rolling a single barrel of money through the unforgiving desert landscape in the sixtieth episode of the series, "Ozymandias."[10] For me, this bloodstained barrel evokes cinematic memories of *Seven Men from Now*, Boetticher's personal favorite of all of his films, and vivid memories of Bill Masters (Lee Marvin) standing over a Wells Fargo box in the middle of the desert, with his eager hands reaching for the guns strapped to his hips, ready to give up his life for the contents of that precious box: $20,000 in stolen gold. Though Walter's barrel contains considerably more loot than $20,000, the emotion evoked by the image is very similar indeed. Inflation may alter the specific digits involved, but the consequences of blind ambition remain unchanged. Early in season five of *Breaking Bad*, Walter references the ancient Greek myth of Icarus flying far too close to the sun to explain the untimely death of a former business associate, not understanding that the same myth could apply to himself just as well.

Other Boetticher obsessions loom over Gilligan's epic narrative. Stepping away for a moment from Boetticher's collaborations with Randolph Scott, consider in his earlier films the recurring theme of primal secrets lurking just beneath the thin veneer of modern life. In Boetticher's 1948 noir thriller, *Behind Locked Doors*, Richard Carlson stars as private detective Ross Stewart who pretends to be insane in order to infiltrate a criminal conspiracy operating behind the walls of an insane asylum baring the innocuous name of "La Siesta." It is not hard to see the considerable influence of *Behind Locked Doors* on far more famous films such as Samuel Fuller's *Shock Corridor* (1963) and Miloš Forman's *One Flew Over the Cuckoo's Nest* (1975). In *Behind Locked Doors*, which was Boetticher's eighth film, a respectable doctor named Clifford Porter (Thomas Browne Henry) is working with organized crime to hide a wanted criminal from the authorities. In *Breaking Bad*, a respectable businessman (the aforementioned Gustavo Fring) uses his popular fast food chain, Los Pollos Hermanos, as a cover for an array of criminal conspiracies. Similarly, Walter uses his position as a high school chemistry teacher to cover up his growing drug manufacturing operation.

This theme can also be found in one of Boetticher's final films, *The Rise and Fall of Legs Diamond* (1960) in which gangster kingpin Arnold Rothstein uses his cover as a respectable businessman to run illegal liquor operations in Prohibition-era New York. Though *Breaking Bad* makes direct references to Brian DePalma's *Scarface* (1983), going so far as to include a scene in season five in which Walter and his son are happily watching DePalma's film in their living room, the gangster epic that most parallels Walter's gradual ascent—and precipitous fall—in the criminal underworld is Boetticher's *The Rise and Fall of Legs Diamond*. Like Diamond (Ray Danton), Walter White uses his wife's profession as a cover for his criminal operations, has a relative (in Diamond's case a brother, in Walter's case a brother-in-law) shot by a rival drug lord, seizes a gangster's empire by observing the intricacies of his operation up-close, and manages to hold onto that empire for only a brief amount of time before forces larger than himself intervene.

Another clue to Boetticher's influence on *Breaking Bad* could not be more overt. Season three of *Breaking Bad* introduces a character who is assigned to Walter as his lab assistant. This character, Gale (David Costabile), is a libertarian chemist who greatly admires Walter's genius. Gale has turned his back on the confining strictures of academia and the corporate world in order to be free to pursue less orthodox avenues of chemical research. Gale considers Walter to be something of a role model. Though at first the two men seem to get along quite well, eventually Gale becomes an unwitting threat to Walter's continued existence. The cliffhanger of season three revolves around Gale's final fate.

The surname Vince Gilligan chose for Gale is "Boetticher."

Like Gale, Budd Boetticher turned his back on the confining strictures of his profession in order to pursue creative freedom. He abandoned Hollywood, turned down multiple offers to make big budget studio films and, instead, spent much of the 1960s in Mexico working on a documentary about his friend Carlos Arruza, the famous bullfighter. After almost a decade during which the filming was interrupted several times by a long series of personal tragedies, the documentary was at last released in the early 1970s under the title *Arruza*. Boetticher's unflagging obsession with this project cost him his career. After 1971, he never directed another film. Like Gale (and Walter White as well?), perhaps Budd Boetticher had flown too close to the sun.

In many of Boetticher's films, the main character is a lone man who is driven to accomplish a just goal against all odds. Except for *Decision at Sundown*, the protagonist of the film is always heroic, sure of themselves, and upholds basic American values such as truth and justice. These are values Boetticher clearly believed in. The characters portrayed by Randolph Scott were living symbols of those beliefs.

If we can learn anything about the current state of American life by placing Boetticher's sixty-year-old films side by side with Vince Gilligan's twenty-first-century Western saga, *Breaking Bad*, perhaps it is simply this: that Randolph Scott's straight-shooting gunfighter is representative of what we think we once were, and Walter White's desperate trek through the desert behind a bloodstained barrel of cash is what we fear we have all become.

Chapter 3

The Brain(s) That Killed Kennedy

The JFK Assassination as Seen Through Film

1. While My Body Roams the World

THOUGH CINEMA CAN sometimes act as a mirror, reflecting the present trends of society back at itself, it can also sometimes act as a magic mirror: a mirror out of myth and legend that predicts events that have not yet occurred, that reveals secrets not yet unveiled. Cinema can, in rare cases, act as a Cassandra that delivers the bad news of the future to a society that will only accept disturbing developments through the lens of entertainment.

One such case is Edward L. Cahn's *Creature with the Atom Brain* (1955). The script was written by Curt Siodmak, a prolific writer of both screenplays and novels. He is best known for his 1942 science fiction novel, *Donovan's Brain* (which was officially adapted for film at least three times and unofficially even more so), as well as for having written the screenplay for the classic horror film, *The Wolf Man* (1941), starring Lon Chaney, Jr in the title role. The early 1940s was a good time for Mr Siodmak.

But it was not a good time for Siodmak's homeland. Siodmak, along with other German émigrés, arrived in the United States to escape Adolf Hitler's fascist regime in Nazi Germany. Like Thomas Mann and

Bertolt Brecht, Siodmak ended up in Hollywood writing screenplays. Unlike Mann and Brecht, however, Siodmak's specialty was not the sort of gravitas-laden literary tome we associate with German novelists. Siodmak was an ideas man, and some of these ideas were quite bizarre for the time period. *Donovan's Brain*, a fast-paced science fiction thriller with stripped-down prose, remains a taut page-turner even today. Many of the science fiction novels written in the 1940s and fifties, perhaps inevitably, have a dated quality to them. Even the best of them—Alfred Bester's *The Demolished Man*, for example—can only be fully appreciated if the readers can somehow manage to project themselves back into the year in which the novel was written and see it from that perspective. *Donovan's Brain*, on the other hand, seems to transcend its time period, perhaps because Siodmak wasn't attempting to write "Great Literature." While its minimalist prose style feels very modern, the Gothic overtones lend the story a timeless quality not unlike Mary Shelley's *Frankenstein*. In the novel's corner is the fact that its speculative elements and central philosophical issues are still relevant today. This, too, makes the novel similar to Shelley's *Frankenstein*.

The basic plot of the novel involves a maverick scientist, Dr Patrick Cory, who steals the brain of a dying financier, W.H. Donovan, and keeps it alive in his laboratory in Washington Junction, Arizona. Donovan's personality is so strong, however, that the brain begins to assert control over Cory's consciousness. Indeed, Donovan does so to such an extreme degree that Cory finds himself reduced to little more than a remote-controlled puppet being moved about by the businessman's telepathic commands.

At one point in the novel, Siodmak writes:

> The brain's penetration is slow, but irresistibly it has engulfed every part of my cerebellum.
>
> One day it may take over my activities completely. The impulses which prompt my actions will generate in Washington Junction, while my body roams the world directed by remote control.
>
> Thus in a future state a human being could be commanded by a chosen super-brain and be guided robot-like from a central station.[1]

Throughout the 1940s and fifties, coincidentally, this was a primary goal of a dedicated cadre of scientists working for several intelligence agencies throughout the world, the Central Intelligence Agency being the most prominent among them.

In 1942 Siodmak stumbled upon a notion that was only being whispered about among certain scientists at that time. It could very well have been the above passage that attracted the attention of the Office of Strategic Services, for at some point in the early forties the OSS invited Siodmak to join their ranks as an intelligence agent.

In his autobiography, *Wolf Man's Maker: Memoir of a Hollywood Writer*, released a year after his death, Siodmak describes his first day working for the OSS in a chapter called "The War and Hollywood:"

> A colonel with a florid face that telegraphed a coming stroke was intrigued by my Hollywood background. He had my files in front of him and also two copies of *Donovan's Brain*. The OSS obviously was dissecting my life and keeping track of my activities.
>
> "I was informed that this book of yours just came out," the colonel said. He didn't say who informed him. "The title intrigued me, and I ordered half a dozen for our files, because I thought you had written about our boss, General 'Wild Bill' Donovan."
>
> I picked up a copy of my book. I hadn't seen it before, though it might be waiting for me at home. I liked the cover, which was done in good taste. "Sign this copy. I'll send it to the general. Write in, 'For William Donovan from Field Operator 76.' He'll get a kick out of that joke. The OSS is independent. No bureaucracy, no interference from Congress, no senators to screw things up."[2]

After Siodmak returned from the War, the content of several of his films seemed to reflect his experiences in the OSS. His 1954 film, *Riders to the Stars* (directed by one of its lead actors, Richard Carlson), can be seen as semi-autobiographical. The film lays out the step-by-step process of being "invited" into an intelligence agency in very accurate detail that's not at all dissimilar to the events Siodmak describes in his memoir. It's possible to conclude, then, that some of his other 1950s films may very well reveal knowledge he picked up while serving as a spy for both the OSS as well as its later incarnation, the Central Intelligence Agency.

2. Creature with the Atom Brain (1955)

IN 1955 REMOTE-controlled assassins stalked the streets of America. I'm surprised you haven't heard about it. It was in all the papers.

The Brain(s) That Killed Kennedy

"DEAD MEN WALK CITY STREETS" is only one of the many provocative headlines that swirl toward the screen in Edward Cahn's *Creature with the Atom Brain*. The average Joe in 1955 might have been distressed to know that the United States was spending millions of dollars in an attempt to turn men into "zombies" (metaphorically speaking, that is), to create a remote-controlled assassin with no will of its own, but if the same information were presented in the form of fiction he might actually be entertained by it all. *Creature with the Atom Brain* unleashes sensitive intelligence information to the public within the form of fiction.

This film is really about the secret headlines of the world, the ones no one ever sees or hears about, except in the form of myth or rumor. In his 1967 book *Were We Controlled?*, Lincoln Lawrence wrote:

> The public is generally aware of the time lag between the development of advanced scientific weapons of defense and their announcement. Secrecy makes sense on the checker-board of international power politics. The "Manhattan Project" comes all too vividly to mind in this context. [...]
>
> [In 1940] a man named Fred Allhoff felt [...] that we were going to have the very foundations of our existence shaken by the announcement of a scientific advance that was being held back from us. Under the guise of fiction titled "Lightning in the Night" in *Liberty* magazine of November 16 of that year, Allhoff broke through that time lag barrier and his readers were given [...] *advance* information [...].
>
> Wrote Allhoff:
>
> "...The President of the United States resumed, 'As you gentlemen have suggested, the development of atomic energy will mean a revolutionary change in the life of every human being now on earth. It can be an overwhelming force for good or for evil.' ...later... 'We saw its potentialities as a weapon of war, but even more clearly as an unlimited source of heat, of light, of power for peaceful production and transportation...' ...and further on... 'Our goal, I must repeat, was the creation of a new, rich peaceful world for all. To reach that goal, we needed to unlock atomic energy before you (Hitler) could do so; to produce tons of pure uranium-235 before you could do so; and then to master the world through the threat of its irresistible destructive force—a force we hoped would never have to be put to use... a weapon that must inevitably overwhelm and subdue any nation on earth.'"
>
> Mr. Allhoff revealed the major scientific advance of his time *years* before the scientific black-out was lifted.[3]

One might call this type of fiction a "disclosure story," in the sense that it reveals Top Secret information years before it was made available to the public. *Creature with the Atom Brain*, written fifteen years after Allhoff's piece, is just such a "disclosure story." On the surface, the plot of *Creature with the Atom Brain* concerns itself with a police scientist named Chet Walker (Richard Denning) who is trying to solve a series of bizarre murders perpetrated by an unlikely pair: a fugitive ex-crime-boss named Frank Buchanan (Michael Granger) and a German scientist named Wilhelm Steigg (Gregory Gaye). The scientist, using electrical and chemical stimulation of the brain, is able to animate the bodies of dead men and use them as remote-controlled assassins. Clearly, the main gimmick around which the plot revolves (the reanimation of the dead) is a metaphor for a far larger issue: the ongoing attempt by authoritarian forces to develop sophisticated techniques that would render everyone "beneath" them into mind-controlled zombies. Except that this is more than just a metaphor. *Creature with the Atom Brain* borders on pure realism, and Siodmak was in a position to know it.

As a member of the OSS, and later the CIA, Siodmak must surely have known about the experimental—and, later, *operational*—work of Dr José M.R. Delgado. Delgado was an authority in neuro-behavioral research. Both within the laboratory, as well as outside of it, Delgado proved over and over again that he could control animals from afar using electrical and chemical stimulation of the brain. It's doubtful Delgado ever considered reanimating a corpse, but then again that was just the sensational MacGuffin Siodmak used in order to market his tale as a "science fiction/horror" flick. If one removes the aspect of reanimating the dead from the film, what you're left with is a fairly accurate depiction of the top secret experiments Delgado was conducting at the very same time that Siodmak would have been writing the screenplay for *Creature with the Atom Brain*.

According to Delgado's biography, the doctor "was born in Ronda, Spain, and received his medical training at Madrid University, where he was Associate Professor of Physiology until 1950 when he came to Yale University to work with Dr. John Fulton."[4] By the late sixties he had risen to a full Professor of Physiology at Yale where he conducted numerous "experiments" for the Central Intelligence Agency to develop techniques with which to create the perfect assassin: one who could kill on command but not remember anything about his actions, or who was really behind them, after the hit was complete.

Several books were written about Delgado's research, perhaps the most important being the one Delgado wrote himself: *Physical Control of the Mind: Toward a Psychocivilized Society*. Published in 1969, Delgado's book laid out a blueprint for how society could—and would—be governed in the near future. Delgado advocates a *Clockwork Orange* world where everyone follows the rules of society simply because they have no choice to do otherwise, the urge to do "wrong" having been programmed out of them. Or as Siodmak wrote in *Donovan's Brain*, "...in a future state a human being could be commanded by a chosen super-brain and be guided robot-like from a central station." I suspect it was this sentence, above all others, that drew the OSS's attention to Siodmak and his writing.

A pair of important books were written about Delgado and his research in the 1970s. One was *Operation Mind Control* by Walter Bowart (1978) and *The Search for the Manchurian Candidate* by John Marks (1979). Though both detailed the CIA's interest in mind control, the two books could not have been more different. In fact, the differences are evident in the titles themselves. Bowart's book claimed that the CIA's programs were *operational* and had been for years, whereas Marks claimed that the "search" for a Manchurian Candidate was just that: a wrongheaded experiment that never bore any useful fruit. Oddly enough, Marks' book remained in print for years whereas Bowart's book went out of print very quickly despite selling well in its initial run.

Bowart's book boasted an introduction by none other than Richard Condon, the author of the bestselling 1959 novel *The Manchurian Candidate*, which was later adapted by screenwriter George Axelrod and director John Frankenheimer into the 1962 film of the same name. In this introduction Condon reveals that his novel about a remote-controlled assassin who attempts to kill a presidential candidate was never meant to be anything more than a political satire. Condon was later shocked to discover, primarily from the revelations in Bowart's book, that his own crazy imagination had somehow paralleled reality itself.

Condon was not aware of Delgado's research when he wrote his breakthrough novel. And yet Siodmak clearly was aware of it, at least as early as 1955 when *Creature with the Atom Brain* was released. Though B-films were written and produced at a fast clip in the 1950s, I suspect the screenplay was probably written sometime in 1954.

1954. By that year Delgado had published only four articles about his research, all of them in very obscure technical journals: "Permanent Implantation of Multilead Electrodes in the Brain" in the *Yale Journal of Biology* (1952), "Hidden Motor Cortex of the Cat" in the *American Journal of Physiology* (1952), "Technique of Intracranial Electrode Implacement for Recording and Stimulation and Its Possible Therapeutic Value in Psychotic Patients" in *Confinia Neurologica* (1952), and "Learning Motivated by Electrical Stimulation of the Brain" in the *American Journal of Physiology* (1954).

It's possible that Siodmak was reading these journals for fun, but I doubt it. I suspect he found out about Delgado's research through his colleagues in the OSS and, later, the CIA. In fact, given the subject matter of such a popular novel as *Donovan's Brain*, it's more than possible that Siodmak was personally introduced to Delgado. Delgado himself may have requested an interview. Given the intelligence world's penchant for working with science fiction writers from time to time—novelists such as H.G.Wells, Cordwainer Smith, James Blish, and Janet Morris—it's not impossible.

It is known that interested parties with the right connections could indeed earn ingress into Delgado's sanctum sanctorum at Yale University. Lincoln Lawrence wrote about Delgado's research in his 1967 book *Were We Controlled?* In Chapter Five, Lawrence (who may actually have been a former FBI agent named Arthur J. Ford) strongly implies that he visited Delgado in his laboratory without coming out and saying so directly:

> Those who are allowed into the Delgado first floor laboratories in the handsome Yale building in New Haven experience quite an adventure—if they get the permission (rarely granted) to visit the area where the Macaque Mulata monkeys, used by the doctor in his experiments, are kept.
>
> The first-time visitor to those well-lighted cage areas will be shaken by the sight that awaits him. It is one thing to *read* of the experiments, in the neat type of medical reports, and quite another to see the monkeys close up with the tiny metal antennae implanted in the top of their skulls. They are lively enough, and well cared for. They are normal monkeys until the buttons on a small nearby hand transmitter which resembles a walkie-talkie are pressed. And then?...
>
> Then—suddenly—the year 2000—is *now*!
>
> A vital question that would link ESB [Electrical Stimulation of the Brain] research at Yale with advanced RHIC [Radio-Hypnotic Intrac-

> erebral Control] was put to Delgado bluntly. Had the control of the brain been attempted on either humans or animals using radio waves alone… with no implantation in the skull? A guarded look came into the scientist's eyes. "There had been experiments…" That was as much as he would say.
>
> In his paper published in Exerpta Medica International Congress No. 87 (Tokyo 1965), Professor Delgado in reference to chronic radio-stimulation of the brain has this to say in his conclusions: "Radio-stimulations of the brain were applied for five seconds once a minute, more than 20,000 times during fourteen days, with reliable results and without disturbances of thresholds, spontaneous electrical activity, or morphology of neurons. These facts suggest that programmed stimulations of the brain may be carried out perhaps indefinitely."
>
> Remember those words, *programmed stimulations* and *perhaps indefinitely*. As our journey through the structure of The Rumor moves into strange byways, they will reassure you we are not dealing here with science fiction.[5]

No indeed. And neither was Curt Siodmak when he decided to base an entire film around Delgado's research as early as 1954.

You might be asking yourself how one can be so sure that Siodmak was aware of Delgado's research. Isn't it possible Siodmak just stumbled over a fictional parallel, as he had done earlier with *Donovan's Brain*? The answer: No, that's impossible, and this is why: Siodmak practically mentions Delgado's name in the middle of the film.

Here's the scene: About halfway into *Creature with the Atom Brain*, the film stops in order to present a film within the film. I've been increasingly interested in these types of scenes. In several movies that could be described as "disclosure films" there is just such a moment, and they usually occur midway through the film. Similar films-within-films play important roles in three other movies under discussion here: *The Parallax View*, *They Live*, and *JFK*. We'll go more into those examples later.

Such interstitial, intertextual films bear some similarity to the play within the play that occurs at the core of *Hamlet*. Hamlet stages a play titled *The Murder of Gonzago* that mirrors the murder of his father in order to provoke a reaction from the main suspect, Hamlet's uncle (and stepfather), Claudius. Hamlet's play is presented as make believe, but in truth it's a "disclosure story." It presents the secret details of a criminal act in the form of fiction. All the films under discussion here perform the precise same function.

At one point in *Creature with the Atom Brain*, Chet Walker consults with Kenneth C. Norton (Nelson Leigh), a scientist in the Department of Neurology at City Hospital, while on his search for Wilhelm Steigg, a German scientist Walker suspects of being the main culprit behind a rash of mysterious murders that have swept over the unnamed metropolis in recent weeks. Norton reveals to Walker that Steigg "won the 1948 Norton Prize in Amygdala stimuli," a comment that prompts the following exchange:

> WALKER: Amygdala stimuli? What's that?
> NORTON: Ultra shortwave stimulations to specific parts of the brain, producing involuntary movements of the body.
> WALKER: Highly specialized stuff.
> NORTON: Yes. A number of stories have been published about amygdala stimulation of monkeys. Here's one of them. [Norton hands Walker a medical journal, the pages turned to a specific article.] Appropriations have been made for research and development. And there's a doctor in Madrid who's made great advances since this article was published.

This throwaway line can refer to no one other than Dr José M. R. Delgado, the only authority in neuro-behavioral research who was conducting such experiments on monkeys in Madrid. By 1955, however, the year *Creature with the Atom Brain* was released, Delgado had already been well ensconced at Yale for five years. The line that precedes the not-so-subtle reference to Delgado, the one that mentions appropriations having been made for "research and development," no doubt refers to the fact that Delgado's experiments had been "quietly subsidized by grants from the Office of Naval Research" for years.[6] The only way Siodmak could have known such a thing in 1954–55 would be if he had heard the information from his contacts in the intelligence world, or if he knew Delgado personally.

The scene in Norton's office continues, segueing into the aforementioned "film-within-a-film":

> WALKER: Have you been conducting any experiments here at the hospital?
> NORTON: No, but I have a short film I told you about. Would you like me to run it?

WALKER: Well, I'd appreciate it.
NORTON: Fine. Draw the curtains, will you?

Imagine being an average filmgoer in 1955, lured in by the sensationalistic title of this movie. Film historian Bill Warren writes in *Keep Watching the Skies!* that "this film's title sums up the appeal of the science fiction/monster movies of the 1950s. It's lurid, it's to the point, and it deals with (a) monsters, (b) atomic radiation and (c) intelligence, all within a single exploitable phrase."[7] Imagine that this hypothetical filmgoer sits down for an afternoon's "lurid" entertainment and is instead treated to a film-within-a-film that reveals research most people in 1950s America did not realize was being actively pursued by their stalwart intelligence agencies and subsidized by their very own tax dollars. They probably thought this little "film-within-a-film" was pure fiction. But those in the know, like Claudius watching *The Murder of Gonzago* in *Hamlet*, might have been deeply disturbed by—or, conversely, deeply proud of—what was being revealed here.

Chet Walker settles down in his chair while Dr Norton narrates silent footage that depicts a dog being remotely controlled via electrical stimulation of the brain. The entire film lasts about one minute:

> NORTON: This animal looks content, doesn't it? You wouldn't suspect it has eighteen electrodes inserted in its skull. Turning this switch releases a small amount of ultra short waves. Those electrodes are tuned to specific frequencies. As long as the impulse is released, the dog barks. [We see the dog barking in response to the flip of a switch.] By applying another impulse of different frequency, the dog immediately falls asleep. [We see the dog fall asleep.] It will lie there as long as the stimulus is active. Another impulse will make it vicious. [The dog grows angry.] Docile. [Abruptly, he falls asleep.] Hunger can be induced. [We see the dog get up and begin eating from a bowl.] Or it can be made to resent its food. [The dog turns away from the bowl in disgust. While switching off the film and turning on the lights, Norton finishes his speech.] Amygdala stimulations, somato-motor, and viscera-motor effects. Does this satisfy your curiosity?
> WALKER: Almost. [...] Do you think an experiment on humans would have the same result as on animals?

NORTON [a long pause follows as the doctor thoughtfully puffs on his pipe]: We haven't arrived at that stage of our experiment... yet. [Judging from the expression on his face, and the tone of his voice, one isn't entirely sure that Dr Norton is telling the truth here.]
WALKER: Could it be possible that somebody else has tried and already succeeded?
NORTON [evading the question]: Are you trying to connect the experiments with animals with mysterious events of our city?
WALKER: It would answer the riddle, wouldn't it? Remote controlled creatures, their brains powered by atomic energy, roaming the streets, directed from a central point.

Directed from a central point. This line echoes the aforementioned passage from *Donovan's Brain* that no doubt won Siodmak a Willy Wonka Golden Ticket into the OSS: "Thus in a future state a human being could be commanded by a chosen super-brain and be guided robot-like from a central station." This is a major concern on Siodmak's part. He first warns us about the possibility in *Donovan's Brain* in 1942, then hammers the point home again with even more specific details thirteen years later in *Creature with the Atom Brain.*

It's important to note that Siodmak is very careful about how he utilizes his most important metaphor throughout the screenplay. The characters who are transformed into "zombies" (when I use the word "zombie" in this context, I mean human beings whose brains are being "guided robot-like from a central station" thanks to Dr Steigg's E.S.B. techniques) are all authority figures: a beat cop, a military general, a homicide detective. It's as if Siodmak is saying that we can never trust those who have been appointed to protect us. After all, they might be controlled by Someone Else. And, of course, that's always been true, but it was a harsh fact of life rarely discussed in 1950s civics classes. It's a fact of life that's not adequately discussed even now.

The typical American naivety that insists one can trust Those In Power to always do the "right" thing was severely tested in the wake of the John F. Kennedy assassination in November of 1963. For the first time Americans became distrustful of what Those In Power were telling them. Many people came to believe that the official story did not match the facts. Mistrust and paranoia seeped into the fabric of American life like never before. There's a term in psychology to describe the tenuous mental state of a person who is forced to accept two conflicting versions of reality at the same time in order to function on a daily basis. This mental state is called "disassociation." It's a mode of survival often used by children who come from violent homes. When a family wears a false mask of civility and harmony in public, while hiding rampant abuse at home, children often "disassociate" in order to reconcile the paradox. "Disassociation" is simply the state of being detached from one's emotional and physical reality.

After the Kennedy assassination, the United States of America quickly devolved into the Disassociated States of America. Mommy and Daddy were lying to them, but since that was too painful to consider, the American people simply disassociated and went about their daily lives as if nothing at all was wrong. Just forget the pain and go through the motions. Become "psycho-civilized." Reduce yourself to a zombie guided robot-like from a central station—a central station broadcasting a constant barrage of propaganda and lies.

Despite this willful ignorance on the part of the American public, The Rumor began to spread only hours after JFK was murdered in Dallas. Lincoln Lawrence attempts to document, and ultimately verify, The Rumor in *Were We Controlled?* The Rumor is quite complicated and elaborate, but it essentially involves the use of E.S.B. and RHIC, the very techniques Siodmak was warning America about back in 1955, to cause men like Lee Harvey Oswald and Jack Ruby to kill with no memory of having done so. Lawrence spends a great deal of time exploring the research of scientists like Delgado to lay the groundwork, to prove that such a "science fictional" concept is indeed possible.

Were We Controlled? was published in 1967, only four years after the assassination. It predates Jim Garrison's investigation (that which inspired the 1991 Oliver Stone film *JFK*) by several years. *Were We Controlled?* is one of the earliest attempts to offer an alternative scenario to the official conclusion of the Warren Commission Report. Dissatisfied with the official story, and yet too frightened to admit that it could be anything but absolutely true, The Disassociated States of America spends the next fifty years trying to work out what really happened in the form of fiction—in the form of movies, as well as movies-within-movies. Hamlet puts on his little plays decade after decade, and sometimes King Claudius even strikes back at the perceived affront. Some of these filmmakers will end up dead before their films are even released (more on that later). But in each of these cases we see the evolving exploration of a Rumor, and an ongoing attempt to create sense from nonsense, order from chaos, truth from lies, unity from disassociation.

Siodmak came first. He was the Cassandra warning people about the dire reality before it had even been implemented. Then came his offspring, so to speak: John Gillig's *The Gamma People* (1956), John Frankenheimer's *The Manchurian Candidate* (1962) based on the 1959 novel by Richard Condon, Alan J. Pakula's *The Parallax View* (1974) based on the 1970 novel by Loren Singer, William Richert's *Winter Kills* (1979) based on the 1974 novel by Richard Condon, John Carpenter's *They Live* (1988) based on the 1963 short story "Eight O'clock in the Morning" by Ray Nelson, Oliver Stone's *JFK* (1991) based on the books *On the Trail of the Assassins* (1988) by Jim Garrison and *Crossfire* (1989) by Jim Marrs, and Jonathan Demme's remake of *The Manchurian Candidate* (2004).

Through these cinematic touchstones we can trace the anatomy of a rumor, and perhaps the anatomy of reality itself.

3. The Gamma People (1956)

> "The [Central Intelligence] Agency doesn't deal in facts, only rumors. And I have a lot more than rumors."
>
> —Leslie Nielsen, *Columbo: Identity Crisis*, 1975

ONLY A YEAR after the release of *Creature with the Atom Brain*, American audiences were assaulted by an even stranger film: *The Gamma People* directed by John Gillig. It was released during the Christmas season on the lower half of a double bill with, of all films, *1984*. Someone, somewhere, was definitely trying to send a message to the American people. Both films were clearly intended to be anti-Communist propaganda, and yet from the perspective of the present the totalitarian governments in both films seem far more similar to recent developments in the Disassociated States of America. *The Gamma People*, in particular, seems strangely subversive in the sense that it appears to be disclosing details about top secret experiments conducted by various United States intelligence agencies while the film was being made. These experiments have been made public within the past thirty years, so the only way the screenwriters could have been aware of the details is if they had friends on the inside, or if they themselves had access to the information à la Curt Siodmak. A third possibility is that their imag-

HE
COMES
FROM
BEYOND
THE
GRAVE!
CREATURE
WITH THE
ATOM
BRAIN
Based on Scientific Facts!
SHOCK-FULL OF THRILLS!
RICHARD DENNING
ANGELA STEVENS
A CLOVER PRODUCTION • A COLUMBIA PICTURE

GAMMA-RAY CREATURES LOOSE!
PAUL
DOUGLAS
EVA
BARTOK
"the gamma
people"

ination just happened to stumble over the truth.

The screenwriters of *The Gamma People* were John Gillig (the director) and John Gossage (one of the producers). Apparently, the screenplay was based on a story by Louis Pollock. Gillig is not known for making bizarro films, and *The Gamma People* is certainly an anomaly in that respect. He has, however, made other notable films in the science fiction/horror genre. Four years before *The Gamma People*, he directed Bela Lugosi in one of the actor's last films, *Old Mother Riley Meets the Vampire* (1952). A few years after *The Gamma People*, he directed several horror movies produced by Hammer Studios in England, among them *Plague of the Zombies* (1966), one of the most atmospheric and effective films that Hammer released in the late 1960s. As for the other writers involved, there's nothing in any of their careers that even hints at something as strange and paranoid and satirical as *The Gamma People*.

According to an essay by John M. Miller published on TCM.com, Robert Aldrich, the famous director of such classic films as *Kiss Me Deadly* (1955) and *What Ever Happened to Baby Jane?* (1962), contributed to the screenplay in its early stages. Miller writes, "*The Gamma People* evolved from a script treatment originally written in the early 1950s by Robert Aldrich [...]. According to Aldrich biographers Alain Silver and James Ursini, the original treatment was optioned by producer Irving Allen, but 'was shelved when its would-be star, John Garfield, was gray-listed.'"[8] This is suggestive, as Aldrich is known for his highly subversive films. Perhaps the "disclosure" elements in *The Gamma People* can be traced back to Aldrich's contributions?

It's noteworthy that the executive producer of the film was Albert R. Broccoli, who would later become famous as the executive producer of the popular James Bond franchise—not subversive films, by any means, and yet redolent with their own form of paranoia and unintentional surrealism. It's also interesting that *The Gamma People* is the one film on which he worked that Broccoli absolutely refused to discuss, even as late as the 1990s. On April 8, 2012, film writer Tom Weaver posted the following message on The Classic Horror Film Board:

> For some reason, this movie appears to have become kind of a lifelong pet peeve for producer Albert Broccoli. In a 1959 interview, he went off on a tangent to bring it up and mention that he DIDN'T want to make it; I think I've stumbled across at least one other story or inter-

> view where he brought it up out of the blue to complain about it; AND… I had a buddy who was friendly with Broccoli's family, and I asked my buddy to ask Broccoli if he'd talk to me about GAMMA PEOPLE. My buddy later reported back to me that he asked, and Broccoli stiffened up, the temperature in the room dropped about 20 degrees, and the unspoken message of "Don't… say… another… word" hung heavy in the air. This was in the '90s.[9]

It's clear to me that the surrealism in *The Gamma People* is not unintentional, and I can only credit John Gillig for the film's effectiveness. It's not out of bounds to suggest that *The Gamma People* prefigures the social satire and pop cultural paranoia of Patrick McGoohan's 1960s television series, *The Prisoner*. The mixture of dark comedy and scathing social commentary are prevalent in both. They also share the similarity of an outsider (or outsiders) stranded in a vaguely Balkanesque village from which they cannot escape. Though McGoohan's tour de force television series will always be more famous than *The Gamma People*, and justifiably so, *The Gamma People* is nonetheless worthy of reevaluation because of its slipstream quality (i.e., its post-modern mixture of various genres to bring about a darkly satirical effect), something very rare in 1950s American cinema. It's also noteworthy due to the fact that it's clearly a "disclosure" movie.

The movie is about an American journalist, Mike Wilson (Paul Douglas), and a British photographer, Howard Meade (Leslie Phillips), who accidentally wander into a mysterious European village known as "the Democratic Republic of Gudavia" and are held prisoner by a dictator named Boronski (Walter Rilla). Boronski is experimenting with the effects of radiation on certain children in the village in order to boost their intelligence and does not want this information released to the outside world.

Could Robert Aldrich have been aware of the fact that the United States government was performing exactly these types of experiments throughout the 1950s? Though Aldrich couldn't be considered an "insider," like Curt Siodmak, he was indeed the grandson of US Senator Nelson W. Aldrich and a cousin to Nelson Aldrich Rockefeller. Rockefeller, of course, was no stranger to cutting-edge developments in the intelligence world. In the early 1950s, around the same time that Aldrich would have been writing the original story upon which *The Gamma People* was based, Rockefeller was handpicked by President Eisenhower to work closely with the CIA as Special Assistant to the President for Foreign Affairs. According to Cary Reich, author of *The Life of Nelson A. Rockefeller: Worlds to Conquer, 1908–1958*, this position is known to insiders by a less polite name: "Special Assistant to the President for Psychological Warfare."[10] It's possible, therefore, that Aldrich could have had informal access to sensitive intelligence information that wouldn't come to light for forty more years.

In 1995 the Clinton administration formed an Advisory Committee to investigate human radiation experiments that had been conducted on US citizens—many of whom were children—throughout the 1940s and beyond. During their investigation, the Committee uncovered the fact that these radiation experiments on children overlapped with mind control experiments performed on the same victims. Though the mainstream media reported on the radiation experimentation aspect of their investigation, no mention was ever made of the mind control angle, no doubt the main imperative of the experiments in the first place. Over 100 pages of testimony from the survivors of these experiments were recorded by the Advisory Committee to absolutely no avail whatsoever. After hearing the testimony, Ruth Faden, the Chair of the Committee, refused to pursue the matter any further, brushed her hands of the entire affair, turned in her final report, and went on to become a Senior Research Scholar at the Kennedy Institute of Ethics, Georgetown University. Investigative journalist Jon Rappoport, nominated for a Pulitzer Prize in 1982 for his coverage of El Salvador, compiled the survivors' testimony heard by the Advisory Committee in a book titled *U.S. Government Mind Control Experiments on Children.*

In his introduction to the book, Rappoport writes:

> In the exposed and published literature, how far do government CIA (and Army) researchers go with their mind control experiments?
>
> Dr. Robert Heath of Tulane University, as early as 1955, working for the Army, gave patients LSD while he had electrodes implanted deep inside their brains.[11]

Electrodes deep inside the brain. This is exactly the same method of mind control depicted by Curt Siodmak in *Creature with the Atom Brain.* As Rappoport notes, Heath was conducting this research on human beings as early as 1955, the same year *Creature with the Atom Brain* was released in theaters. Very rarely does science fiction predict the future; more often than not it's a mirror reflection of the present. Just as George Orwell's *1984* was about 1948, the seemingly outlandish plot of *Creature with the Atom Brain* was a nearly accurate depiction of top secret experiments that were being funded by US tax dollars only ten years after the United States population had sacrificed so many young men to a war intended to wipe out the Nazi menace, a menace whose scientific methodology was alive and well at Tulane University (and other respectable universities) throughout the 1950s, and perhaps even all the way to the present day.

Electrodes inside the brain. This is the same method of mind control that José Delgado was using on monkeys and other animals during his many experiments at Yale University throughout the 1950s. But as Chet Walker says to Dr Kenneth C. Norton in *Creature with the Atom Brain*, "There's only one step between animals and human beings." I suspect Siodmak did not intend this line to be a mere warning. He was trying to tell the American population something they did not know, and do so in a way that would not result in retaliation against him. How better to disguise a serious political message than within a package that appears to be utterly innocuous?

In her presentation to the Presidential Commission on Radiation Committee, New Orleans therapist Valerie Wolf made the following opening statements:

> I am here to talk about a possible link between radiation and mind control experimentation that began in the late 1940's. The main reason that mind control research is being mentioned is because people are alleging that they were exposed, as children, to mind control, radiation, drugs and chemical experimentation which were administered by the same doctors who are known to have been involved in conducting both radiation and mind control research. [Throughout the Committee's investigation, the doctors that came up over and over again were Sidney Gottlieb, L. Wilson Green, Martin Orne, and Louis Jolyon West, all of whom received funding from many different military intelligence sources as well as the Central Intelligence Agency.] Written documentation has been provided revealing the names of people and the names of the research projects in statements from people across the country. It is also important to understand that mind control techniques and follow ups into adulthood may have been used to intimidate these particular research subjects into not talking about their victimization in government research.

> As a therapist for the past 22 years, I have specialized in treating victims and perpetrators of trauma and their families. When word got out that I was appearing at this hearing, nearly 40 therapists across the country contacted me to talk about clients who had reported being subjects in radiation and mind control experiments. The consistency of people's stories about the purpose of the mind control and pain induction techniques such as electric shock, use of hallucinogens, sensory deprivation, hypnosis, dislocation of limbs and sexual abuse is remarkable. There is almost nothing published on this aspect of mind control used with children and these clients come from all over the country, having had no contact with each other.[12]

One poster for *The Gamma People* depicts four children, all wearing the same uniforms, locked inside a laboratory with their heads encased in strange metal helmets that prevent them from seeing or even turning their heads. The tagline reads, "Fiendish Lab Experiments Are Performed On Innocent Children." If the mainstream media had done their jobs back in 1956, the year the movie was released, that tagline could just as easily have been a newspaper headline rather than a sensationalistic come-on meant to lure in thrill-seeking moviegoers. Did the people who designed the poster realize that this tagline was, in fact, an *accusation* as opposed to mere fictional ballyhoo? A movie poster as political broadside? When investigative journalists refuse to investigate, and judges refuse to mete out justice, and law enforcement agencies refuse to enforce the laws (and instead incessantly *break* them), perhaps the artists and the writers and the poets and, yes, the filmmakers are the only ones left to give a voice to the voiceless and document the untold terrors of the age. After all, perhaps presenting these horrible truths under the aegis of a bizarre sci-fi flick was better than no acknowledgement at all.

It's interesting to note that some of the Project Names of these illicit CIA-sponsored programs seem to reflect the basic plot of *The Gamma People* as well: "Moronic Response & Disfunctions," "Pediatric Radionthology," "Radioactive Waves," "Forced Brain Wave Activity," "Wave-Brain-Mind Authorities," "Frankenstein's Theory," and "Mind Over Matter Evolving."[13]

Midway through the film, journalist Mike Wilson manages to get his hands on Boronski's secret journal. He says to his colleague, Howard Meade, "Hey, just listen to this," then proceeds to read verbatim from the journal. When Wilson says, "Hey, listen to this," I suspect it's not just the character talking to his friend. This is the screenwriters—the filmmakers—speaking to the audience. *This is something important*, they're saying. *Pay special attention to this.*

Here's the quote from Boronski's journal:

> By exposing the immature brain to the gamma ray, or controlled radioactivity, I believe it is possible to determine certain developmental factors, both physical and mental. In the second stage, using this as a premise to work on, it is therefore possible to create geniuses or imbeciles at will. The whole future of the human race is already contained within the germ plasm, and after a million years of evolution, more or less, the full potentiality of the human mind will come to fruition. The gamma ray merely accelerates the natural processes of time.

This passage could have been ripped directly from the journals of any of the doctors (particularly the four mentioned above) involved in the CIA and Army programs to subject children to radioactivity and mind control experiments. Consider one of the Project names listed earlier: "Moronic Response & Disfunctions." In *The Gamma People*, Boronski's main objective is to create geniuses, to "improve the race"; however, he also creates a horde of subnormal "imbeciles" whom he uses as his own personal police force. "[Radiation] has many uses, Mr Wilson," Boronski proclaims near the end of the film. "It can be used to create geniuses [...], future leaders of the world. It can be used to create morons—'goons,' as you call them. They can be very useful also. Very useful, indeed."

According to the testimony delivered to the Advisory Committee, many experiments were performed on developmentally disabled children (exploiting what the CIA doctors referred to as the subjects' "moronic dysfunctions") because they were the most malleable and least likely to talk about the crimes committed against them. According to Dr Sidney Gottlieb, such children "were the LEAST likely to ever spill the beans."[14] Furthermore, one of the objectives of the mind control aspect of the experimentation was to create geniuses, future leaders, who would be controlled (behind the scenes) by their masters, i.e., the doctors who programmed them as children. This is clearly Boronski's objective as well.

Mind control survivor Christine Gentry told the Presidential Advisory Committee:

> It was deemed necessary to methodically control members [*sic*] behaviors and thought processes to fully participate in the cultic goals. Certain of the children were selected, those considered to be the best and the brightest, for future leadership within the organization. At about the age of four or five (1949–50), I was selected for future leadership, and was thus trained by Dr. Green.[15]

If Boronski wasn't based specifically on Dr Delgado, Dr Gottlieb, Dr Green, et al., then the screenwriters' imaginations were uniquely tuned to the dark unconscious of their times.

During her testimony before the Presidential Advisory Committee, a mind control survivor named Claudia Mullen stated that the only explanation given to her for why this type of experimentation was necessary was that she was "serving my country in their bold effort to stop Communism from spreading to my fellow Americans."[16] In 1956, most of the moviegoers who saw *The Gamma People* (and bothered to give it any thought at all) no doubt concluded it was a political satire about the abuses committed by Soviet Russia against its people. And though Soviet Russia may very well have conducted such experiments on its children during the Cold War, the only real documentation of which I'm aware regards crimes perpetuated by *American* doctors on *American* children. This is what a literary professor might call *irony*. Others might call it simply tragic.

Dr Colin A. Ross, MD, author of *The CIA Doctors: Human Rights Violations by American Psychiatrists*, wrote in a letter that was presented to the Presidential Advisory Committee by Valerie Wolf:

> Neurosurgeons at Tulane, Yale, and Harvard did extensive research on brain electrode implants with intelligence funding, and combined brain implants with large numbers of drugs including hallucinogens. In a paper I have, Dr. José Delgado at Yale describes implanting electrodes in the brain of an 11-year old boy and stimulating the boy's brain with a remote transmitter that had a range of up to 100 feet (this research was done in the 1960's). When a button was pushed on the transmitter, a specified electrode fired, and the boy would state that he was unsure whether he was male or female, and that he wanted to marry Dr. Delgado. This behavior occurred only when a specific brain electrode was stimulated.
>
> I mention this research to underline how sophisticated and destructive much of the documented mind control has been. MKULTRA

> [a covert research program into behavioral modification operated by the CIA from 1953 to 1973] alone included four Subprojects on children—one was conducted at the International Children's Summer Camp in Maine by an unwitting investigator. The MKULTRA Subproject file in my possession for this project states that the CIA's interest in this research was in establishing contact with foreign nationals of potential future operational use by the CIA—the children who served as subjects in the project were as young as 11 years old.[17]

Again, as Dr Chet Walker says, "There's only one step between animals and human beings."

At one point in *The Gamma People*, after the goons have murdered an old man in the village for daring to speak back against Boronski, Mike Wilson screams from a mountaintop, "I'll write the story! I'll bring this horror out into the open!" This was, almost without a doubt, the screenwriters speaking through their characters. The crimes of Doctors Delgado, Gottlieb, Green, Orne, West et al. are indeed accurately portrayed in the film through metaphor and thinly veiled disguises. Near the end of the movie, the citizens of Gudavia revolt *en masse* against Boronski's rule by disguising themselves behind grotesque masks and throwing a raucous carnival, just as the filmmakers disguise the historical truths of their accusations behind the grotesqueries of a seemingly standard horror story. And yet, despite Wilson's promise, the horrors that occurred in America never really were brought "out into the open." Most Americans are still not aware of the horrific crimes committed in their names, nor are they aware that an Advisory Committee appointed by President Clinton spoke to the survivors of these experiments face-to-face, and even preserved their testimony for all to see. (Searching for "Human Radiation Experiments Testimony" on YouTube will conjure up some of this archival footage.) The doctors who committed these crimes were never brought to justice. On the contrary, they all died as respected members of their communities, highly regarded in their chosen professions, ostensible bastions of Truth, Justice, and the American Way. But what else could one expect from the "democratic Republic" of America? If you don't like it, leave the country. Try moving to Gudavia. You might have better luck there, you commie-pinko bastard.

4. The Manchurian Candidate (1962)

FIRST ANIMALS AND dead people in *Creature with the Atom Brain*. Then children and "imbeciles" in *The Gamma People*. And now a fully grown, highly intelligent adult in John Frankenheimer's 1962 adaptation of Richard Condon's novel, *The Manchurian Candidate*. We're getting closer to the truth.

The Holy Bible tells us that man is the noblest of all creatures, but one must consider the source. After all, men wrote the Bible. If dolphins had written the Bible, perhaps that famous quote would have turned out differently. We've all been conditioned by a century or more of Darwinian thinking to assume that mankind is the apex of creation, that man is somehow inherently more "rational" and "strong-willed" than the average cat or dog. Surely some random feline would be far more susceptible to the dastardly types of mind control technology described in these passages than even the most slow-witted human being. Surely… yes…?

In his book *Operation Mind Control*, investigative journalist Walter Bowart writes:

> The cryptocracy has gone to absurd lengths to develop remote controlled beings. Victor Marchetti [author of the 1973 book *The CIA and the Cult of Intelligence*] revealed the CIA had once tried to create a cyborg cat. He said the Agency wired a feline for sound in an attempt to use the pet for eavesdropping purposes. The cat was first altered electronically so it would function as a listening device in areas where potential enemy agents would be discussing covert plots.
>
> But problems developed, Marchetti said, and the cat had to be rewired. The cat would wander away from its target area, as cats will, looking for food. The CIA fixed that by inserting wires directly into the hunger center of the cat's brain. The wires were attached to a radio receiver which would suppress the hunger pangs by remote control. But once that problem was solved, the CIA found the cat needed more circuitry in its brain to control its natural urges. After the hunger center was turned off, the cat still would wander away, this time following the sex instinct. The CIA planted more electrodes into the sex center of the cat's brain.
>
> After the electronic feline was at last ready for its assignment, it was turned loose on the street and was followed by a CIA support

> van loaded with electronic monitoring gear. However, before any conversations could be picked up, Marchetti said, "The poor thing got run over by a taxicab."[18]

These little problems didn't crop up with human beings. The more highly evolved the animal, the easier it is to control it from afar.

Richard Condon, author of *The Manchurian Candidate*, the best-selling novel in which Sgt Raymond Shaw is brainwashed into attempting to assassinate a presidential candidate, wrote the foreword to Bowart's *Operation Mind Control* in 1977, only a few months after our country's bicentennial. In this foreword he states:

> "Brainwashing" per se is no news to any of us. Controlled assassins are not known to us only through fiction [...]. Zombie is a quaint, old-fashioned folklore word which, by its meaning, becomes obscene when our children's minds are being controlled by any one of dozens of federal secret police agencies. Have government agencies perfected methods sustained by the taxpayers to control the minds of the people who shot the Kennedys, Martin Luther King, and Orlando Letelier, the former Chilean economist and diplomat? Were the assassins programmed to forget they did it or were they programmed to do it? We may never know for they stand bewildered, idiotically grinning for the cameras. Have the technicians developed a model Giant, Economy-Size Government Assassin which can easily be turned out by the thousands?[19]

By reading Bowart's book, Condon discovered that the outlandish conspiracy he had invented for satirical purposes in the pages of *The Manchurian Candidate* was, in fact, based on real events. He discovered that his imagination paled in comparison to the true scientific data Bowart had coaxed out of government archives through the Freedom of Information Act.

But in 1959, the year Condon's novel was released, the general public was not aware of any of this information; nor were they aware of it on October 24, 1962, the day John Frankenheimer's cinematic adaptation of Condon's novel was released in theaters. Though not a runaway hit financially, the film has since been recognized as a genuine classic. It features an array of stars in their finest roles: Frank Sinatra, Angela Lansbury, Janet Leigh, Laurence Harvey, etc. Released almost exactly a year before the assassination of John F. Kennedy, this film must have been fresh in many people's minds when the news of

Kennedy's death swept across the world.

Condon's imaginative conspiracy was so close to the possible truth that Frank Sinatra, in the early 1970s, arranged to block the film's distribution so that people wouldn't be allowed to make the obvious connection in their minds between the mind control aspects of the plot and the real world assassinations (including *attempted* assassinations) of political leaders like John F. Kennedy, Robert F. Kennedy, Martin Luther King, Malcolm X, George Wallace, and on and on and on. In his book *Keep Watching the Skies!*, film critic Bill Warren claims that the film was actually held back because of "Sinatra's anger at claims by distributor United Artists that it didn't make a profit, meaning Sinatra was denied his percentage."[20] Though seemingly reasonable, this doesn't explain why Sinatra also withdrew his 1954 film, *Suddenly*, which deals with an attempted presidential assassination by the mob.

Sinatra's daughter, Tina, claimed her father helped arrange Kennedy's election by pleading JFK's case to Sam Giancana, the head of the Chicago Mafia from 1957 to 1966. Sinatra assured the mob boss that Kennedy was the right horse to back in the 1960 election. Giancana believed him and gave Chicago to the Kennedys by arranging for a lot of "dead people" to cast votes for JFK (a perennial method of election rigging, particularly among Mafia types). Chicago pushed JFK over the top and allowed him to take the White House. Unfortunately, the second JFK became President he reneged on any deal he might have made with Giancana, at which point Attorney General Robert Kennedy started bringing the hammer down hard on mob bosses all around the country. (See the 1997 book, *The Dark Side of Camelot*, by investigative journalist Seymour Hersh for more information regarding JFK's ill-fated alliance with the Mafia.)

Apparently this so angered the Mafia that the plot to kill President Kennedy was put into effect, one of the main purposes of which was to eliminate Robert Kennedy's influence as the Attorney General. Carlos Marcello, head of the Mafia in New Orleans, promised several of his associates in the autumn of 1962 that the Kennedys would be "taken care of." One of these associates was Edward Becker, who repeated Marcello's threats to the United States House Select Committee on Assassinations on November 8, 1978:

> According to Becker's statement to Congress' Assassinations Committee, Marcello referred to President Kennedy as a dog, with his

If you come in five minutes after this picture begins, you won't know what it's all about!
when you've seen it all, you'll swear there's never been anything like it!
Frank Sinatra
Laurence Harvey
Janet Leigh
The Manchurian Candidate
co-starring
Angela Lansbury Henry Silva James Gregory
Produced by GEORGE AXELROD and JOHN FRANKENHEIMER Directed by JOHN FRANKENHEIMER
Screenplay by GEORGE AXELROD Based upon a Novel by RICHARD CONDON Executive Producer HOWARD W. KOCH
An M. C. PRODUCTION RELEASED THRU UNITED ARTISTS

> brother the Attorney General being the tail. He said, "The dog will keep biting you if you only cut off its tail," but that if the dog's head were cut off, the entire dog would die. The meaning of the analogy was clear—with John Kennedy dead, his younger brother would cease to be Attorney General, and harassment of the Mafia would cease. It was, at very least, a chilling prophecy of exactly what did happen after the assassination of President Kennedy one year later.[21]

Surely Frank Sinatra must have been aware of these Machiavellian developments throughout the 1,000 days of Kennedy's presidency. It's doubtful that he knew any details about the assassination itself, but when the news about Kennedy's death went over the airwaves, it wouldn't have been difficult for Sinatra to put together the pieces of this disturbing puzzle. And if *Sinatra* could put it together, I'm sure he would have understood how simple it would be for the average filmgoer to put the plot together as well. It was in Sinatra's best interest not to have people looking too closely at how Kennedy was elected in the first place. Thus, he removed *both* films from distribution, not just *The Manchurian Candidate.*

The Manchurian Candidate is dangerous on many different levels. Throughout the history of literature, the best satirists are those who don't narrowly focus their attention on one specific target. All great satirical novels have a broad scope; everyone is in the crosshairs. This is true of every satirical masterpiece from Jonathan Swift's *Gulliver's Travels* (1726) to Walt Kelly's *Pogo* (1948–73) to Kurt Vonnegut's *Slaughterhouse-Five* (1969) to Thomas Pynchon's *Gravity's Rainbow* (1973) to Chuck Palahniuk's *Fight Club* (1996) to Trey Parker and Matt Stone's *South Park* (1997 to the present). The satirical aspects of Condon's story are so brilliantly honed that some critics attacked the film for being "anti-American" while others accused it of being "anti-Communist propaganda." The significance of this film can't be overstated. As Bill Warren writes in *Keep Watching the Skies!*, "In some ways, the film has almost as much influence as *Citizen Kane*, but its great impact on moviemakers has rarely been noted [...]. It's as daring as any Hollywood film of the 1960s, and retains most of its power today."[22]

As the complex plot unfolds, the film introduces many of the basic techniques of mind control that had been unknown to the general public before this point. A few years after the Korean War, Captain Bennett Marco appears to be suffering from some form of post-traumatic stress syndrome. He's experiencing recurring nightmares that make him suspicious about what really occurred to him and his platoon during the war. Since there are strong strains of *noir* running throughout the film, it's only appropriate that there be a detective in the story. In a way, Captain Marco is a detective trying to solve the mystery of his own trauma, a murder he's seen only in his dreams. It turns out that Marco and other members of his platoon were taken prisoner by Chinese communists during the war and forced to undergo intense torture and hypno-programming. Marco's fellow infantryman, Sgt Raymond Shaw, is the fruit of this experiment. He was forced by the Communists to murder a fellow soldier right in front of Marco during one of these intense hypno-programming sessions. Marco and Shaw have been programmed to forget these things, but even the best programming can't keep the memories away. Eventually, inevitably, something begins to slip out. This is true in real life as well as in the movies. Sgt Shaw has been molded into a hypno-programmed assassin whose main objective is to kill an American presidential candidate. Shaw, of course, is not aware of this at all, though he too has been suffering from similar nightmares as those experienced by Marco. As stated before, reality has a tendency to fight its way through illusions.

But not easily. *The Manchurian Candidate*, within the form of fiction, shatters many illusions about what hypnotism can and cannot do to the human brain. To this very day, most people believe they can't be hypnotized to perform acts they would not normally perform in real life. The people who perpetuated this myth were hypnotists. The person who's convinced he can't be hypnotized will always make the ideal hypnotic subject because all his defenses are down. He doesn't believe there's anything to guard against and, thus, is completely relaxed and in a receptive state for the hypnotist to perform his dirty work. The truth is that people can be hypnotized to do damn well almost anything, including commit crimes like murder. Most people are willing to take another life as long as they think their life, or the life of a loved one, is in danger. The hypnotist merely has to make the subject think that the person they've been asked to kill deserves to die, or that the act is being committed in self-defense. Such things have happened in real life.

In Paul J. Reiter's 1958 book, *Antisocial or Criminal Acts and Hypnosis*, the author (who was chief of the psychiatric department of the Copenhagen Municipal Hospital) discusses a case with which he was personally involved. Two convicts, Bjorn S. Nielsen and Palle Hardup, became friends while in prison in Denmark. After their respective prison terms were over, the two men continued to remain acquainted. Nielsen used hypnosis to slowly transform Hardup into his zombified servant. At the sight of the letter X, Nielsen was able to make Hardup fall into a deep trance. He then hypno-programmed the man to rob banks in order, ostensibly, to raise money for a political party whose main intent was to unify all of Scandinavia, a goal in which Hardup believed. This genuine belief overrode all reluctance on the part of Hardup. Nielsen had a nice operation going, and the only reason the truth came to light was because Hardup, during one of these bank robberies, ended up shooting and killing two men. He was captured by the police and sent back to prison where he was examined by Dr Paul J. Reiter. Dr Reiter worked with Hardup for over a year and eventually uncovered the true source of the man's crimes; as a result, Hardup was released from prison and Nielsen was given a life sentence for the murders that Hardup had committed.

In Hardup's case, the hypnotic cue was the letter X. In Sgt Shaw's case, the cue is the queen of diamonds from a normal deck of playing cards. Shaw's moral compunctions against murdering two of his fellow soldiers are overridden by the conditioning of a brilliant Chinese neurobehaviorist named Yen Lo (Khigh Dhiegh). At one point, before a gathering of Chinese and Russian communists, Yen Lo mocks traditional beliefs about hypnotism: "I am sure you've all heard the old wives tale that no hypnotized subject may be forced to do that which is repellant to his 'moral nature'... whatever *that* may be." (These last few words are uttered with contempt, as if the notion of morality itself is an old wives tale.) "Nonsense, of course!" Yen Lo concludes.

That Condon was able to intuit real world details from what he claimed was nothing more than a cursory reading of Pavlovian conditioning manuals is a testament to his imagination and his skills as a fiction writer. That learned men of great influence and power dreamed up these techniques years before Condon, outside the world of fictional melodrama, is a testament to the human capacity for evil.

According to the updated, revised edition of Walter Bowart's *Operation Mind Control*:

> The psychological techniques described in *The Manchurian Candidate* had secretly become a reality a decade before Condon saw his story set in type. A decade later it appeared as if Condon's fiction had been used as the blueprint for the creation of an army of hypno-programmed "zombies." Some were assassins prepared to kill on cue.

> Others were informers, made to remember minute details under hypnosis. Couriers carried illegal messages outside the chain of command, their secrets secured behind posthypnotic blocks. Knowledge of secret information was removed from the minds of those who no longer had the "need to know"—they were given posthypnotic amnesia.[23]

Bowart then backs up these statements with a very specific example—a case study from the *Journal of Traumatic Stress*, Vol. 5, No. 4, October 1992. In an article titled "Recall of Traumatic Memories Following Cerebral Vascular Accident," Karen L. Cassiday and Judith A. Lyons discuss the case of a World War II veteran who was living a normal life until his first stroke, at which point a flood of previously forgotten memories of his service as an intelligence officer assaulted him. He recalled that he had been captured by the Japanese during World War II and tortured as a prisoner of war. He managed to escape his abductors and was subsequently debriefed by the American military. During these debriefings he was hypnotized to forget any details about his intelligence service—furthermore, *to forget that he had been an intelligence officer at all.* Cassiday and Lyons wrote, "Additionally while hospitalized, [he] had a flashback in which he mistook IV (intravenous) apparatus for being bayoneted. An Asian physician observed him speaking an Asian dialect during this flashback. Collectively, these data led us to conclude that military events occurred as reported and cannot be dismissed as delusions or fabrications."[24]

Bowart begins his book with this case to make a very important point: that the *fact* very definitely preceded the *fiction*.

The filmmakers clearly wished to anchor their story in the known realities of hypnotism and mind control. The technical advisor they hired to work on the film was none other than Dr William Joseph Bryan, Jr, a CIA asset who operated a successful hypnotherapy practice called The American Institute of Hypnosis on the Sunset Strip in Hollywood. Bryan is a significant figure in the assassination milieu of the 1960s due to the fact that he was accused of being Sirhan Sirhan's programmer by former FBI agent William Turner and investigative reporter Jonn Christian in their excellent 1978 book, *The Assassination of Robert Kennedy*. Turner and Christian believed that Bryan's "fingerprints" were all over Sirhan Sirhan's programming, as revealed by diary entries Sirhan scribbled only days before the assassination. More intriguing still was the testimony of two Beverly Hills prostitutes who claimed that Bryan often boasted he was involved in "top secret projects" and of having hypnotized Sirhan, though it was a proven fact that Bryan had never had any contact with Sirhan *following* Kennedy's death. Bryan was known as a great egoist, which perhaps explains why, only hours after RFK's assassination, the doctor went out of his way to appear on a Los Angeles radio talk show claiming that the killer had been hypnotized to murder Senator Kennedy before any details about the assassin, including Sirhan's name, were even available to the press. Chapter Fourteen of Turner and Christian's book, titled "Tracing the Programmer," delves into these and other data points more thoroughly.[25]

Some film critics insist *The Manchurian Candidate* is "science fiction." As previously noted, Bill Warren includes the film in *Keep Watching the Skies!*, an exhaustive film-by-film analysis of every American SF film released between 1950 and 1962. In his introduction to the book, Warren explains that his cut-off date for the decade of the fifties was the end of 1962 because "what we ordinarily think of as a 1950s-type science fiction movie didn't end when the fifties actually did; trends don't watch calendars."[26] I think the real reason, however, is one of which Warren is not consciously aware. The transformation that occurred in the collective unconscious of America following the assassination of John F. Kennedy deeply affected every aspect of the culture, including its popular entertainment—i.e., science fiction. Warren attempts to codify this transformation in the preface to the "21st Century Edition" of *Keep Watching the Skies*!:

> Some of the appeal of the old [science fiction] films is relatively obvious: they tell simple stories with beginnings, middles and ends, and the heroes are readily identifiable and they overcome bizarre menaces by the end of the film. In a handful of these films the hero dies, but the sacrifice is always in a good cause, always with a sense that, despite this loss, the menace has been defeated. These are simple movies; many, but hardly all, are naïve in a manner films have long since left behind.[27]

This naivety that many associate with 1950s America was stripped aside suddenly by the no longer undeniable encroachment of reality in the form of several bullets to the President's face. If any event inaugurated the chaos of the 1960s, it was this.

In the very first paragraph of *Were We Controlled?*, Lincoln Lawrence writes, "Let us note for future generations that the whispered rumors about the assassination of John F. Kennedy and the printed news stories differed greatly."[28]

Lawrence is right; these rumors did not appear in any official record of mainstream history such as the *New York Times*. For the most part, these rumors emerged in the form of popular entertainment. When you can't get your truth from the *Times*, you have to resort to popular entertainment to understand what's really going on.

Some would regard all rumors as nothing more than tall tales—primitive forms of science fiction, perhaps. In his review of the recent Blu-ray release of *The Manchurian Candidate*, film critic Glenn Erickson notes, "Previously, the Remote Control of Human Beings was only investigated in science fiction films like *Invaders from Mars*. That makes *The Manchurian Candidate* science fiction as well."[29] The first sentence is true while the second is not. Just because the technique of mind control appears in a popular science fiction film does not mean that every film about mind control is science fiction. *The Manchurian Candidate* merely rips aside the living metaphors from *Invaders from Mars* and gives us the truth in a more raw form. From the point of view of the filmmakers, *The Manchurian Candidate* may very well have been a form of science fiction. From the point of view of history, *The Manchurian Candidate* is a less outlandish version of a sad and secret truth. It appears to be science fiction only for those who are ignorant of the facts—the documented facts surrounding the subject of mind control and the important role it played in America from World War II onward.

5. The Parallax View (1974)

MULTIPLE LAYERS OF metaphor gradually peel away as these films evolve from one decade to the next. In the 1950s the entwined subjects of mind control and political assassinations are discussed only in the context of science fiction. By the early sixties one layer of metaphor—the living metaphor of science fiction itself—has shed itself, like a tail dislodging itself from a lizard, leaving in its place a darkly humorous satire disguised as an intense political thriller called *The Manchurian Candidate*. The subject of mind control is brought to the fore, but only in the context of a postmodern reimagining of pulp clichés from several decades before; thus, the main perpetrator of the mind control is a Fu Manchu-like mad scientist, not unlike a character Boris Karloff or Bela Lugosi might have portrayed in the early

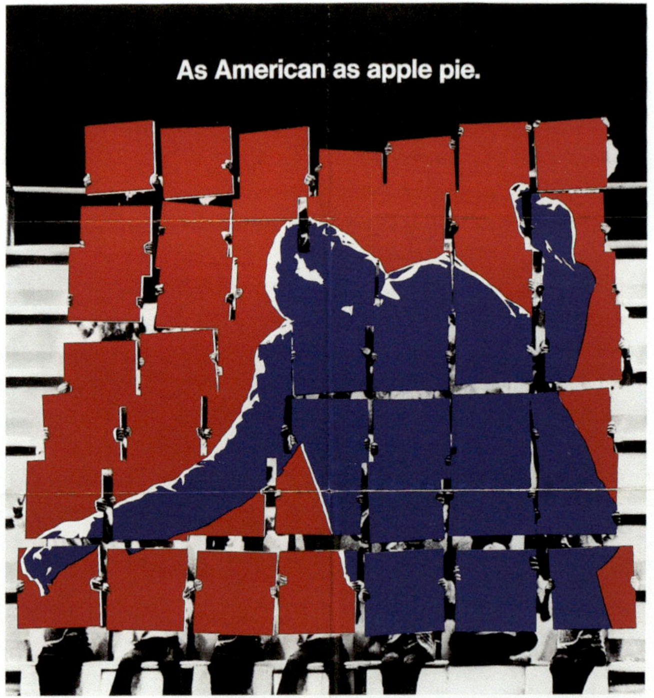

Paramount Pictures Presents
AN ALAN J. PAKULA PRODUCTION
WARREN BEATTY
THE PARALLAX VIEW
Co-starring
HUME CRONYN · WILLIAM DANIELS AND PAULA PRENTISS
Director of Photography GORDON WILLIS · Music Scored by MICHAEL SMALL
Executive Producer GABRIEL KATZKA · Screenplay by DAVID GILER and LORENZO SEMPLE, Jr.
Produced and Directed by ALAN J. PAKULA · PANAVISION® TECHNICOLOR® A Paramount Picture
R RESTRICTED
74/204

1930s. The shadowy villains behind the plot to assassinate the presidential candidate in *The Manchurian Candidate* are Chinese communists and their ostensible sympathizers in the West. This was as far as anyone involved in the film—even artists as forward-thinking as Richard Condon and John Frankenheimer—were willing, or even *capable*, of taking this controversial subject matter in the early 1960s.

By the early seventies, however, America had changed a great deal. By then America had seen, played out in real time on the reflective screens of those strange alien invaders known as television sets, more death and destruction than they had been exposed to before: first the assassination of JFK, then Martin Luther King, Robert F. Kennedy, Malcolm X, the near-fatal shooting of George Wallace, the My Lai Massacre, the Kent State shootings, the Watts Riots, the daily footage shown on the nightly news of young men brought home in body bags for a war no one could understand. World War II had been catastrophic on so many levels, and yet the disturbing fallout—and the word "fallout" is used here both literally and figuratively—was so often hidden behind the veneer of propagandistic news reels seen briefly between patriotic war films at the local movie theater, or presented as a triumphant exclamation point to the "Good War," as journalist Studs Terkel would call it four decades later. The negative effects of World War II were tucked away in the overlooked crevices of civilization, just like the memories of that unnamed World War II veteran mentioned earlier whose brain vomited the truth only after a near-fatal stroke and a protracted stay at a VA hospital jarred them out of their little hiding places. In 1962 the American film audience itself was very similar to Sgt Raymond Shaw: confused victims of a long and complex series of posthypnotic commands—delivered via silver-tongued political stump speeches and catchy advertising jingles manufactured on Madison Avenue—to forget a traumatic past they weren't even aware existed in the first place. They were amnesiacs from birth, these jolly post-war Americans, and almost every single one of them would have preferred to remain that way until death.

But occasionally a little violent jarring of the brain would occur thanks to films like Alan J. Pakula's *The Parallax View* (1974) starring Warren Beatty, Hume Cronyn, Paula Prentiss and William Daniels. Based on the 1970 novel by Loren Singer, *The Parallax View* is a postmodern odyssey in which investigative journalist Joe Frady (Warren Beatty) uncovers evidence of a vast conspiracy being perpetuated by a seemingly omnipotent corporation that can assassinate the most powerful politicians in the country at will. The corporation, known as Parallax, secretly recruits people who can be reshaped into mind controlled killers. If caught, these killers will never be able to point a finger at the true entity responsible for the crime since all memory of their programming has been wiped clean. They will appear to be insane, as so many have appeared after the gruesome details of yet another inexplicable murder has passed across the news between updates on the latest celebrity scandal. "He seemed like such a nice boy." Yes, perhaps he was... before the Bad Brains at Parallax got to him.

It's clear that Loren Singer based Parallax on a very real corporation with a name that's not at all dissimilar: Permindex. Both start with the letter P, consist of three syllables, and end with the letter X. According to William Torbitt, the pseudonymous author of the underground manuscript *Nomenclature of an Assassination Cabal* (1970), Permindex was a Swiss corporation controlled by a "fascist cabal" who engineered the assassination of John F. Kennedy and "planned to lay the blame on honest right-wing conservatives, if their first ploy, to lay the blame on Oswald and the Communists, was not bought."[30]

Founded in 1958 by Major Louis Mortimer Bloomfield, a "former agent with the Office of Strategic Services,"[31] Permindex was an offshoot of a shadowy corporation called the Centro Mondiale Commerciale. According to Jim Garrison, the New Orleans District Attorney who attempted to unravel the mystery behind John F. Kennedy's murder and wrote the 1988 book, *On the Trail of the Assassins* (which documented his controversial investigation in great detail), the Centro Mondiale Commerciale and Permindex were "twin international intelligences combines"[32] composed of disparate parties "apparently representative of the paramilitary right in Europe, including Italian Fascists, the American C.I.A., and similar interests [...]. Before 1962 was out, [the Italian government] had expelled the Centro Mondiale Commerciale—and its half-brother, Permindex—from Italy for subversive intelligence activity."[33] The Italian newspaper, *Paesa Sera*, described Permindex and the Centro as "the point of contact for a number of persons who, in certain respects, have somewhat equivocal ties whose common denominator is anti-communism so strong that it would swallow up all those in the world who have fought for decent relations between East and West, including Kennedy."[34] The Italian press further revealed that Permindex had "among other things, secretly financed the opposition of the French Secret Army Organization (O.A.S.) to President de Gaulle's support for independence for

Algeria, including its reputed assassination attempts on de Gaulle."[35]

In his 1989 book, *Crossfire: The Plot That Killed Kennedy*, investigative journalist Jim Marrs writes, "In tracing the money used to finance the assassination plots against de Gaulle, French intelligence discovered that some $200,000 in secret funds had been sent to Permindex accounts in the Banque de la Credit Internationale."[36]

One of the directors of Permindex was Clay Shaw, the only man to ever be brought to trial for the assassination of President Kennedy. Jim Garrison was responsible for bringing Shaw to trial in January of 1969, though Shaw was eventually acquitted of the charges only two months later. It's since been proven that Shaw oversaw numerous international intelligence operations as an employee of the CIA. Unfortunately, Garrison could not prove Shaw's connection to the Agency during the trial due to several reasons, foremost among them:

1) the sudden and convenient "suicide" of his chief suspect, CIA operative David Ferrie, the day after being released from protective custody (the autopsy later revealed that Ferrie could not have killed himself, despite the presence of two separate unsigned suicide notes left near his corpse, as he had died of a ruptured blood vessel at the base of his brain, a type of aneurysm that could very well have been caused by a blow to the back of the skull; despite this, the coroner's official finding was that Ferrie had perished from "natural causes");

2) unprecedented interference from the judge, Edward Aloysius Haggerty, that burdened Garrison with "constitutional requirements" that had never before existed in a court of law and do not exist to this very day (e.g., the insistence that damning evidence against Shaw was inadmissible because a lawyer had not been present while routine questions were asked of him during his booking);

3) the refusal of several Governors—including John Connolly of Texas and Ronald Reagan of California—to extradite key witnesses such as the enigmatic Gordon Novel, a CIA operative who could have proven Shaw's connection to both Lee Harvey Oswald and the CIA.

Shaw's role in the assassination, according to Garrison, was to set up Oswald as a patsy. His motivation "stemmed from Shaw's history as a CIA operative and his desire, shared by the hardcore cold warriors in the intelligence community, to stop Kennedy's attempts to turn around U.S. foreign policy," particularly with regard to his efforts at reconciliation with the Soviet Union. It was not "until 1979 that Richard Helms, the CIA's deputy director for plans (covert operations) in 1963, first admitted under oath that Shaw had Agency connections."[37] According to Jim Marrs, "...a CIA memo dated September 28, 1967, to the Justice Department—finally made public in 1977—reveals that Shaw had provided the Agency with some thirty reports between the years 1949 and 1956."[38]

Switzerland is a crucial link between Garrison's interest in Permindex and the theories explored by Lincoln Lawrence in *Were We Controlled?* In 1958 Lee Harvey Oswald decided to move to Switzerland under the sponsorship of a mysterious benefactor. Though we know Oswald could not have afforded this move on his own, what we don't know is who exactly provided the funds—or the initial idea—for Oswald to leave the United States. The purpose of this move was for Oswald to attend school in Switzerland in order to (in Oswald's own words) "live in a healthy climate and Good Moral atmosphere" where he could learn the essential foundations of philosophy that he believed were unavailable to him in the United States due to the "inadequate" nature of American universities. He also stated he wanted "to meet Europeans who [could] broaden [his] scope of understanding."[39] He might very well have had his scope of understanding broadened, though perhaps not in the way young Oswald intended. Lawrence contends it's this trip to Switzerland that ensured Oswald's headlong collision with Dr José Delgado's mind control technology. One must ask the question: Is there any significance to the fact that Oswald decided to move to Switzerland the year Major Louis Mortimer Bloomfield established Permindex in the same country?

After Oswald's departure from the United States, claims Lawrence, he was eventually lured to the Soviet Union by his wealthy "benefactor" where he was told that he would assist in "experimental research in the field of electrical stimulation of the brain at No. 5 Krasnaya Street, in the Experimental Section of the Electrotechnical and Instrument Building. Exhibit No. 985 of the Warren Report confirms this indeed was where he worked."[40]

Lawrence makes the case, drawing upon official Russian records, that Oswald became the victim of RHIC-EDOM (Radio-Hypnotic Intra-Cerebral Control-Electronic Dissolution of Memory) on March 30, 1961 when he underwent an eleven-day hospital stay in Minsk. The ostensible reason for Oswald's hospital visit was to fix his hearing problem (a condition that had bothered him since childhood) and remove potentially dangerous polyps from his nose. The real reason, perhaps, was to implant a small electrode "inside Oswald's mastoid sinus. The electrode responded to a radio signal which would make audible, inside Oswald's head, certain electronic commands to which he had already been post-hypnotically conditioned to respond. (The autopsy report in Dallas noted that there was a small scar on the mastoid sinus behind Oswald's ear)."[41]

Lawrence, however, didn't believe that Soviet Intelligence was behind the plot to program Oswald. Instead, he blamed "an international cartel of commodities merchants who sought to make millions by driving the market with the assassination of a president—any president."[42] In other words, Lawrence felt that the true target of the assassination was not JFK, but the office of the presidency itself. This motive differs greatly from Garrison's point of view, but the two theories are not mutually exclusive. There is some significant overlap. It's possible that the *main* goal was to assassinate JFK, but in conjunction with this monumental operation came the irresistible notion of taking advantage of a strategic "coincidence."

> The coincidence of the assassination of a President of the United States… and the simultaneous scandalizing and collapse of the commodities market… *would rapidly drive the stock market down at least 30 points*!
>
> Having advance knowledge of this event… the group would *sell short* on a heavily financed scale… and a profit of perhaps a *half-billion dollars* would be divided amongst its members![43]

I suspect this part of the operation was a bonus, a blood-red cherry on top of the assassination cake. Happy Assassination Day, America. (It's intriguing to note that similar accusations with regard to driving the market began circulating only hours after the tragic events in New York on September 11, 2001.[44])

Lincoln Lawrence wasn't pulling his "mind control theory" out of thin air. People very close to Oswald claimed, only a few years after the assassination, that Oswald had indeed been a victim of advanced mind control techniques. Jack Martin, a private investigator in New Orleans with ties to both David Ferrie and Oswald, was one of Garrison's primary witnesses during Shaw's trial. After Ferrie was found dead, Jack Martin

> came out of hiding long enough to suggest that Oswald had been *programmed* [emphasis mine] by Ferrie to go to Dallas and kill the presi-

> dent. Immediately following the assassination, Martin had reported to the Assistant District Attorney Herman S. Kohlman that Ferrie and Oswald had been friends, and that Ferrie had instructed Oswald in the use of a telescope sight on a rifle. But in 1963 no one followed up on Martin's story.[45]

And Oswald wasn't the only character in this assassination cabal who might have been "programmed." Oswald's killer, Jack Ruby, could very well have been the victim of mind control as well. Bowart claimed that only "an understanding of the techniques of mind control could begin to bring meaning to the fragmented ramblings of Jack Ruby."[46] On June 7, 1964, Ruby was questioned by Chief Justice Earl Warren and future president Gerald Ford. Ruby said to the two statesmen:

> [...] it seems as you get further into something, it operates against you, *brainwashes* you, that you are weak in what you want to tell the truth about, and what you want to say which is the truth [...]. [A] whole new form of government is going to take over our country, and I know I won't live to see you another time.[47]

Ruby died within three years of this interview, but not before admitting to his psychiatrist, Werner Teuter, that the JFK assassination was "an act of overthrowing the government." In a letter smuggled out of the Dallas County Jail, Ruby at last identified one of the masterminds behind the assassination:

> [...] they found some very clever means and ways to trick me and which will be used later as evidence to show the American people that I was part of the conspiracy in the assassination of [the] president, and I was used to silence Oswald.... They alone planned the killing, by they I mean [Vice-President Lyndon] Johnson and others....[48]

As John A. Keel suggests in his 1971 book, *Our Haunted Planet*:

> Jack Ruby pulled his gun and shot down Lee Harvey Oswald after being triggered by an auto horn which suddenly beeped in the basement of the Dallas police station. (No one has ever determined who blew that horn or why.) Ruby claimed to his dying day that he had no memory of entering the police station or firing the shot.[49]

George DeMohrenschildt, one of Oswald's closest friends near the end of his life, appears to have been a victim of mind control as well. Mind control techniques straight out of Richard Condon's imagination could very well have led to DeMohrenschildt's premature death. Like so many of the other colorful characters enmeshed in this melodramatic web of intrigue, DeMohrenschildt had definite ties to the CIA going back to its embryonic OSS days. The CIA's own documents, released through the Freedom of Information Act, prove this connection.[50] DeMohrenschildt, a successful businessman in the oil industry, for no explicable reason, took an interest in the future of an outspoken young Marxist named Lee Harvey Oswald and gave him considerable financial assistance after Oswald's return from the Soviet Union.

During an interview conducted on February 23, 1977 by a man named Willem Oltmans, DeMohrenschildt offered up the following revelations:

> In June, 1976, I completed a manuscript. That's when disaster struck. You see, in that book I played the devil's advocate. Without directly implicating myself as an accomplice in the JFK assassination, I still mentioned a number of names, particularly of FBI and CIA officials who apparently may not be exposed under any circumstances. I was drugged surreptitiously. As a result I was committed to a mental hospital. I was there eight weeks and was given electric shocks and as a consequence I sometimes forget certain details temporarily...[51]

A week after being summoned to testify before the House Select Committee on Assassinations in 1977, DeMohrenschildt was found dead in his Palm Beach, Florida home, apparently having committed suicide by shooting himself in the head. According to Walter Bowart in *Operation Mind Control*, "DeMohrenschildt's daughter, Alexandra, told [Edward Jay] Epstein[52] [author of *The Legend of Lee Harvey Oswald*] she believes her father took his own life after having had a post-hypnotic suggestion triggered by a voice over the telephone in his room."[53]

Though it's easy to attribute nefarious motives to DeMorhenschildt, it's also important to keep in mind that it's not always necessary—indeed, more often than not it's actively *contraindicated*—for every member of an intelligence team to know the precise goal of any given operation. This is true of many top secret projects, including the Manhattan Project. The Manhattan Project was so compartmentalized that many of the scientists working on it didn't even know they were helping to build an atom bomb until the moment it was dropped on Hiroshima. Similarly, many of the agents who worked with Oswald may not have been aware of the operation's goal until the moment Kennedy's head exploded, and maybe not even then. Not until Oswald's name was released to the news media (which, strangely, was not long after the shooting, almost as if these news articles were ready to be printed *before* the tragedy had even occurred) would the realization have dawned on them. By that time, it would have been too late to do anything about it. And those who did try to do something about it, like write a book or grant interviews to journalists researching the assassination, often ended up like DeMohrenschildt. (There's a long list of people connected to Oswald and the assassination who met mysterious ends within fifteen years of the event, but there's no need to repeat that grisly necrology here. I refer you to the chapter in Jim Marrs' *Crossfire* titled "Convenient Deaths" for a more thorough examination of that subject.)

Of DeMohrenschildt, Jim Garrison says the following in *On the Trail of the Assassins*:

> My conclusion that DeMohrenschildt was an unwitting baby sitter [a "baby sitter" is an intelligence agent whose mission is to protect someone from harm until that person's function to the overall mission is fulfilled] for Oswald came not only from publicly available evidence but from my conversations with him and Mrs. DeMohrenschildt. Some years after the assassination, after my investigation was well under way, I established phone contact with DeMohrenschildt. To avoid monitoring, we developed a routine of my calling him at the Petroleum Club in Dallas or his leaving a call for me at the New Orleans Athletic Club. Both DeMohrenschildt and his wife were positive that the shooting of the President, or even of a rabbit for that matter, simply was not in Lee Oswald's makeup. They were vigorous in their insistence that Oswald had been the scapegoat. I was particularly affected by the depth of their unhappiness at what had been done not only to John Kennedy but to Lee Oswald as well.[54]

George DeMohrenschildt died three years after *The Parallax View* was released in theaters and seven years after Doubleday published Loren Singer's original novel. The cultural milieu out of which *The Parallax View* emerged was one of extreme paranoia, distrust, and chaos. Those were bloody times in America, almost as bloody as now. The main difference now is that so often these days the little people getting stepped on by out-of-control intelligence agencies are invisible, lost in the shadows, completely removed from the media spotlight. Whole countries could dissolve in a day under mysterious circumstances, and these events will inevitably be overshadowed by the mainstream media's coverage of yet another celebrity breakup. In the late sixties and early seventies, when the children of even well-to-do white Americans might conceivably be drafted and shipped away in the night to have their limbs blown off in Vietnam, it was becoming increasingly difficult to ignore the destruction and death being caused by Those In Power. The evidence was all around, on the nightly news every weekday at six o'clock, and in the grief-stricken faces of the next door neighbors whose eighteen-year-old son had just been mailed to them in a body bag, and in the angry faces of the teenagers who were protesting outside the White House. By June of 1974, when *The Parallax View* was released, President Richard Nixon was so concerned about what those pissed-off protestors might do to him that he actually feared for his life.

Nixon wrote candidly about the effect the protestors had on him as early as the autumn of 1969 when the Vietnam Moratorium marches "triggered a tidal wave of domestic turmoil."[55] Most prominent on the President's mind at this point, second only to the sounds of the livid protestors gathering outside his bedroom window, was a modest little proposal known to Nixon's inner circle as "Operation Duck Hook." In their 1987 book, *To Win a Nuclear War: The Pentagon's Secret War Plans*, physicists Dr Michio Kaku and Dr Daniel Axelrod describe the plan:

> "I have a secret plan to end the Vietnam War." These prophetic words helped to elect Richard Nixon President of the United States in Nov. 1968. Nixon's secret plan was code named DUCK HOOK, and it called for a dramatic escalation of the war, including dropping the atomic bomb on North Vietnam [...].
>
> Nixon had DUCK HOOK drafted in total secrecy by Admiral Thomas Moorer, Chief of Naval Operations; even Secretary of Defense Melvin Laird was kept in the dark [...]. DUCK HOOK called for a carefully orchestrated series of threats, culminating in dropping a final ultimatum set for Nov. 1, 1969. The November Ultimatum, as Nixon called it, was a direct application of the nuclear war-fighting

> ideas devised by Henry Kissinger [Nixon's Secretary of State and National Security Advisor].[56]

The plans for Operation Duck Hook—named, by the way, after a golf swing—were completed on July 20, 1969. Nixon wrestled with the question of whether or not to implement the plan for several months until the night of October 15, 1969, when a quarter of a million angry demonstrators amassed outside the White House to demand the end of the Vietnam War. This mass demonstration forced Nixon to ask himself a crucial question: If the American people's hatred for him was this vitriolic now, what might they do to him if he dropped an atom bomb on Hanoi?

Years later Nixon wrote:

> I had to decide what to do about the ultimatum... I knew however, that after all the protests and the Moratorium, American public opinion would be seriously divided by any military escalation of the war... On October 14, I knew for sure that my ultimatum failed... A quarter of a million people came to Washington for the October 15 Moratorium...[57]

In his 1983 book, *The Price of Power: Kissinger in the Nixon White House*, Seymour Hersh writes:

> Those Americans who marched in Washington on October 15 to protest the war had no idea of their impact; they were protesting the policies already adopted by the Nixon Administration and not those under consideration. Nixon came out of the crisis convinced that the protestors had forced him to back down. The protestors thought the Moratorium had been largely in vain.[58]

I imagine Kissinger wandering into the Oval Office on that fateful evening of Oct. 15 and seeing a rather disturbing and yet familiar sight. The President of the United States—a chronically depressed, alcoholic lawyer from Yorba Linda—is hunched over his desk, reduced to tears and incoherent mumblings by decades of stress and self-loathing, yet another half empty bottle of Scotch sitting next to his slumped, semi-conscious form. Kissinger, in that strange and pathetic moment, realizes with genuine despair that his precious baby, Operation Duck Hook, is finished once and for all.

Make no mistake: Monumental—perhaps even world-shattering—issues were at stake in the global theater during Nixon's reign in the White House. Tension, Apprehension and Dissension were the true leaders of the country. The atmosphere of paranoia so prevalent in the United States at that time caused even the President himself to live in constant fear. In the case of Operation Duck Hook, that fear served a positive function. It prevented the total nuclear destruction of North Vietnam (and maybe even the start of World War III?). Perhaps Richard Nixon wasn't so far off the mark in 1977 when he told reporter David Frost, "Paranoia for peace isn't bad." Indeed.

But where did all this paranoia come from? Some would say that paranoia in America runs deep, that it's embedded in the soil itself. After all, Indigenous Americans had plenty of reasons to be paranoid with regard to the original settlers from abroad. Black people had much to fear in America as well, before and after the Civil War. For Black Americans, the idealism reflected in cultural artifacts like black-and-white science fiction movies simply did not exist for them before 1963. And yet, despite all this, the JFK assassination remains a cultural nodal point. As Malcolm X said the day JFK died, "All the birds have come home to roost." What he meant was that the violence of white culture had circled back on the source. Malcolm X certainly was not a Buddhist, and yet he was essentially suggesting that JFK had been done in by his own karma. Though this incendiary comment was considered offensive on November 22, 1963, Malcolm X might have been far closer to the truth than even he could have been aware.

Some critics of America's foreign policy made a similar comment on September 11, 2001: that the reason Americans were so shocked by the events of 9/11 was that they had been insulated for far too long from the repercussions of their own foreign policies. After all, other countries had been living with destructive terrorist bombings every day of their lives. Why should Americans feel that they deserved to be protected from the harsh realities to which so many other countries had become resigned long ago?

Whether or not this is a valid point of view is irrelevant for the purposes of this discussion. What is relevant is that the assassination of JFK—or, more specifically, the assassination of Lee Harvey Oswald—represented the moment, the *first* moment, that many Americans had the veil of illusion ripped from their eyes and were forced to see the darkness that had always been lurking in the heart of their country, just beneath the surface, so comfortably out of sight. One assassination by a lone gunman some could accept, and many did. But, two days later, when Oswald was so strategically led into a turkey shoot and slaughtered on live television for all to see, *that* was the moment many Americans refused to accept the official story. A generation of Americans raised on James Cagney/Humphrey Bogart films could hardly fail to recognize a gangland shooting unfolding before their eyes. Many of the most important JFK assassination researchers began their life's work that day: Mae Brussell, Dick Gregory, Sherman Skolnick, Mark Lane, Jim Garrison… on and on and on. Even my father, who worked at US Steel at the time and was hardly prone to questioning consensus reality on a daily basis, remembers thinking, the moment Oswald clutched his stomach in pain as Ruby's bullet tore through him, *Oh, c'mon….*

The ripples caused by the researchers who began their work that day continue to flow outward in time to this very moment. Mae Brussell, called the "Queen of Conspiracies" by some, influenced many through her articles and radio show to question not just the official verdict on the JFK assassination, but the official verdict on damn near everything that occurs in American politics. But in the late sixties, when Loren Singer must have begun writing *The Parallax View*, "conspiracy research" had not yet attained its current status as a recognized subculture of American life. There wasn't a "conspiracy section" in the bookstore. One couldn't punch in the term "conspiracy theories" into Google and invoke a million different responses. One really had to have their ear to the ground in order to pick up this information. One had to be receptive to it.

So how on earth did Loren Singer know enough about Permindex and the entire mind control aspect of the JFK assassination in order to write a very shrewd and thorough fictional examination of it in *The Parallax View*? Perhaps he was an insider, perhaps he knew someone on the inside, perhaps he was an amateur investigator into these matters, or perhaps he just watched movies.

Perhaps he watched *Creature with the Atom Brain* and merged it with *The Manchurian Candidate* and conjured up the truth through intuition? Perhaps.

But I doubt it. The fact is that Loren Singer, like Curt Siodmak, was a member of the Office of Strategic Services. According to his December 23, 2009 obituary written by *New York Times* reporter

William Grimes, the OSS financially sponsored Singer's attendance at Yale University in order to study Malay, the national language of Indonesia. His intelligence experience is reflected in at least two of his other novels: 1974's *Boca Grande* in which "the skipper of a Nassau-Jamaica yacht race carries out a covert mission in Cuba" and 1993's *Making Good* in which "an Army detachment taking inventory of property stolen by the Nazis stumbles into a strange conspiracy when its members uncover a cache of paintings by Klee, Kokoschka and other banned artists."[59] As in Siodmak's work, we see a significant pattern emerging. These are not writers dreaming up fairy tales. Their work, post-World War II, clearly reflects their own lived experience within a dramatic framework. They're not just trying to entertain their audience. They're clearly trying to educate their audience, and they've chosen to do so in the only way that's not likely to result in the author ending up like Senator Charles Carroll, the popular politician in *The Parallax View* whose assassination atop Seattle's Space Needle kicks off the labyrinthine plot. With hindsight, we can see that *The Parallax View* is America's rehearsal for dealing with all the trauma and controversy that will erupt upon the announcement and release of Oliver Stone's 1991 film, *JFK*.

Not only is Senator Carroll referred to as being "too independent for his own good" within the first few minutes of the 1974 film adaptation of *The Parallax View*, but a reporter also mentions that Carroll's point of view doesn't fit easily within either of the two major political parties. Not long after these statements are made, the senator suddenly gets his brains blown out in front of a roomful of witnesses (including the main character, investigative journalist Frady). The filmmakers' message is clear: In "the Land of the Free" being too independent-minded, and advertising that fact on top of it, will get you nothing but killed.

The story then moves forward three years. Six out of eighteen witnesses to the Carroll murder have been bumped off under mysterious circumstances. Frady's ex-girlfriend (ex-wife?), Lee Carter (Paula Prentiss), suddenly shows up at his doorstep. Lee was there in the Space Needle with Frady and is convinced that someone's trying to kill her. Frady disbelieves her. A lot of information is conveyed here, not through dialogue but through the emotions on Beatty's face. We see that he's used to these sorts of emotional outbursts from Lee. Is this one of the reasons he left her in the first place? He's sympathetic, but in the way that a father is sympathetic to a child who's afraid of the dark. You don't want to see your child upset, but at the same time you sort of wish he or she would just calm down and go to sleep.

Abruptly, we move forward a few days to the morgue. We see Lee's corpse and Beatty standing over it. Clearly, he wishes he could go back in time and change this. The character never says this in so many words, but we know he feels the need to rectify this tragedy. He needs to find out who was responsible for Lee's death. His failure to help Lee is a hole in his gut that can be fulfilled only by solving the mystery and bringing the murderers to justice.

In so doing, Frady stumbles on a conspiracy so complex it borders on science fiction. The conspiracy involves a Los Angeles based corporation called Parallax and their covert recruitment of assassins through the simple technique of subtly worded want ads placed in the newspaper. Frady decides to get to the bottom of the mystery by applying for a job at the mysterious corporation.

There's a clear indication in the film that Parallax does far more than just recruit experienced killers. They use highly sophisticated psychological tests to ferret out *potential* killers and mold them to their whims. Essentially, Parallax manufactures these killers through programming. Brainwashing. Mind control.

As Frady discovers, part of this indoctrination process involves being ushered into a sterile room and shown a short film called (in the end credits) the "Parallax Test." This is where we return to the previously mentioned motif of the "film-within-a-film," as we first saw in *Creature with the Atom Brain*. The purpose of the short film within *Creature with the Atom Brain* is to educate the movie-going audience about the truth regarding how *sophisticated* mind control technology had already become by 1955. The purpose of the "Parallax Test" is to approximate the disorientation that some of these mind control victims (including, perhaps, Lee Harvey Oswald and Jack Ruby) report undergoing in the early stages of their indoctrination. Film critic Glenn Erickson was so impressed by this part of the film that he wrote two separate essays about *The Parallax View*, one for the film itself and one for the film-within-the-film. The essay about the film-within-the-film is longer than the essay about *The Parallax View* as a whole. Erickson calls the film-within-the-film "the Incredible Montage."

A barrage of images spliced with simple words presented in bold white letters ("Mother," "Father," "Me," "Home," "Country," "God,"

"Enemy," "Happiness," etc.) assault the viewer. As the innocuous background music speeds up to match the swirling images extracted from both High Culture (e.g., Weegee photographs) and Low Culture (e.g., Jack Kirby illustrations of Thor, the Norse God of Thunder, and a red-faced demon from a Marvel comic book), colliding at full force to create an eighth grade slide show from hell, one truly begins to feel as if the influence of Parallax is creeping into one's brain and is threatening to take over one's consciousness. Several films before this have successfully projected a genuine sense of dread and paranoia in the audience, most of them science fiction. Though Jack Arnold's *It Came from Outer Space* (1953), William Cameron Menzies' *Invaders from Mars*, and Gene Fowler's *I Married a Monster from Outer Space* (1958) are all effective and unique studies in paranoia, Don Siegel's *Invasion of the Body Snatchers* (1956) and John Frankenheimer's *The Manchurian Candidate* are the two films that explore this theme most artfully; however, *The Parallax View* is the only film ever made that succeeds in not just evoking fear, but in also approximating what it might *feel* like to be transformed into a sociopath with cardboard memories, a head full of nothing more than a series of still photos and two-dimensional ethics to match... what it might *feel* like to be bombarded by so many outside influences that one is no longer quite certain what's real, what's important. The test reduces metaphysical concepts ("God") down to just another fragile hook dangling in the placid water of the unconscious. Many of the test's featured precepts ("Mother," "Father," "Me," "Home," "Country," "God," "Enemy," "Happiness") are all strung together in such a way that they begin to blur into one single concept: sex and love and hate and murder all conjoin to form a single dream, the dream in which we're all trapped. Is this a dream worth dying for or just another illusion that fuels our biological imperatives for pseudo-fulfillment, like a car needing gasoline to drive?

This dream-within-a-dream called "the Parallax Test" begins at precisely 0:55:00 and ends at 1:00:00. The short film employs a careful choice of still images: a young, half-naked couple embracing in a messy bed; an American flag waving in the wind; a child screaming in pain; a group of Klansmen burning a cross; a Black man hanging by the neck from a tree; The Mighty Thor of Norse mythology *and* Marvel comic book mythology holding aloft his magic hammer, looking rather like a savior of the Aryan race rather than a simple four-color superhero; a red-faced demon who seems to be lunging at the viewer, eager to eat him or her; a slice of rare beef leaking drops of juice that resemble blood. These are the images that best represent America, say the filmmakers. This is your mad and soulless country distilled down into five minutes of jabberwocky and images as banal as patriotism itself. This is what you're living for, says the test. This is what you're dying for (keep in mind that in 1974, the year this film was released, the Vietnam War was still raging). This is the madness into which the dream of the Founding Fathers has devolved. This is the sum total of the highest aspirations of man. As William Burroughs once wrote in his poem "Thanksgiving Prayer": This country is "the last and greatest betrayal of the last and greatest of human dreams."[60] These five minutes are the best you can ever hope to attain in this country or any other. So why keep struggling? Why keep repressing your rage? Just let it all go, and we'll show you exactly on whom to direct your righteous fury. Trust Parallax. Trust Daddy. Trust the Hand Behind the Still Images. Parallax as Oz. Warren Beatty as Dorothy. As Jack Younger (Walter McGinn), a Parallax agent assigned to be the handler for new recruits, says to Frady at one point in the movie, "I've tried to be a friend to you, haven't I?" Yes, indeed, you have. The best friend a guy could ask for. The guardian at the gate who grants one entrance into the Emerald City where all dreams die and come true simultaneously. Now point me in the right direction and show me who to kill.

The film-within-the-film of *The Parallax View* is a masterpiece of economy and precision, one of the most concise and perceptive deconstructions of American values (or lack thereof) ever committed to celluloid.

Once the Parallax Test has come to an end, the film begins its downward slide into the lower rings of Hell, very similar perhaps to the mythological journey Oswald himself undertook toward his ultimate resting place in the final hours of his life, through Hades and along the shores of the River Styx, through confusion and realization and rebirth into a Christ figure and a fallen angel and a godless heathen all rolled into one, a Rorschach inkblot on which anyone in the world could project their worst fears. Oswald was a commie. Oswald was a CIA agent. Oswald was a tool of the Freemasons. Oswald was a shapeshifting assassin from Mars. Oswald, perhaps most disturbingly, was a lone nut with no one to blame but himself.

Joe Frady, in the last act of the film, crisscrosses the United States attempting to stop the assassinations that Parallax has initiated—

much like Oswald reportedly attempted to stop the assassination of JFK by trying to warn an FBI agent about the coming tragedy three weeks prior to November 22, 1963.[61] Frady must know what Oswald himself was feeling when he realized on November 22, 1963, that almost his entire adult life had been a prelude to a trap in which he was fated to die for a crime he never committed. A dream that led to nothing except chaos. Oswald no doubt understood he'd been a fool for thinking he could play games with people like this. Alas, reality wasn't at all like his favorite TV show, *I Led Three Lives* starring Richard Carlson—an actor who, appropriately enough, also starred in the aforementioned *It Came from Outer Space*. In *It Came from Outer Space* Carlson matched wits with shapeshifting aliens, while in *I Led Three Lives* he matched wits with chameleonic communists attempting to sabotage the American way of life. As Herb Philbrick, Carlson travelled across the United States narrowly halting communist assassinations and nefarious plots at every turn. Was this Oswald's dream, born of a boyhood fascination for cheap melodrama and intrigue? For Oswald the light at the end of the tunnel was not a TV test pattern, but a doorway into Inferno. The illumination of these flames, the full import of their respective mythological journeys, reaches both Oswald and Frady after it's far too late to reverse the path they have created for themselves. Sometimes it's best not to look at the man behind the curtain, or the bony figure obscured behind the cloak that summons you across the black river in its raft constructed of bones. Sometimes the best mystery is the one that remains unsolved.

The next time someone offers you an all-expenses paid vacation to Switzerland, try saying "No thank you" and staying home. In L. Frank Baum's 1900 novel, *The Wizard of Oz*, Dorothy and her companions enter the Emerald City to discover that the legendary metropolis isn't emerald at all. Its citizens are forced to wear eyeglasses made of green-tinted lenses. This is a detail Hollywood altered in the 1939 movie, as well as in every subsequent adaptation.

And keep in mind that the first syllable of "Oswald" is "Oz."

6. Winter Kills (1979)

UNLIKE CURT SIODMAK and Loren Singer, Richard Condon could not be considered a genuine "insider" in the sense that he was most definitely not a member of any particular intelligence organization; however, he did have inside knowledge of the Kennedy family, as he'd had personal dealings with them long before he wrote even *The Manchurian Candidate*. I suspect it was this firsthand knowledge of "Camelot" (the term the mainstream press began to use in reference to the Kennedy administration, further solidifying JFK's ascendance into the realm of mythology) that inspired Condon's 1974 novel, *Winter Kills*, fated to be adapted to the screen as a very peculiar dark comedy that boasts a background story with as many strange twists and turns as the film's labyrinthine plot itself. The protagonist of Condon's novel is Nick Kegan (Jeff Bridges), clearly based on Ted Kennedy, the younger brother of a popular President, Tim Kegan, who was assassinated several years before. Evidence emerges suggesting that President Kegan was not killed by a lone gunman. Nick is given evidence that leads him to a horrifying conclusion: that the President was assassinated by a conspiracy engineered by his own father.

William Richert's *Winter Kills* began shooting in 1976, but was not released in theaters until 1979. Its production history truly does read like a Richard Condon novel. The production was shut down three times due to financial problems. It was the first major film to declare bankruptcy. Before the shooting could even be completed, one of the producers of the movie would be murdered and the other thrown in prison. Producer Leonard J. Goldberg was handcuffed to his bed in his Murray Hill district Manhattan apartment and shot through the head, while producer Robert Stirling was sentenced to forty years on a marijuana conviction. According to Richert, Stirling believes to this day that one of the reasons for his imprisonment was his role in making *Winter Kills*. He told Richert that his ambition was to follow *Winter Kills* with other conspiracy-themed films. Obviously, none of those pictures were ever made.

And *Winter Kills* was almost never completed. One thing working in its favor, perhaps the only element keeping the production afloat, was Richert's youthful enthusiasm and the unusual willingness of the cast and crew to work for free. This was a film originally budgeted at $6 million, no small amount in 1976. It was being shot on six different sound stages at MGM. Richert, a first-time director, had managed to attract an incredibly impressive cast including Jeff Bridges (who was just beginning his rise to stardom at that time), John Huston, Elizabeth Taylor, Anthony Perkins (who turns in the very best performance in a film loaded with terrific performances), Toshiro Mifune, Eli Wallach, Ralph Meeker, and Richard Boone.

The film was based on a bestselling novel. All the stars in the heavens seemed to be lining up over this production. In the eleventh week of shooting, however, the ceiling caved in. The production was halted by the unions whose workers had not been paid by the producers. The soundstages at MGM were suddenly off-limits. After one week, the entire production moved to Philadelphia (where the same cast and crew agreed to work for free). After a week's worth of work, the union shut down the production again. In a 2003 documentary about the making of the film, titled "Who Killed *Winter Kills*?", Richert and other cast and crew members relate examples of the outrageous drama that occurred behind the scenes. According to Richert, at this point in the production "one of the guys who hadn't been paid caught up with John Starke, our production manager. He came with a sawed off shotgun and put it to John's neck until John came up with the cash for his generator." After that the producers began paying the crew with cash, apparently money raised through the dealing of illegal drugs. Vilmos Zsigmond, the cinematographer, commented years later with a smile on his face, "Where that money came from, I have no idea. Nobody ever answered me. I don't know."

Richert had about two weeks' worth of shooting left when the production was shut down for the third time. The production was now $4m in debt to 400 different creditors. It was at this point that producer Leonard J. Goldberg was found murdered in his New York apartment. According to Richert, "That shook us all up," no doubt an understatement. A month later Richert had regained his bearing and came up with a scheme to finish the picture. He co-wrote a screenplay with Larry Cohen for a completely unrelated film, a light comedy titled *American Success Company* (one wonders if the title didn't contain a hint of wish fulfillment on Richert's part), and arranged to shoot this new picture in Germany with some of the same cast and crew from *Winter Kills*, including Jeff Bridges and his co-star, Belinda Bauer. Somehow, the profit generated by *American Success Company* managed to raise enough money to pull *Winter Kills* out of bankruptcy. After a two year hiatus, Richert reassembled his cast and completed the film. After this Herculean effort, despite the fact that the film was very well received by critics, *Winter Kills* was pulled from the theaters after a single weekend. Around this time Richard Condon wrote an article for *Harper's Magazine* titled "Who Killed *Winter Kills*?" in which he speculated that the film's theatrical release was purposely sabotaged by Avco Embassy, the film's distributor. According to Richert, "Avco Embassy had major defense contracts and [...] the Kennedys somehow were involved in those contracts or business dealings, and Ted Kennedy was going to run for President during that time, so they didn't want that movie around, and it *wasn't* around. So once you start thinking conspiracies and connections, they're everywhere."[62]

Richert, who began the production with a rather skeptical viewpoint regarding the reality of the conspiracy theories around which Condon's plot revolves, ended his journey with a broader knowledge of the power these conspiratorial forces have over the lives of others.

Oddly, Richert's own mythological journey from innocence to awareness mirrors the cinematic journey taken by *Winter Kills'* protagonist, Nick Kegan. Richert conceived of the film's structure as an *Alice-in-Wonderland*-like fairy tale in which Nick equals Alice. Indeed, film critic Vincent Canby of the *New York Times* called the film "a funny, paranoid fable...." A fable it is, but all fables have a dash of truth in them, just as all myths have a dash of truth in them. Let's examine the truth that underlies this particular myth.

Winter Kills, at its core, is a cinematic updating of the ancient Greek myth of Cronus, the titan, forced by his own fears and insecurities to eat his son, a terrifying scene so brilliantly realized in Goya's painting titled *Cronus Devouring His Children* (c. 1819–1823). In Goya's painting we can see the forlorn expression in Cronus's eyes as he begins to thrust his son into his own mouth. He doesn't want to eat his son, but he knows he must lest he himself be destroyed. Instinctually, we know this action is contrary to the natural order. Most parents would, without hesitating, sacrifice themselves for their children. To do the opposite is so repellant that we want to shrink away from Goya's painting in utter disgust and fascination. And yet we keep looking.

Just as we keep looking at the evidence swirling around the events in Dallas on November 22, 1963.

Was Cronus to blame for Kennedy's death? According to Condon, yes.

The scenario Condon lays out in fictional form is not difficult to swallow. According to Condon, Kennedy's father, Joseph Kennedy, pulled a lot of strings and promised a lot of favors in order to push his son into the White House. The second JFK took office, however, the new President turned his back on his father's advice and began "going rogue," as they say in the military. Kennedy immediately reneged on the promises to the Mafia and the military-industrial-complex his father had pledged on his behalf and began creating his own policies. Because he genuinely wanted to make decisions that would help his fellow Americans and the citizens of Earth, or because he was just an arrogant son of a bitch who felt he needed to make his *own* mark on the world? The film is not clear on this point.

Either way, the end was the same. Kennedy's father was forced to order the hit on his own son, otherwise he himself would have been destroyed. Eat or be eaten. Joseph, according to Condon, chose the former strategy.

Condon based his characterization on his firsthand knowledge of the Kennedys. According to Richert, Condon observed up-close how Joseph Kennedy would treat his son. Joseph was in the habit of forcing JFK to wait outside his office until he was ready to speak to his dutiful son. One time Condon approached the office and saw JFK sleeping in a chair out in the hall; that's how long Joseph had kept him waiting. It's not surprising, therefore, that JFK would take the first opportunity he could to turn his back on his father. No doubt, he assumed the office of the Presidency trumped the power of his father. Perhaps he was wrong.

To what extent did Condon believe in the veracity of his own conspiracy theory? It's possible that Condon intended this scenario to be taken as pure metaphor. In a sense, Joseph Kennedy was indeed responsible for his son's death simply because he spent every waking moment engineering JFK's ascendency into the Oval Office and everything that came with the position—including that fateful limo ride through Dallas in 1963.

The film alludes to this interpretation at one point. Nick Kegan is in his father's office discussing new evidence he's uncovered that strongly suggests the President's death was the result of a conspiracy. Kegan's father (John Huston) turns to look at old photographs of his late son hanging on his wall and says, "All that time, after and before and during, everything I did, every dime I spent, I was just leading Tim further along the road to meet that bullet."

Nick replies, quietly, "Sounds like that's just what you were doing, Pop."

"What?" asks the elder Kegan, as if unsure he's heard his son correctly.

Nick says, with a more positive tone of voice this time, "Leading Tim along."

The same sentence, depending on the delivery, can either be an accusation or a compliment. Buried beneath the compliment lies the accusation. And the truth.

For this scene is a foreshadowing of the revelation to come. Near the end of the film, Nick interrogates his father's right hand man, John Cerruti (Anthony Perkins), inside a subterranean chamber that's so vast it looks like it's been transplanted from the 1950s science fiction extravaganza, *Forbidden Planet.* It's an intelligence depot that contains all the dirt on almost every important statesman and businessman in the world. Because he's the keeper of the secrets, Cerruti is the brains behind the elder Kegan's entire empire. It's Cerruti who tells Nick that his father was responsible for the President's death. Perkins was the perfect actor to play this part. Essentially, he's the opposite of Franz Kafka's Joseph K (a role Perkins played in Orson Welles' 1962 film adaptation of *The Trial*); he's the omnipotent all-seeing eye, what Frank Zappa called "the Central Scrutinizer" in his 1979 rock opera, *Joe's Garage*. Cerruti is the guy who frames the Joseph Ks of the world and enjoys it. Nick doesn't want to believe Cerruti and yet a part of him has known this obvious truth all along.

Later, when Nick confronts his father, the elder Kegan blames it all on Cerruti. He claims Cerruti is the one who's really in charge and ordered the death of the President in order to keep the Kegan empire running smoothly. There was little the elder Kegan could do to stop him. Do we believe Kegan? The film leaves a slight room for doubt. It's possible Nick's father is telling the truth. This might explain the otherwise uncharacteristic action that the elder Kegan takes at the end of the film when he's cornered by Nick, with nowhere left to turn: He commits suicide. Nick, however, does not appear to believe his father.

Condon's theory was considered blasphemy by some. Richert reports being spit on by some moviegoers who couldn't stand the fact that an American filmmaker would defame American royalty in this way. And yet Condon's theory, as outrageous as it seemed in the late seventies, would soon be outstripped by the truth.

The protagonist of Jack Womack's 1996 novel, *Let's Put the Future Behind Us*, is a Russian named Max Alexich Borodin whose job is to fabricate documents for various high-paying clients. At one point he manages to forge a document proving that JFK ordered a hit on *himself.* Womack, of course, intended this to be the ultimate in absurdist revisionism—far stranger even than claiming that JFK's father was responsible for his assassination.

Surprisingly, government documents released in the wake of Oliver Stone's 1991 *JFK* film might have proven Womack to be more correct than he could possibly ever have imagined.

But we'll have to delay that analysis until a little later....

For now, let's leave Cronus and his son resting (peacefully?) in their graves. For no matter who eats who first, the grave swallows both father and son in time.

7. They Live (1988)

BY THE 1980S, Americans stopped questioning.

Not just the facts behind the Kennedy assassination, but everything.

Too much had happened. Too many scandals had been uncovered in the sixties and seventies. Everyone was numb, and they just wanted to go to sleep. Eat. Mate. Spawn. Die.

The Watergate Scandal that brought down the Richard Nixon administration was first exposed by conspiracy theorist Mae Brussell before mainstream journalists, Bob Woodward and Carl Bernstein, picked up the story and ran with it. Woodward and Bernstein received a Pulitzer Prize for their troubles. Brussell didn't receive a damn thing except the constant accusation that she was nuts. Woodward and Bernstein's story was adapted into the 1976 film, *All the President's Men*, starring Robert Redford and Dustin Hoffman and directed by none other than Alan J. Pakula who had previously directed *The Parallax View*. It's difficult not to see the latter film as a sequel to the first. Since the second film is based on truth, it's not impossible to extend the same view to Pakula's previous political thriller (which, coincidentally, also featured an investigative journalist determined to uncover the truth behind a vast political conspiracy theory). But such political thrillers seemed to die out in the 1980s, replaced instead by an incessant stream of masked serial killers slaughtering young girls naughty enough to engage in premarital sex (the girls who refused to have sex of any kind would very often survive till the end of the movie). The classic Grimm's Fairy Tales that Walt Disney had gone to so much trouble to purify, to Americanize, had been reborn in the form of undead axe murderers, German-style, authoritarian finger-wagging implicit in every downward stroke of the blade. An appropriate through-line for a decade in which the Moral Majority, fully supported by the policies of the Ronald Reagan administration, incessantly equated "sexual diseases" such as AIDS with God's punishment for the wicked. Even James Bond stopped having casual sex in the reinvented series starring Timothy Dalton as Secret Agent 007. The puritans had always perceived sex to be evil and punishment to be godly, but never before had the Christian Right had such a stranglehold over public policy. The influence of the Moral Majority, and such silver-tongued televangelists as Oral Roberts and Jim Baker (both of whom would be destroyed by their own embarrassing sex scandals before the decade was finished) was ubiquitous in the 1980s, so much so that my sex education teacher at Torrance High, a German named Mr Boerger who wore golf pants every day and doubled as the driving instructor, felt complete freedom to tell my class on the very first day of the semester that "the anus is an exit, *not* an entrance," and that any homosexual in the classroom could "stand up and get the hell out of my classroom right now." A couple of people complained, but nothing happened to Mr Boerger as a consequence. He uttered opinions like this almost every day. It's difficult to imagine a high school teacher getting away with such comments today. During the Reagan administration, this point of view was considered to be "common wisdom." Mr Boerger was simply an amanuensis, channeling the collective thoughts of a nation too exhausted from the previous decade's wars and conflagrations to question consensus reality any longer. On December 8, 1980, within a few weeks of Reagan's election to the White House, only one year after *Winter Kills* was released in theaters, John Lennon was gunned down by yet another improbable drone with hypnosis swirls painted on his eyes, and yet no one cared to question the political implications of assassinating one of the last living symbols of hope from a previous decade. During his investigation into the Kennedy assassination, Jim Garrison encouraged Americans to ask the question, "Who benefits?" No one asked that question with regard to Lennon's death. They were no doubt tired of asking the same question over and over again and never receiving any answers.

Perhaps it's appropriate that in the same year John Lennon was murdered by yet another "creature with an atom brain," Curt Siodmak's title should be reborn in the landscape of pop music. In 1980 rock musician Roky Erickson and his band, Roky Erickson and the Aliens, recorded an album, *The Evil One*, that included a song called "Creature with the Atom Brain." The song seems to be permeated by a fear of psychotic delusions, focusing on depersonalization (or derealization), a psychological state that causes people to perceive the events around them as unreal or distant from their own personal experience, which ties in with the most disturbing aspects of Edward Cahn and Curt Siodmak's science fiction film. Though Dr Wilhelm Steigg's victims in *The Creature with the Atom Brain* are controlled remotely by others, their real personalities sometimes rise to the surface, as when the undead police detective Dave Harris (Saul John Launer) forces himself to stalk out of Chet Walker's house in a rage before he's compelled to hurt Walker's young daughter. Imagine the horror of having to harm or even murder innocent people against your will while being forced to watch this real world violence unfold on a grainy television screen always visible inside your mind, a view from which you can never turn away. Scenes of surgical body horror from the film are emphasized by Erickson's rock song in the form of a simple refrain: "No one stitches like that." Erickson's lyric seems to suggest that some medical horrors are too fantastic to be accepted as reality.

One wonders what Erickson's special interest in Cahn and Siodmak's film might have been. Perhaps he was just a fan of 1950s sci-fi films? Or perhaps the subtext of the film held a deeper meaning for him, a meaning of which he may not even have been fully aware.

Erickson began his music career two years after the assassination of John F. Kennedy when he co-founded a band called The 13th Floor Elevators. According to the July 12, 2007 edition of the *Austin American-Statesman*, in an article titled "The Fall and Rise of Roky Erickson," the twenty-one-year-old musician suffered an abrupt mental breakdown while performing on stage in San Antonio, Texas in 1968. Doctors diagnosed Erickson with paranoid schizophrenia, shipped him off to a psychiatric hospital in Houston, and forced electroconvulsive therapy on him.

Could this possibly have been the same Houston mental hospital (i.e., Bellaire Hospital) in which a peculiar gentleman named Marshall Applewhite was confined around the same time period? Applewhite married one of his nurses, was released in the early seventies (just like Erickson), and later began claiming that he was in contact with extraterrestrials. Eventually, Applewhite gathered a substantial following and formed a full-fledged cult in San Diego called "Heaven's Gate." Some people found Applewhite's story so convincing that, in 1996, thirty-nine of them agreed to commit suicide with the charismatic cult leader just to come face-to-face with the aliens on a massive starship supposedly hidden behind a comet called Hale-Bopp.[63]

In 1972, the same year Applewhite met and married his psychiatric nurse at the aforementioned Houston mental hospital, Roky Erickson was also released from a Houston hospital for the criminally insane. Just like Applewhite, he soon began to claim he was in contact with extraterrestrials. In fact, he went a few steps further and insisted that a "Martian" had taken possession of his body. In 1974 he formed a new band called Bleib Alien, which later transformed into Roky Erickson and the Aliens who recorded "Creature with the Atom Brain" in 1980 for CBS Records.

This background information casts the lyrics of Erickson's song in a completely different light. Knowing what Erickson went through, the song seems far more emotionally resonant and haunting than it might appear to be at first glance.

Considering the fact that Erickson incorporates actual samples from the film into the song, it's clear that he's attempting to draw the audience's attention to the movie itself: This is important, he's saying. Pay attention to its twenty-five-year-old message. Pay attention. Pay attention. Who "treated" Erickson and Applewhite in that Houston hospital? Is it known as a "hospital for the criminally insane" because it *cures* the criminally insane or because it *creates* them?

After all, no one stitches like that. No one stitches like that.

Significantly, Curt Siodmak's oddly titled film continues to influence pop culture to this very day. 2004 marked the birth of an experimental Belgian rock band called Creature with the Atom Brain whose latest album was released in 2015. The band cites Roky Erickson, and in particular his 1980 song, as their main influence. Oddly enough, their first two EPs were released through a label called Conspiracy.

Three months after John Lennon was killed, on March 30, 1981, President Reagan was himself gunned down by yet another "lone nut," this one seeming to be even more of an organic-robotoid straight out of a 1950s sci-fi flick penned by Curt Siodmak than the one who had preceded him. Instead of being triggered by the Queen of Hearts, like Raymond Shaw in *The Manchurian Candidate*, this latest "creature with an atom brain" appeared to be triggered by an obsession with the actress Jodie Foster (co-star of Martin Scorsese's 1976 film, *Taxi Driver*, which was also about a "lone nut" assassin who plans to gun down a politician in public). In his comprehensive book, *Rule by Secrecy*, published in 2000, Jim Marrs writes:

> [...] little more than two months after taking office, President Reagan was struck by an assassin's bullet which, but for a quarter of an inch, would have propelled Bush into the Oval Office seven years before his time. Oddly enough, the brother of the would-be assassin, John W. Hinckley, had scheduled dinner with Bush's son Neil the very night Reagan was shot. Hinckley's Texas oilman father and George Bush were longtime friends. It should also be noted that Bush's name—including his then little-publicized nickname "Poppy"—along with his address and phone number were found in the personal notebook of oil geologist George DeMohrenschildt, the last known close friend of Lee Harvey Oswald. The existence of a 1963 FBI report mentioning a "George Bush of the CIA" in connection with reactions of the U.S. Cuban community to the JFK assassination drew media attention during the 1992 election.[64]

When asked why his name had appeared in this FBI report back in '63, Bush claimed the notation was not in reference to him, but to a *different* George Bush who also worked for the CIA at the same exact time. Mainstream journalists bought Bush's answer *en masse*.

The October 21, 1981 edition of the *New York Times* reported that John Hinckley had admitted in writing, while imprisoned, that "he was part of a conspiracy when he shot President Reagan and three other men March 30." To make matters even stranger and more suspicious, FBI documents reveal that only five months before the assassination attempt Hinckley had also been stalking the "Queen of Conspiracies" herself, Mae Brussell, the aforementioned amateur journalist who broke the Watergate scandal well before Woodward and Bernstein.

On May 5, 1985, President Reagan made his true alliances clear when he visited Germany and prayed at the graves of Nazi soldiers. Afterwards, in response to the storm of criticism that erupted in the wake of this public display of either unthinking callousness or outright villainy, Reagan said that the Nazis were just as much victims in World War II as the Jews and deserved the same amount of respect. Mae Brussell and her successor, political researcher Dave Emory, considered this the defining moment of Reagan's presidency.

As the "me decade" wore on, President Reagan became embroiled in so many intricate scandals that most Americans these days neither understand nor remember them—and, even more distressing, perhaps have never even heard of them in the first place. Most Americans thirty-five and under will just stare at you blankly if you mention the word "Iran-Contra." The Iran-Contra scandal revealed that the Reagan administration was heavily involved in illegal arms deals with Iran. There was a time when it looked like President Reagan might be impeached for his involvement in these crimes. After studying the scandal one can come to either one of two conclusions: that Reagan approved of these illegal operations and therefore was not fit to be President, or that he wasn't aware of them at all (despite the fact that they were occurring literally under his nose—Col. Oliver North was running the operation from the White House basement) and therefore was not fit to be President. The conclusion was obvious and inevitable either way. Fed up with seeing their presidents tarnished or impeached, the American public just shrugged and said, "Oh, well, illegal arm sales with Iran doesn't affect me none. I'd rather go to sleep. Eat. Mate. Spawn. Die."

In the midst of this national somnambulism came John Carpenter's *They Live* (1988), perhaps the ultimate commentary on the 1980s and the three decades that preceded it. Though more well known for his proto-slasher film *Halloween* (1978), his science fiction dystopia *Escape from New York* (1981), which had a considerable impact on such well-respected science fiction novelists as William Gibson and Jack Womack, and supernatural thrillers like *The Fog* (1980), I consider *They Live* to be Carpenter's greatest triumph. Sometimes people will ask me, "So what are your favorite films?" The difference between "favorite" and "best" is a subtle but significant distinction. *2001: A Space Odyssey* (1968) could very well be one of the best films I've ever seen, but I have almost no need to see it again. Your "favorite" movies are the ones you could watch over and over again. Without fail, *They Live* makes it into my pantheon of top ten favorites every time someone asks me that question.

They Live offers the perfect metaphor for America's disassociated psychological state following the JFK assassination and all the other cultural upheavals of the sixties and seventies. It's also the most paranoid alien invasion movie ever made—an impressive feat in a subgenre bursting with nightmarishly paranoid delights.

The film is based on a tight, economical short story titled "Eight O'clock in the Morning" by Ray Nelson, one of only two writers who ever collaborated with Philip K. Dick on a novel, 1967's *The Ganymede Takeover*, which is about an invasion of Earth by worm-like aliens. "Eight O'clock in the Morning" was published in 1963, the same year as the JFK assassination. I first read the story roundabout 1999 when I came across a moldering paperback anthology titled *The Others* in a now defunct used bookstore, Book Buddy, in downtown

Torrance, California. Published in 1969, the same year as José Delgado's *Physical Control of the Mind*, *The Others* is a collection of paranoid science fiction tales edited by Terry Carr. The tagline on the front cover reads, "Do strange beings from out there control our lives?" The back copy reads:

THE OTHERS
are all around us—with their third eyes hidden, with
their schemes for tyranny concealed. A very few of us are
in on the secret. Can you afford not to be?

The cover painting, looking somewhat like a Max Ernst collage, depicts two beings—a bird-faced man wearing a blue suit and a reptilian woman wearing a nurse's outfit with a clipboard in her human-like hand—standing in the foreground while behind them a screaming man in a suit and tie seems to be struggling to escape from a giant golden birdcage. When you open the book, the reader is immediately assaulted by three questions:

Are there other intelligent beings in the universe?
Are some of them watching us, waiting for their chance to take over?
Or are they already in control?

Ray Nelson's story is included in this anthology. I suspect Carpenter must have come across the story for the first time in this particular book. One element of the film not included in the original story is that of the "Hoffman lenses," sunglasses that, when worn, reveal who's really an alien and who isn't. The back cover copy of the book reads

THE
OTHERS—
—can be seen only through very
special glasses.

This tag line is actually a reference to Daphne Du Maurier's story "The Blue Lenses," the second story included in the book. (Du Maurier is more famous for her Gothic novel, *Rebecca*, and her short story "The Birds," upon which Alfred Hitchcock based his 1963 film.) "The Blue Lenses" is about a woman whose sight has been restored thanks to an operation performed on the lenses of her eyes. The delicate surgery not only grants her sight, but allows her to peer deeply into the souls of the people around her by transforming them into animals, thus revealing their true personalities. Those with evil intentions towards her, for example, resemble snakes or vultures. I suspect Carpenter's imagination latched onto the tag line on the back of the book and transposed it over Nelson's paranoid alien invasion story.

Nelson's story manages to be suspenseful, disturbing, and funny all at once as it documents the accidental awakening of one man in a society of mind-controlled drones, as well as humanity's subsequent defeat of an invading army of reptilian aliens—all in seven pages. The majority of the story is written from a limited third person point of view, which puts the reader in a subjective viewpoint. All the information we perceive about reality is filtered through George Nada's eyes. He certainly *believes* that he can distinguish aliens from humans, but judging from the reactions of those around him the reader quickly begins to suspect that Nada has lost his mind. And when he begins exterminating the aliens—and their slug-like children—by knifing them to death, we're convinced we know what type of story this is. Like Kurt Vonnegut's novel, *Slaughterhouse-Five* (published in the same year as *The Others*), this is a story in which aliens ostensibly interact with humans, but the author has written the tale in such a careful manner that the reader can also interpret it as a psychological story about one man's mental breakdown.

But no, it's not that kind of story at all. In the last three sentences, Ray Nelson abandons the subjective viewpoint. We learn through an omniscient narrator that Nada's efforts to subvert the aliens' hypnotic control of the population have paid off. He uses their own tool—television—against them, and manages to wake everyone up by broadcasting the truth while imitating one of the aliens: "...and the city did awake for the very first time and the war began." Unfortunately, Nada himself dies soon afterwards from a posthypnotic command implanted in his mind by "his control" (an alien masquerading as a cop) the previous day: "George did not live to see the victory that finally came. He died of a heart attack at exactly eight o'clock."[65]

Despite the fact that the original story is only seven pages long, and the screenplay no doubt at least ninety pages, *They Live* actually manages to be more faithful to Nelson's vision than most film adaptations of literary works. All the most important plot points are included in the film, including a few lines of dialogue. Nada's command to "wake up" near the end of the short story, for example, is echoed in the first few minutes of the film when a street preacher is delivering a sermon about the aliens to a group of bystanders in a park.

Carpenter manages to set the tone for the entire film in this opening sermon, establishing the religious subtext that weaves in and out of the storyline. The preacher is one of the first people Nada (Roddy Piper) encounters upon walking into LA from a train depot on the edge of the city. It's clear from the first time we see him that Nada has arrived in town by riding the rails. A pedestrian in LA: this already makes him a statistical outlier, a man on the margins. Nada enters the margins *from* the margins, and immediately comes across a blind Black preacher delivering what sounds like an old style fire-and-brimstone sermon about the temptations of Lucifer… but the devils this preacher is concerned about are of a different sort entirely. This sermon is Carpenter's thesis statement. Everything you need to know about the fictional world of *They Live*—as well as the real world of the moviegoers sitting in the theater—is embedded in the preacher's opening salvo:

> They use their tongues to deceive. The venom of snakes is under their lips. Their mouths are full of bitterness and curses. In their paths, nothing but ruin and misery. The fear of God is not before their eyes. They have taken the hearts and minds of our leaders. They have recruited the rich and the powerful, and they have blinded us to the truth. Our human spirit is corrupted. Why do we worship greed? Because outside the limit of our sight, feeding off us, perched on top of us from birth to death, are our *owners*. Our *owners*! They have us! They control us! They are our masters! Wake up! They're all about you, all around you!

Of course, that last sentence also echoes the closing warning delivered by Dr Miles Bennell (Kevin McCarthy) in *Invasion of the Body Snatchers* as he stumbles about on the highway, shaking his fists at the sky, screaming directly into the camera: "You fools! You're in danger! Can't you see? They're after you! They're after *all* of us! Our wives, our children, everyone! They're here already! You're next! You're next!"

There's also a strong hint of Charles Fort here, particularly in the line about "they" being "our *owners*." Fort once wrote, "I think we're property,"[66] and this viewpoint has never been more purely expressed in cinema than in *They Live*. Since overt references to Fort

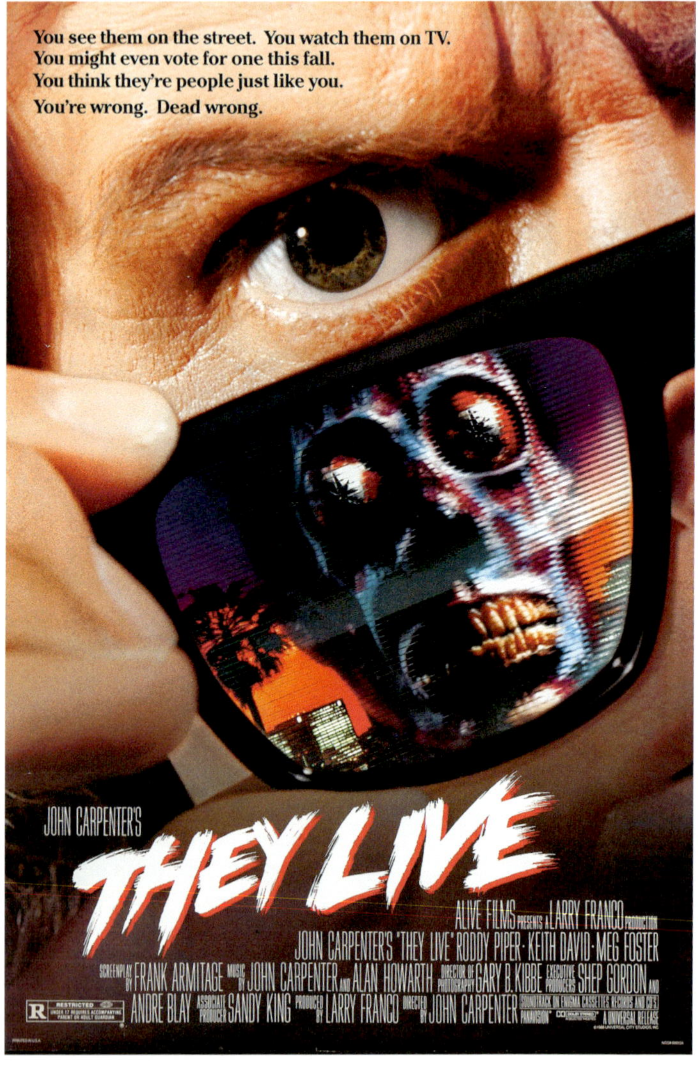
You see them on the street. You watch them on TV.
You might even vote for one this fall.
You think they're people just like you.
You're wrong. Dead wrong.
JOHN CARPENTER'S
THEY LIVE
ALIVE FILMS PRESENTS A LARRY FRANCO PRODUCTION
JOHN CARPENTER'S 'THEY LIVE' RODDY PIPER · KEITH DAVID · MEG FOSTER
SCREENPLAY BY FRANK ARMITAGE MUSIC BY JOHN CARPENTER AND ALAN HOWARTH DIRECTOR OF PHOTOGRAPHY GARY B. KIBBE EXECUTIVE PRODUCERS SHEP GORDON AND
ANDRE BLAY ASSOCIATE PRODUCER SANDY KING PRODUCED BY LARRY FRANCO DIRECTED BY JOHN CARPENTER
SOUNDTRACK ON ENIGMA CASSETTES, RECORDS AND CD'S
PANAVISION
A UNIVERSAL RELEASE
R RESTRICTED

occur in other John Carpenter films (in his 1995 remake of *The Village of the Damned*, for example), I think it's fair to assume that Fort was firmly in Carpenter's mind when he wrote this sermon.

They Live reunites us with the previously mentioned "film-within-film" motif ("video-within-film"?). Once again vital information is transmitted to the audience in the form of speeches (perhaps these could also be called sermons) that appear from time to time on television screens within the movie. Human hackers periodically interrupt television broadcasts with revolutionary speeches in order to disrupt the brainwashing signals the aliens are using to control the minds of human beings. These speeches interrupt broadcasts three times throughout the film; the first and third broadcasts are themselves divided into three parts. As in fairy tales, everything important happens in threes.

The first broadcast occurs about five minutes into the film:

> *Our impulses are being redirected. We are living in an artificially induced state of consciousness that resembles sleep. The Movement was begun eight months ago by a small group of scientists who discovered, quite by accident, these signals being sent through—*
>
> [The transmission is interrupted briefly]
>
> *The poor and the underclass are growing. Racial justice and human rights are nonexistent.* They *have created a repressive society and we are their unwitting accomplices. Their intention to rule rests with the annihilation of consciousness. We have been lulled into a trance. They have made us indifferent—to ourselves, to others. We are focused only on our own gain. We—*
>
> [Another interruption]
>
> *Please, understand,* they *are safe as long as they are not discovered. That is their primary method of survival. Keep us asleep, keep us selfish, keep us sedated.*

The second broadcast occurs about twelve minutes into the film:

> *They are dismantling the sleeping middle class. More and more people are becoming poor. We are their cattle. We are being bred for slavery. The revo—*
>
> [Another interruption]

> *We cannot break their signal. Our transmitter is not powerful enough. The signal must be shut off at the source. We have—*

The third and final broadcast occurs about one hour and nine minutes into the film:

> *There is a signal broadcast every second of every day through our television sets, even when the set is turned off.*
>
> *Look around at the environment we live in. Carbon dioxide, fluorocarbons, and methane have increased since 1958. Earth is being acclimated. They are turning* our *atmosphere into* their *atmosphere.*
>
> *We are like a natural resource to them. Deplete the planet, move on to another. They want benign indifference. They want us drugged. We could be pets. We could be food. But all we* really *are is livestock.*

As with the educational film about the José Delgado mind control techniques that Curt Siodmak embeds within *Creature with the Atom Brain*, Carpenter embeds his own "educational" moments within *They Live*. It's an effective technique that allows the filmmaker to rebuke the movie-going audience, to preach and scream at them, without them even being aware of it. These moments are the truth hidden within the fiction. Ray Nelson's metaphor of a hidden alien invasion, dreamed up within his brain the same year as the Kennedy assassination, is the perfect metaphor for what occurred to the Disassociated States of America after the President's death. Numerous psychological studies have found that children will often obscure memories of abuse (both sexual and otherwise) at the hands of their parents by creating a "screen" that will put the blame on some outside source, perhaps even an imaginary being. At least one psychologist, Dr Kenneth Ring, discovered that children who have suffered sexual/emotional abuse are more likely to report having been abducted by aliens. (See Dr Ring's 1992 book, *The Omega Project*, for more in-depth information on that subject.) Though this does not explain *all* alien abduction experiences, it does indicate that the human mind is an expert in survival. It will do whatever it can to overcome tremendous psychological pressures. If that entails distorting reality, then reality will be distorted. Sometimes whole families will willingly distort reality in order to withstand the ongoing stresses of living day in and day out with an alcoholic family member. And sometimes whole nations can distort reality, as in Nazi Germany when entire communities claimed not to know that Jews were being burned in the concentration camps right next door to their pleasant little homes. Perhaps they weren't lying. Perhaps they really didn't know. Perhaps they chose not to see the evidence that was right there before their eyes.

Sometimes it's easier to blame the Other ("Illegal aliens are to blame for me losing my job," or "I drink because my boss is a son of a bitch" or "some lousy Commie shot the President") because it's harder to deal with the consequences of an uncomfortable truth ("I cut myself out of a job when I voted for so-and-so," or "I drink because I'm weak" or "the current President helped gun down our last President because he's clearly a power mad tool of a fascist cabal").

And sometimes it's even easier to blame the wholly mythological ("God gave up on me" or "Satan tempted me" or "I'm broke because the Illuminati's in control of the world banking system") rather than oneself ("God didn't give up on me, I did" or "Satan didn't tempt me, I just love having sex with hookers" or "the Illuminati didn't blow all my money on blackjack in Las Vegas, I did").

The central metaphor of *They Live* is the natural outgrowth of over twenty years of suppressing the evidence of an obvious truth: that the vast majority of the population of the United States sat by and did nothing while a fascist coup played out right in front of their eyes in real time—and on live television. The Kennedy assassination was the first reality TV show, and its producers knew that fact long before the first bullet was fired. Entertainment always trumps truth.

Graffiti scrawled on the inside of a dilapidated church in *They Live* says it best: THEY LIVE, WE SLEEP.

The film-within-film motif recurs in *They Live* on at least one more occasion, about thirteen minutes in, and it's a significant one. Amidst a montage of *faux* commercials, fleeting satirical swipes at the "divine excess" (one of the commercials—this one advertising a clothing line—actually uses that phrase) of 1980s consumer culture, we see a snippet from John Sherwood's *The Monolith Monsters* (1957). Unlike Carpenter's exaggerated commercials, this clip is actually appropriated from a previous film, and therefore it stands out. It also stands out because it's black-and-white, the only black-and-white footage we see in the film until Nada puts on his "Hoffman lenses" (more on that later) at the half-hour mark and sees the world as it truly is for the first time in his life. The scenes meant to show reality as it is, stripped of all mind control-induced illusions, are presented in black-and-white. Given the fact that *The Monolith Monsters* is the only other black-and-white footage seen in the film, this suggests something important: that the world of *The Monolith Monsters*, a cheap 1950s B-film helmed by a minor director, is more "real" than the world of "free enterprise" ("The fall collection *revels* in freedom of expression," boasts one of Carpenter's *faux* commercials) that Nada appears to inhabit. Carpenter is saying: Stop a moment. Wait. Look at this. These 1950s science fiction films are telling you something important, but none of you are listening.

In his 2010 book-length analysis of *They Live*, Jonathan Lethem writes:

> No matter how ominous, the grainy "reality effect" of this footage seems to call up a better, deeper world than that of the satires of contemporary television around it. One of the functions of films like *The Monolith Monsters*, in the fallout-shelter fifties, was to insert contemplations of death into an atmosphere of remorseless cheer, just as part of film noir's duties was to open up a space for the despair of returning World War II veterans in a culture that didn't want to hear about it. Here, the fifties are made to seem a whole lot deeper than the eighties. At the very least a black-and-white Jack Arnold movie [here Lethem is mistaken, as Jack Arnold did not direct *The Monolith Monsters*, though he did co-author the story upon which it's based] is something John Carpenter certainly likes (it's a movie, for one thing), in a world drowning in his obvious dislikes (television commercials, and the kind of television that might as well be a commercial). Seeing the old movie, and probably liking this kind of thing ourselves, we lean forward.[67]

At this point Lethem chooses to focus on the fact that *The Monolith Monsters* is a movie, arguing that Carpenter clearly favors film over television. In *They Live* television is always equated with mind control, whereas movies are not. But this harkens back to Nelson's original story:

> A TV set in the window of a store caught George's eye, but he looked away in the nick of time. When he didn't look at the [alien] in the screen, he could resist the command, "Stay tuned to this station."
>
> George lived alone in a little sleeping room and as soon as he got home, the first thing he did was to disconnect the TV set. In other rooms he could hear the TV sets of his neighbors, though. Most of the time the voices were human, but now and then he heard the arrogant,

> strangely birdlike croaks of the aliens. "Obey the government," said one croak. "We are the government," said another. "We are your friends, you'd do anything for a friend, wouldn't you?"
>
> "Obey!"
>
> "Work!"[68]

In this sense, Carpenter is sticking very close to Nelson's vision. I think what's most important about Carpenter's choice of *The Monolith Monsters* is not the medium itself, but the content. I'm sure Marshall McLuhan will forgive me for momentarily altering his famous dictum that "the medium is the message." In this case, "the monster is the message." The titular "Monolith Monsters" are non-sentient extraterrestrial rocks that grow to immense heights when exposed to water. They just keep growing until they reach a certain height, topple over, crumble into pieces, then begin growing all over again, each individual fragment producing yet another monolith monster. It's like dealing with a slow-moving avalanche that never ends and multiplies like cockroaches. In the context of *They Live*, it's a perfect visual metaphor for the alien conspirators themselves. When one is killed, more arrive from the home planet to take their place. In the context of the real world, one can extend the metaphor further: When one President is impeached for a federal offence that should lead to serious jail time, here comes another President right behind the last, all ready to pardon the crook he's replacing. Push one monolith out of office, here comes another one hurtling out of the sky to begin its own peculiar brand of destruction. And the impotent townsfolk stand on the edge of the town looking up at the destruction, too dumbfounded to do anything about it.

The image could also be seen as a hopeful one. Carpenter chooses to appropriate a shot of the monsters *toppling over*, perhaps foreshadowing that victory over these seemingly implacable foes is indeed possible. Perhaps the Monolith Monsters aren't as monolithic as they appear.

Of course, one of the simple reasons Carpenter probably chose *The Monolith Monsters* is that it's a Universal film—just as *They Live* is a Universal film, and therefore the rights for the footage would have been easy to clear. Still, there were plenty of other films Universal produced in the 1950s that Carpenter could have chosen. He specifically chose a black-and-white science fiction/horror film that connects us all the way back to the era in which, Cassandra-like, Siodmak unleashed his *Creature with the Atom Brain* on an unsuspecting world.

The broadcasts that interrupt the aliens' brainwashing signals is the little white rabbit that lures Nada, like Alice, off the well-worn path of objective reality. One particular broadcast inspires Nada to investigate a church across the street from a homeless encampment in LA where our itinerant hero is staying temporarily. It turns out that the church is the headquarters of this revolutionary group. Nada stumbles on a cache of their specially made sunglasses that disrupt the mind-distorting signal being transmitted by the aliens. When one puts on the glasses, one can see reality for what it actually is. One can distinguish between the humans and the aliens. Whenever Nada slips on the glasses, the world becomes black-and-white. Humans remain humans, but aliens are revealed as cadaverous, walking nightmares. The end credits refer to them as "ghouls," and indeed they do somewhat resemble the rotting ghouls that "Ghastly" Graham Ingels was so expert at drawing during EC comics' 1950s horror comic heyday. Many times over the years, John Carpenter has mentioned the grip EC comic books such as *Tales from the Crypt* and *Weird Science* held on his imagination when he was growing up in the 1950s (he described *Tales from the Crypt* as "insurrectionary to the culture of Eisenhower and Walt Disney"), so it's not impossible that the "ghouls" in *They Live* were designed to resemble the exaggerated, undead monstrosities in which Ingels specialized before dropping out of the comic book industry in the late fifties.[69]

Not only do the sunglasses reveal the true visages of the aliens, they also reveal the pervasive mind control methods constantly flashed in our faces without our conscious knowledge. Significantly, the main source of the aliens' hypnotic signals is an extraterrestrial machine disguised as a television antenna. (In an odd sense, this is the most realistic aspect of the film—if only on a metaphorical level, of course. Of course.) The symbolism here is obvious. In fact, *all* of the symbols in the film are obvious; that's part of the tale's considerable power. As Stephen King once wrote of Ray Bradbury's work, "The symbolism [in Bradbury's novel *Something Wicked This Way Comes*] is large, crude, and apparent [...]. Bradbury pulls it off nonetheless, mostly out of sheer fearlessness. He deals his archetypes large, like those bridge-sized [Tarot] cards."[70] This film is drunk on symbolism, so much so that it might be argued that the symbolism overrides rationality. The film ends with our hero destroying the TV antenna/mind control machine with a single bullet as the aliens mow him down.

Some critics of the film have questioned this. Could one man-made bullet decimate a complex extraterrestrial device upon which the security of an invading alien race and a decades-long psychological operation *depend?* Well, perhaps. Who am I to say "no"? I've never encountered complex extraterrestrial mind control devices, so I couldn't vouch for their durability. Besides, in recent US history a single commandeered plane was used to destroy the center of economic trade of the entire Western world. Sometimes the most diligent brains overlook the smallest details, and Nada is, if not the smallest detail, a seemingly insignificant one. But questions like this miss the point. The point is best represented by those "bridge-sized" Tarot cards Stephen King mentioned earlier, not perfunctory details of the ostensibly science fictional plot. Nada triumphs and Nada dies: Nada as Christ, but also Nada as Osiris and Odin and so many other mythological martyrs. As Ernest Hemingway once wrote, "Our nada who art in nada, nada by thy name thy kingdom nada thy will be nada as it is in nada."

Though this film truly is a paranoid's worst nightmare, it's also a highly religious film (and if one stops to think about it, one realizes this is not a paradox at all), its seemingly Christian roots extending at least as far back as the early Gnostics. Lethem himself identifies this Gnostic strain: "Our ostensible satire of the Reagan yuppie generation, specific in time and place, keeps gesturing toward corruptions of the human spirit and species as ancient as Lovecraft's Cthulhu, or some other force even more fundamentally Gnostic."[71]

When wearing the Hoffman lenses, the secret messages lurking behind reality—behind every billboard, magazine, paperback book, commercial, and television soap opera—are revealed to Nada in a sudden instant of near-mystic illumination: OBEY, SURRENDER, STAY ASLEEP, WATCH TV, CONSUME, MARRY AND REPRODUCE. As Lethem writes, "*They Live* is an entertainment that sneaks in a lesson in reading, an episode of *The Electric Company* for grownups."[72] This sequence, which begins around the half-hour mark of the film, lifts *They Live* from the mainstream thrillers of Carpenter's previous oeuvre and into a completely different realm altogether, a realm that straddles both the lurid and the divine, a realm in which hermetic wisdom is disguised as popular entertainment; it's one of those rare moments where B-film collides with Art film, and the two immediately decide to get better acquainted by making violent love. In mythological terms, this sequence represents the lifting of the veil of Maya from the eyes of our hero. He is reluctantly expelled from the world of darkness ("Nada") into the world of light. Nada has, like Alice tumbling into Wonderland 123 years before him, become enflamed by the secrets that lay hidden behind the thin curtain of the quotidian.

In this sequence Nada is somewhat akin to a Masonic initiate. Blindfolded, hoodwinked by the notion of objective reality his entire life, he has wandered from town to town looking for the American Dream (as Nada himself says at one point, "I still believe in the American Dream"), his rightful place in the sun. Only after great confusion and chaos can "nothing" (*Nada*, a blank slate) be reborn into "something," in this case a gun-toting martyr willing to sacrifice his own life in order to tear aside the veil of Maya for the rest of humanity, even if only for a few minutes until the back-up alien generator kicks in. For those conspiracy theorists who wish to see Masonic symbolism in almost everything, it's tantalizing to mention here that Nada slips on his glasses at exactly thirty-two minutes into the film. There are thirty-two degrees in Scottish Rite Masonry, plus one honorary degree, the 33rd, reserved for only the most special candidates. The film is precisely one hour and thirty-three minutes long. When Nada first puts on the glasses, he's standing in front of the Los Angeles Athletic Club, one of the main meeting places for The Royal Order of the Jesters, a little known secret society that only 32nd Degree Masons can join. The Royal Order of the Jesters has been accused of various forms of covert skullduggery over the years, including manipulating politicians and the police force from behind the scenes. One of the symbols of the Jesters is a cadaver dressed as a court jester with a skeletal face not at all dissimilar to those of the ghouls in *They Live*.

Of this revelatory sequence, in which Nada is abruptly thrust into a higher form of reality, Lethem writes:

> ...I can easily think of two dozen directors I personally hold above Carpenter. But, given the imperative to preserve just a dozen sequences from film history in a time capsule, the rest to evaporate from human memory, I might pick the next six, or eight, or ten minutes of *They Live*. I'd pick them to stand for the eighties, and for the minor tradition of the "self-conscious B-movie," and for that side of science fiction cinema devoted to what critic Darko Suvin calls "cognitive estrangement" (as opposed to wish fulfillment, thrills, action, techno-lust, or horror). And I'd pick them out of affection. This, for me, is *They Live's* hard, chewy, delicious center. If I had the powers, I'd slow these minutes down and expand them, somehow, into a world in which to linger and

explore like an interactive DVD or video game—flipping through more of the "translated" magazines, gazing at the revelatory architecture and signage, eavesdropping on further conversations.[73]

Significantly, wearing these glasses, seeing reality as it is for any great length of time, always induces a headache. In Carpenter's world, true illumination can come only with physical pain. And that's never more true than in the virtuoso six-minute fight scene that occurs about fifty-five minutes into the film in which Nada attempts to convince his friend, Frank (Keith David), to put on the Hoffman lenses and see reality as it truly is, alien conspirators and subliminal mind control messages and all. Frank refuses to do it. Once all forms of verbal persuasion fail, Nada does the only thing he can do. He begins beating the crap out of his friend, trying to force the glasses over his eyes.

It's the only cinematic fight scene I know of that operates as a perfect metaphor for transmitting "illumination" to someone else. Frank is getting the third degree, as it were, and Nada seems more than happy to give it to him. The two friends even exchange smiles during the fight, a peculiar moment of self-consciousness and embarrassment, a silent and subtle overture to end the battle and start over from the beginning, what Lethem calls "one of the fight's weirdly serene micro-interludes."[74] But neither side is giving up. For Nada, it's the Hoffman lenses or nothing. Nada knows what's really at stake here. Frank is defending his right to remain ignorant. Nada is defending all of reality itself. Of course he's going to win.

The culmination of the fight scene is tantamount to the last three sentences of Nelson's short story. It's the moment when Nada's reality is confirmed—in this case by another human being rather than an omniscient narrator. Once Nada succeeds in placing the lenses on Frank's face, it's all over for Frank. He's seen his world decoded. He can't go back to his wife and family, not unless he gets glasses for them too, and there's only one pair. From now on Frank and Nada are joined at the hip, stars of their own doomed buddy picture, strapped into a grim Gnostic rollercoaster ride into Hell, or the nearest stand-in located beneath an LA TV station—provided courtesy of the alien ghouls.

I have a very clear memory of seeing this movie on opening night when I was sixteen. My girlfriend and I were sitting outside in the lobby waiting for the previous showing to end. When the final credits rolled, all the moviegoers filed out. A teenage couple almost passed by us, then paused and said hi. I had no idea who they were, but apparently they were classmates with my girlfriend.

After exchanging several innocuous pleasantries, my girlfriend asked, "So how was the movie? I've heard all different sorts of things about it."

The guy waved his hand in the air dismissively and said, "Aw, I don't know. It gets kinda silly near the end. It has the worst fight scene ever."

His girlfriend laughed and said, "Yeah, it goes on and on and on. We just wanted it to end already."

I don't remember what I thought about that comment; I do know, however, that the only fight scene I'd ever liked up to that point was the one at the end of John Ford's *The Quiet Man* (1952), and I would have been skeptical that Carpenter could trump Ford, so perhaps I was gearing myself up for something tedious. What I got was something quite different indeed.

Halfway through the fight scene in question, I began laughing uncontrollably and turned to my girlfriend and said, "Your two friends didn't know what the fuck they were talking about! This is *great*!"

At that moment I decided it was the single greatest fight scene ever committed to celluloid. Over twenty years later, while walking to CSU Long Beach to teach an English class, I came across a section of a newspaper someone had abandoned on a bus bench. For some reason the paper caught my eye, so I picked it up and took it with me. It was the entertainment section of the *L.A. Times* and contained an interview with the director of a new action adventure film starring Nicolas Cage. The interviewer asked the director how he developed the uniquely brutal, bare knuckle fight scene featured in the film. The director replied that he had been tearing his hair out trying to decide how to stage this scene so it would look different from all the recent stylized, ballet-like fight scenes that had accrued on the screen in the wake of *The Matrix* (1999). He said he had bought a DVD called *The 50 Greatest Fight Scenes Ever* and watched the entire disc. "Then," he said (I'm paraphrasing from memory), "I got to the scene in this film called *They Live*. Man, I thought it was the best fight scene I'd ever seen! I decided to base my fight scene on that one!" Well, this enthusiastic plagiarism didn't spur me on to see the Nicolas Cage film, but it was the first time I'd heard anyone else echo my opinion about that particular sequence in *They Live*. I don't think I'd heard anyone even mention *They Live* in the preceding twenty years since I'd seen it, though scenes from that film would periodically float back up into my consciousness, prompted by whatever insidious new paranoid nightmare was cropping up in the news that week.

So *They Live* refused to die. Memories of the film might recede into the background for a little while, and then it would crop up again in the most unusual way.

In 1995 while reading Michael A. Hoffman's book *Secret Societies and Psychological Warfare*, I came across a reference to *They Live* on the back cover. Hoffman strongly implies that the sunglasses in the film, referred to fleetingly as the "Hoffman lenses," is a direct reference to *him* and his tireless investigation of Masonic conspiracies. Some claim the lenses are named after Albert Hofmann, the Swiss chemist who created LSD. Given the fact that Carpenter's 2001 film, *The Ghosts of Mars*, contains a blatantly pro-drug, pro-consciousness-expansion subtext, I agree that Mr Hofmann (Albert, not Michael) is more than likely Carpenter's main inspiration.

Seven years later, in 2002, I joined my own vast *They-Live*-like conspiracy when I became initiated into Freemasonry. By 2004 I had worked my way up through the ranks and officially became a 32nd degree Scottish Rite Freemason. One day a fellow brother emailed me and told me I should drop by the lodge because a "famous actor," Roddy Piper, was being initiated into the first degree at my Mother Lodge in Torrance, CA. I wrote back and told him that Piper was the star of one of my favorite films, *They Live*. He'd never heard of *They Live*, but said he was coaching Piper to help him memorize all the oaths in order to move on to the second degree. Unfortunately, I had to teach a class that night, so I couldn't make it to Piper's initiation. Still, I was stunned that "Nada" and I were now officially lodge brothers.

In 2010 Soft Skull Press debuted their "Deep Focus" line of books (each volume features long form criticism of a single film by a well-known writer) with a 163-page analysis of John Carpenter's *They Live* written by Jonathan Lethem, bestselling writer of such phildickian science fiction novels as *Gun, with Occasional Music* and *Girl in Landscape*. Lethem's analysis is in-depth, devilishly clever, and leaves almost no cultural stone unturned. I was particularly impressed that his research into the sub-sub-sub-cultural tributaries of the film was so comprehensive that on p. 43 he actually mentions Michael A. Hoffman's egotistical appropriation of the "Hoffman lenses."

I just learned a few days ago that Shout! Factory has recently released a new version of *They Live* on Blu-ray (a previous no-frills version of the film was released by Universal in 2003) that includes various special features, including a commentary track by John Carpenter.

The film continues to thrive, despite its initial failure at the box office in 1988, because it speaks to unacknowledged truths that most people are aware of only at a subconscious level: that something or someone secretly took over the reins of this country a long time ago ("When did it start?" Frank asks Nada at one point, not long after his six-minute-long beating/initiation into the Mysteries, "how long have they been here?" to which Nada has no answer), and they're not letting go until every resource has been bled out of the earth. Including human beings.

> *We are like a natural resource to them. Deplete the planet, move on to another. They want benign indifference. They want us drugged. We could be pets. We could be food. But all we* really *are is livestock.*

Or as Charles Fort said, "I think we're property."

By the way, I think the obsessive synchronicity-hound in me would be remiss if I didn't mention the fact that the Best Boy Electrician who worked on *They Live* was named "John Kennedy." In case you were skeptical of my thesis before, you can now relax, assured that the spirit of our deceased President does indeed live on in the end credits of a science fiction/horror flick from the late 1980s. As Lyndon Johnson discovered to his dismay, the spirits of martyrs are sometimes hard to get rid of.

They live, indeed.

8. JFK (1991)

THEY LIVE ON in the dreams of men, and some of these dreams evolve into stories and plays and comic books and paintings and radio shows and movies. What once was subtext inevitably becomes text. Living metaphor eventually becomes literal. Truth begets rumor begets fiction begets documentary begets myth.

What was too dangerous to talk about openly in 1955 (the year *Creature with the Atom Brain* was released), except in the form of B-movie metaphors, is at last tackled head-on by writer/director Oliver Stone in his film, *JFK* (1991). After thirty years or more, the hidden subtext was revealed. Enough time had passed, enough rumor and mythmaking had made the rounds of the collective unconscious (in the form of films like *They Live*) that the American people had inoculated themselves to the poisonous truth. Without films like *Creature with the Atom Brain* and *They Live*, a film like *JFK* could never have existed. The shock of undiluted truth would have been too much for most people. All the films under discussion here—plus other films not included in this study—helped pave the way for what really is one of the best films of the 1990s, and probably one of the best films of the past fifty years. One need not even accept the film's thesis to agree with this. When this film was first released, I recall hearing Robert Anton Wilson (co-author of *The Illuminatus! Trilogy*) say that upon first seeing *JFK* he realized he'd seen a film that was as important as Orson Welles' *Citizen Kane* was to cinema in 1941.

I should pause here to mention that I'm not an Oliver Stone cheerleader. Most of the Stone films people tend to rave about leave me cold. I found *Natural Born Killers*, for example, to be shallow and tedious to an extreme degree. Stone's excesses, on full display in that film, tend to overwhelm the story he's attempting to tell. His style is emblematic of the self-conscious filmmaking endemic to the 1990s (and beyond) that makes me want to burrow back into the unpretentious B-movie aesthetics of Edward Cahn. *JFK*, on the other hand, is a different matter. I suspect the restrictions of the narrative, being pushed toward absolute and *unselfconscious* clarity by the complex nature of the plot, somehow restrained Stone's natural tendencies toward excess and forced him to use the camera to *tell the story* with as few frills as possible. In *Natural Born Killers* the star is the camera; the people and the story are incidental. In *JFK* it's the exact opposite; the camera is in service of the story. The stars are human beings, not a steady cam, and the results are imaginative and stunning.

Stone employs a variety of cinematic techniques in order to allow an extremely complicated story to unfold with seeming effortlessness. Over the years I've encountered at least two film buffs who are ardent skeptics of any conspiracy theory, and particularly conspiracy theories involving the JFK assassination, who nonetheless contend that *JFK* is one of the best films they've ever seen. The editing alone is masterful and deservedly received an Academy Award. The screenplay by Oliver Stone and Zachary Sklar, which reduces thirty years' worth of information into a dramatic framework that never falters or seems tedious, was also worthy of every award Hollywood could have heaped upon it in 1992. Instead, the Academy Award for Best Adapted Screenplay went to Ted Tally for *The Silence of the Lambs* (1991), the apotheosis of America's serial killer obsession that began the same year as Richard Nixon's resignation from the presidency with the release of Tobe Hooper's *The Texas Chain Saw Massacre* (1974). It's intriguing to note that *Texas Chain Saw Massacre* was inspired by "the massacres and atrocities in the Vietnam War," according to Hooper, which means that one could draw a straight line from Dealey Plaza to JFK's corpse to the resultant deepening of America's involvement in Vietnam to no less a cultural icon than Leatherface himself.[75] *The Texas Chain Saw Massacre's* more respectable progeny, *The Silence of the Lambs*, also took home the Academy Award for Best Film in 1992. Of course, it's always worth keeping in mind that *Citizen Kane* only won a single Academy Award in 1942 (for Best Original Screenplay).

JFK returns us once again to the film-within-a-film motif. In fact, the first seven minutes of the film is a whole series of films-within-film. The rectangular screen is reduced down to a small square, and in that square is contained everything we need to know about post-World War II American history that will lead to a barrage of bullets being pumped into the President's skull on November 22, 1963. Somehow, Stone and Sklar compress this complex history down to its essentials without misrepresenting the facts. Wisely, they choose to begin the film with President Eisenhower's January 17, 1961 warning to the American people to beware "the military-industrial complex," a salvo against the nascent intelligence community that was just beginning to spin its web around Washington, D.C. I think if we had Nada's glasses on, we'd be able to tell that Eisenhower was no ghoul.

Seven minutes into the film we catch our first glimpse of the most important "film-within-the-film" in *JFK*, and that's the infamous "Zapruder film," the home movie footage taken by Abraham Zapruder on the day of the assassination. Purely by chance, Zapruder recorded a crucial moment in history, and it was this film that would undo the official story as told by the Warren Commission, the committee assigned by President Lyndon Johnson to investigate the assassination. The Zapruder film will play an important role in our narrative later on.

When the shots ring out, the tiny square of history expands to fill the entire screen, and the film proper begins. Stone's imperative was to populate the film with familiar faces, American icons, that would help guide the audience through this most difficult subject matter. His

PRESIDENT KENNEDY
DEATH BY ASSASSIN
SHOT
DALLAS
He's a District Attorney.
He will risk his life,
the lives of his family,
everything he holds dear
for the one thing he holds sacred...
the truth.
KEVIN COSTNER
AN OLIVER STONE FILM
JFK
The Story That Won't Go Away
WARNER BROS. PRESENTS

feeling was that these familiar faces would subliminally make the audience feel secure, assured that the information they were seeing was reliable. Interestingly, William Richert used the same approach in *Winter Kills* fifteen years prior to *JFK*, and in both cases the technique more or less works as intended.

Stone spurs an all-star cast to some of their best performances. Although some of these scenes are quite short, the actors involved all make an impression and own their individual moments. Kevin Costner, Gary Oldman, Tommy Lee Jones, Joe Pesci, Donald Sutherland, Ed Asner, Jack Lemmon, Walter Matthau, and John Candy all excel in their parts. *JFK* is one of those rare movies in which the director manages to cast the perfect actor for each role. It's hard to imagine, for example, a better David Ferrie than Joe Pesci, or a better Lee Harvey Oswald than Gary Oldman.

A brief anecdote about Oldman's performance: A friend recently told me a story about how he was chatting with an acquaintance one day about various actors, and the subject of Oldman came up. His friend was raving about Oldman's chameleon-like qualities as an actor. "Who else," this guy said, "could play Sid Vicious, Dracula, and Beethoven all within a few years of each other?" My friend replied, "Yeah, that's true. You know, I really love his performance in *JFK*." The acquaintance, who had seen *JFK* at least once, just looked at my friend blankly for a moment, then said, "Who does he play in *JFK*?"

That's how good Oldman's performance is.

Some of the actors bring with them the resonance of previous roles. It's difficult to watch Donald Sutherland's breathless rendition of L. Fletcher Prouty (AKA Mr X) without thinking of Philip Kaufman's *Invasion of the Body Snatchers* (1978). In that remake of the 1956 Don Siegel film, Sutherland finds himself up against a metropolis full of human-appearing aliens intent on taking over the world. When we hear Mr X's conspiratorial monologue (which takes up twelve pages of the screenplay) delivered with such ostensible effortlessness on Sutherland's part, we can't help but feel that this guy knows exactly what he's talking about. After all, he's dealt with these alien sons of bitches before, hasn't he? Once again slipping on Nada's sunglasses for a moment, it's clear to us that Sutherland is no red herring sent in to confuse our hero. No, this guy's human.

And there's no doubt that Garrison is human as well. There are a lot of similarities between Nada and Garrison. Both characters are seen to be "naïve" at the beginning of their respective story arcs. In

They Live we have the scene in which Nada tells Frank that he still believes in the American Dream: "I'll do a hard day's work for my money. I just want the chance. It'll come. I believe in America. I follow the rules." In *JFK* private investigator Jack Martin (Jack Lemmon) explicitly tells Garrison, "You are so naïve." The Gnostic journey from ignorance to illumination undertaken by Nada is the same journey taken by Garrison. Both characters refer to themselves as having been liberated from a dream world. Nada to Frank (after Nada has just given Frank the "third degree"): "You ain't the first son of a bitch to wake up out of his dream." Garrison to his wife (Sissy Spacek): "God damn it, Liz, I've been sleeping for three years." (For the Masonic symbolism buffs out there, please note that this comment occurs exactly thirty-three minutes into the film.) Five minutes later, Assistant DA Bill Broussard (Michael Rooker) says to Garrison, "Good lord, wake me up, I must be dreaming." This is a significant comment, as this character will betray Garrison later in the narrative. After having been shown incontrovertible proof of what's really happening in the world, Broussard chooses to accept the cover story given to him by a government agent that there was indeed a cover-up of the Kennedy assassination, but for a very good reason: The commies were behind the assassination, and if the American people were to discover this it might trigger World War III. Garrison sees through the ploy, but Broussard chooses to retreat back into his fantasy world, back into the dream. When Broussard says to Garrison, "Good lord, wake me up, I must be dreaming," Garrison has already woken up. In fact, he replies without hesitation, "No, you're awake, Bill, and I'm deadly serious." In other words, Garrison's reality is Broussard's dream. This single exchange of dialogue operates as a subtle form of foreshadowing, indicating that Broussard will never be able to handle the state of pure knowledge, pure illumination, pure reality, what might be called *gnosis*.

The state of *gnosis* is referenced once again at about 1:05:00. Garrison says to his team of investigators: "Y'all gotta start thinkin' on a different level, like the CIA does. Now we're through the looking glass here, people. White is black, and black is white." Here Garrison is deconstructing consensus reality itself. As the Freemasons like to say, "What is above is like what is below; and what is below is like what is above."[76] The little fables that have been fed to the public have literally prevented them from seeing, or acknowledging, the obvious. They've been trained *not* to trust their senses. The fun-house mirror world is the one we're living in. When Alice tumbles through the looking glass she's not leaving behind reality, but a world of fantasy.

This Alice imagery was implicit in *Winter Kills* as well. As mentioned before, during one of the supplements included on the 2003 DVD of *Winter Kills*, the director, William Richert, states that the protagonist, Nick Kegan (Jeff Bridges), was intended all along to be an Alice-like character, that Kegan's journey from naivety to awareness parallels Alice's fall from the chilling shallowness of everyday life into a burning world devoid of all false assumptions. All the heroes of the narratives under discussion can be tied together in this way: Alice is Dr Chet Walker is Mike Wilson is Bennett Marco is Joe Frady is Jim Garrison.

Garrison's declaration that "white is black, and black is white" has further implications that once again links the narrative back to *They Live*. In *They Live*, Carpenter uses black-and-white to visually distinguish the coded world from the decoded world, the subliminal from the liminal, the dream world from the reality. As Jonathan Lethem has pointed out, Carpenter turns *The Wizard of Oz* upside down. In the 1939 Victor Fleming adaptation of L. Frank Baum's novel, the real world is in black-and-white and the dream world is in color. In *They Live*, when Nada slips on the Hoffman lenses (unlike the emerald glasses in Baum's novel, the Hoffman lenses reveal reality rather than take it away), the decoded world is stripped of color. In *JFK* Oliver Stone also uses black-and-white to visually distinguish truth from lies. In present time, in color, we see Garrison meeting with some of the witnesses who were present in Dealey Plaza on the day of the assassination. He reviews with these witnesses, line by line, the Warren Commission's transcripts of the interviews conducted with them and discovers that the transcripts were altered substantially before being entered into the record. Some of the witnesses claim that words have been put into their mouths and other comments entirely deleted. Any comment that seems to contradict the final conclusion of the Commission—i.e., that there was a single assassin named Lee Harvey Oswald—has been censored. When Garrison is reviewing the records with the witnesses, we see what *really* happened played out before us... in glorious black-and-white.

In a metafictional moment, Jim Garrison himself—the human being and not the character portrayed by Kevin Costner—makes an appearance in the film at around 1:14:00. He appears, puckishly enough, as Chief Justice Earl Warren, the head of the Warren Commission. We see Warren (Garrison) interviewing Jack Ruby (Brian Doyle-Murray) in prison as Ruby utters the desperate words we quoted earlier in the section concerning *The Parallax View*. Garrison has five lines of dialogue: "Mr. Ruby, I don't see why you don't just tell us [the truth] now." In response to Ruby's request to be taken back to Washington, D.C. with the Chief Justice, Warren replies: "No, that could not be done. There would be no safe place for you. We're not law enforcement officers. Mr Ruby, there's a great deal at stake in this matter." Garrison himself, the totem around which this ceremonial dance/tribal exorcism is being performed, first appears to us in black-and-white.

I suspect the reason for this approach on the part of Carpenter and Stone, whether consciously or unconsciously, is the same. Both directors associate the black-and-white aesthetic with a simpler time, a more naïve time, a time that precedes the JFK assassination. (Perhaps it's not a coincidence that in his breakthrough film, *Halloween*, Carpenter sets the first murder committed by his unstoppable serial killer, Michael Myers, on October 31, 1963, just twenty-two days before the JFK assassination.) Though both writer/directors wish to rip through the façade of what's "only apparently real and get at what is really real," as Philip K. Dick once said, both also wish to return to that simpler and more naïve time before their innocence was murdered by illumination.[77]

There are further links between the worlds of Oliver Stone and John Carpenter. In Carpenter's film, certain human beings have sold out and aligned themselves with the aliens in exchange for money and prestige. A homeless man that Nada encounters at the beginning of the film, a character named Drifter (George "Buck" Flower), is later revealed to have joined up with this "human power elite." In Carpenter's world there are three types of characters: 1) Human beings trying to fight for the truth, 2) the human power elite, and 3) the ghouls. In Stone's world there are three types of characters as well: 1) Human beings trying to fight for the truth, 2) the human power elite and/or the unwitting tools of the conspiracy, and 3) the conspirators themselves. Though Drifter is a human being, Carpenter seems to despise him more than the ghouls, for not even Hoffman lenses can reveal this ignoble brand of perfidy. In *JFK*, Stone seems to pity—if not outright disdain—the people who crumble under pressure, characters with shifting alliances like Bill Broussard, who betray Garrison and the fight for truth even after having seen the evidence laid out clearly before them.

If we can slip on Nada's glasses once more, I think we would see that people like Jack Ruby aren't ghouls at all, but human beings who got caught up in something far too large for them to fully comprehend until it was too late, hopeful members of the human power elite who were sacrificed before receiving their promised rewards.

At around 2:14:00 Garrison says to his wife, Liz, "My eyes have opened. And once they're open, believe me, what used to look normal seems insane." Liz replies, "I don't want to see, god damn it. I'm tired. I've had enough. I just want to raise our children and live a normal life. I want my *life* back." This is a replay of the Nada/Frank fight over the Hoffman lenses: the eternal struggle between those who, like Cassandra, are compelled to tell the truth and those who would prefer to exist in a world of lies as long it makes life easier.

Because Garrison has had his eyes opened, he arrests Clay Shaw (Tommy Lee Jones) in the hopes of attaining a platform—Shaw's trial—from which to open the eyes of others. Garrison says to his team at one point, "In the court of public opinion it could take another twenty-five to thirty years for the truth to come out." Of course, he's right; it did indeed take that long. What Garrison could not have known was that it would take a major Hollywood film to tilt the balance.

One of the major purposes of the Shaw trial is to prove that there was indeed a conspiracy behind the assassination. Though the jury eventually found Shaw not guilty, all of them believed Garrison had indeed proven that a conspiracy had been involved in JFK's murder. One of the major pieces of evidence in Garrison's favor was the Zapruder film, which we see played out in real time at around 2:43:00 accompanied by Garrison's commentary: the culmination of the "film-within-the-film" motif that we've explored up to this point. The jury and everyone in the courtroom have their eyes opened to reality thanks to the intervention of synchronicity and happenstance. It was only by chance that Zapruder happened to be standing in the right spot to capture the kill shot on camera. Garrison points out how Kennedy's head snaps "back and to the left" (a phrase repeated five times, like a mantra), the opposite direction expected if the kill shot had hit him in the back of the skull by Oswald's final bullet. Because of the existence of the Zapruder film, the members of the Warren Commission had to fit their "lone nut" theory within a specific time frame: only three shots in 8.4 seconds. And those three bullets had to account for so many different wounds—not only on Kennedy, but on several others in Dealey Plaza as well—that the Warren Commission was forced to dream up the "magic bullet" theory: a single bullet that defied the laws of physics and changed direction in midair several times in order to perform its unusual form of acrobatics. Garrison demonstrates in court how ridiculous this theory is by reenacting the supposed path of the bullet. Stone stages this scene well and demonstrates how flimsy the Warren Commission's conclusions really were when held up to any scrutiny at all.

Just as *They Live* gave us the longest fight scene in cinematic history, *JFK* gives us the longest courtroom scene in history. The trial begins at around 2:38:00 and continues all the way to the very end of the film almost an hour later. The trial takes nearly a third of the entire film, and the film is three and a half hours long. And yet this courtroom scene never drags. It's staged and edited in such a way that it feels far, far shorter than an hour.

Kevin Costner gives the performance of a lifetime when he intones Garrison's summation speech, growing more and more emotional as he realizes what's at stake and how low the country has sunk since Kennedy's assassination, and it's in this scene where all the metaphors we've discussed previously are thrown out the window and naked reality floods in upon the viewer. "The ghost of John F. Kennedy confronts us with the secret murder at the heart of the American Dream," says Garrison at 3:08:00, leading to his warning two minutes later that the form of government we now have in America (in 1969) is not democracy but "fascism," which propels us towards his conclusion at 3:15:00 when Garrison/Costner looks first at the jury, then directly into the camera (i.e., the moviegoers themselves) and says, "It's up to *you*."

The fourth wall has now been broken. All artifice is gone. Gone are all the movie metaphors we've discussed and analyzed and autopsied up to this point. Gone are all the gamma people and the creatures with their atom brains. No more subtle warnings wrapped in atomic age fables. No more parables. No more stories. Just a plea delivered from an actor, no longer playing a character, directly to the human beings sitting in the darkened movie theater: "It's up to *you*."

And indeed it was up to them, to us, as it always had been. The DVD version of *JFK* ends with a message from the filmmakers: "As a result of this film, Congress in 1992 passed legislation to appoint a panel to review all files and determine which ones would be made available to the American public."

This is true, but few people have since discussed the results of that legislation. Because of Stone's film, numerous secret documents were indeed released to the American people, but as with all such research involving the review of government documents it took a very long time for researchers to comb through these papers and uncover the kernels of important information tucked away within them.

This research, hardly publicized at all, has led to startling revelations that shed light on a whole new aspect to the constricting web of events that led up to the murders of John F. Kennedy and Lee Harvey Oswald.

Upon entering the White House, President John F. Kennedy and his brother, Attorney General Robert F. Kennedy, were intent on proving their Cold Warrior status by secretly assassinating Fidel Castro. They built a complicated undercover operation with which to accomplish this, an operation that later became known as "Project Freedom." The network of spies they assembled to kill a foreign leader (a violation of US law and therefore an impeachable offense) was cleverly hijacked by someone else. These hired thugs and hitmen were no doubt offered a much higher price to turn their guns on the very man for whom they were ostensibly working: John F. Kennedy. Government documents released in the wake of Oliver Stone's *JFK* indicate that this is what occurred.[78]

As Edward T. Haslam writes in his revelatory book, *Dr. Mary's Monkey*:

> Officially, the officer of the U.S. Government who has the final word on whether you have lost or renounced your citizenship is the Attorney General. In 1961, the U.S. Attorney General was Bobby Kennedy. The normal administrative request to resolve a question of whether one had renounced one's citizenship would have come to his desk. At that time, Bobby had his own set of problems. He was busy fighting a war against the Mafia (particularly Carlos Marcello) and was trying to figure out what the CIA was really doing with the millions of dollars missing from its budgets. Bobby was particularly concerned about renegade CIA paramilitary operations involving the Mafia, since they defied the authority of the White House. Bobby needed one or more competent undercover agents to get inside these operations and report back to him (through intermediaries, of course). Lee was a trained spy who had done undercover work in the Soviet

> Union. Normally, the AG would rely on the FBI for this type of counter-intelligence help, but the FBI Director was his sworn enemy, was blackmailing his brother the President, and had connections to the Mafia himself. So Bobby needed his own off-the-books agents to do this work. Bobby Kennedy arranged for Lee and his family to return to the U.S. The price: You work undercover for me […].[79]

When the news hit the wires that a man named Lee Harvey Oswald was the main suspect in the President's death, imagine the shock to Bobby Kennedy. One of his own secret agents had ostensibly shot his brother. The wheels in his brain would have been spinning and spinning and spinning, trying to figure out how the hell all of this had unfolded. His paranoia, quite justifiably, would have been working overtime. This explains why "[u]pon hearing that Lee Harvey Oswald had been arrested, Bobby Kennedy picked up the phone and called CIA director John McCone, and asked him if the CIA had killed his brother. Bobby and McCone had been working together to track down renegade CIA operations […]."[80] Bobby Kennedy would have known that his operation had been hijacked by someone else—someone who knew about Oswald's connection to the Kennedys, a connection the Attorney General could never talk about publicly.

Now, let's return to one of the main sources we drew upon earlier: Lincoln Lawrence's 1967 book, *Were We Controlled?* Lawrence's scenario, that Oswald was a victim of José Delgado's mind control technology in a Minsk hospital and that the main purpose of the assassination was to make a killing on Wall Street, seems far-fetched. And yet, buried in the middle of Chapter Eight, we find a significant passage that prefigures the revelations regarding "Project Freedom" found in the recently released government documents:

> For certain things… Lee Oswald… had money… make no mistake about it. Not for Marina or his home particularly… but for expediting his *actions*.
>
> Did this money come from the CIA, FBI, State Department, Castro or the Soviets? No, not according to The Rumor.
>
> But it was there to be had… made available to him by some group… for a reason.
>
> The simple fact is the most convincing argument to men who follow the professional intelligence craft… that he was "somebody's man."

> The Rumor crystallizes a picture of Lee Oswald as a "high-jacked sleeper." In intelligence jargon that simply means that he was selected by one group and maneuvered into the orbit of *another* group which trained and prepared him for work in the future when they (the second group) might have need for his "special" qualifications. The first group had secretly spotted him as an ideal person to use *as a tool* in a very special operation. His desirability was even higher because the blame for his actions (should he be caught) would fall quite naturally on the second group. He was the man high-jacked by some of the most amazing and sophisticated methods known to modern science and secretly—without his own conscious knowledge—used as a key man in the plot to kill John F. Kennedy and "rig" the Stock Exchange. He was to play a major role in the crime of our century![81]

This scenario, laid out so precisely by Lawrence only four years after the assassination, hints at some amount of insider knowledge on Lawrence's part. According to the late researcher, Jim Keith, Lawrence was actually a journalist named Arthur J. Ford who had intelligence agency contacts.[82] Other researchers, such as Dr Armen Victorian (author of *The Mind Controllers*), claim that Ford was also a former FBI agent.[83] How much did Lawrence/Ford know about this "high-jacked sleeper" scenario? Was he only releasing part of the story in his book? When he suggests that Oswald was "somebody's man," could he have been referring to the Attorney General?

Haslam further explores Bobby Kennedy's dilemma from the perspective of the conspirators:

> If you're planning to shoot Jack Kennedy in the head with high-powered rifles in broad daylight, you'd better spend some time thinking about his brother. His brother is Bobby Kennedy, the Attorney General, and he has the power and the resources to come after you. In order to get away with killing Jack, you must neutralize Bobby at the critical moment. If you stymie Bobby, you might get away with it. If you don't, you could be in really big trouble.
>
> The question: *How do you paralyze Bobby at the critical moment?*
>
> *The answer:* By publically accusing one of his agents of the crime!
>
> If Bobby says, "But Lee's legitimate; he's with me," then J. Edgar Hoover is able to say, "If Lee's with you, then you have just murdered your own brother, you ambitious little bastard."[84]

And so we circle back to Richard Condon's *Winter Kills*. Was JFK murdered by his own family? Given what we now know, one might have to answer "yes" to that question. Imagine the guilt Bobby Kennedy must have experienced upon realizing that he had set up the very network of trained assassins who, unbeknownst to him, would eventually kill his own brother. He must have felt as if he'd helped pull the trigger(s) himself. And, in a sense, he had.

Does this explain Bobby Kennedy's transformation from aspiring Cold Warrior who desperately wanted to assassinate Fidel Castro at the beginning of JFK's administration to the vehemently anti-Vietnam candidate who planned to retake the White House in 1968 using a pro-peace message? Does it explain his reckless behavior during the '67 campaign, the way he would interact with the public with little or no security around him, as if daring the shooters to try again? Was he suffering from survivor's guilt? In his final moments, after having been gunned down by the same network that had assassinated his brother, did he realize that this was inevitable? Did he feel that he deserved it somehow?

Los Angeles novelist Steve Erickson witnessed Robert Kennedy's brazen behavior up-close when the senator made a campaign appearance in LA in 1968. Over four decades later, Erickson's youthful observations found their way into his phantasmagoric 2012 novel, *These Dreams of You*, capturing a moment in time that's both prophetic and eerie:

> But more than anyone, he provokes the killer out there. More than anything he provokes his own fate. Campaign assistants draw the curtains in hotel rooms, and she watches him get up and open them and frame himself in the window: I'm here. You out there on one of those rooftops, here I am. *Ready, aim.* Here I am, take… me… out. Stepping from a doorway out onto the sidewalk, his bodyguards trying to bustle him into the waiting car, she sees how he resists, stops, lingers a moment at the street's edge: You. Up there in one of those windows—I know about high windows. I know about their vantage points. *Fire.* I know about high-powered fifty-two millimeter Italian Carcano rifles, I know how the flimsiest of men and circumstances can change the world.[85]

When Jack Womack dreamed up the satirical notion, in his novel *Let's Put the Future Behind Us*, that JFK put a hit out on himself, he couldn't have known that this—the most ridiculous theory of them all—was also the one that was closest to the truth, a truth now reinforced by official government documents that the American people would never have seen if not for the release of Oliver Stone's *JFK*.

Which brings us to an important point: The purpose of art is not always to serve as an encoded palliative for the nation's collective woes (though this function has its own value, of course) or as a secret warning to those few who might be paying attention to the message hidden between the lines, but as an actual agent of change in the real world. Writer Alan Moore, author of such bestselling graphic novels as *V for Vendetta*, *Watchmen*, *From Hell* and *The League of Extraordinary Gentlemen* (all of which have been adapted into films, almost always to Moore's displeasure), once said that the people most feared by Those In Power during medieval times were not the rogues and assassins attempting to dethrone them, but the bards. If an assassin cut you down with a knife in the back, you only died once. If a bard managed to create a clever and catchy song that satirized you and destroyed your reputation, that song might exist for generations upon generations. Not only would *your* name be ruined, but so too would the names of your children and your grandchildren and your great-grandchildren.[86]

The types of people we're talking about here, the types of people who manufacture creatures with atom brains in order to ascend the ladder of power, are concerned most of all with their legacies. They obsess about it. What will history say about them? Rick Santorum, the infamous right-wing Republican from Pennsylvania who's vehemently anti-homosexual, had his reputation permanently destroyed in the eyes of popular culture when, in 2003, a very clever blogger named Dan Savage suggested that everyone on the planet begin referring to the residual drops of lubrication and fecal matter that seep out of the anus after anal sex as "santorum." Seven years later, Stephanie Mencimer of *Mother Jones* magazine wrote that this creative re-definition may very well have contributed to Santorum's defeat by Robert Casey in 2006. I suspect this is the main reason Santorum so desperately wanted to win the Republican nomination in 2012. The main reason this man needed to become President was so that, when he passes away, the first line of his Wikipedia page would read "Rick Santorum was the 45th President of the United States" instead of "Rick Santorum was a Republican Senator from Pennsylvania whose last name has become synonymous with the residual drops of lubrication and fecal matter that seep out of the anus after anal sex." At least if he was President, this information would probably drop down to the second paragraph.

Lyndon Johnson was so concerned about his legacy that, in September of 1969, he gave an interview to Walter Cronkite in which Johnson strongly implied that he'd always suspected President Kennedy had been killed as a result of a conspiracy. He knew full well that many Americans believed he had, like Macbeth shoving the knife into the back of King Duncan, been involved in a conspiracy to kill the President. So he tried, at the last minute, to reposition himself in the eyes of history by being *on record* as suspecting that Oswald was not the lone assassin. ("Oh, well, Johnson couldn't have been involved if he, too, believes there was a conspiracy!") In 1973 the *Atlantic Monthly* quoted Johnson as saying, "I never believed that Oswald acted alone although I accept that he pulled the trigger."[87] Perhaps someone didn't appreciate this move on the part of the ex-President, for Johnson died the very same year—ostensibly of heart failure.

Legacies are everything to these people, but the sad truth (for them) is that history is not judged by voluminous government reports like the Warren Commission. History is judged by what survives. The cultural artifacts that survive from the seventeenth century, that still remain in our collective consciousness today, are the tragedies and comedies of William Shakespeare, not the thousands of unreadable and deadly dull government documents churned out by Parliament. What we know about Victorian London comes from the novels of Charles Dickens, not the newspapers of the day. What we understand about America in the 1920s comes from F. Scott Fitzgerald and Ernest Hemingway, not the *New York Times*. In 100 years the Warren Commission will be a mere footnote to an enduring cultural artifact known as *JFK* directed by Oliver Stone.

If you want to understand the hidden ground of the 1950s, you'll learn more from *Creature with the Atom Brain* and *The Gamma People* than the *Wall Street Journal*.

If you want to try and comprehend the formless shadows closing in on the Kennedy administration in the 1960s, watch *The Manchurian Candidate*, not archival footage of the *Huntley-Brinkley Report*.

If you want to get into the minds of Those In Power who made millions off rampant chaos and violence in the 1970s, watch *The Parallax View*, not the CBS Evening News.

If you want to trace Alice's plunge from a world of no worries and perpetual tea parties to a subterranean realm where the laws of physics have turned upside down, watch *Winter Kills*, not the vacuous "Happy Talk" news programs that began to emerge on TV outlets in the early 1970s.

If you want to penetrate the layers of obfuscation surrounding the opaque Reagan administration, put on a pair of Hoffman lenses and watch *They Live*, not Ted Turner's Cable News Network.

If you want to understand the evolving attitudes of the American people, their slow conversion from illusion to a fleeting glimpse of *gnosis*, watch *JFK*, not the *MacNeil/Lehrer NewsHour.*

And if you want to follow the trail of covert mind control operations to its latest incarnation in the twenty-first century, it wouldn't hurt to watch Jonathan Demme's remake of....

9. The Manchurian Candidate (2004)

THIS VERSION OF the classic 1962 John Frankenheimer film is one of the few remakes from the past thirty years that actually justifies its own existence. (John Carpenter's 1982 remake of Howard Hawks and Christian Nyby's *The Thing* is another example that leaps immediately to mind.) According to Bill Warren, the film "came about because Frank Sinatra told his daughter Tina the movie was ready to be remade. Over several years, she ushered the project through, and the result was largely satisfying."[88] One can't know why Frank Sinatra felt the film was "ready to be remade," particularly after having spent so much effort keeping the original out of circulation for so long, but given Sinatra's intimate connections to Those In Power during the Kennedy administration, it's not at all unlikely that Sinatra understood in a very real way that the Machiavellian political environment that had given birth to the first film had become even more vicious, not less so.

In this version Marco and Shaw's relationship is very similar to the one in Condon's novel; however, enough new twists have been added to the plot that the film feels new even to ardent admirers of the original. These twists don't feel at all forced. In many remakes twists are added to the plot in an obligatory manner; not so here. Every addition, subtraction, or seeming tangent feels very natural and appropriate. In this version the "Manchurian" referred to in the title is not a Fu Manchu stereotype, but instead a multinational corporation similar to the fictional Parallax or its real world analogue, the Centro

Mondiale Commerciale. It's described at one point, by an exiled Southeastern European scientist named Delp (Bruno Ganz) whose specialty is neuro-behavioral research (interestingly, Delp is not at all dissimilar from DrWilhelm Steigg in *Creature With the Atom Brain*), as "a god damn geopolitical extension of policy for every president since Nixon." Manchurian Global seems to be a hybrid of the Carlyle Group, the infamous global asset management firm, and Blackwater (now named Academi), a private security firm used by the US State Department to provide "protective services" for Coalition Forces in Iraq. Manchurian Global abducts an entire platoon of Army soldiers, transports them to a remote island, and in three days programs them to kill via remote control. Their purpose is to stage a coup d'état in the United States by planting their own wind-up Vice-President (Shaw) on the Republican ticket while using another wind-up toy (Marco) to assassinate the President; this parallels the real world attempt in 1982 to eliminate President Ronald Reagan for the alleged express purpose of elevating Vice-President George Bush Sr. into the Oval Office. As in the film, the shooter was not entirely successful at his appointed task.

James Joyce once wrote that "pastimes are past times,"[89] meaning that what's popular among the masses now is often a generation out of date. In the original film version of *The Manchurian Candidate* we see fairly straightforward hypnosis and torture techniques being used to brainwash Raymond Shaw. In the 2004 version we see the José-Delgado-like mind control technology that was the hidden ground of the first film fully realized on screen for all to see. It's clear that the character of Dr Atticus Noyle (Simon McBurney) is at least partially based on Delgado himself. At 1:24:00 Dr Noyle claims that one of the main benefits of his technology will be to treat various mental disorders like schizophrenia and "offset the ravages of dementia." This is precisely what Delgado claimed in his book *Physical Control of the Mind*. At about 1:08:00 we see monkeys with wires trailing out of exposed brains, looking as if they were modeled on the numerous photographs that Delgado published in his book with obvious pride. At one point we see Major Marco (Denzel Washington) and Raymond Shaw (Liev Schreiber) hooked up to EDOM and RHIC devices that look almost exactly like the ones we first encountered in *Creature with the Atom Brain* way back in 1955. The Delgado machines we see in the mind control sequence, about twenty-four minutes into the film, could have been lifted right out of *Creature with the Atom Brain*, the only difference being that this time they were filmed in color.

There are other, more subtle hints that connect the film back to the sci-fi B-film aesthetic one associates with the 1950s. The sharp eye will notice that director Roger Corman, famous for such 1950s B-films as *It Conquered the World*, *Not of This Earth*, and *Attack of the Crab Monsters* (this latter film, by the way, is also about the human mind being taken over and subjugated against its will), appears as a minor but highly visible character named "Mr Secretary." To the uninitiated Corman's presence seems incongruous here. After all, he was not associated with the original production in any way and is not known as a character actor, and yet he pops up at least three times in the background of major scenes. Near the end of the film, we can see Corman applauding and smiling widely just behind Meryl Streep as she and her son are being lined up in the assassin's crosshairs.

It could be that Corman appears in the film to act as a cultural signpost pointing back to that naïve "before time" when this arduous journey from ignorance to awareness first began. The quiet disclosure, the slow release of suppressed memories and censored truths, first occurred in obscure science fiction B-films in the 1950s, and someone involved in the production doesn't want us to forget that fact. After all, Corman began his low budget directorial career in 1955, the same year *Creature with the Atom Brain* was released.

Once again, the hidden ground has become the figure. Subliminal has become liminal. Subtext has become text.

By the time Hollywood got around to showing José Delgado's technology in all its horrifying glory, Dr Delgado was eighty-nine years old and living a happy life of retirement in sunny San Diego, CA (he finally died in 2011 at the age of ninety-six). I remember Walter Bowart, author of *Operation Mind Control*, calling me on the phone not long after the movie had premiered in July of 2004 and asking me if I had seen the film yet. I told him yes.

"So what'd you think of it?" he asked.

"It was very clever," I said. "I thought it was impressive that they figured out how to update the story without destroying all the subversive subtext of the original. What did you think of it?"

"It was a bunch of *bullshit*!" he said. "These Hollywood guys have absolutely no idea what's going on. The kind of technology they used on those soldiers in Kuwait is at least twenty years out of date. They don't even *need* to put implants in you anymore. They don't have to plug wires into your brain. That's what Delgado was doing way back in the 1950s. Nowadays, they can just tune in on the particular frequency of your brain without having to perform any invasive surgery at all."

Around the time I first met Walter in 2002, I had just finished writing an article about thought control in the American education system titled "Concentration Campus." (Later, this article became Chapter Six of my first book, *Cryptoscatology: Conspiracy Theory as Art Form.*) When I told Walter what I was writing, he asked to read it. He gave me some very helpful comments on the piece. Next to one particular paragraph he added five words that he suggested I insert into my essay.

The original paragraph read: "Mind control has morphed into thought control. No implants required." Walter pointed out to me that thought control (a term he associated with brainwashing) came first, later followed by the more sophisticated *mind control* technology of José Delgado and friends. Walter rewrote the sentence to read: "Thought control has morphed into mind control, mind control into soul control."

Soul control.

Walter had invoked the perfect phrase to describe the dark evolution of these "psychocivilization" methods. Only someone with Walter's substantial background in researching the complex history of secret US government mind control programs could make a distinction as subtle as that, and yet it's a completely valid one. I don't think Walter meant it metaphorically. He meant it literally. It's possible this phrase was inspired by Ray Kurzweil's book *The Age of Spiritual Machines*, a book I know Walter was reading at the time. In that book Kurzweil rhapsodizes about a near future in which humanity and technology will merge, becoming virtually indistinguishable from one another.

In the future, machines will have simulated souls while genuine souls are stamped out and reduced into mere machine-like reflexes; this mirrors Raymond Shaw's dilemma in Jonathan Demme's version of *The Manchurian Candidate*. In defiance of Kurzweil's ideal future, the entire ending of the film hinges on the ability of the human soul to rise above the remote-controlled orders of a sophisticated artificial programmer. As Marco says to Shaw near the conclusion, "We are connected, and that's something *nobody* can take from us. You could've had me locked up, but you didn't. That's proof that there's something deep inside, there's a part that they can't get to, and it's deep inside of us, and I think that's where the truth is. That's our only hope. That's what you and me need to tap into, and that's what you and I are gonna use to take them out, Raymond, but we don't have much time."

The connection is real, and so is the truth, and that truth erupts in the form of dreams. Richard Condon couldn't have predicted that numerous mind control survivors, despite layers upon layers of safeguards implanted in their consciousness by their programmers, would first access these denied memories through recurring dreams. Once again, Condon's artistic intuition ferreted out the truth without even intending to do so.

My connection to the subject of mind control is not merely an academic one. I'm friends with one woman, a successful attorney, who survived intensive mind control programming for which she was "volunteered" by her father (a judge in Washington State) as a very young child beginning in the 1950s. The memories first erupted out of her subconscious through her dreams. She then used her lawyerly skills to track down what really happened to her through genuine research, much like Major Marco does in the 2004 version of *The Manchurian Candidate*.

This woman liked the film very much, and one of the aspects of the films she particularly appreciated was the end. She felt the filmmakers must have had some specific knowledge of the mind control programming that people like her had undergone back in the fifities and sixties. The victims who managed to survive into adulthood and piece their shattered lives together often felt compelled to return to the place where the original programming had occurred in order to create a sense of closure. Major Marco does exactly this at the end of the 2004 film. In a way, he's seeking closure for the entire United States. The first words of the film are "Somebody help me." The last words are "There are always casualties in war, sir." In our case, the case of the United States of America, the most serious casualty has been that of democracy itself. As Bowart once told me, "We don't have a democracy anymore. We have a cryptocracy" (i.e., "rule by secrecy"), a word originally coined by French writers Jacques Bergier and Louis Pauwels in their seminal 1960 book, *The Morning of the Magicians*, to describe the true structure of world governments in the twentieth century.[90] One of Walter's goals was to get the word "cryptocracy" into the *Oxford English Dictionary*. After all, you have to diagnose a problem before you can cure it. You have to name Rumpelstiltskin before you can control him. Walter wasn't successful in this goal during his lifetime, but eventually, if the legacy of Kennedy's death is to mean more than a *faux* eternal flame and a monument that doubles as a tourist attraction, the American people have to decide that it's time to put a name to the evil imp that's manipulating them from behind the scenes. They have to shirk off the invisible chains of psychocivilization, slip on the Hoffman lenses, and see the subliminal commands that are all around them. Aliens did indeed invade the United States a long time ago, non-human intelligences called "fascists" armed with technology to which Hitler never had access.

Film is a powerful medium in ways that most people never stop to comprehend. In his 1990 novel *A Graveyard for Lunatics*, which takes place in 1954 (a year before the release of *Creature with the Atom Brain*), Ray Bradbury wrote about "the idea of films falling off theatre screens to run the world. Every damn city in Europe is starting to look like us crazy Americans, dress, look, talk, dance like us. Because of films we've won the world, and are too damn dumb to see it."[91] For the most part films are made merely to keep people distracted from the real concerns of the world. If religion is the opiate of the masses, then film is the crack cocaine of the masses. Nonetheless, sometimes the medium of film is used to preserve the truth in encoded form. In a country where news reporters disseminate misinformation so casually, without even being aware of it sometimes, it's appropriate that one must resort to a medium famous for its pretty lies in order to get at the truth. As Jim Garrison says in *JFK*, "We're through the looking glass here, people. White is black, and black is white." Everything is upside down. And in an upside down world, sometimes you have to stand on your head to see reality for what it actually is. Sometimes, *sometimes*, we enter into a rabbit hole called a theater and wake up briefly from our collective dream. "It's up to you," Garrison tells the audience near the end of *JFK*.

The medium of film can be valuable in creating cultural artifacts, but when working at its highest level it can also enact change in the dream we call the real world. *JFK* did that when it encouraged the American people to lobby their Congressmen in order to bring about the committee that released formerly secret documents, thus revealing hitherto unknown information about the Kennedy assassination, information that has moved us much closer to comprehending what really happened to the United States of America on November 22, 1963. So often the moviegoer, like the typical American, is a passive entity that sits and waits for life to happen to people around them. The first step in waking up the creatures with atom brains that lumber around us on a daily basis is to extinguish that dependent attitude in ourselves.

All the films in this litany are about mind control in one form or another, whether literally or metaphorically, whether imposed from without or invited upon oneself with open arms. *JFK* never mentions the phrase "mind control," never hints that Oswald or Ruby were victims of Delgado-like technology, but that doesn't matter. In the end, the entire film is about nothing other than mind control. Or perhaps I should say it's about *thought* control, the first stage in the process. As Delp says to Major Marco at 52:00, "We've all been brainwashed, man."

In the end, it's not relevant at this point if Dr Delgado (or his CIA cohorts) physically invaded Lee Harvey Oswald's brain. What's relevant is that, based on textual evidence within the book, Lincoln Lawrence's *Were We Controlled?* was clearly written by a professional with insider knowledge of what would have been very sensitive intelligence matters in the 1960s; here was a professional familiar enough with Delgado's operative top secret technology that he suspected "The Rumor" *might* be true, so much so that he went to the trouble of anonymously publishing a book about mind control at a time when very few people even knew that such science fictional devices existed, practically kicking off the entire JFK conspiracy theory subgenre as a result.

Was Oswald a victim of advanced mind control techniques? When he volunteered to join the US military in 1956, he might as well have been. Was the most impactful influencer in Oswald's life Delgado's cutting edge technology or propagandistic US television shows like *I Led Three Lives?* Which affected the brains of more American boys (i.e., future military fodder) reaching their maturity in the Eisenhower/Disney era of the 1950s?

The answer to that question should be obvious.

> "In their propaganda today's dictators rely for the most part on repetition, suppression and rationalization—the repetition of catchwords which they wish to be accepted as true, the suppression of facts which they wish to be ignored, the arousal and rationalization of passions which may be used in the interests of the Party or the State. As the art and science of manipulation come to be better understood, the dictators of the future will doubtless learn to combine these techniques with the non-stop distractions

which, in the West, are now threatening to drown in a sea of irrelevance the rational propaganda essential to the maintenance of individual liberty and the survival of democratic institutions [...].

"Thanks to compulsory education and the rotary press, the propagandist has been able, for many years past, to convey his messages to virtually every adult in every civilized country. Today, thanks to radio and television, he is in the happy position of being able to communicate even with unschooled adults and not yet literate children.

"Children, as might be expected, are highly susceptible to propaganda. They are ignorant of the world and its ways, and therefore completely unsuspecting. Their critical faculties are undeveloped. The youngest of them have not yet reached the age of reason and the older ones lack the experience on which their new-found rationality can effectively work. In Europe, conscripts used to be playfully referred to as 'cannon fodder.' Their little brothers and sisters have now become radio fodder and television fodder [...].

"Brainwashing, as it is now practiced, is a hybrid technique, depending for its effectiveness partly on the systematic use of violence, partly on skilful psychological manipulation. It represents the tradition of *1984* on its way to becoming the tradition of *Brave New World*. Under a long-established and well-regulated dictatorship our current methods of semiviolent manipulation will seem, no doubt, absurdly crude [...]. On the road to the Brave New World our rulers will have to rely on the transitional and provisional techniques of brainwashing."

—Aldous Huxley, *Brave New World Revisited*, 1958

"Although no one has yet planted a closed circuit control device in a human (as far as we know... peculiar rumors come to us from behind the Iron Curtain), that day cannot be far off. As recently as 1969, Yale researcher José Delgado implanted radio sets in the skulls of animals and transmitted signals that caused them to perform in as Pavlovian a manner as Dr. Delgado might have wished, even to the point of distinctly altering their emotional states from rage to calm.

"The gap between radio-controlled cattle stimulated to graze in productive patterns over vast pasture lands and computer-guided people ordered to and from routine production line jobs is narrower than we might think, and closing with every advance in biochemistry and electronics. A terrifying thought. Perhaps only a wry and vagrant vision of a fantasist, or perhaps an ominous shadow on the horizon. Are you keeping your eyes open?"

—Harlan Ellison, *Vertex*, June 1974

I once heard a radio interview with the comedian Mort Sahl who, unbeknownst to many people, was instrumental in helping Jim Garrison with the JFK investigation back in the late sixties. Sahl coached Garrison for days to help him prepare for his interview on an episode of *The Tonight Show* which featured Garrison as the sole guest. The host, Johnny Carson, tried to decimate Garrison's investigation, but instead the audience rallied to Garrison's side. You can hear the entire audio of this interview on YouTube (under the title "JFK Assassination Debate: Jim Garrison vs. Johnny Carson").

Years later, in the early 1990s, I heard Sahl reflecting on his decades-long friendship with Garrison. Sahl recalled appearing with his old friend on a radio talk show in New York not long before Garrison's death in 1992. At this point Garrison was a frail old man, dying of an aggressive form of cancer. He and Sahl were strolling away from the studio, trudging through an unusually thick carpet of snow that had fallen on New York in the past few days. He and Garrison paused on the corner to wait for the stop light next to a wealthy old woman walking her dogs.

Sahl turned to Garrison and said, "Wow, look at all this snow. It's going to swallow us up. I've never seen it build up this fast before."

The woman, looking completely disgusted, snapped her tongue against the roof of her mouth and said, "I *know*! It's shameful, isn't it? Why doesn't the government *do* something to clean up this mess?"

With a straight face, Garrison turned toward the old woman and said: "Lady… hasn't the government done enough already?"

"When the president bleeds, all of us have to sleep in it."

—Carl Oglesby, *The Yankee and Cowboy War*, 1977

Chapter 4

One Chants Out Between Two Worlds

It Came from Outer Space, Twin Peaks, and the Legacy of Jack Parsons

1. "Kind of an Outsider"

JACK ARNOLD'S *IT Came from Outer Space* debuted in May of 1953, becoming an immediate smash hit with audiences. Available on the recent Blu-ray release of the film is a supplementary documentary titled *The Universe According to Universal*, which includes an interview with award-winning science fiction illustrator Vincent Di Fate, who comments at length on the significance of the film in pop culture. Not only was it the first film written by a young Ray Bradbury, not only was it the first 3-D science fiction film, but it was also the first film to depict "alien perspective" (i.e., the audience views the action through the cyclopean eye of the extraterrestrial who has landed on Earth).

It also supplied us with a character-type never before seen in American cinema. Before *It Came from Outer Space*, scientists were usually depicted as lunatics bent on criminal activity, à la Henry Frankenstein (Colin Clive) in James Whale's *Frankenstein* (1931) or Dr Mirakle (Bela Lugosi) in Robert Florey's *Murders in the Rue Morgue* (1932). When scientists weren't involved in some form of malfeasance, they were often depicted as glasses-wearing, clueless milksops, like Dr Jackson (portrayed, appropriately enough, by none other than Richard Carlson[1], the star of *It Came from Outer Space*) in Arthur Lubin's 1941 horror-comedy, *Hold That Ghost.* With the arrival of *It Came from Outer Space*, American audiences were introduced to the idea of a scientist not only being adventurous, but attractive as well.

In the words of Vincent Di Fate: "One of the important images that emerges from *It Came from Outer Space* is the establishment of the scientist/hero through the person of Richard Carlson: handsome, erudite, dark-haired, ruggedly good-looking, [and yet also] kind of an outsider [...]. *It Came from Outer Space* establishes that archetype."[2]

While listening to Di Fate describe Carlson's character in the film, it suddenly occurred to me that this very same description could be applied to Jack Parsons.

2. The Jack Parsons Project

UNEXPECTEDLY, JACK WHITESIDE Parsons appears to be ubiquitous these days. Parsons was the sorcerer-cum-scientist who helped establish Jet Propulsion Laboratory in Pasadena, California, and was instrumental in developing the rocket fuel that propelled the United States to the moon. There's a crater on the moon named after Parsons to commemorate his contributions to the aerospace industry. Parsons is also the author of what novelist Robert Anton Wilson once called the greatest libertarian manifesto ever written, *Freedom Is a Two-Edged Sword*, which should be required reading in high school civics courses.

Infamously, sadly, Parsons blew himself up in his Pasadena home while experimenting with unstable chemicals. Or *did* he blow himself up? Some claim Parsons was assassinated, or that his death was faked as part of a complicated "brain drain" covert operation conducted by the US government, or that... well, the speculations go on and on.

At one time Parsons was the hidden ground of 1940s/1950s Southern California history, serving as inspiration to only a select few, such as the writers Anthony Boucher and Philip K. Dick. Boucher based a character on Parsons in his 1942 mystery novel, *Rocket to the Morgue*. Philip K. Dick, whose career Boucher was instrumental in launching when Boucher was serving as editor of *The Magazine of Fantasy & Science Fiction*, reportedly based a character on Parsons in his 1960 novel, *Dr. Futurity*.

During the past few years, I couldn't help but notice that Parsons has been popping up in more and more unlikely places. Parsons, along with his wife Marjorie Cameron (who, subsequent to Parsons' death, evolved into an accomplished painter and actress and was featured in such cult films as Kenneth Anger's *Inauguration of the Pleasure Dome* and Curtis Harrington's *Night Tide*), appear as characters in Mark Frost's 2017 novel, *The Secret History of Twin Peaks*. There are oblique but crucial references to both Parsons and Cameron in Mark Frost and David Lynch's Gnostic parable, the eighteen-episode TV series, *Twin Peaks: The Return*. Parsons also appears, disguised under a fictional veneer, in the 2017–2018 comic book mini-series titled *Bettie Page: Bettie in Hollywood* by David Avallone and Colton Worely, which revolves around the imaginary exploits of the infamous pin-up queen in 1950s Hollywood. Perhaps more significantly, Parsons is the subject of a recent CBS television series based on George Pendle's 2006 Parsons biography, *Strange Angel*. This series was created by Mark Heyman, who co-wrote Darren Aronofsky's *Black Swan* (2010), and was produced by Ridley Scott, director of *Alien* (1979), *Blade Runner* (1982), *Prometheus* (2012), and *The Martian* (2015). In 2021 James Tynion IV wove Parsons and his legend into the fourteenth issue of his conspiracy thriller comic book series, *The Department of Truth*.

Is all of this Parsons-related activity an example of what conspiracy theorist Michael A. Hoffman would call the "Revelation of the Method" (i.e., the unveiling of certain sinister hermetic obsessions on the part of the political elite in the form of popular entertainment), or is this simply a sign that the mass audience has evolved to the point where they can at last contemplate the importance of transgressive, fringe figures like Parsons in the make-up of America's post-World War II development?

Back in 1996 I wrote a phantasmagorical short story titled "A Babe of the Abyss" about Parsons' connection to the creation of the Church of Scientology that I sold on first submission to a British anthology which was to have been called, if memory serves, *The Creation of the Beast*. The story was scheduled to appear side by side with contributions by such writers as Alan Moore and Grant Morrison (in fact, if you happen to have a copy of the comic book *The Invisibles Vol.*

I No. 25, you will see that Morrison makes a reference to this anthology in the letters page). At one point the editor of the anthology, D.M. Mitchell—who had previously edited a superior Lovecraft-themed anthology titled *The Starry Wisdom*—mailed me a cryptic letter, still filed away in my office somewhere, in which he expressed his concern about being hounded by Scientology lawyers when my story eventually appeared in print. I was never paid for the story, and the anthology—as far as I know—was never even published.

Only a few years later, roundabout 2000, Alan Moore and Melinda Gebbie's Jack-Parsons-inspired comic book story, "Brighter Than You Think," was outright censored by DC Comics, reportedly due to the same fears regarding legal reprisals from the Church of Scientology. Perhaps it just wasn't time for Parsons' story to be fully explored? Perhaps...

But these recent fictional representations are not the first time the spirit of Jack Parsons emerged in pop culture. Soon after his death, certain aspects of his life and philosophy began to appear (disguised) in American cinema.

3. It Came from Outer Space: The Parsons/Adamski Connection

A TEENAGE RAY Bradbury first met Jack Parsons in the late 1930s. According to George Pendle's *Strange Angel*:

> Following [a Los Angeles Science Fiction League] field trip to Caltech, during which the young members must have stopped by the [Guggenheim Aeronautical Laboratory] test shack, Parsons was enticed to speak at the meeting held on May 1, 1938. He cut quite a figure when he arrived, immaculate as ever in suit and tie. "My impression of him was like a young Howard Hughes," remembered [Forrest] Ackerman [Bradbury's first literary agent]. He talked about the latest developments in rocketry at Caltech, about his group's successes and failures, and about the future and the moon. He roused his audience, especially one of its junior members, a young Ray Bradbury.
>
> Bradbury was an eighteen-year-old newspaper boy at the time, still living with his parents in Los Angeles. He had a great interest in science fiction and had found out about LASFL through the letters page of the pulps—the great forum of debate for science fiction fans.

> He had always wanted to be a fantasy writer, and LASFL provided him with a community which shared his enthusiasms and understood his ambitions. When Parsons finished speaking, Bradbury asked him a barrage of questions. Many years later Bradbury remembered the incident well. "A young man, some six or seven years older than myself, was there, talking about Rockets and the Future," he recalled. "He was wonderful. I chatted with him, after, but was afraid of him because I was an uneducated non-student, a newsboy... and with no way of joining the rocket society the gentleman spoke of." Little did Bradbury realize how lacking in credentials Parsons was himself.
>
> Though he eschewed membership in LASFL just as he had in the Communist Party, Parsons visited the group on occasion. He even invited a few of the members out into the desert to watch him and [Edward] Forman set off some of their homemade black powder rockets. It must have been heartening for Parsons to be among real enthusiasts.[3]

And it must have been equally heartening for a blossoming Ray Bradbury to discover a scientist who was neither a lunatic nor a milksop, like those he had seen in the Universal horror films he'd grown up watching. One can only wonder if any aspect of Parsons' adventurous/outsider persona found its way into the "young amateur astronomer" around which *It Came from Outer Space* revolves—a scientist described by other characters in the film as "intense" and "odd," a "man who thinks for himself" and risks his own life to protect a group of extraterrestrial visitors in danger of being destroyed by the small-minded Earthmen who populate the tiny desert town in which the scientist works. Does a possible clue lie in the fact that Bradbury chose to christen his protagonist "John Putnam," a scientist/hero who shares Parsons' initials?

Parsons was certainly a man who thought for himself, at a time when such individuality was almost seen as tantamount to treason. In Mike Bara and Richard C. Hoagland's 2007 book, *Dark Mission: The Secret History of NASA*, the authors have this to say about Parsons' unorthodox life and career:

> What eventually became NASA's "Jet Propulsion Laboratory" [...] actually began in the 1920s as an aerodynamics testing facility, under the fledgling "California Institute of Technology" in Pasadena [...]
>
> In 1926, the lab was put under the direction of [Theodore] Von Karman. Von Karman's chief experimental "rocket scientist," formally hired in

> 1935, was John Whiteside Parsons—brilliant chemist and engineer who ultimately made huge strides in the field of solid-rocket propulsion.
>
> Parsons, however, led an amazing double life [...]. Parsons had a long fascination with magic and the occult, and regularly practiced ritual sex orgies in his Pasadena mansion. His compatriot in many of these bizarre rites was one L. Ron Hubbard, who later went on to form the controversial "Church of Scientology"—which is still a major influence in Hollywood today.
>
> Parsons took many of his most bizarre occult ideas from the equally controversial Aleister Crowley, the self-proclaimed "wickedest man in the world." After Parsons spent several years as a member of Crowley's Pasadena lodge, Crowley ultimately appointed Parsons to *head* this Southern California center of Crowley's world-wide organization—while, *simultaneously*, Parsons was still employed by Cal Tech to develop rockets for the U.S. Army [...].
>
> Parsons [developed] one breakthrough after another in rocket propulsion [...]. Parsons' personal quest was to create powerful *solid-fuel* boosters, which could someday—by being far simpler, thus cheaper and more reliable—supplant the liquid fueled complexities (and spectacular accidents) of [Robert] Goddard and [Wernher] Von Braun's painful efforts at practical rocket development.
>
> Parsons' ultimately simpler (and more cost-effective) vision is directly embodied in NASA and the Department of Defense today—a result of the chemistry breakthroughs in solid-rocket fuels that Parsons' essentially singlehandedly achieved.[4]

Parsons believed that these achievements were brought about through magic—or "magick" (Crowley's preferred spelling). Many of these "magick" rituals engaged in by Parsons took place at night while surrounded by the isolation of the desert—the Mojave Desert, to be exact.

Let's now return to Vincent Di Fate discussing the significance of *It Came from Outer Space*: "It's the first of the desert science fiction films. There would be later films like Jack Arnold's *Tarantula*—films of that ilk—which use the terrestrial [desert] environments as if they were the bleak landscapes of other worlds."[5] Di Fate is correct in saying that *It Came from Outer Space* is the first film to juxtapose otherworldly images with the desert landscapes of North America; however, the merging of bleak, desert landscapes and extraterrestrials did not begin with Ray Bradbury; it didn't even begin in film.

It began in the real world, with the rituals of Jack Parsons.

According to Jacques Vallee's 1979 book, *Messengers of Deception: UFO Contacts and Cults*, Parsons claimed to have "met in the Mojave Desert in 1945 a 'Spiritual Being' whom he regarded as a Venusian."[6] This encounter prefigures the even more dramatic assertions of an "amateur astronomer"—described as such in the April 4, 1950 edition of the San Diego *Tribune-Sun*[7]—named George Adamski, who in November of 1952 claimed to have spoken with a "Venusian" named Orthon in the Colorado Desert, near a city called Desert Center in Riverside County, California. This meeting—if it indeed happened—occurred between Bradbury writing the 100-plus-page first draft of *It Came from Outer Space* in September and October of 1952, during Harry Essex's rewriting of Bradbury's screenplay, and before the film went in front of cameras in the Mojave Desert (yes, the exact location where Parsons claimed to have encountered a "Venusian" seven years earlier) on February 4, 1953. Clearly, Adamski's claims about his November 20th encounter with Orthon were not influenced by Bradbury's screenplay; however, Adamski's desert stargazing, which had already produced many published photos of alleged flying saucers zipping through the Southern California skies, had been the subject of numerous major newspaper articles since at least March of 1950, plenty of time for Bradbury to have come across several of them.[8]

Adamski's story about encountering Orthon in the desert didn't become widely publicized until the September 1953 release of his bestselling book, *Flying Saucers Have Landed*, coauthored with Desmond Leslie, a former Spitfire pilot in the Royal Air Force who eventually transitioned into becoming a professional screenwriter. (Among Leslie's produced screenplays is Burt Balaban's *Stranger from Venus* [1954] starring Patricia Neal, who also co-starred in Robert Wise's superior UFOlogical 1951 film, *The Day the Earth Stood Still*. When she made *Stranger from Venus*, Neal was married to celebrated children's book writer Roald Dahl, who, like Desmond Leslie, served in the Royal Air Force during World War II. In 1972, Dahl wrote his own extraterrestrial-themed tale, *Willy Wonka and the Great Glass Elevator*.) Though *Flying Saucers Have Landed* wasn't published until four months after the release of *It Came from Outer Space*, it's important to underscore the fact that Adamski's claims about photographing vehicles from outer space in the middle of the desert had already appeared in newspapers such as the *San Diego Journal* and the *San Diego Tribune-Sun*.[9] Therefore, it's reasonable to assume that Brad-

FANTASTIC SIGHTS LEAP AT YOU!
IN 3-DIMENSION
AMAZING! EXCITING!
SPECTACULAR!
IT CAME FROM OUTER SPACE
From Ray Bradbury's great science fiction story!
Starring
Richard CARLSON · Barbara RUSH
with CHARLES DRAKE · RUSSELL JOHNSON
KATHLEEN HUGHES · JOE SAWYER
Directed by JACK ARNOLD · Screenplay by HARRY ESSEX · Produced by WILLIAM ALLAND · A UNIVERSAL-INTERNATIONAL PICTURE

bury was well aware of Adamski's stories at the time he began writing the first draft of *It Came from Outer Space*.

It appears as if the John Putnam character is, at heart, a fictional amalgam of Adamski's "amateur astronomer" persona and Parsons' outsider reputation. If you think this conclusion is unwarranted, consider the fact that Bradbury's childhood best friend, pioneering special effects artist Ray Harryhausen, went out of his way to visit Adamski in the "amateur astronomer's" home during the 1950s. Since the early 1940s, Adamski and his wife had been living at the base of Palomar Mountain, location of the legendary Palomar Observatory in San Diego.[10] According to Harryhausen:

> I did a lot of research [while working on special effects for Columbia Pictures]. I even went out and talked to George Adamski. He wrote that book, *Flying Saucers Have Landed*, and he was the first person to claim he'd spoken to people from outer space. So I went out to San Diego to meet him. He was building a brick wall around his house. He gave [a] very convincing impression that he *had* talked to these people, and I was impressed with him. Then I went back to see him a year later and he started spouting that [...] flying saucers had landed, and he went inside, and they took him up to Jupiter, and they were playing cards while they were going up. So, you know, I lost interest in him after that.[11]

Despite his eventual disillusionment, Harryhausen felt these encounters with Adamski were important enough to discuss with director Tim Burton in an interview included on the 2008 DVD release of Fred F. Sears' 1956 film, *Earth vs. the Flying Saucers,* over forty years after Adamski's death. It's more than possible that Bradbury may have shared his best friend's initial enthusiasm for Adamski's early claims. Also, consider the fact that Harryhausen was responsible for bringing to life the memorable extraterrestrial spaceships featured in *Earth vs. the Flying Saucers*. These craft bear a striking resemblance to the saucers allegedly photographed by Adamski only a few years before the film's release.

Like Adamski, Putnam spends most of *It Came from Outer Space* trying to convince his fellow man of the unprecedented desert landing of a UFO and his subsequent, face-to-face encounter with "strangers from outer space." Like Adamski, this zealous mission puts him at loggerheads with established scientists, as in the scene in which Putnam confronts university astronomer Dr Snell (George Eldredge) and Snell's young assistant, Bob (Bradford Jackson), about the unbelievable fact that extraterrestrials now walk among us:

> PUTNAM (to Snell): I don't know what's odd and what isn't anymore, but I do know I expected you to be more open to the idea than the others. You're a man of science!
> SNELL: And therefore less inclined to witchcraft, John.
> PUTNAM: Not witchcraft, Dr Snell—*imagination*! Willingness to believe that there are lots of things we don't know anything about! Look, there was a time when people thought the Earth was a level plane between two mountains that were set there to hold up the sky and that the stars were lamps hung from that sky. Then a better idea came along and people were willing to listen.
> SNELL: Be realistic, John. We've worked together before. In the meantime, you can do an article for us.
> PUTNAM: Yeah. Here. I already have. [Putnam hands a manuscript to Snell, then walks away.]
> SNELL (to Bob): An intense young man.
> BOB: Yeah, and an odd one too.
> SNELL: More than odd, Bob. Individual and lonely. A man who thinks for himself. [He reads aloud the title of Putnam's manuscript.] "Report on the Arrival of Strangers from Outer Space." [Shakes his head in pity.]

The reaction Putnam receives from Bob and Dr Snell mirrors the criticisms faced by Adamski in the real world. Ironically, Bradford Jackson, the actor playing Snell's skeptical assistant, shared many of Adamski's (and Parsons') unorthodox beliefs. In his 2017 book, *Universal Terrors, 1951–1955*, Tom Weaver writes:

> According to *Los Angeles Times* columnist Edwin Schallert (February 6, 1953), Jackson—future star of Roger Corman's *The Saga of the Viking Women and Their Voyage to the Waters of the Great Sea Serpent* (1957)—had been brought to Universal's attention by Shelley Winters and was making his debut in *Outer Space*. In the movie, Jackson's character calls John Putnam "odd," but his *Viking Women* co-star Jay Sayer told me that in real life, Jackson was the odd one. "He thought he was the reincarnation of Rudolf Valentino [...]."

> "He was *really* into reincarnation—he was into all that really occult stuff," said Kenny Miller, who appeared with Jackson in the supernatural drama *The Search for Bridey Murphy* (1956). "In fact, he was so spooky about it, that's one of the reasons people wouldn't *hire* him. He was a great-lookin' guy and a good actor, but he was so involved in that kind of stuff."[12]

It sounds like Jackson and Parsons might have had a lot to discuss. Alas, by the time Bradbury began writing *It Came from Outer Space*, Parsons had already been dead for about three months.

June 17, 1952 marked Parsons' last day on Earth, the day a catastrophic explosion ripped through his Pasadena laboratory. Apparently, he had been trying to complete a rush job for a motion picture that had hired him to create special effects. According to Parsons' biographer George Pendle:

> Don Harding, a criminologist involved in his first major investigation since his assignment to the Pasadena police department, found residue of fulminate of mercury, a highly combustible explosive, in a trash can at the scene of the explosion. He also found bits of coffee tin shredded into shrapnel and theorized that Parsons had been using the tin to mix the chemical in when he had accidentally dropped it. Knowing the fulminate was so volatile, Parsons had quickly stooped down in an attempt to catch it. He had been too late. The can had hit the floor, the explosive had ignited, and Parsons' searching right arm and right side of his face had borne the full brunt of the blast. The explosion had then ignited other chemicals in the room, causing the holocaust. A man of promise and genius had been lost to a terrible accident.[13]

Since Parsons' May 1, 1938 lecture had clearly left a permanent imprint on Bradbury, it's hard to believe that such a dramatic, fiery death—widely publicized in American newspapers nationwide with lurid headlines such as "SLAIN SCIENTIST PRIEST IN BLACK MAGIC CULT" and "VENTURES INTO BLACK MAGIC BY BLAST VICTIM REVEALED"[14]—would not have been hovering near the forefront of Bradbury's mind when Universal Studios approached him to dream up an appropriately sensationalistic plot for their first UFOlogical film. Perhaps this is why Bradbury's hero soon evolved into an "intense," "odd," "lonely" scientist who "thinks for himself." Perhaps this is why the entity Putnam encounters in the desert first appears in the form of pure flame.

What follows is a sentence that appears early in Bradbury's screenplay: "Across the night sky a vast, roaring furnace, a bright blazing stream of fire, like a gush of molten metal from the stars, races from horizon to horizon."[15] Bradbury could just as easily be describing the tumultuous arc of Parsons' life and death.

In his 1992 book, *Hecate's Fountain*, ceremonial magician Kenneth Grant wrote:

> An excellent and comparatively recent example of tangential magick occurred in connection with the Babalon Working performed by John W. Parsons, shortly before Crowley's death in 1947 [...]. On February 28th, 1946, [Parsons] performed an invocation in the Mojave Desert, California. A Force which he intuited as Babalon responded, and it was not long before it obsessed him and commanded him to write *The Book of Babalon (Liber 49)* [...] It was Parsons' belief that *The Book of Babalon* contained the "record of a magical experiment relating to the invocation of an elemental, and thereafter of the Goddess of Force called Babalon, and the results thereof." He believed also that the Aeon of Horus [...] related to Fire and to Mars, which he interpreted in terms of war and similar violences [...]. [*Liber 49*] is of some historic interest as containing several accurate prophecies, including an unequivocal indication of the ordeals that lay ahead of him [...]: the mode of death by flame.[16]

There are many indications in Bradbury's screenplay, as well as in Jack Arnold's completed film, that the entities who appear in a ball of flame in the opening scene of *It Came from Outer Space* are not merely physical beings from another planet, but elementals, the very same type of interdimensional entities that Parsons was attempting to invoke in February of 1946.

Throughout the film, the aliens—called "Xenomorphs" in all the contemporaneous publicity materials[17]—are depicted as beings that can transition from a physical to a nonphysical state almost instantaneously. It's implied more than once that they can transform into pure energy and travel through power lines. The first implication of this comes when Putnam and his girlfriend, Ellen (Barbara Rush), ask two telephone linesmen, Frank (Joe Sawyer) and George (Russell Johnson), if they've seen anything unusual in the desert since the arrival of the "meteor" the night before. Frank replies that he hasn't seen anything, "But I sure am hearing things!" Frank invites Putnam to join him at the top of the pole and listen to "the [darnedest] sound you ever heard." At this point the film transcends itself, becoming less of a genre picture and more of an atmospheric experiment in mood and tone. Frank delivers a very memorable speech about working in the desert:

> After you've been working out in the desert fifteen years like I have, you hear a lot of things. See a lot of things too. The sun in the sky, the heat, all that sand out there with the rivers and lakes that aren't real at all. And sometimes you think that the wind gets in the wires and hums and listens and talks... just like what we're hearing now. Still hear it?

Not long after this, Frank and George are driving down the highway in their truck. We see the truck from an aerial perspective with the telephone lines in the foreground, as if the wires themselves are somehow *spying* on Frank and George. Frank even looks up at the wires with a curious expression on his face, as if he's suspicious of them (or at least senses that there's something peculiar about them). Seconds later, a Xenomorph materializes in the middle of the highway, right in front of the truck, as if it's materialized out of nowhere—or perhaps from the telephone wires above them. Similar scenes of these telephone wires "spying" on our protagonists from above recur throughout the film.

4. "From Pure Air We Descended": The Twin Peaks Connection

IN MANY WAYS, the Xenomorphs of *It Came from Outer Space* behave like the immaterial beings that populate David Lynch and Mark Frost's television series *Twin Peaks* (1990–91), Lynch's 1992 film *Twin Peaks: Fire Walk With Me*, and Lynch and Frost's recent follow-up, *Twin Peaks: The Return* (2017). As mentioned before, *Twin Peaks* has buried within it several subtle—and not so subtle—references to Jack Parsons and the Babalon Working he performed in the Mojave Desert. Take, for example, Lynch's *Twin Peaks: Fire Walk With Me*, a prequel that followed the cancellation of the initial television series. The screenplay was co-written by Lynch and Robert Engels, one of the key staff writers on the series. During one scene early on in the film,

FBI agent Chet Desmond (Chris Isaak) is investigating the bludgeoning death of a young woman named Teresa Banks (Pamela Gidley) in a seedy motel room located in the middle of a small town called Deer Meadow, Washington. His investigation has led him to the Fat Trout Trailer Park where Banks used to live. While Desmond drinks coffee with the manager of the trailer park, Carl Rodd (Harry Dean Stanton), the scene abruptly shifts. We now find ourselves outside the trailer. The soundtrack music grows ominous. Because of a subjective tracking shot, seen through the eyes of an unknown person, we know that someone is approaching the trailer slowly. Now we return to the interior of the trailer where we see an old woman, whose face is covered in what looks like black soot, open the door and glance around, as if she's searching for someone or something. Perhaps she's investigating Desmond, just as he's investigating the people of Deer Meadow? Carl appears not to recognize the woman at all. Desmond asks her a question, but the strange woman does not respond and merely backs away. Then we return to the exterior of the trailer. We see a telephone pole in the exact center of the screen. The woman has vanished. Now the camera slowly pans up the telephone pole and focuses on the wires, as if the strange woman has returned to the realm of electricity from which she came. Later, we see Agent Desmond inspecting these same wires again when he returns to the trailer park to search for a green ring stolen from Banks' hand after her death. It's as if he suspects there's something strange and unexplainable lurking in the wires.

Tellingly, in one of the scenes deleted from the theatrical release, which can be viewed in a bonus feature titled *Twin Peaks: The Missing Pieces* included on the 2017 Criterion Blu-ray release of the film, one of the denizens of The Black Lodge (an otherworldly limbo occupied by an array of malevolent beings that feed off the "pain and sorrow" of human beings), a dwarf known as The Man from Another Place says, "From pure air we have descended. From pure air. Going up and down. Intercourse between the two worlds." Meanwhile, in this same scene, FBI Regional Bureau Chief Gordon Cole (David Lynch) and Agent Dale Cooper (Kyle MacLachlan) attempt to interrogate Agent Phillip Jeffries (David Bowie), who has been missing for two years. Desperately, Jeffries tries to explain what happened to him: "I've been to one of their meetings. It was above a convenience store. It was a dream. We live inside a dream!" As we see disjointed images of this interdimensional space where this "meeting" occurred, we hear The

Man from Another Place say, "*Electricity*." Behind the dwarf, what appears to be a bearded lumberjack fiddles with a weird machine that generates sudden bursts of electricity, conduits of power through which these beings apparently go "up and down… between the two worlds."

These lines echo the cryptic poem recited by another interdimensional being, this one named The One-Armed Man (Al Strobel), in Episode Three of *Twin Peaks'* first season:

Through the darkness of future's past,
The magician longs to see.
One chants out between two worlds
Fire walk with me.

The One-Armed Man then delivers the following monologue: "We lived among the people. I think you say, convenience store. We lived above it. I mean it like it is… like it sounds. I too have been touched by the devilish one. Tattoo on the left shoulder. Oh, but when I saw the face of God, I was changed. I took the entire arm off. My name is Mike. His name is Bob." ("Bob," portrayed by Frank Silva, is the main antagonist of *Twin Peaks*, another malevolent being that dwells within the Black Lodge.)

In *Fire Walk With Me*, during a scene that takes place inside this Lodge, the Man from Another Place identifies himself to Agent Cooper as "the arm." Parsons, a magician who was torn between two worlds (the worlds of science and sorcery on one level, and the worlds of the noumenal and the phenomenal on another), had his left arm burned and his right arm completely amputated during the explosion that killed him, causing his unbound spirit to metaphorically "walk with fire." It's strongly implied in *Fire Walk With Me* that The One-Armed Man's amputated arm evolved into The Man from Another Place. Both The One-Armed Man and The Man from Another Place, non-physical beings whose origins lay in an unknown plane of existence, certainly seem to feed off the "pain and sorrow" of Earth's physical beings. Apparently, Bob's main function is to deliver this "pain and sorrow" to those who dwell in the Black Lodge.

Like the Xenomorphs from *It Came from Outer Space*, these non-material creatures utilize electricity to travel from place to place while on Earth; other similarities between the Xenomorphs and the interdimensional beings in *Twin Peaks* is their ability to shapeshift (e.g., The One-Armed Man's arm metamorphoses into The Man from Another Place, who then metamorphoses into an even more peculiar being called The Evolution of the Arm in *Twin Peaks: The Return*) and create doppelgangers of human beings. In fact, John Putnam and Special Agent Dale Cooper are compelled to face exact replicas of themselves at the conclusions of both *It Came from Outer Space* and *Twin Peaks: The Return*.

During a crucial scene in *Fire Walk With Me*, we see "Bob" invade the bedroom of Laura Palmer (Sheryl Lee), the teenage protagonist of the film, and rape her, perhaps adding another layer of meaning to the dwarf's phrase "intercourse between two worlds." The morning after, still stunned by what occurred to her the night before, Laura walks down the street toward school in a somnambulant state. She keeps staring up at the power lines above her, as if afraid of them, as if she knows the beings that are stalking her are somehow connected to those lines. For a moment, we see the image of grayish snow on a television set superimposed over the black wires, as if to underscore the connection between electricity and Laura's hopeless plight. Like Parsons, Laura is torn between two worlds, though in her case this fatal situation is not under her control.

The connection between electricity and interdimensional beings, hinted at in the original series as well as in *Fire Walk With Me*, is made explicit in *Twin Peaks: The Return*, Lynch and Frost's belated conclusion to the series. When Dale Cooper finally manages to escape from the otherworldly Black Lodge in which he has been trapped for twenty-five years, we see him emerge on Earth through an electrical socket. He spends many episodes unable to remember his Agent Cooper persona until, at last, he plunges a metal fork into another electrical socket, the resultant shock putting him into a coma, then restoring him to full consciousness.

In *The Secret History of Twin Peaks*, Mark Frost makes the connection between *Twin Peaks* and Jack Parsons even more transparent, having Parsons appear as a character in the book. In a fictional top secret FBI field report prepared by none other than Lieutenant L. Ron Hubbard (who has infiltrated Parsons' Pasadena mansion on behalf of Congressman Richard Nixon), Parsons is quoted as saying:

> JP: Alchemy isn't only about "chemistry" or turning base metals to gold. The medieval philosophers and alchemists know this—even Isaac Newton knew it—but their knowledge was lost until Crowley

brought it back. You see, alchemy actually speaks to *internal* processes, and a radical revolution in our spiritual development; transforming the "base metal" of primitive man to the "gold" of an enlightened soul. Rockets and magick are both about breaking through the animal boundaries of space and time that hold us back from realizing our potential. Either, maybe both, will someday take us to the moon and the stars beyond. I truly believe that. Magick is just the name we've always given to things we don't yet understand…

(He stares at me a moment with his dark brown eyes, then turns his gaze to the statue of Pan, gets a faraway look and mutters something under his breath.)

JP: The magician longs to see…

LRH: Excuse me, what's that?

(He trails a hand along one of the walls.)

JP: I've often felt there were spirits in this wood…

(He looks at me again, suddenly focused.)

JP: You'll have to excuse me. I must attend to my other guests.[18]

By having Parsons quote the second line of the poem first recited by The One-Armed Man in the original *Twin Peaks* series, he's clearly signaling to the reader that the "magician" mentioned in the poem is Parsons himself. Another important Parsons connection to the narrative involves Teresa Banks' aforementioned missing ring. In *The Secret History of Twin Peaks*, during a scene in which L. Ron Hubbard notices that Parsons is "worrying a ring on his right ring finger, a flat green stone, maybe jade, etched with some sort of inscription,"[19] Frost implies that Teresa's ring once belonged to Parsons himself. In Episode Eight of *Twin Peaks: The Return*, we receive several implications that the combined cosmos-rupturing influences of the detonation of the atom bomb in 1945 and Parsons' Babalon Working (the preparations for which began in 1945 and culminated in 1946) opened a dimensional doorway that allowed this bizarre array of immaterial beings to enter our world.

This very same notion had been percolating in the UFOlogy field for several decades. The first person to suggest this scenario in print was ceremonial magician Kenneth Grant in his influential 1980 non-fiction book, *Outside the Circles of Time*. Over a decade later, UFOlogist George C. Andrews popularized the idea even further in his 1993 book, *Extra-terrestrial Friends and Foes*:

> The purpose of the series of ceremonies performed by Parsons and Hubbard was to unseal an inter-dimensional gateway that had been sealed in deep antiquity, thereby allowing other-dimensional entities known as "the Old Ones" access to our space/time continuum. The culmination of the ceremonies was described as having successfully resulted in extra-terrestrial contact. As Grant puts it: "Parsons opened a door and something flew in; he supposed it was Babalon and the fourth chapter of the *Book of the Law* [a 1904 book by Aleister Crowley]; others have supposed other things but all are in agreement that something unusual, something inexplicable by mundane laws, occurred around that time."[20]

That oft-quoted line by Kenneth Grant ("Parsons opened a door and something flew in") is echoed by Mark Frost in *The Secret History of Twin Peaks* in the form of a footnote written by FBI Special Agent Tammy Preston (portrayed by Christa Bell in *Twin Peaks: The Return*). This particular footnote is commenting on a transcript of a 12-3-49 dialogue between Parsons and Major Douglas Milford (a role originally written for novelist William S. Burroughs, who shared many of Parsons' Gnostic beliefs, though the character was ultimately portrayed by character actor Tony Jay in *Twin Peaks'* second season):

> He [Milford] seems to be suggesting that Parsons' ritual somehow "opened a gate" that resulted in aliens showing up in Roswell. I'm not endorsing this jibber-jabber as fact, but I have done my own research now into the Arroyo Seco [described by Milford earlier in the transcript as "a forbidding and desolate 25-mile-long dry river canyon [...] where, after founding JPL, Parsons first began enacting his bizarre 'Thelemic' rituals"]. The Native Americans who lived here were in fact wary of the place, and did call it the Hell Gate, claiming they could "hear the devil's laughter in the waterfall."[21]

Clearly, Frost is having fun playing with these outré speculations in a fictional framework; however, it's important to keep in mind that the connection between Parsons' magical activities and UFOlogy originated neither with Kenneth Grant nor George C. Andrews. They originated with Parsons and his second wife, Marjorie Cameron. Like Hubbard, Cameron participated in the Babalon Working and served in the US Navy during World War II. As previously mentioned, after Parsons' death, she appeared in several important cult films such as

IN A TOWN LIKE TWIN PEAKS
NO ONE IS INNOCENT.
A FILM BY DAVID LYNCH
TWIN PEAKS
FIRE WALK WITH ME
NEW LINE CINEMA AND FRANCIS BOUYGUES PRESENT A CIBY PICTURES PRODUCTION OF A FILM BY DAVID LYNCH TWIN PEAKS-FIRE WALK WITH ME SHERYL LEE MOIRA KELLY
DAVID BOWIE CHRIS ISAAK HARRY DEAN STANTON RAY WISE AND KYLE MacLACHLAN AS SPECIAL AGENT DALE COOPER PRODUCTION DESIGN BY PATRICIA NORRIS EDITED BY MARY SWEENEY
DIRECTOR OF PHOTOGRAPHY RON GARCIA MUSIC COMPOSED BY ANGELO BADALAMENTI PRODUCED BY GREGG FIENBERG EXECUTIVE PRODUCERS MARK FROST & DAVID LYNCH
R RESTRICTED UNDER 17 REQUIRES ACCOMPANYING PARENT OR ADULT GUARDIAN
WRITTEN BY DAVID LYNCH & ROBERT ENGELS DIRECTED BY DAVID LYNCH NEW LINE CINEMA
SOUNDTRACK ALBUM AVAILABLE ON WARNER BROS. RECORDS
DOLBY STEREO
FILMED IN PANAVISION

Kenneth Anger's *Inauguration of the Pleasure Dome* (1954) and Curtis Harrington's *Night Tide* (1961). (In this latter film, appropriately enough, Cameron co-starred with a young Dennis Hopper, the actor destined to play Frank Booth, the antagonist of David Lynch's 1986 neo-noir film, *Blue Velvet*.) Parsons believed he and Hubbard had summoned Cameron through a magic ritual performed at his "favorite place" in the Mojave Desert in January of 1946. In *Strange Angel*, George Pendle describes this location as follows:

> [Parsons'] favorite place was marked by the intersection of two massive power lines, their source and goal lost in both horizons. The sagging cables emitted an ominous, enveloping drone, as if they were the antennae of an almighty cicada buried deep beneath the ground. At sunset the two men stood beneath them and suddenly Parsons felt the tension snap. "I turned to him and said 'It is done,' in absolute certainty that the operation was accomplished. I returned home, and found a young woman answering the requirements waiting for me." Parsons had summoned his elemental.[22]

That "elemental," of course, was Marjorie Cameron. In October of 1946, less than a year after meeting for the first time, the two would marry. They remained married until Parsons' sudden death. In Spencer Kansa's 2011 biography of Cameron, *Wormwood Star: The Magickal Life of Marjorie Cameron*, we learn:

> [B]arely a week after her husband's death, Cameron conducted her first blood ritual, in a desperate attempt to reach Jack on the other side [...] A week later, Cameron read about the fleet of UFOs that were recently sighted, hovering over the Capitol Building in Washington, D.C., and took it as a cosmic response to her husband passing.[23]

That Cameron would associate UFOs with her husband's death is not entirely unexpected, as Parsons himself considered UFOs to be vitally important when he performed the Babalon Working early in 1946. Evidence for this was discovered by Cameron after Parsons' death:

> Cameron personally subscribed to [the idea] that *she* was the chosen vehicle for Babalon's manifestation. She saw proof of this in another letter Jack wrote to Crowley, in which he anticipated Babalon coming to him bearing a secret sign. Now it turned out that during those first

> early weeks together, Cameron spotted a silver, cigar-shaped UFO moving soundlessly in the sky as she sat out in the back garden of [Jack's home at] 1003 [S. Orange Grove Avenue in Pasadena]. When she mentioned the sighting to her [future] husband later that day, he remained silent on the subject, and it was never raised again. Now, sifting through his papers, Cameron discovered that Jack had indeed marked the momentous sighting, by drawing a symbol of the UFO—a circle with a trine set within it—in the marginalia. To her mind, this was the celestial sign he had been waiting for.[24]

UFOs continued to fascinate Cameron throughout her life. Only a year after Parsons' death, she wrote a letter to Jane Wolfe, a former silent film actress and a founding member of the Pasadena Agape Lodge to which Parsons belonged, in which she expressed her belief that a flying saucer would eventually transport her and her "peculiar few" to Mars, which she considered to be her true home.[25]

5. The Culmination of the Babalon Working

IN WHAT CAN only be described as an example of cosmic synchronicity, on February 28, 1953, the seventh[26] anniversary of the culmination of the Babalon Working (to the day), Jack Arnold and crew shot the key scene in *It Came from Outer Space* in which John Putnam at last comes face-to-face with an alien being, seeing its true form for the first time, when it emerges from the darkness of a mine shaft located in the middle of the desert.[27]

According to John Carter's 1999 biography of Jack Parsons, *Sex and Rockets: The Occult World of Jack Parsons*, Bradbury only met Parsons "once, when I was a teenager and he came to lecture at the Los Angeles Science Fantasy Society in the late thirties… I was merely part of a small audience of about 20 or 30 who were fascinated with his ideas about the future."[28] Taking Bradbury's word that he met Parsons only once, it's nonetheless important to keep in mind that Bradbury and Parsons shared many mutual friends and acquaintances, including Jack Williamson (author of the 1940 novel *Darker Than You Think*, the supernatural themes of which exerted a tremendous impact on Parsons), A.E. Van Vogt (who in 1950 became the head of the California branch of Dianetics), L. Ron Hubbard (who, in 1946, married Parsons' ex-girlfriend, Sara Northrup, a key figure in the creation of Dianetics and the Church of Scientology), Robert A. Heinlein (author of the 1961 science fiction novel, *Stranger in a Strange Land*, rumored to have been heavily influenced by Parsons' life and philosophy), and the aforementioned Forrest J Ackerman (who, despite claiming not to believe in the paranormal, certainly seemed to share Parsons' interest in the occult; I myself observed him attempting, with all apparent sincerity, to get in contact with his deceased wife, Wendayne, via a midnight séance at the Egyptian Theater in Los Angeles in 2002). The idea that Bradbury might have heard about Parsons' 1945 desert encounter with an extraterrestrial being from a mutual friend or acquaintance, and subsequently woven that story into his screenplay for *It Came from Outer Space*, is not at all far-fetched. The world of science fiction enthusiasts in Los Angeles was much smaller in the late 1940s and early 1950s than it is today; every science fiction fan or writer tended to know each other. The continuing misadventures of someone as outré as Jack Parsons would have been hard to overlook, particularly when his occult exploits were being described in major Southern Californian newspapers as "sexual perversion[s]" and "intellectual necromancy."[29]

Some truths, however, are too taboo to deal with in their raw form. When Parsons was alive, most Americans would have gone out of their way *not* to acknowledge the implications of this man's brazen dismissal of almost every stricture upheld by Western society. The inextricable link between the world of the occult and the beginnings of the space program is not something the typical American can easily comprehend in the twenty-first century, much less back in the 1940s and 1950s.[30]

What is not acknowledged consciously emerges in the ethereal realms of the subconscious in the form of fiction. And fiction, in its cinematic form, eventually evolves from metaphor to unadulterated truth. We can see this process in the context of the uncomfortable truths represented by Parsons' life and career.

His life's work first emerges symbolically (in cinema) in the form of a fictional character, John Putnam, an "odd" and "lonely" outsider who "thinks for himself" and defies the common wisdom of his peers in order to make direct, face-to-face contact with otherworldly beings in the middle of the desert—in February, no less, the same month in which the Babalon Working culminated, the month in which *It Came from Outer Space* takes place, as evidenced by a calendar clearly visible in the background of the police station when Putnam is trying to convince the sheriff that extraterrestrials have indeed arrived on Earth. Over the next few decades, Parsons' occult philosophies begin to trickle slowly upwards out of the collective unconscious thanks to Marjorie Cameron's contributions to avant-garde cinema in the form of her collaborations with Kenneth Anger and others. Then, over thirty years later, Parsons' philosophies invade the mainstream once again in the form of a hit television show, *Twin Peaks*, which inarguably altered the landscape of television forever. Only one year after *Twin Peaks: The Return* concludes, the taboo nature of Parsons' life is at last unveiled in naked form in Mark Heyman's television series, *Strange Angel*, in which Jack Reynor (who memorably appeared in another occult-influenced project, Ari Aster's 2019 film *Midsommar*, as a young man named "Christian" whose final fate synchronistically mirrors Parsons' own fiery immolation) portrays Parsons in a historical drama that makes much use of the rocket scientist's interest in UFOs and related esoteric phenomena.

Robbie Graham's 2015 nonfiction book, *Silver Screen Saucers: Sorting Fact from Fantasy in Hollywood's UFO Movies* (mentioned further in Chapter Six), is valuable because it makes the case for a truth I myself noticed many years ago: that science fiction films tend to borrow from UFOlogy, not the other way around. Many skeptics insist that most UFO sightings and abduction reports are due to the witnesses involved having seen far too many science fiction films. But it can be demonstrated over and over again that the UFO sightings generally *predate* the appearance of such images on screen. In the astral realms of cinema, the folklore (and, occasionally, folk *truth*) of UFOlogy more often than not predates the more easily digested contributions of professional dreamers like Jack Arnold, Ray Bradbury, Mark Frost, David Lynch, and Mark Heyman.

Chapter 5

The Man from Planet X

Hollywood's First Invasion from Outer Space

1. Invasion USA

MUCH HAS BEEN written about the science fiction films of the 1950s. Prominent in this ongoing discussion are the classics with which all science fiction cinema buffs are intimately familiar: Howard Hawks and Christian Nyby's *The Thing* (1951), Robert Wise's *The Day the Earth Stood Still* (1951), William Cameron Menzies' *Invaders from Mars* (1953), Byron Haskin's *The War of the Worlds* (1953), Jack Arnold's *It Came from Outer Space* (1953), Joseph Newman's *This Island Earth* (1955), Fred M. Wilcox's *Forbidden Planet* (1956), Don Siegel's *Invasion of the Body Snatchers* (1956), Fred F. Sears' *Earth vs. the Flying Saucers* (1956), even Ed Wood's *Plan 9 from Outer Space* (1958).

All of these films, with the exception of *Forbidden Planet*, involve aliens either surreptitiously infiltrating the earth or outright assaulting it, a plot that certainly did not die out with the 1950s. The film industry reincarnates this scenario almost every year in a new form, ranging from the ridiculous to the sublime and everything in between, whether it be Nicholaus Webster's *Santa Claus Conquers the Martians* (1964), Steven Spielberg's *Close Encounters of the Third Kind* (1977), Eliseo Subiela's *Man Facing Southeast* (1987), John McTiernan's *Predator* (1987), John Carpenter's *They Live* (1988), Roland Emmerich's *Independence Day* (1996), Tim Burton's *Mars Attacks!* (1996),

M. Night Shyamalan's *Signs* (2002), Michael Bay's *Transformers* (2007), Neill Blomkamp's *District 9* (2009), Jon Favreau's *Cowboys & Aliens* (2011), J.J. Abrams' *Super 8* (2011), Guillermo del Toro's *Pacific Rim* (2013), Doug Liman's *Edge of Tomorrow* (2014), Chris Columbus' *Pixels* (2015), Roland Emmerich's *Independence Day: Resurgence* (2016), or *Avengers: Infinity War* (2018).

The film that started it all, however, is not often spoken about, and yet it's possibly the most significant since it represents such an important milestone in film history, a missing link as it were between the Gothic horror that dominated Hollywood cinema throughout the 1920s, thirties and forties, and the abrupt turn toward the genre of science fiction in the early 1950s as technological progress continued to speed along at a pace that many Americans found dizzying. The science fiction films of the fifties fed off that discomfort and confusion by both condemning and glorifying technological progress at the same time.

Many Americans were suffering from fears brought on by their own government's use of the atom bomb against the Japanese in 1945. Genuinely frightened by the prospect that other nations were developing their own version of the A-bomb, Americans hunkered down for the End of Days in concrete bunkers that would sustain them as the air of the surface world darkened, corrupted for generations with the poisonous winds of radioactive fallout. Even non-science fiction films like Alfred E. Green's *Invasion USA* (1952) drew upon this paranoia in order to create pro-military propaganda in the form of popular "entertainment." In the early fifties, if *Invasion USA* is an accurate measuring stick, "entertainment" meant being frightened half to death by depictions of major urban centers being destroyed by Russian atom bombs and watching nubile young women raped by vodka-toting Russian troops. (But don't worry, Amurrica, the young lady in question jumps out the window of a multi-storey building and kills herself before those nasty, bear-like Russians can have their way with her. The message is clear: That's what's going to happen to *your* daughter if you people don't shape up and jump on the anti-commie bandwagon.) The film's lurid advertisements included this promise from popular gossip columnist Hedda Hopper: "IT WILL SCARE THE PANTS OFF YOU!"

Albert Zugsmith, the producer of *Invasion USA*, later collaborated with Jack Pollexfen and Aubrey Wisberg on several low budget science fiction films such as *Captive Women* (1952) and *Port Sinister*

(1953). Pollexfen and Wisberg were the co-writers and co-producers of a very different kind of "invasion" movie released a year before *Invasion USA*; in fact, it was the very first Hollywood film to depict an invasion from outer space: Edgar G. Ulmer's *The Man from Planet X* (1951) starring Robert Clarke, Margaret Field, and William Schallert. Thanks to an intelligent script by Jack Pollexfen and Aubrey Wisberg, the film succeeds in setting the pattern for the invasion-from-space movies to come while also functioning as a link to the generation of Gothic horror films that preceded it.

2. Edgar Ulmer, the King of Poverty Row

EDGAR G. ULMER, the director of *The Man from Planet X*, began his career in 1920s Vienna where he worked with the early German Expressionists Carl Boese, Fritz Lang, F.W. Murnau, and Paul Wegener. He worked on such expressionist classics as *Der Golem* (1920) directed by Boese and Wegner, F.W. Murnau's *Sunrise* (1927), and Fritz Lang's groundbreaking films *Metropolis* (1927) and *M* (1931). Ulmer is one of many German immigrants who settled in California in the early 1930s and proceeded to transform the typical Hollywood film style with his expressionist obsessions. Working within the parameters of the studio systems offered such talented German immigrants as Michael Curtiz, Karl Freund, Fritz Lang, and Robert Siodmak the opportunity to alter not just the look of a Hollywood film with their expressionist philosophies, but also bring a deeper, darker subtext to the psychological makeup of the characters. It just so happened that the rise of the American horror film coincided with the arrival of many of these directors, thus offering the perfect vehicles in which to cloak their subversive goals. Such expressionist approaches can be seen in horror and noir films such as Michael Curtiz's *The Mystery of the Wax Museum* (1933) and *The Walking Dead* (1936), Karl Freund's *The Mummy* (1932) and *Mad Love* (1935), Fritz Lang's *Fury* (1936) and *Scarlet Street* (1945), and Robert Siodmak's *The Phantom Lady* (1944) and *The Dark Mirror* (1946). Freund, it should be noted, greatly influenced the expressionist look of other classic Hollywood films in the 1930s as a cinematographer. His contributions to Tod Browning's *Dracula* (1931) and Robert Florey's *Murders in the Rue Morgue* (1932), to name only two examples, are often cited by film scholars as being just as invaluable—if not more so—than those of the actual directors involved.

And then there's Edgar Ulmer. Ulmer's first major project made specifically for the mainstream Hollywood studio system also turned out to be his last: *The Black Cat* (1934), the first film that paired Boris Karloff and Bela Lugosi. Though the heads at Universal decided to market the film as an adaptation of the famous Edgar Allan Poe short story "The Black Cat," in truth the plot and themes are wholly original to Ulmer and his co-writer, Peter Ruric. The title refers to Poe only in spirit, functioning more as a postmodern reference to the transgressive obsessions we associate with Edgar Allan Poe—what his legacy represents in the popular imagination—than a Hollywood-esque attempt at false advertising.

As film historian Tom Weaver writes in his 2007 book, *Universal Horrors: The Studio's Classic Films, 1931–1946*:

> Not only did *The Black Cat* come to symbolize the unalterable status of its star players (Lugosi would hereupon assume a subordinate position in terms of billing and salary to his professional rival, the mystically-billed KARLOFF), the production was an invaluable proving ground for its director, Edgar George Ulmer. The Austrian-born filmmaker transformed a studio property into an intensely personal work. Keeping his adaptation faithful to the "spirit" if not the word of Poe, the psychologically-scarred Ulmer integrated into the work his personal quirks, including a childhood Oedipal complex and a fascination for such larger than life personalities as the notorious Satanist and all-purpose degenerate, Aleister Crowley.[1]

The term "personal quirks" is quite an understatement. *The Black Cat* looks and sounds like no other American film from the 1930s. If one were to stumble across this film randomly on Turner Classic Movies, one might think the station was in the midst of a von Sternberg classic foreign film festival—if not, that is, for the presence of its instantly recognizable Hollywood stars, Karloff and Lugosi. John Waters, director of *Pink Flamingos*, once observed—half-jokingly—that there were some American films whose status would be much higher among scholars if only they possessed subtitles. *The Black Cat* is one of these. Despite the fact that *The Black Cat* was a huge hit at the box office in Depression-era America, it really is a statistical outlier in terms of its aesthetics and atypically grim philosophy. By no means does it feel "American" in any way. During its brief sixty-five minute running time, the films packs in enough cultural taboos for a whole decade's worth of films: incest, necrophilia, Satanism, human vivisection, rape, voyeurism, sadism, insanity induced by wartime trauma, and good old-fashioned murder. In large part it was due to the perceived depravity of *The Black Cat*, Louis Friedlander's *The Raven* (Universal, 1935), which once again paired Karloff and Lugosi in an ostensible Poe adaptation, and Karl Freund's aforementioned *Mad Love* that initiated England's all-encompassing ban on horror films in 1936; in turn, this ban forced American studios to end its production of all horror films for about three years. It's no coincidence that the Motion Picture Production Code went into effect in 1936 as well. If Edgar Ulmer had wanted to make *The Black Cat* for a major studio only a couple of years later, the film would never have made it past the planning stages, much less the first reel. The Production Code, of course, remained in effect in the United States until the late 1960s.

Despite having written and directed Universal's highest grossing film of 1934, Edgar Ulmer was never asked to helm another Universal production. According to Tom Weaver, "Months after the release of *The Black Cat*, Ulmer's romantic relationship with Carl Laemmle's nephew's wife became known and the director became *persona non grata* in virtually every major Hollywood studio."[2] Ulmer was forced to find a niche for himself outside the major studios, at first specializing in so-called "ethnic films" such as the Yiddish *Green Fields* (1938), and then in the 1940s drifting toward the "Poverty Row" studios where he directed B programmers that have now attained the status of cult films. Ulmer's *Bluebeard* (1944), starring John Carradine, is without question one of the best horror films produced in the 1940s and certainly the best horror film with which Carradine or PRC studios were ever involved. Ulmer's *Detour* (1945), starring Tom Neal and Ann Savage, is generally considered by fans and scholars alike to be one of the best—if not *the* best—film noir ever made.

By the 1950s and early sixties Ulmer began turning his talents toward low budget science fiction movies such as *The Amazing Transparent Man* (1960) and *Beyond the Time Barrier* (1960), both of which were shot in the same two-week period. Indeed, most of Ulmer's films—even the ones now considered classics—were shot in under a week. *The Black Cat*, despite having a major studio behind it, was given only a fifteen-day shooting schedule. Ulmer finished the film in sixteen.

Of his later science fiction films, *The Man from Planet X* is the best on an aesthetic level and the most significant from a historical perspective as well, deserving of a special position in Ulmer's *oeuvre*. As mentioned before, *The Man from Planet X* functions as a missing link in the evolution of cinematic horror and science fiction. This link is evident in the very first shot.

3. The Man from Planet X

WE BEGIN WITH a shot of the clouds drifting past a full moon, a scene that would not be out of place in a Gothic horror film from twenty years before. And yet the credits now filling the screen resemble shards of metal that have been bolted together haphazardly, suggesting a juxtaposition between the old style horror audiences have come to expect and the new horrors lying in wait in the future. Of course, with the advent of atomic energy the future had already arrived in ways that the science fiction writers of the previous century had never even imagined. The future could now be considered the present time of April 27, 1951 (the night of the film's premiere).

We segue from the full moon to an establishing shot of the Scottish moors. In these initial moments we're not quite sure where we are, in terms of location and time and even genre. We could easily be in the first reel of the Sherlock Holmes mystery, *The Hound of the Baskervilles* (1939), another film that crossbred two distinct forms: the Gothic horror film and the detective story. According to both Edgar Ulmer and Jack Pollexfen, the reason the story was set in the Scottish moors was to make use of standing sets left over from Victor Fleming's big budget epic, *Joan of Arc* (1948), starring Ingrid Bergman, Francis L. Sullivan, and J. Carrol Naish.[3]

This illustrates how Ulmer's instincts as an improvisational, low budget director became invaluable. On an Ulmer set pragmatism and style could entwine. Peter Bogdanovich, director of such films as *Targets* (1968) and *The Last Picture Show* (1971), wrote of Ulmer in his 1997 book, *Who the Devil Made It*:

> [N]obody had ever made good pictures faster or for less money than Edgar Ulmer. What he could do with nothing (occasionally in the script department as well) remains an object lesson for those directors, myself included, who complain about tight budgets and schedules. [...] That he could communicate a strong visual style and personality with the meager means usually available to him is close to miraculous.[4]

This resourcefulness is certainly on display in *The Man from Planet X*. The location of the moors, forced upon the director due to budget constraints, ultimately functions as a visual metaphor when juxtaposed with the gleaming space age vehicle that will soon be found within its murky depths. The location serves to underscore *The Man from Planet X*'s status as a hybrid, transitional film between the pre-Space Age Gothic horrors of the Depression and the far more existential horrors of post-World War II atom bombs and mutually-assured destruction.

Gothic horror didn't emerge as a powerful force in Hollywood until 1931 with the release of *Dracula*. The genre continued to be a major box office draw until the end of the Second World War. In the 1930s and forties the classic film monsters were very much linked to the uncertainties of the economic unknowns that faced the entire world at that time, even the idle rich. The wolf was always at the door, and it was human, but it was hard to know exactly what it looked like or when or where it might erupt. During the thirties, as the vampire known as the Great Depression sucked the country dry, the main question on everyone's mind was a primal one: "What do we eat tonight?" Immediately after the atom bomb had been dropped on Hiroshima and Nagasaki, after the infrastructure of the United States had been buttressed by the economically-sound business venture known as World War II, literature, theater, and the arts in general began turning more and more toward existentialist attitudes, and the main question seemed to become: "Though we've attained all the material goods we could ever want, what does it matter when we feel spiritually hollow inside?"

It's at this point that the Brothers from Outer Space begin to descend from the skies in order to save our souls. In the early reported contacts with these ostensible beings from elsewhere, the meetings often occur in solitary areas cut off from the rest of civilization. This is true of both George Van Tassel and George Adamski, two of the earliest "alien contactees." This is true as well in man's many encounters with mystical God-figures in ancient mythology. And the same occurs in *The Man from Planet X*.

Into this eerie Gothic setting arrives our protagonist, American investigative journalist Lawrence portrayed by Robert Clarke, whose very presence in the film serves as a link to the classic horror films from a decade before, as Clarke also worked with Boris Karloff and Bela Lugosi in Robert Wise's *The Body Snatcher* (1945) and again with Karloff in Mark Robson's *Bedlam* (1946). He appeared twice more with Lugosi: in Gordon Douglas's *Zombies on Broadway* (1945) and Leslie Goodwins' *Genius at Work* (1946).

This archetype of The Outsider, specifically one leaping into The Great Unknown, follows the pattern of any number of Golden Age Gothic horror films, many of which begin with a naïve American—sometimes even a group of them—penetrating a remote, foreign world of the strange and supernatural. *Dracula* (1931), *White Zombie* (1932), *The Mummy* (1932), *King Kong* (1933), and Ulmer's own *The Black Cat* are just a few of the Depression-era horror films that fit this description.

We soon discover that Lawrence has been summoned to this isolated location, a Scottish island called Burray in the Orkneys, by his friend, Professor Elliot (Raymond Bond), an astronomer who wants to give Lawrence the chance to break what might be the biggest story of his career: the imminent arrival of a wandering planet designated X. According to Elliot, Burray will be the spot on Earth closest to Planet X during its passage. Working with the professor is a scientist named Mears (William Schallert) who has recently served time in prison for an unnamed crime.

True to form, the scientist has a beautiful daughter named Enid (Margaret Field, mother of Sally Field). While Lawrence and Enid are getting acquainted out on the moors, the first hint of strangeness occurs. They see lightning, but no thunder accompanies it. Not long afterwards comes the second level of strangeness: They stumble across a peculiar metal object that stands about three feet tall. Though it looks like it should weigh a ton, Lawrence attempts to pick it up and is surprised when he's able to lift it into the air easily. "There's nothing to it," he says with wonder in his voice. This is an intriguing moment in the film, perhaps a prescient one, as rumors of extraterrestrial objects made of lightweight metal will later become an oft-repeated detail in reports involving the fabled "Roswell Crash" of 1947. This detail doesn't appear in print, however, until 1980, with the publication of the book *The Roswell Incident* by Charles Berlitz and William L. Moore.[5]

Lawrence and Enid take this object back to Professor Elliot and Mears who study it thoroughly. The object turns out to be similar to an atmospheric probe. Mears wonders aloud about how much money could be made from back-engineering such a unique metal.

Later that night Enid drives Lawrence to his hotel in town, but while on the way back her car breaks down, necessitating a walk through the middle of the moors. The young female forced to trek through a threatening setting all by herself—even by 1951 this was a cliché in horror films. However, rather than being attacked by the Hound of the Baskervilles or a similar Gothic "bogie," Enid discovers the source of the strange light she and Lawrence had seen earlier: a large metal craft that looks somewhat like an oversized diving bell carefully lowered into the atmosphere of Earth, just as we would lower a bathyscaphe to the bottom of the ocean floor. Enid peers through one of the portholes and comes face-to-face with the Man from Planet X himself, a grayish "gnome" (as Mears calls him at one point) with slits for eyes and an oversized head encased in a cumbersome, transparent helmet. She runs home, then guides her father back to the craft. A beam erupts from the ship and hits her father in the face; it turns out the beam is some kind of hypnotic ray that renders the Professor lethargic and highly suggestible, an effect that soon wears off.

The next day, Lawrence and Professor Elliot return to the ship and experience a close encounter of the third kind. The Man from Planet X emerges from the ship and points a weapon at them. Lawrence and Elliot raise their arms in the air.

What happens next is open to interpretation: Either the Man's air supply cuts off accidentally, or the Man shuts off his air supply on purpose, potentially sacrificing his own life in order to put these Earthmen to the ultimate test, much like the Greek Gods would often descend to Earth in a helpless disguise in order to test the integrity of their mortal subjects. Will the Earthmen turn the air supply back on or will they let him die?

After only a moment's hesitation, Lawrence approaches the gasping alien and turns the lever that will replenish the Man's air supply. Lawrence and Elliot then back away and lift their arms in the air again, resuming their subservient position. The alien rises to his feet and slips his gun into his holster. He extends his arms outward in a gesture of friendship. Lawrence and Elliot attempt to communicate with the Man, but it's no use. They decide to back away slowly, then hightail it to the professor's observatory.

When Lawrence and the professor reach their destination, they're surprised to discover that the Man has followed them home. They decide to give the alien shelter, but make the mistake of leaving him alone with Mears. Mears figures out how to communicate with the alien through the universal language of mathematics. He discovers that the Man is from the wandering planet now hurtling toward Earth. Later, Mears informs Lawrence that the Man is "[E]stablishing a wireless directional beam to his planet. At midnight, when the planet is at its closest approach to Earth, an invasion will be launched. He comes from a planet that's dying. It's turning to ice. If his people do not escape from the planet before it swings back along its route through space, they will be doomed."

It's not clear, however, if the word "invasion" is Mears' interpretation of what the Man told him, or if the aliens really do intend on causing harm to the people of Earth. It seems as if the last remnants of this dying race wish to migrate to Earth merely to save themselves, not to conquer anybody.

Mears tortures the Man in order to wrest from him valuable secrets that could be used to replicate the lightweight metal out of which the alien's atmospheric probe was constructed. It's clear from his prior actions, however, that the Man would have shared these secrets willingly without having to be brutalized.

After this horrendous encounter with Mears, the Man concludes that human beings aren't quite as trustworthy as they had at first appeared. Using his portable hypnotic ray, the Man abducts Enid and Mears. Later, he also abducts Professor Elliot and dozens of random villagers. After his ray transforms them into zombified drones, the Man uses these workers to help him build a protective barrier around his ship.

Lawrence turns to the local constable (Roy Engel) for help. At first some of the villagers are suspicious of Lawrence and don't want to bother with him. Establishing another link to the Gothic horror stories of old, Professor Elliot and his associates are considered to be suspicious simply because they're engaged in scientific research. The villagers seem to equate astronomy with "bogie doin's," in the frightened words of one of the villagers. In one scene this same villager stares at a simple telescope with open disgust and fright, as if it's a tool forged by the devil. The villagers in this movie become the metafictional stand-ins for the fading audience of the traditional cinematic Gothic tale. Back in the 1930s, the blatant moral of many of the horror stories seemed to be that scientific exploration of any kind could only lead to blasphemy (or rather, that's how many of the audience members at the time *interpreted* these films). We see this theme not just in *Frankenstein* (1931) but also in *Dr. Jekyll and Mr. Hyde* (1931), *Murders in the Rue Morgue* (1932), *Doctor X* (1932), *Island of*

The
WEIRDEST
visitor
the Earth
has ever
seen!
The MAN FROM PLANET X
Sherrill Corwin presents
"The MAN from PLANET X" starring ROBERT CLARKE · MARGARET FIELD · WILLIAM SCHALLERT
Directed by Edgar G. Ulmer · Written and Produced by Aubrey Wisberg and Jack Pollexfen · Released thru United Artists

Lost Souls (1933), *The Vampire Bat* (1933), *The Invisible Man* (1933), *Bride of Frankenstein* (1935), *The Invisible Ray* (1936), *Son of Frankenstein* (1939), and *The Return of Dr. X* (1939).

In *The Man from Planet X* it seems as if the filmmakers are almost satirizing this backwards perspective, underscoring how impotent it had become by the beginning of the 1950s. Back in the 1930s, at the very least, the angry villagers would have had the pleasure of destroying the monster in the final reel; here they become the "monster's" slaves with little or no struggle, and their anti-intellectualism acts as nothing more than a brief irritant to Lawrence, our protagonist.

In the hands of Ulmer, Pollexfen and Wisberg the traditional tropes of a Gothic horror story are turned inside-out. The true scientific genius in this film is, of course, neither Professor Elliot nor Mears but the Man from Planet X himself. And this benign visitor is assassinated not by a mob of torch-bearing Balkan villagers, but by the British military. After Lawrence and the constable send a distress signal to a passing ship, Scotland Yard and the military arrive and decide to drop a bomb on the Man's ship—along with his human slaves—because they can't risk the Man signaling his native planet during its closest approach to Burray.

Lawrence manages to save the zombified workers just before the military decimates the Man and his ship. Planet X swings by at that exact moment, causing extreme winds and other earth changes as a result of its near passage.

Perhaps the most significant part of the film is the epilogue in which this exchange occurs between Lawrence and Enid....

> Enid: Is it true that no one will ever know what happened here?
> Lawrence: Knowledge would only bring more fear in a world already filled with it.
> Enid: Can such a thing be kept secret?
> Lawrence: No, but it can be reduced to gossip.

This might be the most original twist on the Gothic tale in the entire film. In the 1930s and forties even simple-minded villagers were able to handle the knowledge that they had just undergone an encounter with the supernatural, and yet—apparently—a planet full of sophisticated, post-World War II Earthmen, who have just survived the most technologically-advanced war ever waged, must be kept in the dark about the "bogie doin's" in Burray. Even at this advanced stage in their ostensible evolution, the human race is not yet ready for the implications of the Man from Planet X's existence.

Like Klaatu in *The Day the Earth Stood Still*, by the third act the Man emerges as a clear Christ figure; unlike in that far more famous film, however, in which the entire population of Earth is aware of Klaatu's demands, the Man's arrival and subsequent crucifixion are "reduced to gossip" by the machinery of the National Security State while our ostensible "hero," Lawrence, the intrepid investigative journalist, seems perfectly willing to go along with the cover-up. After all, as Lawrence himself says, "Knowledge would only bring more fear in a world already filled with it." Here the message of the story is made evident, the ultimate inversion of the traditional Gothic tale now complete: The true hero of the story is the Man who only wishes to bring knowledge to a backwards race. The villains are the humans who not only refuse to accept the knowledge that could have been theirs, but then cover up what little illumination they have attained by manipulating the free press. This subtle touch of politically-astute, ironic, dark humor is lacking in even the best science fiction films of the 1950s, most of which tend to be marred by an idealism that seems dangerously naïve by today's standards. This is one of many reasons why *The Man from Planet X* holds a far more significant position in cinematic history than is often ascribed to it.

The Christ symbolism in the film is by no means a new concept; however, its absence from the other classic science fiction films of the 1950s, with the exception of *The Day the Earth Stood Still*, is telling. Both *The Man from Planet X* and *The Day the Earth Stood Still* were no doubt in production at the same time. This couldn't be a case of one production company copying the other. Therefore, it seems as if these films were reflecting—either on purpose or through sheer happenstance—the needs of the collective unconscious at this unique moment of time at the very beginning of the 1950s, in which destructive forms of technology seemed to be growing out of control and the Cold War was just beginning to ice over... perhaps forever, it seemed, until one side inevitably decided to wipe out the other's existence. With such a stalemate in the offing, who could possibly intervene to avert certain destruction? Not the United Nations, surely. A greater power was needed, and humans looked to the sky for this new hope.

The Day the Earth Stood Still is the Old Testament template of this heavenly intervention, *The Man from Planet X* the New Testament version. In *The Day the Earth Stood Still* Klaatu arrives like a disapproving Jehovah and concludes his visit with a stern, paternal talking-to and the threat of a very bad spanking, then takes off. In *The Man from Planet X* the Man extends his hands to the first Earthmen he meets, weaponless, gives them valuable scientific knowledge, is tortured by a greedy Judas, and blown to atoms for his selfless efforts, even his decimated remains reduced to nothing more than gossip and rumor.

4. The Secret of the Saucers

KLAATU AND THE Man mirror the extraterrestrial Christ figures in the alien contactee books that emerged at around the same time. Both in cinema and the UFO literature of the early 1950s the initial "invaders" from space did not want to conquer us, but to cure our sickened souls.

The first flying saucer sightings occurred not long after the end of World War II. In June of 1947, pilot Kenneth Arnold claimed to have seen strange metal discs flying in formation above Mt Rainier in Washington State. This caused a sensation during that summer of '47, paving the way for a whole slew of saucer sightings that regularly appeared on the front pages of all the major newspapers well into the 1960s. The Saucer Craze had officially begun.

In 1950 journalist Frank Scully wrote the first UFO bestseller *Behind the Flying Saucers*, the source for the later stories of saucer crashes in New Mexico. In that same year came another UFO bestseller: *The Flying Saucers Are Real* by Major Donald E. Keyhoe, which later became the official source material for the film *Earth vs. the Flying Saucers*. In 1952 Kenneth Arnold teamed up with *Amazing Stories* editor Ray Palmer and wrote *The Coming of the Saucers* that detailed his surreal experiences following his initial saucer sightings. In that same year came *I Rode A Flying Saucer* by George Van Tassel, architect of the Integratron, a strange saucer-shaped construction built as a meeting place with the Gods From Space located in the middle of California's Joshua Tree Desert, a building that can still be visited to this very day.

Van Tassel's claims of alien contact were followed by 1953's *Flying Saucers Have Landed* by George Adamski and Desmond Leslie. With the publication of those two books, the field of UFOlogy was altered forever. The first books about UFOs offered journalistic reportage regarding the UFO phenomenon, but the authors of those books never suggested they had *interacted* with aliens personally. Van Tassel and Adamski changed all that. They were the first public "contactees" who claimed to have met with extraterrestrials in the isolated deserts of Southern California. Then the floodgates opened wide and other contactee books began appearing. In 1954 alone came Daniel Fry's *The White Sands Incident*, Truman Bethurum's *Aboard a Flying Saucer*, and George Hunt Williamson's *The Saucers Speak*. In 1955 Orfeo Angelucci arrived on the scene with his *The Secret of the Saucers*. In 1959 came Howard Menger with *From Outer Space to You*. By 1962 the High Weirdness factor of UFOlogy was suddenly amped up to eleven with the appearance of *Flying Saucers and the Three Men* by Albert K. Bender, the man who first presented the world with the now-archetypal image of The Men in Black.

What was similar about all these books is that none of the aliens wished to invade Earth. They were here either as benign forces, intending to observe the activities of the human race at a distance with little or no interference, or they were here to save us from ourselves using the contactees as their conduits, their latter-day disciples, to spread the cosmic message of truth and universal understanding.

The religious implications of these early contacts are palpable. In his 1961 book, *Flying Saucers Farewell*, his last book about UFOs, George Adamski writes:

> Many people want to know if the space people are Christians. I would say they are better Christians than we are. We have never believed in the teachings of Jesus. We have rehearsed them and that is all. We have done this in order to keep the "Christian" label and His name before the people. But this is all. Anything a man believes, he lives, and we have never lived Christ's teachings.
>
> Had we lived the teachings of Christ we would not have the pains, aches, sorrows or the threat of annihilation hanging over us today. If His teachings were applied to our everyday living, these conditions would not be present. A virtual heaven on earth would have been established.
>
> Every now and then we rehearse Christ's teachings—on Sunday, Christmas, Easter—then we go right out and forget all about them until the next time we are reminded. We have never taken hold of them to the point of living them. Now again we find the messengers are warning us.

> When I asked the "boys," [Adamski's term for his extraterrestrial acquaintances] as I stated in *Inside the Space Ships* [Adamski's second book], "If we should shoot you down or get you in the sights of our guns so we could shoot you down, would you defend yourself with the power you have?" they answered, "No. We would have to die, because we could not take advantage of our brothers who do not understand." Did not Jesus say the same thing when He was on the cross? "Father, forgive them for they know not what they do." We would have asked for revenge.[6]

Carl Jung examined this link between religion and UFOs in his last book, *Flying Saucers: A Modern Myth of Things Seen in the Sky* (1959). Jung did not use the word "myth" to indicate something that was untrue, but instead a psychological framework worthy of study if only because of what it says about the hopes and fears—the dreams and nightmares—of modern culture. Jung read many of the contactee books published in the fifties and was particularly impressed by Orfeo Angelucci's *The Secret of the Saucers*. Jung wrote:

> The psychological experience that is associated with the Ufo consists in the vision of the *rotundum*, the symbol of wholeness and the archetype that expresses itself in mandala form. Mandalas, as we know, usually appear in situations of psychic confusion and perplexity. The archetype thereby constellated represents a pattern of order which, like a psychological "view-finder" marked with a cross or circle divided into four, is superimposed on the psychic chaos so that each content falls into place and the weltering confusion is held together by the protective circle. The Eastern mandalas in Mahayana Buddhism accordingly represent the cosmic, temporal, and psychological order. At the same time they are *yantras*, instruments with whose help the order is brought into being.
>
> As our time is characterized by fragmentation, confusion, and perplexity, this fact is also expressed in the psychology of the individual [...].
>
> The Ufo vision follows the old rule and appears in the sky. Orfeo [Angelucci]'s fantasies are played out in an obviously heavenly place and his cosmic friends bear the names of stars. If they are not antique gods and heroes they are at least angels. The author certainly lives up to his name, for just as his wife, née Borgianini, is in his opinion a descendant of the Borgias of unhappy memory, so he, an earthly copy of the "angels" and a messenger bringing Eleusinian tidings of immortal-

ity, must style himself a new Orpheus, divinely appointed to initiate us into the mystery of the Ufo.[7]

It could be said that the contactee books, such as those written by Adamski and Angelucci, reflected a need in this new science-dominated age for "secular proselytizing": religious figures who were not gods, but something far more comprehensible, a higher being that might exist even in the cosmology of an atheist. The aliens featured in the films released at the very beginning of the science fiction craze, predating the earliest contactee books by a full year, descend to earth like technological angels, the intangible aura of secular mysticism encircling their humanoid bodies like halos.

With the exception of the alien in Howard Hawks and Christian Nyby's *The Thing*, our first visitors from cinematic space were by no means hostile. *The Man from Planet X*, *The Day the Earth Stood Still*, W. Lee Wilder's *The Phantom from Space* (1953), and *It Came from Outer Space* all presented us with martyred aliens oppressed and hunted by a hostile human race too ignorant to recognize a genuine savior when they saw one. With the box office success of 1953's *The War of the Worlds*, however, that pacifist outlook gave way to paranoia. It's no coincidence that 1953 was also the year President Harry S. Truman declared that the US had developed a hydrogen bomb, followed only a few months later by the counter-announcement of Prime Minister Georgi Malenkov that the Soviet Union had their *own* hydrogen bomb and were more than willing to use it. Destruction was on everyone's mind at this time, even in the field of UFOlogy. The following year marked the publication of Harold T. Wilkins' book, *Flying Saucers on the Attack*, in which the peaceful view of the Space Brothers was tarnished by endless reports of saucers shooting airliners out of the skies and setting forest fires all over the world (see, in particular, Chapter V: "The Martian Cat Among the Pigeons," pp. 69–88).

Hollywood producers must have decided that cosmic destruction meant a surefire recipe for success, since almost every single alien who visited the Earth after *The War of the Worlds* was here to burn the planet to a cinder, a trend that continued for several decades. It continued for so long, in fact, that later films from the 1970s and 1980s, ones that featured peaceful aliens such as Steven Spielberg's *Close Encounters of the Third Kind*, *E.T.*, and John Carpenter's *Starman*, seemed innovative to audiences simply because the movie-going public had been programmed by that time to *expect* hostile invaders in their science fiction films; in truth, these directors were merely retrieving the aesthetic of the earliest trend in science fiction cinema. A trend begun by *The Man from Planet X*.

5. Hollywood Haunts the World

BY THE 1980S *The Man from Planet X* had acquired the status of a rarely seen cult film. Science fiction fans had no doubt heard of the film, but few had seen it. In his 1982 encyclopedic book, *Keep Watching the Skies!: American Science Fiction Movies of the Fifties*, Bill Warren concludes his assessment of *The Man from Planet X* by saying that he regrets "its virtual inaccessibility today."[8]

That situation has changed. In 2017 the film became available on Blu-ray, courtesy of Shout! Factory. Not long ago, the film received significant scholarly attention in the anthology *Edgar G. Ulmer: Detour on Poverty Row* edited by Gary D. Rhodes (Lexington Books, 2008). In 2001 MGM released a DVD version of *The Man from Planet X* as part of their Midnight Movies series. Five years before that the film secured for itself an obscure niche in American mythology when Col. Philip J. Corso mentioned the film in his 1997 bestselling memoir, *The Day After Roswell.* Corso had an impressive military career that spanned the years of World War II, the Korean War, and beyond, including performing wartime intelligence duties for General Douglas MacArthur, as well as serving as Chief of the Pentagon's Foreign Technology Desk in Army Research and Development in the early 1960s. This solid background in the field of military intelligence made it all the more surprising when he claimed in his book that he had been involved in the back engineering of extraterrestrial technology retrieved from a UFO crash in Roswell, New Mexico. He also claimed that his military team influenced from behind the scenes the production of such films as… yes, you guessed it.

Corso writes:

> [A]s each new [UFO investigation committee] project was created and administered, another bread crumb for anyone pursuing the secrets to find, we were gradually releasing bits and pieces of information to those we knew would make something out of it. Flying saucers did truly buzz over Washington, D.C., in 1952, and there are plenty of

> photographs and radar reports to substantiate it. But we denied it while encouraging science fiction writers to make movies like *The Man from Planet X* to blow off some of the pressure concerning the truth about flying disks. This was called camouflage through limited disclosure, and it worked. If people could enjoy it as entertainment, get duly frightened, and follow trails to nowhere that the working group had planted, then they'd be less likely to stumble over what we were really doing.[9]

If either Jack Pollexfen or Aubrey Wisberg, the writers and producers of the film, operated as a witting tool of Col. Corso's military team, they certainly took the secret to their graves. Whether or not one considers these claims far-fetched or plausible, the mere fact that Corso chose *The Man from Planet X* to buttress his controversial claims does represent the rising visibility of a film that at one time had been considered just another in a long line of cheesy programmers from the early fifties.

Whether Corso was telling the truth or not, certainly the UFO reports of the late forties did indeed influence the making of the film. When Jack Pollexfen and Aubrey Wisberg began writing their screenplay for *The Man from Planet X*, they had no doubt seen the flying saucer stories that had been appearing in newspapers since Kenneth Arnold's sighting in 1947. In the early 1950s it was impossible *not* to have seen them. A quick glance through the microfilm archives of the major newspapers at that time will reveal that almost every newspaper in the late forties and early fifties printed UFO stories on their front pages nearly every day.

Flying saucers were everywhere. Not only did they sell newspapers, but serious-minded people were concerned about them. Having read through several newspaper articles published at that time, it becomes clear that the consensus opinion among the general public seemed to be that flying saucers were unquestionably real and being piloted by Russians. In fact, that's the idea of the very first flying saucer film—which is *not* science fiction, by the way—titled, simply, *The Flying Saucer* (1950). However, many of the writers and directors who were responsible for the earliest science fiction films had a genuine interest in the subject matter of UFOs beyond being a convenient source for money-making ideas. Robert Wise, director of *The Day the Earth Stood Still*, went on record several times stating that he genuinely believed in flying saucers and extraterrestrial visitations and did so even before he was asked to direct the film in 1950. Ray Harryhausen, the guiding force behind *Earth vs. the Flying Saucers*, also stated on many occasions that he had an intense interest in the UFO phenomena. According to Burl Lampert, an actor who collaborated closely with Jack Pollexfen during the last seven years of his life, Pollexfen was very skeptical of UFOs, and indeed was skeptical about most subjects that hinted at the mystical in any way.[10] Nonetheless, whether skeptical or not, it's clear that Pollexfen and his co-writer were well-versed in the UFO lore that had been published up to that point.

Certainly they must have read Frank Scully's *Behind the Flying Saucers* and Donald E. Keyhoe's *The Flying Saucers Are Real.* The first two chapters of Scully's book are infamous, as they mark the first time that reports surfaced in print regarding what would later be known as The Roswell Crash. Scully claimed that an inside military source had given him information regarding several saucers that had crashed in the desert near Aztec, New Mexico in 1948. The military had retrieved the saucers as well as the tiny corpses that were inside. The source even claimed that three of the bodies were still alive when they pulled them out of the wreckage.[11]

Whether Scully was given accurate information, false information, or fabricated the whole story is not known; however, the book created quite an impact upon its first publication, though it seemed to have nothing but a negative effect on the author's journalistic career after the initial flurry died down, particularly when *San Francisco Chronicle* reporter J.P. Cahn published a major article in a 1952 issue of *True Magazine* that called into question the validity of Scully's anonymous sources.

But Scully's story never really died. It has morphed slightly and expanded over the years thanks to Scully's posthumous collaborators, and is now the subject of several books by authors who may never have read Scully's original book or even heard of it; nonetheless, what began as mere filler for Scully's *Variety* gossip column in 1950 has since taken on a life of its own and entered the rarified realm of modern mythology, a mythology that began to be built upon and exploited the second the story appeared. For example, fans of EC comics will recognize Scully as the basis of the character Frank E. Keely in "Flying Saucer Report," the lead story in *Weird-Science Fantasy* #25. All of Scully's information about the crashed saucers in the Southwest appears in this 1954 story illustrated by the famous comic book artist Wally Wood. It must have been quite a hit with the readers, as it influenced the contents of the next issue. *Weird Science-Fantasy* #26 was dedicated entirely to a documentary-style report that summarized all the major UFO sightings up to that point, complete with footnotes. Scully's work is clearly the source material for much of this issue as well.

Not only did Scully inspire a character in an obscure comic book back in 1954, but in the 1990s he also became the basis of the character Dana Scully in Chris Carter's long-running TV series, *The X-Files*. Before all of that, however, it's clear that Scully's presence can be felt in the script for *The Man from Planet X*. For example, it's very likely that the design for the alien in *The Man from Planet X* was based on the descriptions of the captured aliens in Scully's book. Like the aliens in *Behind the Flying Saucers*, the Man from Planet X is diminutive. Scully writes:

> Three of the four [crashed saucers], [Scientist X] added, had been captured and had been inspected by men with whom he was currently identified in geophysical research. Thirty-four men, measuring between thirty-six inches to forty inches in height had been found dead in three of the saucers discovered.[12]

Keep in mind that this was at a time when the *de facto* image of an alien had not yet been nailed down in popular consciousness. In the late 1940s and early fifties no one had any preconceived notions as to what an alien was "supposed" to look like. Would they be bigger versions of us? Smaller versions? Something entirely different from a biped? Would they even be carbon-based life forms? Reading through the vast array of UFO literature published in the early 1950s, what immediately strikes one is the fact that people reported encounters with alien beings that ran the gamut of possible life forms. With straight faces, people reported contacts with hairy giants, gnomes the size of your fist, cyclopean robots that hovered in midair, beautiful women with golden tresses, creatures that resembled giant owls, and on and on and on. By the 1980s, the vast majority of UFO literature coalesces into a single icon: the gray alien, the type made famous by the cover of Whitley Strieber's 1987 bestselling memoir, *Communion*.

Hollywood haunts the world. In the ancient days druids used to gather in secret groves to cast spells with wands they thought were capable of casting magic spells—illusions. The wands were made out of a special type of wood: Holly. Hollywood. Therefore, it makes sense that the modern day druids, filmmakers, should choose "Hollywood" as the name of their own special little grove where they cast spells on the rest of the world.[13]

More often than not, Hollywood locks down our visual image of archetypes. When we think of a vampire, we generally think of Bela Lugosi (or perhaps Robert Pattinson these days). And when we think of an alien, we generally think of a small gray man with an oversized head. This expectation is based on an incessant flood of images seen in commercials, children's toys, music videos, comic books, coloring books, and films. *The Man from Planet X* was the first movie to depict an alien that fits that exact image, an image now forever intertwined with our concept of what to expect from an alien. The fact that the extraterrestrials in Scully's book and the title character in *The Man from Planet X* share the same basic physical characteristics, therefore, is not necessarily a mere coincidence. The filmmakers went out of their way to find an actor who was both diminutive as well as capable of moving in slow-motion, as if his body was not used to dealing with the gravity of Earth. According to Pollexfen, the alien was played by a vaudevillian who "did a slow-motion act that combined dance and acrobatics. And he was quite small [...]. I don't remember his name."[14]

Imaginative but economical touches like these help add a certain amount of realism to the outlandish scenario and lifts *The Man from Planet X* above its low budget origins. In *Keep Watching the Skies!,* Bill Warren writes:

> Obviously, *The Man from Planet X* was one of the things [Edgar] Ulmer did for money's sake. But his integrity and artistic goals resulted in the first science fiction gothic horror film, probably the only one until *Alien* (1979). The picture is very graceful and flowing, maintaining a good pace [...].
>
> The alien, played by an unidentified midget actor (possibly Billy Curtis), is of an unusual though anthropomorphic design. His face is described in the script as being distorted by pressure. It somewhat resembles a ritual mask from some primitive tribe. In actuality, of course, it *is* a mask, but is more convincing than most, despite being totally immobile; the believability is created by lighting and camera angles.
>
> The alien also has a distinctive character. He means no harm to Earth people at first, and even bravely puts his life into their hands deliberately by turning off his air supply. (He's accompanied by the loud hissing of the gas wherever he goes.) Only the intercession of a

> greedy villain causes the Man from Planet X to turn hostile, and even then the alien's primary motivation seems to be to protect himself. There's little justification in the script for Lawrence's conclusion that the alien is building an army to conquer the world. To the viewer, the Man simply seems to be digging in for self-preservation. The writers, Aubrey Wisberg and Jack Pollexfen (who were also the producers), apparently thought that simply having come from outer space was enough reason for the alien to be killed. But even more than the aliens in *It Came from Outer Space*, this alien seems more sinned against than sinning [...]
>
> Thanks to Ulmer's atmospheric direction and his unusually intelligent and sympathetic attitude toward the alien (not present in the script), *The Man from Planet X* was one of the best of the low budget independent SF films of the 1950s [...].[15]

It could be that Warren has underestimated the screenwriters here, particularly Pollexfen. But before we address that point, something should be said about Aubrey Wisberg, Pollexfen's co-author. According to Burl Lampert, Wisberg's function was not to work on the script at the idea-stage; therefore, he did not come up with the initial concepts for *The Man from Planet X*. Wisberg mainly polished Pollexfen's dialogue after the first draft of the script had already been completed. Pollexfen himself has said, "Normally I would write the first draft of the script; Aubrey would *enhance* the dialogue. Another of the reasons we split [i.e., stopped working together]."[16]

The entire theme of the film, clearly, is the fact that human beings are far less trusting, far more prone to paranoia and hysteria, far less "human" than the Man from Planet X. The theme is encapsulated in the title itself. A far more commercial title could have been slapped on this film. It could have been called *The Thing from Planet X*, or *It Came from Planet X*, or *The Creature from Planet X*. Instead it's called *The MAN from Planet X*. The sympathies of the screenwriters are with the Man, not with the humans who perceive the Man as something less than human. *The Man from Planet X* does not have a happy ending. It's a tragedy in which the title character, the true hero of the film, is destroyed in the last act by a pack of domesticated primates who have misinterpreted his actions. The screenwriters hint at this at the end when Enid says to Lawrence, "You know, I think that creature was friendly. I wonder what would have happened if Dr Mears *hadn't* attacked him."

During his interview with Jack Pollexfen for his 1988 book *Interviews with B Science Fiction and Horror Movie Makers*, Tom Weaver addresses this error in Warren's assessment:

> WEAVER: A recent book on sci-fi films insists that the most intriguing part of the story—depicting X as a harmless visitor and certain Earthmen as heavies—was *not* written into the screenplay and therefore must have been introduced into the story by director Edgar Ulmer.
>
> POLLEXFEN: *Wrong*. Making the Earthlings—or some of them—the heavies was a key part of the script from the first. Oddly enough, the idea has been seldom copied.[17]

Given the preponderance of "alien invader" movies in cinematic science fiction, Pollexfen is justified in saying that the idea has been "seldom copied." Pollexfen is, of course, referring to the genre of science fiction as it exists in *film*, not as it exists in literature. According to Burl Lampert, Pollexfen was never particularly interested in literary science fiction aside from Jules Verne. His major influences were classic adventure writers such as Frederick Maryat whose 1836 semi-autobiographical novel, *The Adventures of Mr. Midshipman Easy*, set during the Napoleonic Wars, was Pollexfen's favorite.[18] This is another reason to believe that Pollexfen was more influenced by the prominent saucer stories in the newspapers at that time than by any prior literary description of aliens.

According to Lampert:

> Jack told me once that *The Man from Planet X* came to mind as he was at a cocktail party in 1949 or 1950, and the topic de jour was flying saucers, and was there life on Mars? Now Jack listened to all the theories, and when they came to him for comment, he just sort of snorted something noncommittal, but was thinking "…Idiots!"
>
> He thought, and I agreed, that space men were Jesus was Zeus was Grunt. All bullshit. But Jack being Jack, filmdom's quietest pragmatist, wondered how to turn that night's party talk into next quarter's highest-earning second feature. Jack's movie inspirations were always what would bring in the most for the least. But he didn't really press this talent—it just happened […].

> But innovation, however inadvertent, happened to him a lot—he created the little space man as a benevolent visitor from the unknown—now, is that Jack or what? Not an invader, but a neighbor, praising our lawn.
>
> Jack was proudest, however, that he made *The Man from Planet X* in nine days for $41,000… and that it was good.[19]

Given this insider's view of Pollexfen, I think we can conclude that Jack Pollexfen was, as a man, a pragmatist, but as an artist he was an inspired amanuensis dictating the collective hopes and anxieties of his generation in the form of a low budget Gothic horror film cloaked in the vestments of a secular religion for a New Dark Age.

Chapter 6

Golden the Film Was—Oh! Oh! Oh!

Cinema and the Art of Perception Management

1. Shaping the Direction

THE PREVIOUS CHAPTER first appeared in the October 2010 edition of David Hartwell's *The New York Review of Science Fiction*. Upon the article's publication, I assumed I had exhausted everything I wanted to say regarding the subject of Edgar Ulmer's *The Man from Planet X* and its connections to the enigmatic world of UFOlogy.

Over the years, I've heard *The Man from Planet X* brought up from time to time by both cinema historians and UFOlogists. The former generally scoff at the notion that the film could have received covert support from the US government; on the other hand, the latter seem to buy the notion with little critical thinking at all. Both attitudes seem inadequate. It might be beneficial to dig a bit deeper into the precise ways that cinema can be used as a tool of consciousness alteration on a mass scale. *The Man from Planet X* will be the rabbit hole through which we enter this shadowy realm, but by no means is it the only film under discussion in this chapter.

Here's the main question: Could a Hollywood production be influenced by outside sources without the creative talent being aware of such an influence? For the answer, we need not refer to some conspiratorial tome filled with quasi-rumors and urban myths, but instead to a recent memoir written by a successful writer/producer who was called "one of the hottest screenwriters in Hollywood" by the *Los Angeles Review of Books* as recently as 2019. In that same year said screenwriter, J. Michael Straczynski, published a harrowing memoir titled *Becoming Superman: My Journey from Poverty to Hollywood.* In Chapter 26, Straczynski describes how his science fiction television show, *Babylon 5*, was ripped off by Paramount Pictures and transmogrified into a *Star Trek* spin-off called *Deep Space Nine*.

It's worth pausing here for a moment and mentioning that *Star Trek*—no stranger to incorporating into its storylines UFOlogical details inspired by eyewitness accounts—was created by the late Gene Roddenberry, who was a veteran of the United States Army Air Corp and also served as the speech writer for the LAPD's Chief William Parker during the 1950s. According to Bruce Rux, author of *Hollywood vs. the Aliens: The Motion Picture Industry's Participation in UFO Disinformation*, "[S]ome of his associates all at various times confirmed that Roddenberry was not only in the department, but was actually Chief William Parker's personal protégé for police chief, beginning with Parker's making him the LAPD official historian."[1] Rux also notes that "the LAPD was a notoriously corrupt bureaucracy" under Chief Parker's reign. Rux elaborates further:

> Five-year intelligence officer for the LAPD, Mike Rothmiller, wrote a 1992 best-seller called *L.A. Secret Police: Inside the LAPD Elite Spy Network*, documenting that since 1959's dictatorial and ambitious Chief Parker (he wanted J. Edgar Hoover's job), there was a secret and nearly omnipotent spy network within the police, "operating like the KGB, blessed with power." This same Chief Parker was [...] Roddenberry's personal mentor [...].[2]

According to his biographer, David Alexander, Roddenberry was surprised when Chief Parker revealed to him that he had been exploiting his privileged position as Police Chief with the express intention of introducing the young man to Hollywood producers with the hopes that the right connections at the right time would help launch Roddenberry's professional screenwriting career. Chief Parker clearly had high hopes for Roddenberry's writing talents.[3] The question is: Why?

Roddenberry probably had no problems transitioning from LAPD bureaucrat to Hollywood producer, as a Machiavellian talent for deception and betrayal can be helpful in both walks of life, as evidenced by the following tale related by Straczynski in his aforementioned memoir. Though Roddenberry himself was dead by the time *Deep Space Nine* debuted, it's certainly fair to note the irony underlying a scenario in which a popular science fiction parable that espouses utopian hopes for a one world future should stoop to the level of outright thievery in its day-to-day business dealings. One wonders what Roddenberry would have thought of the following scenario….

During the late 1980s and early 1990s, Straczynski spent nearly five years pitching his concept for *Babylon 5*

> to every network, studio, and production company in town, only to be told there was no room for a space-based science fiction series other than *Star Trek*. We even pitched the show to Paramount, which was still producing *Star Trek: The Next Generation*, giving them the pilot script series bible, and concept art. This led to a flurry of phone calls intimating that a deal was possible. Then the studio abruptly went radio silent and the door closed.[4]

Despite this, Straczynski persisted and the *Babylon 5* pilot was greenlit by the Prime Time Entertainment Network (PTEN), a division of Warner Bros. In November of 1991, the show was officially announced. Soon afterwards, the plug was almost pulled on the production when Paramount announced a *Star Trek* spin-off called *Deep Space Nine*. Quoting Straczynski:

> For thirty years, the various *Star Trek* series had been set aboard starships. That's the textbook definition of a trek, a journey from *here* to *there*. By contrast, the *Babylon 5* pilot was about an Earth-sponsored space station, identified by a name and a number, located in neutral territory, that served as a meeting place for alien races and diplomats, with a bar, a casino, a female second-in-charge, and a shape-changer […].[5]

Straczynski soon learned from veteran *Star Trek* actor Walter Koenig that the plot of *Deep Space Nine* involved:

> an Earth-sponsored space station, identified by a name and a number, located in neutral territory, that served as a meeting place for alien races and diplomats, with a bar, a casino, a female second-in-charge, and a shape-changer […].

> During the five years spent pitching *Babylon 5* we'd given Paramount all of our development material. This led to several discussions with the executives that seemed to be going in a positive direction when suddenly they went radio silent. It never occurred to us that someone inside Paramount might have looked at that material and thought, *Hmmm... a companion series to* Next Gen *about a space station, that's a great idea. But why do we need* these *guys?* [...]
>
> In the years since *Babylon 5* went on the air, science fiction fans have debated whether or not Paramount ripped off our show to create *Deep Space Nine*. My belief at the time was that the studio co-opted the material we gave them only *after* they knew we were going into production in order to kneecap PTEN in favor of their own new network. I also accept [...] that the *Star Trek* producers were blameless. But studio executives higher up the food chain can easily shape the direction of a show without explicitly telling the producers the source of their suggestions. *Hey, listen, guys, we really like your idea for a new* Trek *series, but instead of doing another starship show or something on a colony, let's think outside the box... how about a space station, you know, a port of call, with a casino, cargo ships, lots of different alien races coming through... a* Casablanca in Space *kind of thing. Give it some thought, roll it around for a while, and let's discuss it next week.*[6]

In 2013, Steven Hopsaken, the "marketing specialist who had worked as a copywriter and editor for Dick Robertson's Warner Bros. International Television Distribution from 1993 to 1994, the years that marked the birth of *B5* and *DS9*," admitted, in a statement that first appeared on the website io9.com, that Paramount "purposely took what they liked from the *B5* script and put it into the *DS9* script. In fact, there was talk of leaving the *B5* script intact and just setting it in the *Star Trek* universe. I had to keep rewriting press release drafts while they were trying to make the final decision."[7]

Straczynski wraps up his story with the following statement: "[I]n the end, only the top studio brass on either side of the contretemps really know the truth of what happened, and they ain't talking."[8]

2. A Revolving Door

WHAT DOES THIS have to do with *The Man from Planet X* and UFOs?

As stated in the previous chapter, there are many elements in *The*

Man from Planet X that presage certain core elements of the modern UFO field.

There are at least two conclusions one could draw from these telltale connections, one far more outré than the other: 1) Ulmer's film directly inspired what would later become staple elements of a modern fairy tale built upon decades of lies and shared delusions, or 2) the people who made *The Man from Planet X* were somehow privy to top secret information derived from a high level government cover-up of UFOs.

At this point skeptics would no doubt invoke Occam's Razor, the principle that the simplest solution is generally the most reasonable. On the surface, the average person might assume that the former conclusion is indeed the simplest; however, the fact that it requires dismissing decades of eyewitness UFO accounts—including testimonies from thousands of reliable, trained observers—might render this conclusion somewhat problematic. Another common mistake, when dealing with any aspect of UFOlogy, is the false dichotomy of limited choices, a fallacy committed by film historian Tom Weaver during his audio commentary on the 2017 Shout! Factory Blu-ray release of *The Man from Planet X*. Weaver begins his commentary by stating:

> Jack Pollexfen and Aubrey Wisberg: the men who wrote and produced *The Man from Planet X*. Did they make it at the behest of the government? We find that implication in the 1997 bestseller *The Day After Roswell* by Col. Philip J. Corso who, after decades of military service, wrote that book in which he claimed to have stewarded the Roswell alien artifacts [...]. [In regards] to Col. Corso's claims that *The Man from Planet X* was made with the encouragement of flying saucer "cover-uppers"... is it true? Well, in order to believe that Corso was telling the truth about that, you'd first have to accept that there really was a "Roswell Incident" and alien artifacts. I think *The Man from Planet X* was made for a much more mundane reason: to make a buck off the back of another movie. [The movie Weaver is referring to is Christian Nyby's *The Thing from Another World*, which was produced by Howard Hawks for RKO Pictures and released only a week after *The Man from Planet X*.] Howard Hawks was a major producer/director, he was making the first man-from-space movie, it was being made by a major studio. *The Thing* must have had potential written all over it. And, sure enough, Wisberg and Pollexfen bing-bang-boomed *The Man from Planet X* together, started and even finished it while *The Thing* was

> still shooting. In fact, within days of *The Thing* finally wrapping in March 1951, the Paramount Theater employees in San Francisco were standing outside the theater dressed as The Man from Planet X as [*The Thing*] began playing there.[9]

It's undoubtedly true that Pollexfen and Wisberg were trying to make quick cash off *The Man from Planet X* by beating *The Thing from Another World* into theaters. The likelihood of this statement does not, however, cancel out the possibility that the production was "encouraged" by certain elements in the US government for the purpose of perception management, exactly as Corso claimed in his memoir. Ironically, Weaver appears not to be aware of the fact that *The Thing from Another World* itself has been a subject of debate for years among certain UFOlogists due to the film's many striking parallels with the events of the alleged Roswell Crash of 1947, as reported by so many eyewitnesses over the decades. These parallels were first noted by author Bruce Rux in Chapter Two of his 1996 book, *Architects of the Underworld*, as well as in Chapter One of his 1997 book, *Hollywood vs. the Aliens*. (For a comprehensive analysis of these parallels, I refer the interested reader to the latter book.)

In *Hollywood vs. the Aliens*, Rux comments on the possible behind-the-scenes influences on *The Thing*'s production:

> RKO, as a subsidiary of Time-Life, was directly connected to the CIA—which should be no surprise, since RKO was owned by billionaire industrialist/aeronautic engineer Howard Hughes, whose very name was synonymous with government interests. Many other studios and directors who made low budget science fiction pictures, especially those dealing with flying saucers, were similarly connected to the CIA and other agencies. In 1957, Hughes sold RKO, at which time Metro Goldwyn Mayer bought its last flying saucer film, made in Japan with Toho: *The Mysterians*. MGM has turned out more UFOlogical movies than any other studio except United Artists, and (as if to emphasize the point) MGM and United Artists fused into a single corporate entity in 1980. Many of the people involved behind the scenes in the production of those movies, at the highest level—including one of the most prominent CIA figures in mind control, William Joseph Bryan, Jr.—are to be found working on the same projects at other studios, such as the next most prominent on the UFOlogical list, American International Pictures... which, as Orion Pictures Corpora-

> tion, is presently being taken over by MGM/UA. Such a surfeit of bad flying saucer movies [...] would be produced in ensuing years, from these and other studios, that they would become first a laughingstock and ultimately a nostalgic institution, which was precisely what they were intended to be from the outset. A psychological strategy was employed to deflect public attention from the subject by ridicule, that both then and now has been perhaps the most successful counterintelligence program ever undertaken.[10]

In Chapter Three of his 2015 book, *Silver Screen Saucers: Sorting Fact from Fantasy in Hollywood's UFO Movies*, author Robbie Graham also notes the parallels between *The Thing from Another World* and real life events, then quotes filmmaker Paul Davids' opinion on this issue:

> The parallels between *The Thing from Another World* and the Roswell incident have not gone unnoticed [...] in Hollywood. Filmmaker Paul Davids, who wrote and produced the popular TV movie *Roswell* (1994), starring Kyle MacLachlan and Martin Sheen, notes:
>
> "*The Thing* was the story of a flying saucer crash... all the themes of the Roswell Incident were there. The military covered it up. A newsman pleaded for disclosure. There was buried saucer wreckage. There was an alien body (that turned out to be still alive). There was secrecy. And, in the movie, there was danger."
>
> Davids wondered if the purpose of *The Thing* may have been to take a factual and highly sensitive event and to couch it in fiction, the goal being to ridicule the idea of saucer crashes by associating them with superficially outlandish sci-fi cinema, and/or to subtly drip-feed these realities into the popular consciousness. Hawks' movie was based on a science fiction story called *Who Goes There?* by John W. Campbell Jr., "But there are thousands of science-fiction stories," says Davids, "and only a small fraction of them are produced as films. Was it a coincidence that a great producer put this tale to film just three years after [the Roswell incident]?"[11]

For decades, well before the publication of Corso's book, UFOlogists have discussed the possibility that the mass perception of the UFO phenomenon was being subtly managed from behind the scenes through science fiction films, particularly those that deal with the subject of UFOs. If true, it's natural to assume that this perception management began with *The Man from Planet X*, the first film that revolved around an all-out invasion from outer space. Had Corso heard these rumors, inspiring him—or his co-author, William J. Birnes—to mention *The Man from Planet X* in *The Day After Roswell* for the sake of verisimilitude? Perhaps. We can't dismiss such a possibility. But for the moment, let's take Corso's claims at face value and follow through on this "perception management" scenario in a deeper way.

In my 2015 nonfiction book, *Chameleo: A Strange But True Story of Invisible Spies, Heroin Addiction, and Homeland Security*, scientist Richard Schowengerdt, who possessed top-secret clearance for decades, told me:

> It's possible for [the government] to keep a deep, dark secret, and they do. However, sometimes they *want* to leak it out. They want a controlled leak. And I firmly believe that the UFO phenomenon has been leaked out in a very controlled manner since about the 1950s and '60s. They started releasing to the media the ideas of the Roswell findings, and I really believe that much of this has been stimulated by leaks from the government. And that it was deliberate. The reason I say that is because there's just too many coincidences and too many connections, and a lot of executives from the CIA, for example, have moved back and forth into the movie industry. It's like a revolving door between the CIA and the movie industry, and the media, the national media. And the whole idea behind it is that it's a form of conditioning and control, that if you condition the people that this is the way it's gonna be, then when it finally comes, they're not going to be shocked out of their mind, you know. And I think it's worked pretty well, because right now, I think, if we saw UFOs and they really did land, we wouldn't go into panic like we would have back in the '30s, when Orson Welles came out with his thing. I think today that people would be a lot more mature about it, because I've heard the polls say that seventy percent or more of people believe in UFOs, and so if they did appear, and with all the movies we've had and all the conditioning, I think that it wouldn't be a great shock. There would be some people maybe that would commit suicide. I think there'd be some people who would go bananas. But they would be some of the less stable people in society. Yes, I think the military can keep a deep, dark secret, and I think they have done that to a degree with Roswell. But they've also leaked it out, which is kind of a paradox.[12]

If Schowengerdt is right, and the American film industry has been conditioned and controlled for at least seventy years, how does such

HOW DID IT GET HERE ?
WINCHESTER PICTURES CORPORATION
Presents
HOWARD HAWKS'
Astounding MOVIE
THE THING
from another world !
Directed by CHRISTIAN NYBY
Producer—HOWARD HAWKS
Associate Producer—EDWARD LASKER
Screen Play by CHARLES LEDERER

he's got the world in an
UPROAR!
The UNFORGETTABLE CAST... of
"A GREAT NEW CARTOON MOVIE!"
"IT'S TERRIFIC!" - WALTER WINCHELL
LOUIS DE ROCHEMONT'S
ANIMAL FARM
Color by TECHNICOLOR
Based on GEORGE ORWELL'S Brilliant Best-Seller
Produced by Halas & Batchelor
"YOU'LL HAVE THE LAUGHS OF YOUR LIFE!"

conditioning and control take place? How exactly does the military-industrial-entertainment complex *operate*?

Few cinema goers ever even think about such hidden influences when they pay money to see the latest blockbuster. Those who do think about it, like the dedicated/obsessed UFOlogists I mentioned earlier, no doubt assume that this process happens in a strictly Orwellian fashion—that the idea for a propagandistic film is generated by members of an unnamed US intelligence agency, then pushed into production, financed, and promoted by said agency. In fact, it can be proven that some films came about in precisely this manner. Perhaps one of the most documented cases is the subject of its own book, Daniel J. Leab's *Orwell Subverted: The CIA and the Filming of Animal Farm*, published by Pennsylvania State University Press in 2007.

According to Leab:

> More than five years intervened between the idea of a movie version of *Animal Farm* and its 1954 theatrical premiere. During those years the CIA, and the "dirty tricks" division within the agency responsible for initiating the project, changed dramatically. In part these changes resulted from what an analyst has described as America's "ever-grimmer" responses to the escalating Cold War, and from a restructuring of the agency during the Truman administration, which established it.
>
> The government personnel directly involved in making Orwell's book into a movie remained constant, but the bureaucrats directing the agency changed, as did the approach to the kind of covert action that financing a movie entailed. However, the Truman and, after January 1953, the Eisenhower administrations remained committed to psychological warfare underlying the production of such propaganda, even if the "psywar" decision makers changed [...].
>
> Covert action (ranging from paramilitary efforts to propagating misinformation) was placed in the hands of a newly created Office of Special Projects, quickly renamed the Office of Policy Coordination (OPC), an "anodyne name" for what became a powerful policy instrument that in the late 1940s "was almost as secret as the Manhattan Project had been while producing the atomic bomb."
>
> OPC, a hot potato if ever there was one, was lodged in the CIA "but as a completely separate entity." The CIA supported it logistically with "quarters and rations" but formally and practically had little say over it. The secretary of state selected OPC's head. Policy guidelines for OPC were laid down by a special "10/2 Panel" of representatives

> from Defense and State; any policy conflicts were "mediated" by the NSC. The chain of command did not include the CIA's director, but, while wearing a hat as director of central intelligence, that person received reports of OPC's activities [...].
>
> [Frank] Wisner [who committed suicide in 1965] and his OPC associates recruited for the psywar workshop from what a later CIA administrator characterized as "our inner circle of people," which meant, as a policy wonk subsequently explained, that they had begun their careers in many of the same places. As a Yale professor later put it, this cohort was "heavy with Ivy League, Virginia, Wisconsin, and Chicago" and "elitist by educational background." A number of these people played key roles in the production of the movie version of *Animal Farm.*[13]

This represents a more direct involvement with the film industry on the part of the intelligence world. It's unlikely that this approach would be taken with films such as *The Man from Planet X*. It would be costly and counterproductive to go about a mass program of perception management in such an obvious manner. Yes, certain key projects (like the above mentioned adaptation of *Animal Farm*, which was shown to high schools all around the country, including my own, even decades after its initial release) would receive undeniable, documented, direct involvement from the military-industrial complex. Other projects, more than likely, would be nudged into production in far less direct ways.

If Philip Corso was not lying, if his "working group" did indeed influence the creation of *The Man from Planet X*, then wouldn't Jack Pollexfen and Aubrey Wisberg have been aware of this fact? The answer: No, not necessarily.

How many UFO-themed screenplays were floating around Hollywood in the early 1950s? Obviously, not that many. The science fiction trend had not yet taken off. Indeed, it was only because of the success of *The Man from Planet X* and *The Thing from Another World* that other producers began jumping on the science fiction bandwagon. Keep in mind that having agents embedded within the Hollywood dream machine—making sure that diligent, trained eyes were permanently on the ground in the film capital of the world—is a practice the intelligence community had been following since the beginning of the Cold War. Once again quoting Robbie Graham:

> Letters penned in 1953 by an executive at Paramount Studios provide stunning insight into just how deeply the Agency was able to penetrate the film industry in the early days of the Cold War. The letters are significant for their revelation that the movie executive in question, Luigi Luraschi, was simultaneously a CIA asset reporting to the government's Psychological Strategy Board (PSB). His identity was not discovered until five decades after the fact by British academic David Eldridge. In letters to his CIA handler, Luraschi described how he had secured the agreement of several Hollywood casting directors to subtly plant "well dressed negroes" into films, including "a dignified negro butler" who has lines "indicating he is a free man" in *Sangaree* (1953), and in a golf club scene in the Dean Martin/Jerry Lewis vehicle *The Caddy* (1953). Luraschi also arranged for the removal of key scenes from the film *Arrowhead* (1953), which questioned America's treatment of Apache Indians, including a sequence where a tribe is forcibly shipped and tagged by the US Army. Such changes were not part of a ham-fisted campaign to instill what we now call "political correctness" in the populace. Rather, they were specifically enacted to hamper the Soviets' ability to exploit the United States' poor record in race relations and served to create a peculiarly anodyne impression of America, which was, at that time, still mired in an era of racial segregation.[14]

It's important to note as well the other verifiable connections between Paramount and Universal Studios and the military at this time. According to award-winning journalist David L. Robb, author of the 2004 book *Operation Hollywood: How the Pentagon Shapes and Censors the Movies*:

> [John] Horton, a major in the army during World War II, [went] to work as a location manager for Warner Bros. after the war. In 1948, he was recalled to active duty as a lieutenant colonel and was named chief of the army's motion picture department, where in 1949 he helped write the Department of Defense's original policy for providing assistance to commercial filmmakers. He left the army the next year and went back into the movie business, serving as Universal Pictures' representative in Washington, DC, and then as a producer at Universal and Paramount Pictures.[15]

Later, Horton "started his own consulting firm, specializing in coordinating cooperation between Hollywood and the military." According to Robb, Horton spent the next four decades helping "hundreds of producers navigate the Pentagon's maze of regulations" he created in the first place.[16] This is a classic example of what's referred to by a certain breed of social engineers as the "Hegelian Dialectic." Step One: You create the problem. Step Two: You offer the solution to a crisis that never would have existed without your initial meddling. Using this strategic advantage, Horton was able to steer numerous pro-military propaganda films from the initial planning stages to the big screen, including that infamous 110-minute Navy recruitment commercial titled *Top Gun*, starring Tom Cruise and Val Kilmer, a commercial hit that grossed $356m in 1986. In his June 12, 2006 *Los Angeles Times* obituary, Horton is quoted as saying that *Top Gun* was "one of the most personally satisfying projects" in which he was ever involved.[17] This begs the question: What other perception management projects was Horton involved in behind the scenes while working at Universal and Paramount during the 1950s? Perhaps it's just a coincidence that Universal and Paramount produced a bumper crop of extraterrestrial-themed films at this same time, including *It Came from Outer Space* (1953), *The War of the Worlds* (1953), *This Island Earth* (1955), *Conquest of Space* (1955), *The Monolith Monsters* (1957), *The Blob* (1958), *I Married a Monster from Outer Space* (1958), and *The Space Children* (1958).

3. The Right Money Being Placed in the Correct Hands

GIVEN THE INTELLIGENCE community's strategic presence in Hollywood at the beginning of the 1950s, it would have been relatively easy to locate those few unsold science fiction screenplays that would serve as ideal vehicles for pushing forward the desired agenda of UFO information/disinformation dissemination. Once these scripts had been found, then it would be a simple matter of encouraging an investor—in the case of *The Man from Planet X* that would have been independent exhibitor Sherrill C. Corwin and United Artists—to distribute the project. Conveniently, Pollexfen and Wisberg need never know of this help from outside sources.

Referring once again to Bruce Rux's *Hollywood vs. the Aliens*:

> Ex-CIA Assistant to the Deputy Director, Victor Marchetti, and for-

mer State Department official John D. Marks document in their groundbreaking exposé of the Agency, *The CIA and the Cult of Intelligence*, that "As part of their formal clandestine training at 'The Farm' [the CIA's Williamsburg, Virginia, training facility]... CTs [Career Trainees] are regularly shown Hollywood spy movies, and after the performance they collectively criticize the techniques used in the films," strongly implying that Agency personnel are indeed behind the making of many of those very spy movies. They quote a former clandestine operator whose April 1967 testimony in *Ramparts* helps strengthens the idea: "We were shown Agency-produced films depicting the CIA in action, films which displayed a kind of Hollywood flair for the dramatic that is not uncommon inside the Agency."

In light of these facts, it is most interesting what [UFO researcher] Jenny Randles was told by a high-ranking establishment figure at the House of Commons bar, after "a talk to a gaggle of Lords, Barons and MPs" on the subject of UFOs, days before Rendlesham Forest ["Rendlesham Forest" refers to a series of dramatic UFO sightings that occurred at a US Air Force base in England in December of 1980]. Though he was credible, "a source in the House of Lords," she didn't believe what he had to say at the time, treating it as a joke. He had claimed, perfectly seriously, that there was an "educational program" afoot at the official government level to gradually release the truth about UFOs—that the world had to be prepared, which necessarily took some time. He claimed that films like Steven Spielberg's *Close Encounters of the Third Kind* were part of that program, "financed by the right money being placed in the correct hands at the appropriate time."[18]

From a "perception management" perspective, United Artists was indeed the "correct hands" in which to place the fate of *The Man from Planet X*. As already stated earlier, United Artists was responsible for a deluge of UFOlogical films and TV shows in the 1950s and beyond. According to Rux, United Artists was "one of the three most prolific studios involved in disseminating accurate UFOlogical material".[19] Such productions included *Red Planet Mars* (1952), *Phantom from Space* (1953), *The Magnetic Monster* (1953), *The Twonky* (1953), *Gog* (1954), *U.F.O.* (1956), *The Creeping Unknown* (1956), *The Flame Barrier* (1957), *It! The Terror from Beyond Space* (1958), *Invisible Invaders* (1959), *The Flight That Disappeared* (1961), *The Outer Limits* (1963–65), *Message from Space* (1978) and *Invasion of the Body Snatchers* (1979), among others.

The amount of "former" military and intelligence agents involved in developing these projects is substantial. A partial list includes *Red Planet Mars* director Harry Horner, who served in the US Army Air Forces during World War II; *The Magnetic Monster* scriptwriter Curt Siodmak, who, in his 2001 memoir, *Wolf Man's Maker*, claimed to have been recruited by the Office of Strategic Services, the forerunner of the CIA, not long after the publication of his 1941 bestselling science fiction novel, *Donovan's Brain*; *The Magnetic Monster* and *Gog* producer Ivan Tors, who served in the United States Army Air Corps before also transferring to the Office of Strategic Services; *The Twonky* producer Sidney W. Pink, who "served in the Army Transportation Corps and Special Services" (as reported in an obituary published in the October 17, 2002 edition of the *Los Angeles Times*); *U.F.O.* documentary subject Albert M. Chop, who served as the US Air Force public information officer in charge of fielding questions from the public regarding the UFO phenomenon throughout the 1950s; *The Creeping Unknown* producer Anthony Hinds, who served as a pilot in the Royal Air Force during World War II; *The Flame Barrier* producers Arthur Gardner and Jules Levy, both of whom served in the Army Air Forces' First Motion Picture Unit, which churned out more than 400 propaganda and training films for the US military between 1942 and 1945; *Invisible Invaders* star John Agar, who appeared in numerous science fiction films in the 1950s and sixties after serving in both the Navy Air Corps and the United States Army Air Corps; *The Outer Limits* producer Leslie Stevens, who "attained the rank of captain in the Army Air Corps during WWII" and served "in Intelligence for three years in Iceland."[20]

One might argue that it's completely natural and expected for these influential professionals of the 1950s to have had military connections, given the fact that World War II was only a few years in the past when the decade began; however, what's not at all natural and expected is the preponderance of men on this list with connections to intelligence agencies and experience in crafting propaganda for the military.

4. Hollywood Wargaming

FROM AN INTELLIGENCE perspective, one of the many reasons for backing "perception management" films is to create the cinematic equivalent of "training exercises" in the form of fictional dramas. In other words, Cinema as Wargame Scenario.

Hollywood Haunts the World

During Professor Tricia Jenkins' December 2, 2009 interview with Michael Frost Beckner, the creator of the action-drama television show *The Agency* (2001–03), which glorified the Central Intelligence Agency, the writer/producer went into great detail about being supplied specific ideas for his series by "former" CIA undercover operative Chase Brandon. The following excerpt is from Jenkins' 2012 book, *The CIA in Hollywood: How the Agency Shapes Film and Television*:

> [Beckner] suggested that the CIA may have been using the series to workshop threat scenarios, as they were already doing with the University of Southern California's Institute for Creative Technologies (ICT). This idea is not as crazy as it sounds. Shortly after 9/11, President Bush sent his senior adviser, Karl Rove, to Los Angeles to meet with entertainment leaders to discuss ways they could "encourage volunteerism and offer support for American troops." Screenwriters and directors such as David Fincher and Spike Jonze also "brainstormed with Pentagon officials about creative ways to prevent future terrorist attacks," all as part of a larger Hollywood-military effort.
>
> The ICT often organizes such efforts to unite government officials and Hollywood creators. According to Richard Lindheim [former executive vice-president of the Paramount Television Group], the institute's peacetime purpose is to set the "best minds of the entertainment industry to the task of creating state-of-the-art training exercises for soldiers," and more recently, to create possible terrorist scenarios for government consideration. "Fortunately or unfortunately," Lindheim argued, "art has often led the way to reality, and art and writers and motion pictures and ideas coming from writers have often been the inspiration for reality." (Tom Clancy's 1994 novel *Debt of Honor* is often cited in such discussions, as it featured a disgruntled Japanese pilot intentionally flying an airplane into the U.S. Capitol Building, thereby killing most of the top government officials.) In 2002, the CIA formally recognized the link between entertainment and reality, too, as it began working with the ICT on a video game that would allow Agency analysts to assume the role of terror-cell leaders, members, and operatives in order to help the United States avert future attacks.
>
> Beckner claims that he was asked to join the ICT think tank while working on *The Agency* [...]. When Beckner followed up with Chase Brandon regarding the opportunity, however, Brandon told him that he "really shouldn't waste [his] time with that": "He told me that what you're doing with *The Agency* certainly makes us happy enough."

> This comment certainly is cryptic, and Beckner did not elaborate. Nonetheless, it suggests that in Brandon's eyes, Beckner's work on *The Agency* served the same purpose as the ICT think tank, which uses screenwriters to think through terrorist attacks and other threats to national security. By suggesting particular plotlines, then, Brandon may have been feeding Beckner ideas that the CIA wanted to see developed, explored, and analyzed precisely because it knew they were serious threats […].[21]

At the same time, Brandon was clearly exploiting his connection to Beckner for another very valuable strategic purpose: as a vehicle for the dissemination of disinformation. Brandon admitted as much to Beckner, and Beckner, in turn, admitted this to Professor Jenkins during her 2009 interview with him:

> According to Beckner, while he often consulted with Chase to enhance the realism of the show's surveillance and computer-based technology, Brandon once suggested featuring a highly advanced biometric system that would allow officials to detect almost any terrorist entering the United States. Beckner remarked that at first, he was unsure why Brandon was pushing the plotline in their conversations given that the device was so futuristic. "It would've been such a great tool in the war on terrorism if we had actually had it," he remarked. Brandon conceded that the technology was not real, but "he told me to go ahead and put it in the episode anyway," because "it would scare them." The "them," of course, meant plotting terrorists, since, according to Chase, "terrorists watch TV, too."
>
> This exchange between Beckner and Brandon suggests that Chase was using *The Agency* to scare potential and existing terrorists by exaggerating the CIA's ability to track their activities and ultimately to capture them […]. Admittedly, the strategy was a smart one, as Brandon is right that many terrorists consume American media. Simultaneously, however, the strategy belies the CIA's claim that it is invested in Hollywood only to portray accurately the Agency and to educate viewers about the CIA's role. Indeed, these examples suggest that the CIA had started to use the American media much as it did in the Cold War—not just as a tool of self-aggrandizement, but also as part of a psychological warfare strategy.[22]

This brings us back to the science fiction films of the 1950s. In what way were these films intended not just for the consumption of entertainment-starved Americans with a growing appetite for UFO-logical dramas, but for foreign entities as well? The same, by the way, can be said for numerous UFO reports—some of them sincere efforts to report the truth, some of them a deft mixture of truth and untruth, and some of them completely manufactured from whole cloth—that were being planted in American newspapers throughout the Cold War.

5. Manufacturing the Golden Ships

LET'S TURN NOW to the father of psychological warfare. Paul Linebarger not only helped create the US Army's first psychological warfare section and taught classes in psychological warfare for the CIA, but also wrote boundary-warping, *sui generis*, incendiary science fiction under the name Cordwainer Smith. According to an article titled "The Big Con at Dealey Plaza" by William E. Kelly (one of the original founders of The Coalition on Political Assassinations):

> The best black [ops] artists in the CIA during the Cold War were trained by Professor Paul M. A. Linebarger (1913–1966), whose book on *Psychological Warfare and Propaganda* (Combat Forces Press, 1948; 1954) is the classic textbook on the subject. In his classes, Linebarger didn't just use his own book *Psychological Warfare*, but had his students read David Maurer's *The Big Con* for examples of how successful covert operations are planned and executed.
>
> Besides being professor of Asiatic Studies at Johns Hopkins, Linebarger was also a part time professor at the School of Advanced International Studies (SAIS), a transparent front for a CIA think tank. CIA recruits who were invited to take Linebarger's SAIS classes, which he taught at his home at night, were required to use tradecraft in avoiding detection to get there so as to avoid being followed.
>
> Among Linebarger's students were E. Howard Hunt, David Atlee Phillips and Ed Lansdale, three of the most prolific covert operators during the Cold War [...]. When Paul Linebarger gave his lectures to young CIA officers, he warned them that these techniques should never be used domestically or it would totally destroy our form of democracy.[23]

Judging from what I know of Linebarger, based mainly on his writings—both fiction and nonfiction—I strongly suspect he would not have approved of his students' severe misapplication of these techniques. No doubt he would have recognized the pedigree of his own stratagems upon seeing them played out on such a massive scale in the geopolitical scene of the chaotic 1960s. Perhaps this is why, only a year after the assassination of President Kennedy and the subsequent escalation of the United States' involvement in Vietnam, Linebarger wrote, while hiding behind the mask of his literary alter ego, Cordwainer Smith, "I'm a machine, but I used to be a person, long, long ago," a passage from his classic short story "The Dead Lady of Clown Town" (1964).

Another classic Cordwainer Smith story is "Golden the Ship Was—Oh! Oh! Oh" (1959), in which a ninety million mile long, golden ship ("a gigantic dummy, the largest scarecrow ever conceived by the human mind") is created by the rulers of Earth in order to win an interstellar war against a far stronger foe.[24] As in Linebarger's optimistic dreams, psychological warfare saves the day.

At one point in the story, Lord Raumsog, the dictator of Earth's enemy planet, comments to a subordinate about the fantastic legend of this "golden ship": "There is no such ship that size. The golden ships are just a story. No one ever saw a picture of one."

The subordinate gives Raumsog a picture of one of the golden ships, to which Raumsog replies, "It's a trick. Some piece of trick photography. They distorted the size. The dimensions are wrong. Nobody has a ship that size. You could not build it, or if you could build it, you could not operate it. There is just not any such thing—"[25]

But Raumsog's logic fails in the face of such well-crafted lies. The legend of the golden ship's ferocity is more effective, in the end, than Occam's Razor and the most sophisticated firepower in the universe.

In Chapter Three of the story, Smith describes Earth's "scarecrow" ship like so:

> The cabin was small, twenty feet by thirty. The control area of the ship measured nothing over a hundred feet. All the rest was a golden bubble of the feinting ship, nothing more than thin and incredibly rigid foam with tiny wires cast across it so as to give the illusion of a hard metal and strong defense.
>
> The ninety million miles of length were right. Nothing else was.[26]

Given Linebarger's intimate connections with the US military and the CIA, one can't help but wonder if this story is an allegory for the Cold-War-era UFO phenomenon itself.

In 2011, journalist Annie Jacobsen published a bestselling nonfiction book titled *Area 51: An Uncensored History of America's Top Secret Military Base*. She began researching the book after being approached at a Christmas Eve dinner party by a retired physicist named Edward Lovick, who had "played a major role in the development of aerial espionage for the CIA."[27] According to Jacobsen, Lovick claimed that the otherworldly object that crashed near the deserts of Roswell, New Mexico in July of 1947 was, in truth, a plane filled with children made to look like aliens as part of Joseph Stalin's plot to create panic in the United States, à la Orson Welles' *War of the Worlds* radio broadcast of 1938.

I'm not certain that Lovick ever related such a story to Jacobsen, and if he did he might very well have been asked to do so by his (former?) employers. Given Stalin's reported interest in the subject of UFOs (see, for example, Chapter Three of Don Berliner and Stanton T. Friedman's 1992 book, *Crash at Corona*[28]), it's more than possible that elements of the Roswell story—whether such elements were accurate or not is immaterial—were purposely leaked to the American press in order to create a panic among the leaders of the Soviet Union. In other words, the story fed to Jacobsen might very well have been a strategic inversion of reality, just another in a long line of ever-changing cover stories regarding the "truth" behind the now legendary Roswell Crash of 1947.

As in "Golden the Ship Was—Oh! Oh! Oh!," when Lord Raumsog tries to reason with his frightened subordinates, he fails. An extravagant lie—in this case a cleverly faked photograph—almost always win over logic. During the Cold War, cinema was a convenient conduit for such lies. But that situation did not end with the death of the Cold War.

6. Programming Awareness

TAKE, FOR EXAMPLE, the case of Paul Bennewitz, an American physicist and inventor who, beginning in the early 1980s, was harassed by US intelligence agents with a psychological warfare cover story involving UFO stories to such an extreme degree that Bennewitz ended up being committed to a mental health facility three times before ultimately dying of "exhaustion" in July of 2003. Richard Doty, an agent for the US Air Force Office of Special Investigations, has admitted that he was given the assignment of hoaxing UFO information in order to prevent Bennewitz from learning the truth about certain sensitive operations being conducted at Kirtland Air Force Base in New Mexico. Because Bennewitz was actively monitoring what he believed were UFOs hovering over the base, the Air Force feared he might accidentally record and release top secret information to enemy agents. To prevent this, they orchestrated complex scenarios to make Bennewitz believe that mind-controlling aliens were on the verge of invading the Earth. As Greg Bishop wrote in his 2005 nonfiction book, *Project Beta: The Story of Paul Bennewitz, National Security, and the Creation of a Modern UFO Myth*, "Apparently, someone was beaming degraded video of some of the wackiest scenery this side of 1950s schlock cinema into Bennewitz's receiver setup" (located at his Albuquerque electronics company, Thunder Scientific Corporation), in order to help convince him of this mad scenario.[29] An entire Hollywood-style dream team was cranking out some creative science fiction soap operas during the 1980s, and Bennewitz was their (unfortunate) audience of one. Later, however, those stories that had been manufactured specifically for the consumption of Bennewitz alone soon leaked out into the mainstream of UFOlogy, and from there into Hollywood science fiction films and television shows.

Richard Doty insists that in the 1990s, while Bennewitz descended into insanity due to these operations, Doty graduated from Air Force Special Agent to working as a consultant on Chris Carter's hit television series, *The X-Files*. According to Greg Bishop:

> In time, he also wrote the screenplay for an episode, "The Blessing Way," which aired on September 22, 1995, although producer Chris Carter received writing credit. Doty also appeared as an extra in two episodes: "Anasazi," which aired on May 19, 1995, and "Paper Clip," shown on September 29 of the same year. He tried to write another, but says that it was "killed" by a government agency that he was required to run everything past before turning any of it in for production. After the final season of the show, *X-Files* producer Chris Carter was reportedly spotted at the Los Angeles FBI shooting range, which makes one wonder who was courting whom.[30]

Due to the fact that Doty is a disinformation specialist, everything he says must be questioned. According to Mark Pilkington, author of the 2010 book, *Mirage Men: A Journey Into Disinformation, Paranoia, and UFOs*, it's unlikely that Doty ever worked with Chris Carter in any capacity at all, much less wrote scripts for *The X-Files*. While conducting research for *Mirage Men*, Pilkington interviewed both Chris Carter and Frank Spotnitz (the two most important executive producers of the series) and asked them pointblank about Doty's claims to have written for the show. Pilkington states, "They said they'd never heard of him. I also tried hard to spot Doty's alleged extra appearances and failed to find him. I think Doty was just telling me what he thought I wanted to hear, to be honest, as he's done with so many other people."[31]

Where does truth end and disinformation begin? If a government propagandist ghostwrote an episode of a hit TV series with a heavy anti-government vibe, I could see why the creator of the show might not want to advertise that fact. This is why Doty's claims are so perfect from the perspective of a disinformation specialist. One can always find reasons to doubt one conclusion or the other. Consequently, such claims can remain hovering safely in a gray, indeterminate limbo for eternity, with no repercussions for the man who spread the claims in the first place. Of course, whether Doty's assertions are true or not, the fact that he even tried to attach his name to a TV show that revolves around government conspiracies, UFOs, and extraterrestrials is telling in and of itself. The very claim of intelligence involvement in *The X-Files* merely succeeds in reinforcing the popular notion that extraterrestrials are an active and ongoing concern for the government.

In a December 2005 interview, actor/comedian Dean Haglund, who portrayed Richard "Ringo" Langly on both *The X-Files* and its spin-off, *The Lone Gunmen*, briefly discussed what he called the "creepy" intersection between Hollywood and the intelligence community:

> Chris Carter was at a cocktail party, and he felt very out of place, and apparently was tucked away in the corner. And this psychic came over to him and said, "Whatever you're working on now is going to make you a ton of money." And that was just before he did *The X-Files*. Well, [I talked to] that psychic. I go, "What were *you* doing at that Hollywood party?" She goes, "I was hired by the CIA to go to parties and then just go home and email what I talked about." So the CIA has

> been tracking Hollywood parties since the '80s in order to determine—because, you know, Hollywood films set foreign policy, sort of. So they want to make sure that all the producers and the writers—that nobody is thinking anything so radical or doing a movie that will completely undermine their foreign policy plans. And they do that through sending women to parties and having them email [the CIA]. It's the weirdest thing. It's kind of creepy. Everybody I tell in Hollywood, all my actor friends, are kind of freaked out about it. And this becomes—you know, as an actor, the question is: Well, are you going to audition for [a project backed by the CIA]? There's a part where the tire hits the road when you're in Los Angeles, where suddenly you are called to audition for parts that are questionable... not just is it a good film/bad film, but now you're actually seeing—you know, the more I research this stuff—you're seeing part of that machine coming right through your own back yard. It's very, very creepy.[32]

As far as I know, the first time anyone published the suggestion that UFOlogical films were being used as a means of "perception management" was George Hunt Williamson in his 1954 book, *The Saucers Speak*. In Chapter Six, "Radio Diary," we find this sentence: "The movie, *The Day the Earth Stood Still* was for a purpose and was more fact than fiction."[33] This message, among many others, was spoken by "Zo" (who claimed to be an alien from Neptune) to Lyman H. Streeter, a radio operator who worked for the Santa Fe Railroad in Winslow, Arizona. Streeter was convinced that he had begun receiving messages from extraterrestrials through his ham radio set in August of 1952. According to Williamson, Streeter "had a great deal of experience in his field and held a commercial license as well as an amateur ham license."[34] In the original edition of *The Saucers Speak*, Williamson avoided naming Streeter and identified him only by the pseudonym "Mr. R." In a 1963 reissue of the book, Williamson added two new chapters in which he disclosed Mr. R's identity:

> Lyman had good reasons for not wanting his identity known. First of all, he had never used his call letters during his communication with the space intelligences and he never logged any of his receptions. If these facts were made known, he knew he would lose his license, and this was the very last thing he wanted, for to him radio was his very life.[35]

Streeter's involvement with these "space intelligences" put a great deal of strain on his life, pushing him into a continual state of fear and paranoia. In 1963, Williamson suggested that this strain played an important part in his death: "Needless to say, the extreme mental anxiety and pressure placed upon Lyman Streeter didn't exactly place him in a state of exuberant health. He was a very young man to die, but I feel certain that [he] had done his job and had completed the mission he came here to do."[36]

The undeniable parallels between Streeter's monitoring of "space intelligences" in the 1950s and the activities of Bennewitz in the 1980s should certainly be considered. Perhaps Bennewitz was not the first person to fall victim to the space age cover stories cooked up by US intelligence agents.

The May 1991 issue of *UFO Universe Magazine* contains what purports to be an exclusive interview with "a three star general" originally conducted on July 9, 1989 and July 14, 1989. The interviewer is identified only as "Bill" (a member of the Alien Information Technology Research and Development group, founded in 1988 by Kim Mikules). Of course, there's no way to verify whether or not "Bill" or the "three star general" even exist; however, certain statements made by the "general" during the course of this conversation overlap so perfectly with our main topic that I think it would be worthwhile quoting a brief segment here. From the mouth of the "general" himself come these words:

> The Awareness Program [the purpose of which, according to the "general," is to covertly disseminate information about "Alien contact" to the public] calls for the funding of movies, specials and books. All of the "front" money will filter its way to fund a TV series or movie if it is deemed worthy of friendly, helpful alien contact. An idea is passed along to the big named producers and directors and if it takes hold, everything will fall in place and the funding starts. It is really unique how it all works. No way to trace it to the government and the people involved truly believe it is their own creative work. Everyone gets into the act and no problems. After the movie hits the public, the reaction and interest of the masses are carefully monitored.[37]

Whether or not this "general" actually exists is almost beside the point; the fact is that this is exactly how creative talents like Pollexfen and Wisberg may have had their idea for *The Man from Planet X* slightly altered and influenced from behind the scenes without their express knowledge. One of Straczynski's key statements bears repeating here: *[S]tudio executives higher up the food chain can easily shape the direction of a show without explicitly telling the producers the source of their suggestions*. Compare this to the "general's" statement: *It is really unique how it all works. No way to trace it to the government and the people involved truly believe it is their own creative work.* When it comes to a prolific and successful writer/producer such as Chris Carter, what incentive does he have to reveal the full extent of any help he might have received from his paid "consultants"? When one is being praised for one's outlandish concepts, why would one admit during an interview, "Oh, actually, I didn't come up with that one—some frog-faced government disinformer fed that one to me while we were working on Season Three. And you know what's funny? *He* didn't even make that up! Some committee of anonymous psychological warfare hacks stationed at Kirtland Air Force Base originally came up with it back in the 1980s! Isn't that hilarious? I didn't even have to pay the crafty son of a bitch for it! It was already in the public domain!"

How did all those telltale UFOlogical details end up in trailblazing 1950s science fiction films like *The Man from Planet X* and *The Thing from Another World*? It's important to underscore the fact that *The Thing*, like many other science fiction films, was derived from previously published source materials. *The Thing* was based on John W. Campbell's famous novella *Who Goes There?* (which was published in the August 1938 edition of *Astounding Science Fiction* thirteen years before the release of the film). The aforementioned UFOlogical details in *The Thing* are—for the most part—unique to the film adaptation. So who was responsible for adding these details into the production?

This is an impossible question to answer definitively, but I would suggest that a clue might be found in Straczynski's comment (which was admittedly made in a context slightly different from this one): "[I]n the end, only the top studio brass [...] really know the truth of what happened, and they ain't talking."

Chapter 7

Invisible Ghosts

The Films of Bela Lugosi as Borderline Surrealism[1]

1.

> "Write quickly, without any preconceived subject, fast enough so that you will not remember what you're writing and be tempted to reread what you have written."
>
> —André Breton, "Manifesto of Surrealism," 1924

THE ABOVE ADVICE was offered by André Breton, the founder of surrealism, to budding artists who wished to practice surrealism themselves. But this mode of artistic creation was not the sole property of avant-garde surrealists. It was also, by necessity, the working method of a whole generation of screenwriters pounding out storylines for the masses throughout the 1930s to 1950s. This surrealist methodology applies not just to the writing of screenplays, but to the actual act of committing these stories to film. B-films were often written within three or four days and sometimes shot in an equal amount of time. No one involved in the production had much time to prepare—not the actors, not the director, and least of all the screenwriters.

A young Ray Bradbury once hung a sign on his typewriter that read, "DON'T THINK." Before his death, the poet Charles Bukowski requested that the following two words be etched into his tombstone: "DON'T TRY." The beauty of not thinking, of not trying, when creating any kind of art is that mysterious and wondrous ideas sometimes erupt from the sleeping brain and sneak out into the real world while one's consciousness isn't paying attention. The early surrealists in France wished to evoke this mysterious phenomenon, on purpose, via the method of automatic writing—simply putting pen to paper and allowing the words to flow with neither rhyme nor reason. Purely by accident, half a world away, a whole community of writers were also practising automatic writing. But most of them knew nothing about surrealism, and few of them were interested in making "Art." They were little "a" artists who were interested in grinding out a product in order to make money. In Hollywood, particularly during the 1930s and forties, strict deadlines necessitated that the most productive writers were those who *didn't think* about what they were writing and *didn't try* to produce anything of any social value whatsoever. It just so happened that these were also the goals of committed European revolutionaries who called themselves surrealists. The screenwriters under discussion in this chapter called themselves "hacks" and were probably proud of it. Breton, a committed Marxist to the day of his death in 1966, would be appalled at the very notion that the basic tenets of capitalism could actually be the unwitting accomplice of surrealism. Breton believed that surrealism and revolutionary Marxism were inextricably linked; without one, the other could not exist. Breton was wrong.

But he's not the only genius who was ever wrong about something.

Breton believed that surrealism could be a medium with which to introduce revolutionary ideas into the minds of the masses, to shock them out of their somnambulism with beautifully disordered nonsense. Breton was *right* about this. What he didn't realize is that he and his colleagues would not be the ones to introduce surrealism to the masses. Breton and his colleagues were avant-garde artists who held the common man in contempt. They published their works in obscure literary magazines in Europe that would never be seen by the "besotted underclass." The very "sheeple" Breton wished to liberate from the shackles of reality would never waste precious time in between work shifts at the local steel factory by reading nonsensical poetry jotted down by effete Frenchmen. But what these average people *did* like to do was see movies.

Without knowing it, thousands of filmgoers in the 1920s, thirties, forties, and fifties were introduced to surrealist techniques and philosophies in the form of cheapjack B-films. Even more poetically, the filmmakers themselves—for the most part—did not know they were making surrealist movies. This is the perfect surrealist conspiracy, for neither the conspirators nor the victims of the conspiracy were aware it was happening. One might consider this to be the ultimate exercise in automatic writing and telepathy, conducted on a mass scale by unwitting vessels of the surrealist spirit itself, a strange behavioral experiment that could only be comprehended in full several decades after the conspiracy had long been completed.

The very process of making B-movies, a process that remained in place in Hollywood until the early 1960s, encouraged and necessitated surrealist methodologies. A few filmmakers, the cutting-edge ones who understood their place in the Hollywood hierarchy and used it to their advantage, might very well have been aware of this, but most were not. The basic method of churning out these little celluloid dreams and nightmares enabled industrious filmmakers the ability to write, direct, edit, and distribute their films within a very short space of time—within a matter of months, or even weeks, sometimes. Very often the small-minded businessmen who ran the movie studios didn't care what was actually *in* the films just as long as they generated money. This process was a veritable breeding ground for all manner of surrealist techniques and obsessions: automatic writing (as mentioned before), synchronicity, chance, happenstance, coincidence, telepathy, etc. It's a breeding ground that no longer exists in modern-day Hollywood. There's too much at stake now, economically, to allow chance or happenstance to have anything at all to do with producing a finished film. Every detail is planned out well in advance. Modern Hollywood has so many safety measures in place that art can't even happen by accident.

In the Golden Age of Hollywood, however, art almost never happened *except* by accident, and that was never more true than in the case of the B-films.

2.

> "[E]ver since I have had a great desire to show forbearance to scientific musing, however unbecoming, in the final analysis, from every point of view. Radios? Fine. Syphilis? If you like. Photography? I don't see any reason why not. The cinema? Three cheers for darkened rooms."
>
> —André Breton, "Manifesto of Surrealism," 1924

BELA LUGOSI HAS often been referred to as the "King of the B-films." After briefly enjoying mainstream success via his successful turn as Bram Stoker's Count Dracula, as well as in other starring roles in major studio productions such *The Black Cat* (1934) and *The Raven* (1935), the bottom fell out of the horror market in 1936 due to a ban on such gruesome fare in England. Since England was one of the major markets for such films, Hollywood initiated its own unofficial ban on horror films that lasted almost three years. When this ban was finally lifted late in 1938, Lugosi found himself appearing in the occasional "A-film" such as *Son of Frankenstein* and *Ninotchka*, but for the most part the rest of his career would be spent starring in B-films.

Word spreads fast around Hollywood, and always has, even back during its Golden Age. Everyone in town knew that Lugosi was in financial trouble. His name had marquee value, and you could get him pretty cheap. Perfect. As Lugosi was quoted as saying in 1939, signifying his grudging surrender to the dark gods of Hollywood, "Lugosi. Horror. Box office. Fine. And I am horror."[2] As a result, Lugosi (perhaps more than any other actor) starred in the vast majority of these films that could be categorized as works of "accidental surrealism." One might say that Lugosi represents the spirit of accidental surrealism, or perhaps "surrealism for the masses." His association with such films predates his financial troubles in Hollywood. Even during his heyday, while basking in the glory of his post-*Dracula* successes on stage as well as on screen, he chose to star in Poverty Row films that owed more to surrealism and hermetic esotericism than to traditional American popcorn fare. These strange bastard children of sensationalism and expressionism permeated the nightmares of a generation lost in the crippling financial troubles of the Great Depression. These celluloid dark fantasies in which Lugosi was often the main attraction were, for the most part, surrealist at their core.

The titles of these films, some of them cinematic masterpieces and most of them nonsensical dross, unreel in one's mind like a nomenclature of the absurd: *The Thirteenth Chair* (1929), *Dracula* (1931), *The Black Camel* (1931), *Murders in the Rue Morgue* (1932), *White Zombie* (1932), *Chandu the Magician* (1932), *Island of Lost Souls* (1933), *Night of Terror* (1933), *International House* (1933), *The Whispering Shadow* (1933), *The Black Cat* (1934), *Return of Chandu* (1934), *The Mysterious Mr. Wong* (1935), *Mark of the Vampire* (1935), *The Raven* (1935), *Murder By Television* (1935), *Shadow of Chinatown* (1936), *The Invisible Ray* (1936), *Son of Frankenstein* (1939), *The Dark Eyes of London* (1939), *The*

Phantom Creeps (1939), *Black Friday* (1940), *You'll Find Out* (1940), *The Devil Bat* (1941), *Spooks Run Wild* (1941), *The Wolf Man* (1941), *Black Dragons* (1942), *The Ghost of Frankenstein* (1942), *The Corpse Vanishes* (1942), *Night Monster* (1942), *Bowery at Midnight* (1942), *Frankenstein Meets the Wolf Man* (1943), *The Ape Man* (1943), *Ghosts on the Loose* (1943), *Return of the Vampire* (1944), *Voodoo Man* (1944), *Return of the Ape Man* (1944), *The Body Snatcher* (1945), *Zombies on Broadway* (1945), *Scared to Death* (1947), *Abbott and Costello Meet Frankenstein* (1948), *Mother Riley Meets the Vampire* (1952), *Bela Lugosi Meets a Brooklyn Gorilla* (1952), *Glen or Glenda* (1953), *Bride of the Monster* (1955), *Plan 9 from Outer Space* (1958).

But perhaps none of them are more absurd than Joseph Lewis' *Invisible Ghost* (1941).

3.

> "This world is only very relatively in tune with thought, and incidents of this kind are only the most obvious episodes of a war in which I am proud to be participating. Surrealism is the 'invisible ray' which will one day enable us to win out over our opponents. 'You are no longer trembling, carcass.' This summer the roses are blue; the wood is of glass. The earth, draped in its verdant cloak, makes as little impression upon me as a ghost. It is living and ceasing to live that are imaginary solutions. Existence is elsewhere."
>
> —André Breton, "Manifesto of Surrealism," 1924

The shadow of an ape?
The portrait of a beautiful woman.
Good evening.
Dinner's served.
Good evening to an invisible woman?
Is this guy nuts?
Clarence Muse serves the ghost.
Mirror image.
Daughter. Virginia.
"They're" having dinner.
Ralph enters.
What's all the mystery about?
After dinner, we're taking a long walk.

BELA LUGOSI
INVISIBLE GHOST
RELEASED THRU
ASTOR PICTURES
CORP.
ASTOR PICTURES CORP.
POLLY ANN YOUNG
JAMES McGUIRE · CLARENCE MUSE
LITHO IN USA

It must seem weird to someone who's never seen it before.
Never forgets.
I guess he's not the only one who resorts to make believe.
An uncanny feeling.
Cecilia?
I think this is a crazy house.
Jules.
I'll show you where we keep our linens.
Little mousy man stealing food?
Mrs. Kessler. In the basement?
I want to go home.
I can't go home now… can I?
More mirrors.
Late again, Jules.
All these horrible murders….
Amnesia.
Virginia's been cheated on, just like her dad?
Hello, Casanova.
Have you gone crazy?
The servants see all.
The maid's a stalker?
I promise I'll make you a good wife, Ralph, I promise I will.
Love? He's a fine boy.
Thank you for the dinner.
The dirty secret emerges.
A psychic link?
Cut in half by a window.
Somnambulism.
Hypnotism?
A trance.
Automatic killer.
A lateral shot through the wall.
Sleepwalking fiend.
What's that music playing?
1940s popular music.
The beautiful maid.
Kessler comes undone.
Radio.
Creeps toward the camera.
Has he always been insane, or has his wife made him so?

Exercise lessons on radio.
Dead body in bed.
Contrast.
Lateral shot through wall.
I tried to wake the new maid….
The chauffeur.
How many murders have there been?
I'm practically engaged to a Ralph.
Ralph Dickson.
He never loved her.
Engineer.
I thought they were married.
Dickson sentenced to die.
Slanting, diagonal shadows in a prison.
Ralph Dickson takes the final walk—
—juxtaposed with Lugosi reading from the Bible.
Ralph is executed.
It's all over.
Overhead shot.
Ralph returns from the dead.
My name is Dickson.
It can't be.
Apparently your brother never told you about me.
Sorry to have startled you.
Do I look pale? I feel pale.
Fire in the foreground.
Secret emerges from the basement again.
Paul Dickson.
There's the wife again.
(How much more effective these scenes would be without a musical score.)
Grabs heart.
Back into the trance.
Uh-oh.
Pulling off robe.
Going to kill the butler.
Changes his mind.
Wants to kill wife.
Kills others instead?
Shadows in the kitchen.

Gardener gets it.
Early serial killer movie?
Gardener died on the linoleum floor.
The butler discovers the body again.
Calls police. The body has not been touched.
Murdered?
Strangled. Well, here we go again.
You're wanted in the kitchen.
Am I seeing things?
He's the image of 'im.
Jan. the 13th.
Have you had your coffee yet?
What does he mean by "the others"?
We can't leave.
If you want the truth, always talk to the servant.
There's been quite a lot of them.
He's waitin' for his wife to come back.
Well, this isn't a very pleasant way to entertain a guest.
She has eyes like Virginia.
She'll be back someday.
Coroner's Office.
Mr. Kirby.
The gardener's wife.
Another lateral shot.
Coroner leaves her alone with the body.
Mr. Mason.
He's alive!
He's not dead.
Jules Mason.
Did you recognize the man who tried to kill you?
It was ghastly.
Just a few moments longer….
Talking about murder over dessert.
The new cook.
Burning the roast.
I want to stay.
Ever read the newspapers?
What you don't know….
Lightning and chess.
It's getting late.

Invisible Ghosts

Such an elegant dinner.
Roast beef.
Wait until you taste my apple pie, Mr. Kessler.
Oh, he's a wonderful man.
What did I do wrong?
Slowly I turn.
The face at the window….
Cut in half by the window.
Almost kills Dickson… backs away….
Belt on the bathrobe.
Kill his daughter?
Lightning flash… breaks him out of trance….
Chance… coincidence….
Mr. Kessler?
Are you ill?
Hello, Paul.
I must have walked in my sleep.
The face at the window.
Fists grasping air.
The torn portrait.
"I wonder if anyone was hurt."
Ryan.
A dead cop behind the curtain.
Disappearing food.
The thread in the portrait.
All we want to know is if he's crazy.
That's easy.
Is it possible for someone to be normal and then go crazy only for an hour or two?
Lights go out!
We want to talk to you.
The secret enters the house.
Okay, sister, it's yours.
I'm going home… have to see my husband and my daughter.
I'm dead.
I know that woman. She's wicked. She can't go home. Mrs. Kessler….
I'm dead, Charles. Do you hear me? I'm dead.
I'm afraid to come home.
The secret dies.
She's dead.

What happened here?
We've got the murderer.
I knew you'd come back.
Kessler dies.
The invisible ghost ends.

4.

"The simplest Surrealist act consists of dashing down into the street, pistol in hand, and firing blindly, as fast as you can pull the trigger, into the crowd. Anyone who, at least once in his life, has not dreamed of thus putting an end to the petty system of debasement and cretinization in effect has a well-defined place in that crowd, with his belly at barrel level."
—André Breton, "Second Manifesto of Surrealism," 1930

IN HIS 1993 book, *Poverty Row Horrors!: Monogram, PRC and Republic Horror Films of the Forties*, Tom Weaver describes *Invisible Ghost* as "almost *surreal*," but I would go just a tad further and say that it *is* surreal—or at least as close as a Hollywood film could get to being surreal in the early 1940s.[3] The same could be said of many of Lugosi's 1940s "poverty row" films, particularly the nine that he made for Monogram studios between the years 1941 and 1944, but here we will focus on only one, the very first: Joseph Lewis' *Invisible Ghost*.

In *Invisible Ghost*, Lugosi plays Dr Charles Kessler, a far more psychologically complex character than was typical for 1940s poverty row films. Indeed, Kessler's not typical of *any* American film of the 1940s, including those made by the major studios. On the surface Kessler appears to be a kindly old man who loves his daughter and yet at the same time appears to be utterly insane. Once a year, on his wedding anniversary, Kessler hosts an elaborate dinner for his absent wife who, years before, ran off with his best friend and never returned. He even makes sure there's a place for her at the table and talks to her as if she's actually sitting there. It seems odd for a man to go crazy only once a year, and yet he appears to do just that. His loving daughter, as well as his servants, grudgingly humor the sad old man's eccentricities. The fact that he continues to long for a woman who betrayed him in a heartless manner seems to suggest a masochistic streak in Kessler's personality. But perhaps this streak is more than just a streak, and perhaps it's far more than merely masochistic.

It will become clear that Kessler, the gentle old doctor, wishes to kill his wife for what she has done to him. Because he can't face this ugly truth about himself, he suppresses this transgressive impulse. And by suppressing the impulse, it emerges only when Kessler's asleep.

André Breton, and the surrealists in general, believed a great deal in the power of dreams and sleep and self-induced hypnotic trances. They believed everyday waking life was an illusion, the dream life infinitely more tangible and meaningful. Therefore, what was revealed in one's dreams said far more about one's "true" personality than anything one had ever thought or done in the "real" world.

Kessler suffers from somnambulism. He walks in his sleep. And while walking and dreaming simultaneously, he also pursues another odd pastime. He kills.

Breton, a champion of using self-induced hypnosis to conjure forth surrealist works of art, once said—no doubt rhetorically, of course—that mass murder was the "simplest Surrealist act."[4] Kessler combines several surrealist tendencies into one. He's a hypnotist, a hypnotic subject, and a serial murderer all at the same time.

Charles Kessler is an unwitting surrealist.

But then again, Breton believed *everyone* was an unwitting surrealist, at least when they were asleep, and they could even be so when they were awake just as long as they were willing to drop their everyday, shallow façades and penetrate to the core of what was genuinely "real" about themselves—or rather "surreal," those secrets that lay hidden deep beneath the surface of their dream lives. The mysteries tucked away in the basements of their brains.

Sigmund Freud was an immense influence on Breton and the surrealists. They felt that Freud offered humanity the tools by which to remove themselves from the shackles placed upon them by organized religion and penetrate the previously unexplored depths of the human mind. Breton's positive attitude toward Freud never wavered, though by the end of his life he did believe that Freud's knowledge had been perverted into yet another trap for human beings rather than a means of liberation. *Invisible Ghost* is dripping with Freudian symbolism, most of it no doubt unintentional. The author of the screenplay, Al Martin, was hardly known for his subtlety and layered subtext. He was a reliable craftsman who cranked out scores of scripts, for both film and television, throughout his forty-year-plus career, including the cult classics *Invasion of the Saucer Men* (1957) and *The Eye Creatures* (1965), neither of which are notable for their use of complex symbolism. Nonetheless, such symbolism exists throughout *Invisible Ghost* and could only be the product of the screenwriters (Helen Martin is credited as the screenplay's co-author) or perhaps the director, Joseph Lewis.

This latter possibility is not unlikely. Joseph Lewis was a groundbreaking director who honed his craft on Poverty Row before graduating to the big studios like Columbia where he directed such Gothic/noir hybrids as *My Name Is Julia Ross* (1945). Lewis' masterpiece, however, is *Gun Crazy* (1950). Many film critics claim that *Gun Crazy* is the best film noir ever made, and one would be hard pressed to disagree with that assessment. Throughout Lewis' oeuvre, we see him committing to film abstract representations of reality in order to tell darkly psychological stories about damaged people who transgress against the traditional social strictures of the day. This certainly describes *Gun Crazy*. Despite the fact that the film is a gritty, realistic tale of two murderous outlaws, I suspect Breton would have held some sympathy for the film and its two main characters. As Breton wrote in his very first Surrealist Manifesto in 1924:

> The mind of the man who dreams is fully satisfied by what happens to him. The agonizing question of possibility is no longer pertinent. Kill, fly faster, love to your heart's content. And if you should die, are you not certain of reawaking among the dead? Let yourself be carried along, events will not tolerate your interference. You are nameless. The ease of everything is priceless [...].
>
> I believe in the future resolution of these two states, dream and reality, which are seemingly so contradictory, into a kind of absolute reality, a *surreality*, if one may so speak.[5]

One can almost imagine one of the two main characters of *Gun Crazy* uttering these same words. Listen to this exchange between the two protagonists, Barton Tare (John Dall) and Annie Laurie Starr (Peggy Cummins), after they've successfully avoided being arrested for armed robbery and murder:

> BARTON: Everything's going so fast. It's all in such high gear that sometimes it doesn't feel like me. If that makes sense.
> ANNIE: When do you think all this?
> BARTON: Oh, at nights. I wake up sometimes. It's as if none of it really happened. As if *nothing* were real anymore.

ANNIE: Next time you wake, Bart, look over at me lying there beside you. I'm yours. And *I'm* real.

BARTON: Yes. But you're the only thing that is, Laurie. The rest is a nightmare.

Of course, these words were written by the screenwriter of *Gun Crazy*, Dalton Trumbo, not Lewis. Nonetheless, it's certainly fascinating to note the repetition of a specific theme from one director's film to another, as it might very well be an indication of that director's attraction to a particular type of subject matter, in this case the fine line between reality and *surreality* in the transgressive mind.

Bart's words could easily have slipped out of the mouth of Charles Kessler… or André Breton.

5.

> "Under the pretense of civilization and progress, we have managed to banish from the mind everything that may rightly or wrongly be termed superstition, or fancy; forbidden is any kind of search which is not in conformance with accepted practices. It was, apparently, by pure chance that a part of our mental world which we pretended not to be concerned with any longer—and, in my opinion by far the most important part—has been brought back to light. For this we must give thanks to the discoveries of Sigmund Freud. On the basis of these discoveries a current of opinion is finally forming by means of which the human explorer will be able to carry his investigations much further, authorized as he will henceforth be not to confine himself solely to the most summary realities. The imagination is perhaps on the point of reasserting itself, of reclaiming its rights."
>
> —André Breton, "Manifesto of Surrealism," 1924

THE FREUDIAN IMPLICATIONS of Kessler's obsession results in a series of brutal murders. Kessler can't get back at his wife for leaving him, and yet he still loves her. Eros and Thanatos entwined. These polar impulses pull his brain in two. No sane mind could handle such stress. And so Kessler's mind snaps, and while asleep he projects his hatred for his absent wife onto the only females who are present in his home and easily accessible to him. It's telling that Kessler never kills outside his own home. Some critics have lambasted the film for this plot point. After all, why don't the police have this house under twenty-four-hour surveillance if so many people have been brutally murdered there? This would be a fair question if this were a realistic story set in a realistic world. But it's not. It's the story about a man's mind slipping into a psychotic dream world, and the house is the physical manifestation of his disordered brain. The police in the film are symbols only, impotent phantoms that prevent none of the violence from occurring because that's not their job. Their job is simply to reveal Kessler's murderous side to himself when the doctor's sleeping brain deems it necessary, when the time is right. The house, and the people that seem to populate it, are nothing more than ghosts that haunt Kessler's troubled dreams. Most critics believe that the seemingly nonsensical title refers to Kessler's wife, since it is her recurrent appearances outside Kessler's bedroom window that seem to trigger his murderous rages. But no. The ghost in the title is everyone other than Kessler. This is Kessler's dream, and his sleeping mind is the only thing that's real. The invisible ghost is the world itself.

We learn seven minutes into the film that Kessler's wife never actually left Kessler. She tried to, but fate intervened. As she and her lover were driving away, they got into a car accident that killed the lover and left Mrs Kessler an amnesiac, brain-damaged wreck. Somehow she made her way back to the estate where the gardener, Jules, found her wandering around in a daze. Instead of taking her to a hospital, as most people would do in the real world, Jules stuffed her away in the basement beneath the garden house. What he's doing with her down there is anybody's guess. According to Jules, he keeps her down there because he feels that Mr Kessler would be unable to handle the sight of his wife in such a condition.

As in most neo-Gothic horror films of this type, very often there's a dirty secret hidden inside the basement or some similar underground grotto. In *The Phantom of the Opera* (1925), the Phantom makes his lair in the elaborate sewers beneath the Paris opera house. In *The Most Dangerous Game* (1932), Zaroff, a psychotic game hunter, displays his human trophies only in the darkness of his basement. In *House of Dracula* (1945), the undead Count hides his coffin in the basement of the physician from whom he's ostensibly seeking a cure for vampirism (not only is Dracula not cured by the end of the picture, but the good doctor turns into a vampire too). In *Psycho* (1960), Norman Bates keeps the corpse of his beloved mother in the basement. In such films, houses—and architecture in general—are transformed into metaphors for the human brain. And the basement, or the underground, become stand-ins for the unconscious itself from which the typical "rational" human mind has become so thoroughly alienated that it does not comprehend its own motivations.

Like Charles Kessler.

6.

> "I have always been amazed at the way an ordinary observer lends so much more credence and attaches so much more importance to waking events than to those occurring in dreams [...]. I have no choice but to consider [the waking state] a phenomenon of interference. Not only does the mind display, in this state, a strange tendency to lose its bearings (as evidenced by the slips and mistakes the secrets of which are just beginning to be revealed to us), but, what is more, it does not appear that, when the mind is functioning normally, it really responds to anything but the suggestions which come to it from the depths of that dark night to which I commend it."
>
> —André Breton, "Manifesto of Surrealism," 1924

THE TROPES OF Gothic fiction fascinated Breton and the surrealists. Despite the fact that Breton considered all fiction to be an "inferior" art form, as storytelling in general required a linear logic that precluded the beautiful non-rationality of surrealism, he granted one exception to the Gothic horror story, and in particular championed M.G. Lewis' 1796 novel, *The Monk*, generally considered to be one of the earliest and most influential Gothic novels. H.P. Lovecraft, in his book-length essay "Supernatural Horror in Literature," deemed *The Monk* "a masterpiece of active nightmare."[6] Breton, too, felt it was a masterpiece, though a masterpiece of proto-surrealism:

> In the realm of literature, only the marvelous is capable of fecundating works which belong to an inferior category such as the novel, and generally speaking, anything that involves storytelling. Lewis' *The Monk* is an admirable proof of this. It is infused throughout with the presence of the marvelous. Long before the author has freed his main characters from all temporal constraints, one feels them ready to act with an unprecedented pride. This passion for eternity with which they are constantly stirred lends an unforgettable intensity to their torments, and to

> mine. I mean that this book, from beginning to end, and in the purest way imaginable, exercises an exalting effect only upon that part of the mind which aspires to leave the earth and that, stripped of an insignificant part of its plot, which belongs to the period in which it was written, it constitutes a paragon of precision and innocent grandeur.

Breton caps off his analysis with the following footnote: "What is admirable about the fantastic is that there is no longer anything fantastic: there is only the real."[7]

Only the real. Breton deconstructs everyday reality by flipping the binary opposites of reality and the fantastic, or *surreality*. In Breton's world, dreams and nightmares represent reality and reality is the insignificant shadow of the fantastic that lurks in the secret lairs beneath our waking life. This exact deconstruction occurs in Lugosi's best films, *Dracula*, *Murders in the Rue Morgue*, *White Zombie*, *Island of Lost Souls*, and *The Black Cat* (the 1934 version) foremost among them. It's not difficult to imagine Breton and his colleagues being sympathetic to these neo-Gothic films, particularly *The Black Cat*. In 1924, in his very first surrealist manifesto, Breton identified Edgar Allan Poe as a surrealist. (Breton would later change his mind about this, claiming that Poe's obsession with rationality, per his proto-detective stories about C. Auguste Dupin, overshadows his otherwise surrealist tendencies). Not only is *The Black Cat* ostensibly based on the Poe story of the same name, not only does it benefit from Edgar Ulmer's German Expressionist interpretation of reality, but it also boasts a screenplay (co-written by Ulmer) that manages to pack in almost every single transgressive "perversity" of which the Marquis de Sade (also identified by Breton as a progenitor of surrealism) himself would have approved. Film critic David Kalat once said of *The Black Cat* that it "was one of the most gorgeous movies ever to come out of Universal in the 1930s. It looked like the Dadaist art of the Bauhaus school had literally come to life, and Ulmer coaxed from Lugosi his most human and endearing performance ever."[8]

If there's any doubt that Breton and his intellectual colleagues would have been attracted to this type of Americanized surrealism as manifested in the form of commercial horror fiction, consider the following excerpt from an article written by Franklin Rosemont, the co-founder of the Chicago Surrealist Group:

> The Second World War, and the Nazi occupation of France, forced André Breton and other surrealists to seek refuge in the U.S. Regrouping in New York, they began a fruitful search for "surrealist evidence" in the New World. Among their greatest discoveries was Howard Phillips Lovecraft and the "Lovecraft circle," including Clark Ashton Smith, August Derleth, Donald Wandrei and Frank Belknap Long.
>
> In the works of these authors the surrealists found confirmations and extensions of their own quest. Appearing in *Weird Tales* and other "pulp" magazines, these works seemed to them more truly poetic than the stuff in *Poetry* or other official organs of High Culture. Lovecraft and his friends reached beyond mere "literature" into the volatile shadows of a new mythology [...].
>
> For surrealists today, the works of the Lovecraft Circle remain a *central source.*[9]

Not all of Lugosi's collaborators were unconscious of the surrealist movement and its potential to be a subversive force in society. Two of Lugosi's best directors, Edgar Ulmer and Robert Florey, sympathized with the surrealist movement and no doubt wished to make such groundbreaking films in America, the kind that Salvador Dali and Luis Buñuel were becoming famous for in Europe. In an interview included on the 2005 DVD release of Ulmer's 1957 horror film, *The Daughter of Dr. Jekyll*, Ulmer's daughter (and sometimes collaborator), Arianne, mentions that her father not only knew Salvador Dali, but was "very close" friends with him.[10] Clearly, therefore, it's natural to assume that Ulmer was intimately aware of surrealist techniques. Cinematographer Paul Ivano, with whom Robert Florey worked on the ill-fated screen test for *Frankenstein* (which Florey was assigned to direct before being switched by the studio executives to *Murders in the Rue Morgue*), once commented on Florey's love of surrealism. Ivano insisted that the test reel for *Frankenstein*, despite the less-than-positive reactions of the studio heads, was expertly realized. Ivano claimed that the use of shadows in the scenes was "very artistic yet nightmarish. Robert loved this for he was very adept in the Germanic style of cinematography, like *The Cabinet of Dr. Caligari*. Even his own experimental films had the same atmosphere: Surrealistic."[11]

But in the early 1930s what studio executive in America would subsidize a surrealist film? Of course, not one of them would ever do so—not knowingly, at least. The trick, therefore, was to slip surrealism in under the radar of the executives. The only way to do this would be to mask a surrealist film under the guise of a popular genre. Would a romantic musical lend itself to surrealism? Not likely. A shoot-'em-up Western? Until Alejandro Jodorowsky's 1970 film *El Topo* (in which Jesus returns to Earth as a gunslinger in the Old West), the answer would be a definite "no." A gangster flick? A swashbuckling pirate adventure in the South Seas? Not likely.

Clearly, the nascent horror film (made possible, and popular, only because of the success of Lugosi's portrayal as Dracula) was the perfect vehicle in which to explore all the surrealist and expressionist techniques being employed by the most groundbreaking filmmakers in France (e.g., Dali and Buñuel's *Andalusian Dog*) and Germany (e.g., *The Cabinet of Dr. Caligari*). Ulmer and Florey, in particular, no doubt saw the potential of the horror film being the perfect vehicle by which to surreptitiously assault dull American minds with their surrealist time bombs. And Lugosi, now firmly established as a horror star as a result of his indelible interpretation of Bram Stoker's most famous creation, was the perfect actor to star in these films.

The only reason Ulmer was able to make *The Black Cat* was because the head of Universal Studios, Carl Laemmle, Sr, happened to be out of the country at the time and wasn't around to disapprove. By the time he returned, this strange little nightmare had already been committed to film. Despite Laemmle's skepticism about the finished product, it went on to become the biggest grossing Universal film of that year. Yes, dull American minds *could* indeed handle a surrealist film—as long as they didn't realize that that's what they were watching. Surrealism, like so many other dirty little secrets in America, had to be hidden away in the basement and called by a somewhat more proper name so as not to disturb the neighbors.

Everything worthwhile in America invariably ends up in the basement, if it wasn't born there in the first place.

7.

> "Nothing, in fact, can any longer prevent this country from being largely conquered. The hordes of words which, whatever one may say, Dada and Surrealism set about to let loose as though opening a Pandora's box, are not of a kind to withdraw again for no good purpose [...]. [C]onsider how far a handful of completely modern works, about which the very least one can say is that a particularly unhealthy

atmosphere pervades them, has already wormed their way, admirably and perversely, into the public consciousness [...]."
—André Breton, "Second Manifesto of Surrealism," 1930

PERIODICALLY, THE GARDENER'S dirty little secret will sneak out of the basement and wander around the grounds of Mrs Kessler's former home. On the night of her wedding anniversary, she looks up at the window and whispers, "I'm afraid to come home. He'd kill me. You'd kill *any*body." What does this mean? Is she predicting the future? Is she making this happen? (A self-fulfilling prophecy?) Or does she understand something about her husband's personality of which Kessler himself is not even aware?

The sight of his missing wife seems to stun and bewilder Kessler. He slips into a sort of self-induced trance and wanders into the maid's room. Here Lewis makes the most of his environment to stage a scene of mounting terror. The use of popular music emerging from the maid's radio in the background serves as an innocuous counterpoint to the grim reality of the murder unfolding before our eyes. It's a disturbing (and, in a way, darkly humorous) technique that has been used often since. Two examples leap immediately to mind: Stanley Kubrick's use of the song "Singin' in the Rain" during a brutal rape scene in *A Clockwork Orange* (1972) and Martin Scorsese's use of Donovan's 1960s folk song "Atlantis" during an equally violent scene in *Goodfellas* (1990).

In this first murder scene Lewis also makes use of very potent close-ups and subjective shots to put the audience in the place of the victim while the murder is occurring, a disturbing technique since exploited multiple times in far less stylish serial killer films produced throughout the 1970s, eighties, and beyond. The fact that Lewis' use of this technique remains effective to this day, due primarily to his subtlety and timing, indicates that this B-film may actually have been slightly ahead of its time rather than several steps behind it, as was suggested in many contemporary reviews. *The New York Daily News*, for example, called Lewis' direction "inadequate" and *The New York Daily Mirror* called it "terrible." Ironically, Lewis' direction is the one element in the film least vulnerable to criticism.

As the maid, Cecile (Terry Walker), shudders in fear and confusion, Kessler slips off his bathrobe slowly and deliberately: a perverse striptease. An expression of both sexual desire and anger flares in

Kessler's eyes, then the kindly old philanthropist proceeds to strangle the woman to death. This is the most arresting scene in the film, the showstopper that remains in one's mind even if one is indifferent (or even hostile) to the rest of the film.

The next morning, when the maid's body is discovered, Kessler has no memory of having committed the crime and is as baffled as everyone else, including the police. Ralph Dickson (John McGuire), the boyfriend of Virginia Kessler (Polly Ann Young), Charles Kessler's daughter, is accused of the crime by the authorities due to the fact that Ralph had been Virginia's lover, was being blackmailed by her, and lacks a strong alibi. Despite the fact that Charles Kessler does everything he can to save the young man (he even appeals to the Governor), Ralph is executed for the crime committed by Charles Kessler.

The Freudian cues couldn't be more obvious, nor could they be overlooked by any true surrealist. Not only is the young maid a stand-in for Kessler's missing, adulterous wife, but by killing the woman Kessler has also eliminated the only rival for his daughter's affections, Ralph. Kessler's intense love/hatred for his wife will soon extend to his daughter as well.

After Ralph is murdered by the state, who should appear on Kessler's doorstep? Ralph's doppelganger, his "ghost," a twin brother belatedly seeking answers to his brother's death. Paul Dickson (also played by John McGuire) wants nothing more than to uncover the real murderer of Cecile. The night of his arrival, Paul almost becomes Kessler's next victim.

Once again Kessler spots his wife through the window, nearly kills Paul, but instead decides to strangle Jules the gardener while the man is in the kitchen retrieving some food for Mrs Kessler. Lewis effectively stages the murder by employing shadows thrown on the walls of the kitchen.

Kessler has managed to merge the waking and dream states into one and fully lives out his nightmares (dreams? secret desires?) without the messiness and inconvenience of having to remember what he's done in the morning. He doesn't even remember not *wanting* to remember. He can be the well-liked philanthropist the town very much wants him to be ("He's an important man around here," a police detective admits at one point, no doubt the main reason none of the policemen accuse him of the murders), while also fulfilling his dream life without any guilt whatsoever. He's gone beyond Dr Jekyll and Mr Hyde. Jekyll at least takes the initiative and brings about his bifurcation willingly. Kessler isn't even aware that he *wants* to be bifurcated. His disassociation is perfect and complete.

In the 1920s Salvador Dali began experimenting with what he called "paranoic" double visions, a perfect melding of two distinct images. His 1929 surrealist painting, *Invisible Man*, in which two fluid landscapes overlap and appear to form a single scene, is a prime example. Perhaps the screenwriters, or even Joseph Lewis himself, were thinking of this painting when they chose the final title for the film (the working title throughout production was *The Phantom Killer*), for Charles Kessler is very clearly a "paranoic" double vision given human form.

This double vision, having easily skirted the law once the body of the gardener is found in his kitchen, imposes itself on the world around him one last time when he sees his wife's face only inches outside his window one rainy night. Lewis' use of noir lighting enlivens this scene considerably. It prefigures his masterful use of lighting in his future noir masterpieces such as *Gun Crazy* and *The Big Combo* (1955). In fact, *Invisible Ghost*, while also being borderline surrealism, could be considered borderline noir as well. Not only does Lewis' involvement with this film underscore this connection, but so does the presence of actor John McGuire, who gave such an effective star performance in what many film critics believe to be the first genuine film noir: Boris Ingster's *The Stranger on the Third Floor* (1940) co-starring McGuire and Peter Lorre. Surrealism? Noir? Horror? Drama? Theater of the Absurd? The film is a mixture of all of these elements, like a dream that meanders from one disjointed scenario to another, or a nightmare that defies convenient analysis. To some extent, *Invisible Ghost* defies any convenient label, including such shallow descriptions as "good" or "bad."

Charles Kessler defies such descriptions as well. He's neither "good" nor "bad" because he never intends on creating any harm. It's clear from his third confrontation with his wife's "phantom" that Kessler is frustrated by his inability to resolve his lingering, psychic connections to his missing wife. At one point, after his wife's spectral visage has vanished into the rain and the darkness, Kessler impotently strokes and claws at the glass, as if wanting to caress and choke his wife at the same time. But he can do neither. So he simply balls his fists in frustration. The scene fades out and resumes the next morning. It's not until later that we learn Kessler has—in the middle of the night—destroyed his wife's portrait, one that he has doted over constantly throughout the film. The second he sees the vandalized painting, Kessler whispers, "I wonder if anyone was hurt," as if he's subconsciously aware of the "paranoic" double vision that he has become. A few minutes later, we learn that Kessler has strangled a police officer in the night (one of the very same detectives posted in the house in order to prevent another murder) and has, rather puckishly (and most improbably), arranged the body so that it appears to be standing behind the curtains in the living room. The second the curtains are parted, the corpse goes tumbling facedown onto the floor.

Though Kessler is surprised by this development, he's far more distressed by the vandalized portrait in the hallway. Paul Dickson finds a thread attached to the painting. The thread matches Kessler's bathrobe. So, naturally (per 1941 American logic), the police suspect Kessler's Black butler, Evans (Clarence Muse), of both the vandalism and the murder. In *Invisible Ghost* Muse manages to turn in a sober and serious performance in what might otherwise have been a clichéd "Step-n-fetch-it" type of role. Despite the rambling script, Muse remains the anchor amidst the dream-like proceedings, the only character who responds sensibly to the strange events swirling around him. Against tremendous odds, Muse succeeds in bringing a great deal of dignity to a minor role. (It should be noted that Muse appeared in a previous film with Lugosi, the Halperin Brothers' low budget masterpiece, *White Zombie*.)

Near the end of the film, Evans is being interrogated by two police detectives, a psychiatrist, Paul Dickson, and Charles Kessler. Except for Kessler, they all seem to suspect Evans of the murder. The look on Muse's face is both amusing and realistic. One can hear the thoughts in his mind simply by reading his expressions: *Well, I knew this had to happen sooner or later.* When it comes down to accusing the wealthy white philanthropist or the Black butler of murder, the butler's always going to lose.

In this film, however, the Black butler does *not* lose. Fortunately for Evans, Mrs Kessler must sneak into the house more and more frequently to scrounge for food due to the fact that her husband has strangled the one person on the grounds who knew Mrs Kessler was still alive. Thus, with the gardener dead, there's no one around to bring her sustenance anymore. A pair of police detectives find Mrs Kessler in the kitchen gnawing on a chicken leg. Due to her rambling, the officers immediately recognize that she's crazy and drag her upstairs. The second Kessler sees her, he slips into another trance and tries to strangle the lead detective. The only person in the room noticeably relieved by this development is Evans.

While Kessler is strangling the detective, Lewis intercuts two scenes of Mrs Kessler dying in another room. Why she's dying now is a mystery that's never explained. There's no reason for it at all. Except...

Except perhaps she's dying because Kessler has no need for her anymore. The secret in the basement of his mind has now been revealed before witnesses. His "paranoic" double vision has been exposed to others, and therefore to himself. Perhaps Mrs Kessler never survived that car crash at all. She even tells her husband in this final scene that she's "dead." Perhaps she *is* a ghost, in a way. Perhaps she's what the Tibetans call a "tulpa," a physical being manifested in three dimensions by the power of the mind—in this case, Kessler's mind. He desperately wanted to see his wife, and he desperately did *not* want to see his wife. He desperately wanted his wife to return to him so he could love her again. He desperately wanted his wife to return to him so he could strangle her to death. This bifurcation in his psyche resolved itself by conjuring up her "ghost." Once that bifurcation was revealed to others, and therefore—by extension—himself, he no longer had any need for her. So she died.

And once the tulpa dies, Kessler is released from her spell—a spell he put on himself by conjuring her in the first place.

The two Kesslers are the perfect melding of two distinct images, as in Dali's *Invisible Man*. Mr Kessler is Mrs Kessler (the fact that she has no first name in the script is certainly suggestive of her lack of individual identity), and Mrs Kessler is Mr Kessler. Both one and the same. Both invisible and visible at the same time. Both entwined on a psychic plane far beyond matrimony. Bonded by pain more than love. Products of the same consciousness. Till death do they part.

And part they do. Mrs Kessler dies (disappears?), and Mr Kessler is led away by the police past the torn portrait in the hall. Kessler stops in front of it for a moment and says, "I knew you'd come back to me." Of course he did. In a way, he'd summoned her in the first place. He'd made her live and breathe again with nothing more than convulsive desire.

8.

"Beauty will be CONVULSIVE, or will not be at all."

—André Breton, *Nadja*, 1928

IF YOU'RE STILL not convinced that *Invisible Ghost* is an example of borderline cinematic surrealism par excellence, then consider this development. In 2002 Martin Arnold, the Austrian avant-garde artist, created a conceptual piece titled *Deanimated: The Invisible Ghost*. Worldscinema, a website devoted to archiving experimental films from around the globe, describes *Deanimated* as:

> [...] an installation piece for projection as a 60-minute loop in gallery spaces. *Deanimated* is literally displaced from the theater environment typical of film spectatorship, slightly blurring the boundaries between the spaces of projection and reception.
>
> *Deanimated: The Invisible Ghost* is based on the 1941 horror film *The Invisible Ghost* with the lead actors Bela Lugosi, Polly Ann Young, and John McGuire. In *Deanimated* the actors are gradually eliminated [via digital manipulation] and thus the narrative loses its coherence. What remains are backgrounds, erratic camera movements that seem to move without focus throughout the room, capturing ghostly changes in light and shadows. In this project, Arnold asks fundamental philosophical questions about human existence and presence in absence. Although the actors are missing, they leave behind traces (such as [...] dust stirring up...) and are experienced precisely in their absence as a ghostly, unreal present.[12]

Deanimated can only be seen as an installation piece, separating it even further from the world of cinema. If one wishes to see it, one can't be a passive spectator. One has to actively seek it out. In *Deanimated* one sees Lewis' camera wandering through empty corridors and basements and dimly lit bedrooms, creating a disconcerting experience. If one has never seen the original film upon which it is based, one is left with a sense of having taken a trip through an alien, haunted world. If one *has* seen the film before, one is left with the feeling of having revisited a familiar world with an altered consciousness, like returning to a childhood home after having been away for many years. The architecture is the same, but all the people you once knew are gone. A sense of deep loss permeates *Deanimated*, and one walks away from the installation imbued with the same sense of desolation and psychic bifurcation that Charles Kessler himself must have felt as the police led him down his own haunted corridor and past the mutilated portrait of his dead wife one final time. *Deanimated* strips the architecture of Kessler's mind down to its bare essentials, revealing what the original film only hints at: Everyone in the film is an invisible ghost, a projection of a disordered consciousness. Kessler's home certainly is haunted; it's haunted by Kessler himself and his inability to let go of the wholly illusory image of his less-than-perfect wife to which he stubbornly grasps. To let go of the past.

Arnold had previously created a similar installation based on the Andy Hardy comedies of the 1930s, forties, and fifties starring Mickey Rooney. In *Alone. Life Wastes Andy Hardy* (1998) Arnold digitally manipulates the original images to reveal the subversive subtext hiding just beneath the surface: transgressive messages of forbidden Oedipal desires and all manner of sexual frustrations that lie festering at the core of any repressed and puritanical society. *Deanimated* is even more successful in peeling away the seemingly shallow veneer of a pop cultural artifact and unmasking the strange face that—like Mrs Kessler herself huddled in fear and confusion beneath the garden shack—lies hidden away just under the surface, waiting for its chance to escape.

Deanimated reifies, in artistic form, what I myself had always thought about the film: that it was far more than what it appeared to be. With digital manipulation, Arnold was able to reveal the truth behind the film: at its core, it's a surreal journey through a fractured man's mind. That surreality, implicit in Joseph Lewis' original, is made explicit by Arnold's manipulation. This is one of those rare cases in which digital manipulation is not being used to distort reality, but instead is revealing the reality underneath.

Arnold's *Deanimated* accomplishes the seemingly impossible. It manages to champion the surrealistic spirit of Lewis' *Invisible Ghost* while also placing the film—including its many flaws and virtues—in its proper historical and sociological context.

It's the ultimate proof that *Invisible Ghost* is, at heart, a work of surrealism.

9.

> "The approval of the public is to be avoided like the plague. It is absolutely essential to keep the public from entering if one wishes to avoid confusion. I must add that the public must be kept panting in expectation at the gate by a system of challenges and provocations."
>
> —André Breton, "Second Manifesto of Surrealism," 1930

> "[W]e have never ceased to maintain, with Lautrémont, that *poetry must be created by everyone* [...]."
>
> —André Breton, "Surrealist Situation of the Object," 1935

THERE ARE SO many surreal images in the films of Bela Lugosi that it would be difficult to name all of them here. Half-remembered images often come floating to the forefront of my brain, almost unbidden. In the middle of the night, teetering on the border of wakefulness and sleep, these images haunt my mind like invisible ghosts, brief flashes of visual poetry laced with silver nitrate, strange memories cast in monochromatic black-and-white: Murder Legendre holding up a white handkerchief in the air—the handkerchief is so white it almost glows—as a horde of half-alive men come shambling toward him out of the Haitian hills; the bestial Sayer of the Law stalking toward the camera, edging into an extreme close-up, while Max-Ernst-like animal-men creep behind him, howling angrily at their flawed creator; a bat-winged woman dressed in a pale white gown descending slowly, dream-like, toward the ruins of a castle; Dr Mirakle genuflecting before the exquisite corpse of a crucified prostitute, as if in deep and respectful prayer; General Petronovich bellowing in a jealous rage while a pistol bends and melts like silly putty in his fist; Vitus Werdegast staring up in sadness and wonder at the preserved carcass of his long-lost wife while surrounded by a stylish art deco hallway decorated with deceased women, all beautiful, all frozen in time; an elegant ballerina—half-woman, half-raven—performing double pirouettes in honor of a tuxedoed man whose eyes are haunted by lust and torture; a Eurasian scientist named Poten tries to burn a man's brain with a fishbowl; amidst expressionist shadows, a broken-necked hunchback with gnarled teeth lovingly strokes the furry chest of a storybook giant, whispering/boasting that the sleeping beast "does things" for him; Dr Paul Carruthers, dripping in perfume, runs in fear from a kite that looks like a giant devil bat; Nardo the Magician gestures proudly toward a cemetery, intoning the words, "The city of the dead. Do they, too, hear the howling of the frightened dogs?" while his dwarf assistant shrugs uncaringly; Dr James Brewster, looking more like a cross between an ape and a penguin than a human being, getting whipped brutally by a stunning blonde in stiletto heels; the face of Armand Tesla melting into wax amidst the smoking ruins of a bombed-out cathedral; Professor Dexter walking down a darkened street with a blowtorch in his hand, searching for an ape who has just emerged from an ice cube; Joseph's crippled and pathetic shadow being strangled by a man named Gray; an undead monkey shambling along with its little arms outstretched before it, as if under a hypnotic spell; a snarling half-man/half-wolf creature wearing a pressed shirt and tattered pants embraces/strangles a bat while launching itself off a cliff-side balcony toward a beach of crashing waves and sharp rocks thousands of feet below; a human being who thinks he's a vampire commands a robot to kill a septuagenarian transvestite; an unnamed spirit intoning the mantra "Beware of the big green dragon that sits on your doorstep. He eats little boys... puppy dog tails, and big, fat snails. Beware, take care... beware!" is superimposed over a horde of stampeding buffalo; Dr Eric Vornoff, wearing platform shoes from the 1970s, wrestles with an impotent octopus in a muddy lake in the 1950s; a grieving old gentleman takes a moment to sniff a beautiful flower before shuffling off to his death, the man's shadow still visible in the frozen frame as he cries out in agony, rising from his flimsy tomb only minutes later with an ivory-faced, obsidian-haired phantasm for a wife.

I could go on and on, but these are the enigmatic images that stand out most in my mind: cinematic riddles, low budget Zen koans, 2:00AM revelations, quasi-religious litanies for a postmodern generation weaned on nightmarish and non-rational images that came dripping out of a glass teat well past midnight, long past one's bedtime, long after all the adults had retreated into sleep. Even in an age when hundreds of different channels haunt the airwaves, long after the tradition of obligatory late-night spook shows have become an artifact of a fading past in which only a handful of channels were once available for the potential viewer, still programmers fill the night air with images of UFOs and ancient aliens and angry poltergeists, though more often than not these days such images will appear in the context of half-convincing documentaries that attempt to prove to the viewer that the non-rational is, in fact, rational. That the surreal is real and, therefore, unworthy of our fear, unworthy of our worship. In between these new and colorful images shot on video, however, one still sees the occasional throwback to a golden age of accidental surrealism.

As Nancy Joyce Peters wrote in the book *Surrealism and Its Popular Accomplices*:

> After the legitimation comedies and the frauds passed off as "news" have left the air, that is, *late at night and in the dark*, we are likely to find roving our television screens ubiquitous and disquieting figures—vampires, werewolves, mummies, zombies, abortive creations of diabolical doctors, and other masked and mutant beings. Monsters and magical practitioners have always been inseparable from the human imagination,

> a fact confirmed in ancient civilizations, rites and myths of tribal peoples, folk tales of peasant societies, the fantasies of childhood and the dreams of "civilized" adults. Only the means of expression changes [...].
>
> In poetry, content, especially latent content, is always sovereign over form. Sometimes the maker of a film is quite unaware of the resonances of the marvelous it emanates. Dream figures of animals appear as regularly as they once did in legends told around fires on starry nights in the past, and their sense of enchantment is not limited to the dialogues concerning radioactive mutation. Transformation into cat, wolf, ape, spider, cobra, alligator, plant, owl, bat, vulture, wasp: an uncannily familiar scenario expressing universal impulses to live outside social regulations prescribed by human law and to recognize deeply felt bonds with earth's other creatures. Here is a potential meeting ground, in film, with the wisdom of non-Western cultures, a hint of a future myth for all humanity which might break the chains of habitual conventions [...].
>
> Under the surface, horror films deal with *essentials*: the exaltation of desire, wishes for the excessive possibility, the truth inhering in the non-rational, and the absolute necessity for transmuting and surpassing present reality. The protagonists are on a quest as authentic as that of a medieval knight or a historic revolutionary. The dreamers are not satisfied. And although the passages of transformation are dangerous, dreamers will change the world [...]. Deprived of love, living a living death, disoriented among the electric rays of the 19th century's magneto apparatus and 20th century weaponry, the monster destroys an alienating world. Portraying in fantasy the images of defiance, negation and revolt, the horror film grants a powerful assent to freedom.[13]

And the films starring Bela Lugosi in particular, perhaps above all others, are overripe with such surrealistic representations of freedom from the knowable and the mundane.

10.

> "As has been proved to me after the fact, the definition of Surrealism given in the first Manifesto merely 'retouches' a great traditional saying concerning the necessity of 'breaking through the drumhead of reasoning reason and looking at the hole,' a procedure which will lead to the clarification of symbols that were once mysterious."
>
> —André Breton, "On Surrealism in Its Living Works," 1953

Invisible Ghosts

NO MATTER WHAT any critic in 1941 said about *Invisible Ghost*, and no matter whether the film is considered by viewers to be "good" or "bad" today, the fact is that the film is unquestionably unique. That Joseph H. Lewis and Bela Lugosi crossed paths for this one project (one artist on his way up in Hollywood, the other on his tumultuous way down) is fortuitous, as it gave Lugosi the chance to demonstrate that he could pull off a sensitive, sympathetic, nuanced performance even while portraying a serial murderer, and it gave Lewis the chance to demonstrate that he was capable of constructing an effective thriller with his own distinctive *noir* touches even within the confines of a screenplay that makes sense only in the context of dream-logic. Both artists benefited greatly from this too-brief collaboration, and it's unfortunate the two men never worked together again.

> "It is common knowledge that Surrealism saw in it the means of obtaining, most often under conditions of complete relaxation of the mind rather than complete concentration, certain incandescent flashes linking two elements of reality belonging to categories that are so far removed from each other that reason would fail to connect them and that require a momentary suspension of the critical attitude in order for them to be brought together."
>
> —André Breton, "On Surrealism in Its Living Works," 1953

Chapter 8

The Suppressed Science of Dr. Mirakle

The Cinematic Ancestors and Descendants of Charles Darwin

1. Mirakle v. Darwin

THE YEAR 2021 marked the 212th anniversary of the birth of Charles Darwin. Most people today are well aware that Darwin is the author of *On the Origin of Species By Means of Natural Selection, or the Preservation of Favoured Races in the Struggle for Life* (1859) and the man credited with the theory of evolution, which stated that human beings—indeed, all life forms on earth—were not created in a single instant by an omniscient deity but had instead evolved over time from simpler life forms, a discovery that shook the foundations of the scientific community and drew accusations of blasphemy from religious quarters around the world.[1] What few people know is that another scientist, a far more obscure one, is on record as having proposed similar theories a full fourteen years before the publication of Darwin's classic book. Given the known facts, it's not outside the realm of possibility to conclude that Darwin attended a lecture by this individual and pilfered his famous theory from him.

Or so Universal Studios would lead us to believe.

The obscure scientist in question was apparently known by a variety of different monikers, but the one by which history knows him is Dr Mirakle. According to director Robert Florey and screenwriters Tom Reed and Dale Van Every, Dr Mirakle visited Paris in the fall of 1845. Mirakle's scientific theories were considered so bizarre at the time that he was ostracized from the mainstream scientific community and forced to continue his research under the guise of a traveling circus. Mirakle's main experimental subject was an ape he called "Erik" who, according to Mirakle, possessed the intelligence of a normal human being. Mirakle's theory, stated hundreds of times during his sideshow presentations, was that human beings were descended from apes like Erik. Conversely, Dr Mirakle contended, apes such as Erik had the capability of adopting human behaviors if trained properly.

Mirakle conducted these experiments 121 years before Dian Fossey began her work with gorillas in Zaire in 1966. Unlike Fossey, however, Mirakle chose to train his experimental subjects to kill with precision rather than communicate peacefully with human beings. As a result, Erik the Ape was responsible for several deaths in the Rue Morgue area of Paris in 1845.

The thirty-two-year-old Edgar Allan Poe must have encountered Dr Mirakle when the traveling circus with which the doctor was associated put down stakes in Baltimore, Maryland, in 1840. Poe must have had some foreknowledge of Mirakle's plans, for he published a short story titled "Murders in the Rue Morgue" in *Graham's Magazine* in 1841, four years before the actual murders occurred. Since no character resembling Mirakle appears in the story, it's reasonable to assume that Poe was attempting to protect the doctor's identity for some reason. Perhaps Poe respected Mirakle's theories and wished to see him free to continue his groundbreaking scientific investigations.

Or so Universal Studios would lead us to believe.

In 1932, Universal produced a feature length film titled *Murders in the Rue Morgue*, ostensibly based on Poe's story. Fans of Poe were no doubt disappointed when they saw the film, as it bears little resemblance to the 1841 short story. On April 16, 1932, the British publication, *Today's Cinema*, called the film a "[v]ery free and greatly elaborated version of Edgar Allan Poe['s] story,"[2] not knowing that the Universal film was based less on the Poe story and more on actual historical events. Because Poe possessed such popular name value, Universal advertised the film as an adaptation of the celebrated Poe tale—and in some respects it was. But the main character of the film,

Pierre Dupin, a young medical student, bears almost no resemblance to Poe's brooding detective, C.Auguste Dupin.

2. Universal's Darwin

THE PRIMARY ARTISTS responsible for the 1932 Universal production of *Murders in the Rue Morgue* were director Robert Florey and his trio of screenwriters:Tom Reed, Dale Van Every and a very young John Huston, who would later win acclaim as the director of such classic films as *The Maltese Falcon* (1941) and *The Treasure of the Sierra Madre* (1948). Appropriately enough, Tom Reed would later co-write *The Loves of Edgar Allan Poe* (1941) while Dale Van Every would go on to write Victor Fleming's *Captain Courageous* (1937), among other notable screenplays. Huston came onto the project late in its development and merely polished the dialogue in Reed and Van Every's initial draft.

Robert Florey's *Murders in the Rue Morgue*, in a famous twist of Hollywood irony, came about because of James Whale's film adaptation of *Frankenstein* (1931). Florey had been the first director assigned the task of bringing the Mary Shelley Gothic novel to the screen with Bela Lugosi—who had portrayed Dracula in the successful Universal adaptation only a few months earlier—featured in the star role as the Monster. Lugosi was reluctant to take the assignment because, among other reasons, he did not wish to play a non-speaking role at that point in his career. (According to Florey, the director first approached Lugosi with the opportunity to play Dr Frankenstein, but the studio heads reversed that decision and insisted Lugosi play the Monster.) Lugosi refused the role, at which point the studio removed both Florey and Lugosi from the project and assigned them to *Murders in the Rue Morgue*, while James Whale and Boris Karloff went on to make cinematic history with *Frankenstein*.

Though no doubt disappointed that such a plumb assignment had been torn from his grasp, Florey did everything he could to make up for it with his expressionistic take on 1845 Paris in his consolation prize. An in-depth analysis of Florey's film can only be beneficial, as it's a telling touchstone that reveals the attitudes towards the theory of evolution at a time in the United States when the subject was still in wide dispute and capable of inflaming great debate among both religious and scientific figures alike. That Florey attempted to address the issue within a semi-fictional framework, within a popular medium like film, was daring in 1932 and is therefore worthy of deeper study now, when the topic of evolution is still capable of stirring anger and controversy in certain quarters.

3. Murders in the Rue Morgue

WE BEGIN OUR story at a carnival where we see exotic dancers from the Middle East (or at least their Hollywood stand-ins) entertaining our protagonists: Pierre (Leon Waycoff, who later became Leon Ames), Pierre's girlfriend Camille (Sidney Fox), Pierre's friend Paul (Bert Roach), and Paul's girlfriend Mignette (Edna Marion). A carnival barker directs our attention toward the dancers, advertising them as "the adorable Arab angels." Special emphasis is placed on the males in the crowd ogling the exotic dancers. Some older, respectable looking gentlemen exchange suggestive jokes about the dancers, and the leering expressions on their faces make their desires obvious.

> FIRST GENTLEMAN (referring to the dancers): Do they bite?
> SECOND GENTLEMAN: Oh, yes. But you have to pay *extra* for that!
> CAMILLE (to her boyfriend): See, Pierre, how *brown* they are. Is that their real color do you suppose, or have they painted themselves?
> PIERRE (smiling): Shall I find out for you?
> CAMILLE: Don't you dare!

Paul asks his girlfriend if she would, for him, learn to dance like the "Arab angels." When she appears offended and says no, Paul replies, "I guess I'll have to join the show."

In these exchanges, we see "civilized" white men lusting after dark-skinned, "lesser" females, and yet the men feel compelled to disguise their lust as playful jokes. Even in 1932, and certainly as far back as 1845, following through on their desires would have been seen as tantamount to bestiality… or at least one's priest would no doubt have said so from behind the pulpit on Sunday morning. And the product of such a sinful union would have been considered an inferior person, a "half-breed."

What the movie audience, as well as the audience at the carnival, does not yet know is that the story's antagonist, Dr Mirakle (Bela Lugosi), plans to prove his theory concerning the connection between mankind and simians by mating a human female with an ape. Mirakle, however, would never consider the product of such a sexual union to be a "half-breed," as he believes that humans and apes are members of the same species. Even in the pre-Code days of Hollywood (the censorious Motion Picture Production Code was not established until 1934), Universal could not have gotten away with stating Mirakle's intended goal quite so bluntly, though Florey attempted to do so in the earlier drafts of the screenplay. In order to suggest the same idea in a more oblique fashion, Florey and his screenwriters have Dr Mirakle claim that he is attempting to "mix" Erik's blood with that of a human, a polite euphemism for the bestial-rape-as-controlled-experiment the doctor intends.

The first shot of the civilized Parisians leering at females of an "inferior" race parallels the obvious lust later expressed by Erik the Ape (portrayed by Charles Gemora) for Pierre's girlfriend, Camille. Florey is bringing civilized man down to the level of an ape—or, conversely, raising civilized man *up* to Erik's level.

Florey seems interested in blurring the traditional line of racial identity, not just in the story itself but in several other aspects of the production. Dr Mirakle's servant/slave "Janos" is portrayed by the Black actor Noble Johnson (who also appeared in several other classic genre films of the period such as *The Most Dangerous Game*, *The Mummy*, and *King Kong*). Though Johnson is listed in the credits as "Janos, the Black One," Florey chose to have Universal makeup chief Jack Pierce make him up in *whiteface*. Though plenty of white actors portrayed Black men in early Hollywood films, very rarely did Black actors portray *white* men.

Matters of race and sexuality hang over the entire film like a shadow, perhaps not just in a metaphorical sense but in a Jungian sense as well. In Dr Carl Jung's psychological framework, a "shadow" is the innate self that rests within us, that mirrors choices by antithesis. In the context of the human ego and self-perception, the Jungian shadow is an ostensibly malignant being; however, the concept of a Jungian shadow may also encompass an incomplete ideal, stifled hopes, or inhibited thoughts, those hidden aspects of ourselves we do not wish to recognize. Erik the Ape is that shadow.

After seeing the exotic dancers, Pierre and his friends are lured into the tent of Dr Mirakle by the lurid promises of a sideshow barker: "Attention! Attention, ladies and gentlemen! Behind this curtain is the strangest creature your eyes will ever behold! Erik the Ape

Man, the monster who walks upright and speaks a language even as you and I! The ruler of the jungle whose giant hands can tear a man in half! Erik the Ape Man! The beast with a human soul! More cunning than a man and stronger than a lion!" Inevitably, perhaps, our protagonists follow the siren's call and enter the sideshow. The triangle-shaped entrance into the tent is decorated with the painting of an ape, its bowlegs straddling the arch. It seems as if the carnival-goers are actually penetrating a cavity between the ape's legs, as if to suggest that the characters are entering the ape's womb—or perhaps *re*entering the ape's womb? This would be appropriate, as these unsuspecting Parisians are about to hear a lecture about humans having *emerged* from apes long ago.

Dr Mirakle's sexual attraction toward Camille is made apparent from the start when he suggests that she take a seat in the front row where she can have a better view of the proceedings. Perhaps Mirakle wants a better view of *her*—or perhaps, even more perversely, he wishes *Erik* to have a better view of the demure ingénue.

Now comes Mirakle's presentation, Lugosi's chance to display all the strange mannerisms and disjointed line reads that made him so effective in the role of Dracula a year before. Standing in front of a painted backdrop decorated with illustrations of sealife evolving into apes and apes evolving into humans, Mirakle paces back and forth across the stage as he delivers a blasphemous lecture about the kinship humans share with simians: "Here, the story of man!" He points toward the chart behind him. "Crawling reptiles grew legs. Eons of ages passed! There came a time when a four-legged thing walked upright. Behold, the first *man*!" He gestures toward Erik in his cage.

The audience's reaction to Mirakle's theories are heated, to say the least—and probably mirror the reaction of many moviegoers in the South and the Midwest who wandered into a film called *Murders in the Rue Morgue* expecting a typical murder mystery, only to be assaulted with a lecture about evolution from Bela Lugosi ten minutes into the movie. This is almost a metafictional, postmodern moment. As the camera draws in on Lugosi's leering face, the audience in the carnival stand in for the audience in the theater watching the movie; just as Mirakle lures the carnival-goers with the promise of sensationalistic entertainment, only to pull the rug out from under them and assault them with heretical scientific theories, Florey as director pulls the same bait-and-switch. One wonders if Mirakle is echoing Florey's own

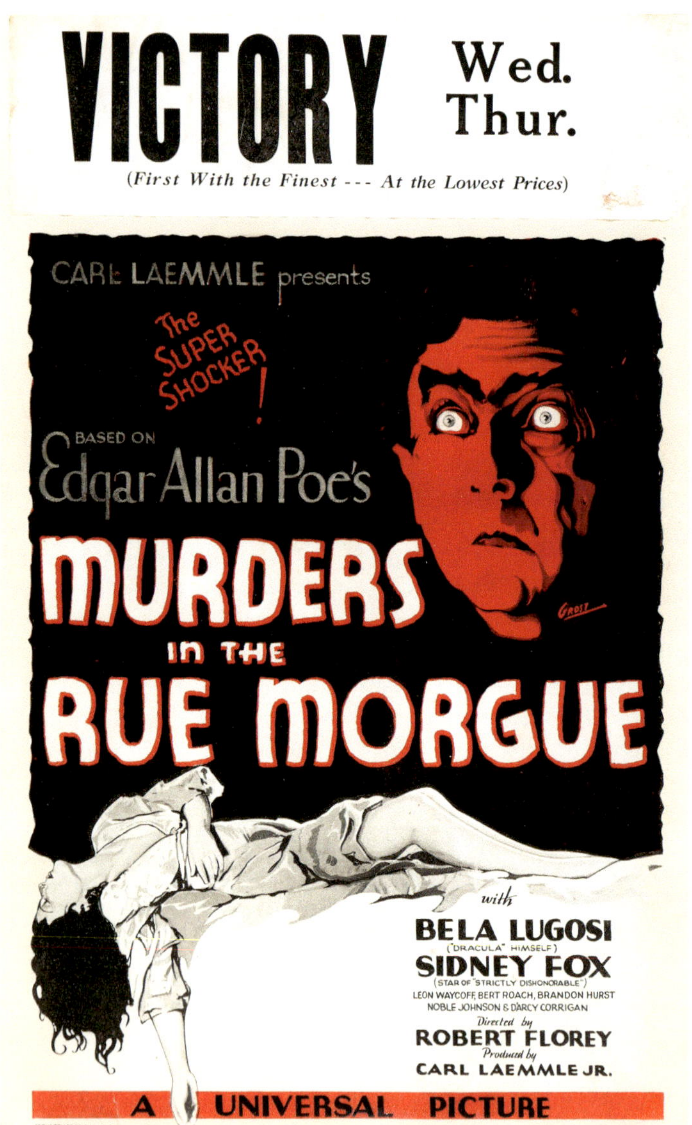
VICTORY
Wed.
Thur.
(First With the Finest --- At the Lowest Prices)
CARL LAEMMLE presents
The SUPER SHOCKER!
BASED ON
Edgar Allan Poe's
MURDERS
IN THE
RUE MORGUE
with
BELA LUGOSI
("DRACULA" HIMSELF)
SIDNEY FOX
(STAR OF "STRICTLY DISHONORABLE")
LEON WAYCOFF, BERT ROACH, BRANDON HURST
NOBLE JOHNSON & D'ARCY CORRIGAN
Directed by
ROBERT FLOREY
Produced by
CARL LAEMMLE JR.
A UNIVERSAL PICTURE

thoughts when he says, "Do you think these walls and curtains are my whole life? They are only a trap to catch the pennies of *fools*."

A man erupts from the audience and accuses Mirakle of spreading heresy. Mirakle replies, "Do they still burn men for heresy? Then burn me, Monsieur. Light the fire. Do you think your little candle will outshine the flame of truth? My life is consecrated to great *experiment*." Florey very nearly breaks the fourth wall when Mirakle stares directly into the camera—perhaps at the audience in the movie theater itself—and whispers, "I tell you I will prove...*your* kinship...with the ape."

Extreme close-ups of Lugosi's face, particularly his hypnotic eyes, almost became a motif of 1930s horror films, appearing and reappearing in *Dracula* (1931), *White Zombie* (1932), *The Return of Chandu* (1934), *The Dark Eyes of London* (aka *The Human Monster*, 1939), and several other films, but never was the technique used to better effect than in this moment when Mirakle is lambasting the entirety of the cinema-going audience of the 1930s for their reluctance to accept the theory of evolution.

In a series of quick cuts, the camera focuses on various audience members as Mirakle continues to insist on their "kinship with the ape." Each of the faces, even the prettiest ones, have a dour and bestial look to them, resembling more the extras in a Fellini movie from forty years later than the traditional background faces in a major Hollywood production. These quick cuts underscore the underlying truth in Mirakle's heretical claims.

As with many of the best and most subversive horror films of the 1930s, the supposed "villain" was the one character allowed to speak the inner thoughts of the filmmakers. Only a villain can get away with uttering heresies. After all, the "bad guys" in a popular medium like film couldn't possibly be speaking the truth. Just as James Whale would use the character of Dr Septimus Pretorius (portrayed by Ernest Thesiger) as his mouthpiece to challenge the religious strictures of his day in *Bride of Frankenstein* (1935), Florey uses Mirakle to assault the movie-going public with statements that would, if uttered by the hero of a film such as this, have caused some of the more fanatically evangelical segments of the audience to burn down the theater.

At one point during this unorthodox sideshow performance, Erik grabs Camille's bonnet and almost strangles Pierre. Mirakle offers to buy Camille a new bonnet merely as a ploy to discover Camille's address. Pierre prevents Camille from doing this and takes her away from Mirakle's tent. Frustrated by the tantalizing vision of Camille being wrenched from his grasp, Mirakle instead takes Janos on a coach ride to prowl along the waterfront and find an appropriate mate for Erik in order to continue his "research."

Dr Mirakle's core dilemma is no doubt a twisted, psychological one. He professes to have only the noblest scientific intentions, yet his essential quest is that of fulfilling his own thwarted sexual desires via Erik. Erik is his proxy. Lugosi's contorted, labored mannerisms hint at the possibility that Mirakle is a tortured man, perhaps suffering from a great deal of sexual frustration that can only be fulfilled through his "great experiment." Mirakle's quest is an impossible one. From what occurs later, we know he's searching for a woman who looks like a whore on the surface, but nonetheless is "pure" inside. This is made evident by his actions after the tempting visage of Camille is taken from him by Pierre (a younger and more virile rival).

Mirakle spots a "female in distress" in the thick fog that plagues the Parisian waterfront. Two potential johns are apparently fighting over the streetwalker (portrayed by a teenage Arlene Francis in her screen debut). The streetwalker stands there and screams as the two men, behaving like alpha-male primates, murder one another. Ironically, the woman is spared the fate of becoming a living prize for either one of the first two human primates only to fall into the hands of Dr Mirakle, who wishes to hand her over to a *genuine* primate.

(Let's pause for just a moment for an interesting side note that demonstrates the continuing influence of Florey's film on subsequent writers and artists. The bestselling 1980s graphic novel *V for Vendetta* by Alan Moore and David Lloyd begins with a scene in which the anarchist V saves a prostitute from the fog-strewn streets of London under very similar circumstances. Later in the story, V puts the girl through a series of physical and psychological tortures as part of his own "great experiment." On the first page of the graphic novel, the reader catches a glimpse of V's secret lair. One of the decorations hanging on the wall above his vanity mirror is an original movie poster for none other than Robert Florey's *Murders in the Rue Morgue*.)

In the film's next scene, one that was censored from many early versions of the film, Mirakle has the prostitute crucified to a large wooden crossbeam in a series of shots redolent with perverse religious imagery made even more twisted by Lugosi's manic performance and offbeat, almost dream-like, line readings. We enter the scene *in media res* as the prostitute whimpers and screams, Mirakle insisting that the pain will last only "a little while longer." Here the doctor's psycho-sexual sadism is made evident by the fact that he is only removing blood from the prostitute's arm, leading to the conclusion that Mirakle has taken a leisurely route to reach this otherwise simple goal.

Mirakle puts the blood sample under a microscope. When he discovers that the woman has "rotten blood," a euphemism for some form of sexual disease, Mirakle grows enraged and shouts in her face: "Your blood is rotten because of your sins! Your beauty was a *lie*!" Mirakle requires a "pure" woman for his experiment, chooses to kidnap a prostitute instead, then flies into a homicidal rage when she turns out not to be "pure." Mirakle has set up for himself and his victims an almost impossible set of standards, similar to the inquisitors in the Salem witch trials who condemned any woman who caused a married man to have an erection to prolonged torture and execution. After all, any woman "impure" enough to illicit such a reaction in a church-going man could *only* be a witch.

The woman's crime is not that she fails to meet Mirakle's standards. She fails to meet the standards that Mirakle has established for *Erik the Ape*. Ironically, the woman's blood must be pure enough to mingle with that of the beast, not the other way around.

The line between human and primate is blurred throughout the film. Many of the actors and actresses have a bestial look to them. Mirakle's own bizarre uni-brow makes him resemble something that's vaguely half-animal. The Morgue Keeper (D'Arcy Corrigan), who plays a prominent role in the film, possesses features that are more akin to ape than human. The Morgue Keeper's assistant, who delivers to him the corpse of the murdered prostitute, is also animalistic and displays morals and ethics as base as that of an unthinking primate. The homeless people camped out by the river are referred to as "waterfront rats" by one of the civilized gentlemen earlier in the film; indeed, they look like vermin, particularly the old woman (portrayed by Tempe Pigott) who delivers these lines about the recent spate of murder victims: "Women, all of them. Life is hard. The river is kind, the river is soft. It rocks them to sleep and asks no pay." These onlookers express no real remorse at the discovery of yet another murdered woman in their neighborhood, only stoic curiosity, as if they're resigned to tragedy as a way of life. Their economic despair has rendered them nothing more than their moniker implies: "waterfront rats," too busy scrounging to survive to indulge in any human compassion beyond a certain quiet envy... envy that this anonymous streetwalker has obtained the restful *rigor mortis* of death while they're forced to deal with the rigors of life.

At one point in the film, Pierre is standing on Camille's balcony talking to her about Paris and the people who live there. Camille says, "Wouldn't it be fun to know all that was going on inside those houses?" Pierre replies, "Perhaps it's just as well that we don't know. Think of what all those walls are hiding." In the context of the entire film, it's very clear what they're hiding: the bestial side of man, the original primate consciousness from which humans evolved.

In a private conversation with his roommate and fellow medical student, Paul, Pierre admits that he sympathizes with Mirakle's theories of evolution and finds him to be a "fascinating man." Paul responds with blustering frustration at this heresy. When Pierre refers to "what all those walls are hiding," he's actually referring to the civilized veneer of modern society that chooses to keep the savage side of human nature hidden away in the shadows rather than confront the obvious: that there's a little bit of beast in all of us, that evolution is not just a theory, but a fact.

The entire movie is about hidden fears. At the beginning of the film, the civilized ladies and gentlemen of Paris observe Arabs and Native Americans on display. A barker refers to the Native Americans as "Blood-thirsty savages from the wilds of America! See the redskins scalp their victims!" The gentlemen in the audience mock the performers because, subconsciously, they fear it's only circumstance and environment which separates them from a similar position, that they're somehow related to these inferior beasts, that perhaps they themselves should be on display.

It's the fear of being related to an ape that causes Sir Arthur Jermyn, the protagonist of H.P. Lovecraft's 1920 short story "Facts Concerning the Late Arthur Jermyn and His Family," to commit suicide. The theme of this pulp story is so similar to that of Robert Florey's version of *Murders in the Rue Morgue*, one wonders if the director or any of the screenwriters were familiar with it. Since the story originally appeared in the pages of *Weird Tales* in the early 1920s, under the title "The White Ape," this is not at all impossible.

Lovecraft's story begins with the ominous sentences:

> Life is a hideous thing, and from the background behind what we know of it peer demoniacal hints of truth which make it sometimes a thou-

> sandfold more hideous. Science, already oppressive with its shocking revelations, will perhaps be the ultimate exterminator of our human species—if separate species we be—for its reserve of unguessed horrors could never be borne by mortal brains if loosed upon the world. If we knew what we are, we should do as Sir Arthur Jermyn did; and Arthur Jermyn soaked himself in oil and set fire to his clothing one night.[3]

Anthony Pearsall offers a thorough summary of the story in his book, *The Lovecraft Lexicon* (2005):

> According to the narrator, Arthur Jermyn was so peculiar-looking that many people with his facial features would have wanted to die; but he has a sweet soul. He is a poet, a dreamer, a scholar, and a First Class Honors graduate—the highest possible rank—of Oxford University. He is the son of Sir Alfred Jermyn and "a music-hall singer of unknown origin." (Music halls were popular forms of working-class entertainment in the nineteenth and early twentieth centuries, featuring a variety of less-than-great singers warbling typically sentimental, comical, or patriotic songs in front of large audiences, on a variety-show bill interspersed with comedians, acrobats, magicians, and so forth. A gentleman's marriage to a music-hall singer in the late Victorian era would have been a social scandal.)
>
> After her husband deserted the family, the mother raised her son at Jermyn House, the family seat, although their circumstances were not especially wealthy. In 1911, Sir Arthur makes an expedition to the Belgian Congo (now simply "Congo"), among the Onga and Kaliri tribes. He meets Mwanu, an elderly Kaliri, and hears some significant stories about a lost city and its inhabitants. In 1912, he finds the remains of the lost city Sir Wade described, which—in a constant characteristic of HPL's lost cities—has passageways that "[seemed] to lead down into a system of vaults," perhaps hiding horrors unrevealed on the surface. In June, 1913, back in England, Sir Arthur is informed by a letter from Monsieur Verhaeren, his Belgian contact in the Congo, that a certain stuffed goddess from the lost city had been found in the keeping of the now-peaceful N'bangu tribe. Sir Arthur receives the mummified relic in a box on August 13, 1913, and opens it privately. The box, he instantly understood, contained the withered and battered corpse of his great-great-great-grandmother, "a mummified white ape of some unknown species, less hairy than any recorded variety, and infinitely near mankind—quite shockingly so." Then, with a

> scream, he races out of the room, douses himself with flammable liquid, and sets fire to himself on the moors beyond Jermyn House. His remains were *not* collected and buried, and some of the Royal Anthropological Institute burn the mummy and afterwards refuse to admit that Arthur Jermyn ever existed.[4]

It's interesting to note that the fear of discovering that one's ancestry can be traced back to far less than "noble" origins lay at the core of another classic Lovecraft story, "The Shadow over Innsmouth," in which the nameless protagonist discovers that he's descended from a long line of "fish-men" who have lived off the coast of Massachusetts for generations. Lovecraft, like many people in the early twentieth century, was haunted by the notion that the veneer of genteel civilization could be wiped out by a single moment of "discovery"... perhaps a metaphor for the advancements of the biological sciences at that time.

As Lovecraft biographer S.T. Joshi writes in *H.P. Lovecraft: A Life* (Necronomicon Press, 1996):

> [W]hat Lovecraft is suggesting is that the inhabitants of this city are not only the "missing link" between ape and human but also *the ultimate source for all white civilization*. For someone of Lovecraft's well-known racialist bent, such a thing would be a horror surpassing any isolated case of miscegenation.[5]

Robert Florey's *Murders in the Rue Morgue*, under the guise of being a mere piece of popular entertainment (just as Dr Mirakle himself disguised his scientific lectures as a sideshow attraction), rubs the faces of its audience in the "demoniacal hints of truth" which caused Sir Jermyn to snuff out his own life. Unlike Lovecraft, however, Florey sometimes transforms this fear into opportunities for dark comedy. Perhaps this should be expected, as Florey also directed the Marx Brothers' first film, *The Cocoanuts*, for Paramount Studios three years before. (From the Marx Brothers to Bela Lugosi... as bizarre a career trajectory as one could imagine in Hollywood's Golden Age.) In one of the only scenes in the book derived directly from Poe's short story, three "witnesses" to a murder—in truth, they only overheard the murder from the hall downstairs—attempt to identify the strange language spoken by the assailant. Of course, none of them realize that the assailant was speaking a completely inhuman language, that of an ape. The German witness insists he heard Italian being spoken. The Italian insists it was Danish. A native of Denmark insists it was German. Their disagreement descends into a heated argument during which none of them can be understood. Their irrational debate makes them seem more like chattering apes in a zoo rather than civilized human beings.

This scene has taken a beating from many recent critics, perhaps because it detracts from the cheap thrills they're so conditioned to expect from a film of this type, but Florey's darkly humorous point (as well as Poe's before him) should be obvious when looking at the story as a whole: Human beings of different races are so alienated from one another that they perceive each other as being nothing more than animals; conversely, they do not realize that *their* language sounds just as bestial to a member of a different race. We can perceive the beast in others, but not in ourselves. It's easy to imagine the human race, in abstract form, being descended from primates, but when the logical implications of this discovery are taken to their ultimate conclusion, one is likely to reject it and instead remain sanguine in the belief that God created Mankind in His own exalted image.

When Erik the Ape first speaks in grunts and growls at the sideshow, Mirakle turns to the audience and says, "Listen to him, brothers and sisters. He's speaking to you. Can you understand what he says, or have you forgotten?" Again, the implication is that humans have forgotten their primate roots and Mirakle's goal is to rub their faces in the ugly truth.

Arthur Jermyn was willing to accept this truth, but he felt his only way to deal with it was to wipe himself out, for living with the knowledge would require readjusting his myopic world view and seeing himself on the same level as the "inferior" races that he, much like Lovecraft himself, had been brought up to despise.

Lovecraft's extreme xenophobia and racism, which rendered him incapable of functioning within a metropolis like New York, has already been analyzed by a number of writers. In 1912, eight years before he wrote "Arthur Jermyn," Lovecraft composed this poem and distributed it to friends and family[6]:

On the Creation of Niggers
When, long ago, the Gods created Earth
In Jove's fair image Man was shap'd at birth.
The beasts for lesser parts were next design'd;

Yet were they too remote from humankind.
To fill this gap, and join the rest to man,
Th' Olympian host conceiv'd a clever plan.
A beast they wrought, in semi-human figure.
Fill'd it with vice, and call'd the thing a NIGGER.[7]

It's easy to see how the man who wrote this poem, if given the news that he was secretly related to a lost tribe of half-human primates in deepest, darkest Africa, might resort to self-immolation in order to deal with the revelation.

In his version of *Murders in the Rue Morgue*, as stated before, Florey often blurs the line between animal and human. Mirakle, however, seems very clear on where the line ends: It *doesn't*. Mirakle continually insists that Erik has not just been trained to act like a human, he *is* human.

At the very beginning of his presentation, Mirakle says, "I'm not exhibiting a freak or a monstrosity of nature, but a milestone in the development of science. The shadow of Erik the Ape hangs over us all—the dark before the Dawn of Man." At which point, Mirakle unveils Erik for the first time. This last line, coupled with Lugosi's venomous delivery, gives the impression that Mirakle is being somewhat sarcastic when he refers to Erik as "the dark before the Dawn of Man." Mirakle doesn't consider the birth of mankind to have been the dawn of anything; it's clear that Mirakle has little use for mankind, except as experimental subjects to prove that humans are no better than animals. (His theatrical moniker, Mirakle, seems laden with sarcasm as well. A modern equivalent would be a biologist like Stephen Jay Gould touring the American South giving lectures about evolution under the name "Dr Kreation.")

When Erik is visibly pleased by the nearness of Camille to his cage, Mirakle says, "Erik is only human, Mademoiselle. He has an eye for *beauty*!" The phrase "only human" again suggests that Mirakle does not hold humanity in high regard, though sometimes Mirakle does find use for "beauty," if only temporarily, until beauty expires prematurely.

Later in the film, Mirakle tracks Camille to the apartment that she shares with her mother. After Camille refuses to be lured into Mirakle's coach, the good doctor sends Erik the Ape into Camille's bedroom to kidnap her. The kidnapping is interrupted, however, by Camille's hysterical mother, Madame L'Espanaye (Betty Ross Clarke). What happens next is one of those rare moments when studio interference can make a scene *more* daring and suggestive than originally intended.

According to the authors of the encyclopedic book, *Universal Horrors: The Studio's Classic Films, 1931–1946*: "Upon the film's completion, Carl Laemmle, Jr., ordered reshoots of several key scenes. In a bid to add to the realism of Erik's scenes, close-ups of an actual monkey, filmed at a zoo, were none-too-artfully edited into the final prints."[8] Bob Burns, an expert in the history of cinematic horror, spoke to the authors of *Universal Horrors* about his 1957 meeting with Charles Gemora, the actor who portrayed Erik the Ape:

> [T]he thing about *Murders in the Rue Morgue* that stuck in Charlie's craw a little was the fact that close-ups of an actual chimp were inserted into the movie instead of the close-ups they'd shot of Charlie in his gorilla suit. When he saw the movie, he said he was in shock because the movie would, all of a sudden, jump from a shot of him in his gorilla suit to a shot of that very different-looking chimp. He wasn't too pleased with that, and could never figure out why they did it. His gorilla face was perfectly mobile, it could do the expressions that were needed.[9]

The ironic result of this tampering on the part of the studio, which was apparently done against Florey's wishes, was that it lent a perverse twist to the murder of Camille's mother. Due to the combination of the angle of the camera, the chimp's frenetic motions, and the actress' high-pitched screams, it appears as if Erik the Ape is *raping* Camille's mother rather than just beating her to death as originally intended. The studio balked at having Mirakle state that he intended on mating an ape with a woman, but then altered the film after the fact by inserting shots that actually seem to *show* the very act the studio heads didn't want Lugosi to mention in a mere sentence.

At the end of the film, Erik the Ape turns against Dr Mirakle and kills him—which is exactly how James Whale's *Frankenstein* ended a year earlier. It could be that this element was a direct carry-over from Florey's adaptation of Shelley's novel. In Bryan Senn's 1996 book *Golden Horrors: An Illustrated Critical Filmography, 1931–1939*, Florey is quoted as saying:

> I wrote the *Rue Morgue* adaptation in a week and directed the film in four. That was during the fall of 1931. In *Rue Morgue*, I used the same device I employed in my *Frankenstein* adaptation. Bela Lugosi became Dr. Mirakle—a mad scientist desirous of creating a human being—not

> with body parts stolen from a graveyard and a brain from a lab, but by the mating of an ape with a woman.[10]

Unlike in *Frankenstein*, however, Erik the Ape turns on his master—not because he's been rejected by him, but because he wants to prevent Mirakle from harming his prize, Camille. Ironically, Mirakle is brought down by the very theory he was attempting to prove. There are two alpha-males in the cage and only one prize. The weaker primate has to go, and he does. The stronger alpha-male prevails. He claims his prize and takes to the highest rooftops of Paris with the unconscious beauty under his arm, much like another primate would do only a year later in a far more dramatic fashion in Merian Cooper and Ernest Schoedsack's *King Kong* (1933). Just like in *King Kong*, Erik is riddled with bullets and falls off the rooftop to his death below while the hero saves the girl from a similar fate.

4. The Scopes Monkey Trial and Its Cinematic After Effects: The 1920s to the 1940s

MURDERS IN THE Rue Morgue was released on February 21, 1932. This was only seven years after the highly controversial 1925 legal case The State of Tennessee v. John Thomas Scopes, also known as "The Scopes Monkey Trial" which later inspired the 1955 hit play *Inherit the Wind* by Jerome Lawrence and Robert Edwin Lee. In Dayton, Tennessee, a high school teacher was arrested for violating the Butler Act which outlawed the teaching of evolution in high schools in any form. Despite his being defended by Clarence Darrow, the most prominent defense attorney of his day, the jury found Scopes guilty on July 21, 1925 and forced him to pay hefty fines. The Butler Act was not repealed in Tennessee until 1967, forty-two years later.

The Scopes Monkey Trial may have kicked off a cinematic fascination with the link between ape and human that lasted through the 1940s, but for some reason this fascination could only manifest itself safely in the form of horror fiction. First came Richard Rosson's *The Wizard* (1927), starring Edmund Lowe, who would later star, alongside Bela Lugosi, in the lead role of Fox's 1932 film *Chandu the Magician*. *The Wizard*, a lost silent film also produced by Fox, was an adaptation of *Balaoo*, a 1911 novel by Gaston Leroux, author of *The Phantom of the*

Opera. Both the book (whose initial English translation was first advertised as *The Mysterious Mr. Noel*) and the movie are about a doctor who turns an ape into a human with predictably disastrous results. Some scholars have cited the Leroux novel as a possible inspiration for Edgar Rice Burroughs' *Tarzan of the Apes*, which first appeared as a serial in the October 1912 issue of *All-Story Magazine*, but *Balaoo* did not make its first appearance in English till 1913. It was one of Leroux's most popular works in its day; it was first filmed as a short the year after its initial publication: Victorin Jasset's *Balaoo*, a mere 352 meters of film that was shown at US carnival sideshows as *Balaoo the Demon Baboon*. It was simply an excuse to show actor Lucien Bataille, in semi-simian makeup, photographed upside down so that he appeared to creep across the ceiling to strangle his victim. Though *Balaoo* would be filmed at least once more and inspire other films by example, Leroux's 1937 sequel, *Les Fils De Balaoo* ("The Sons of Balaoo"), remains untranslated.

Following the box office successes of Universal's *Dracula* and *Frankenstein*, Paramount Studios decided to get in on the act with *Island of Lost Souls* (1932), an adaptation of H.G. Wells' *The Island of Dr. Moreau*. Wells intended his 1896 novel to be a critique of vivisection as well as a socialistic parody of class barriers and organized religion. Directed by Erle C. Kenton and starring Charles Laughton as Dr. Moreau (the cast also includes the ubiquitous Bela Lugosi as The Sayer of the Law), *Island of Lost Souls* remains to this day an atmospheric and genuinely disturbing film, the best cinematic adaptation of H.G. Wells' classic novel (filmed again in 1977 and 1996).

Though Allan Dwan's *The Gorilla* (1939) is an ostensible comedy featuring the Ritz Brothers (a bargain sub-basement version of The Three Stooges, if such an improbability can be imagined), nonetheless the film also has broad horror elements that revolve around the human-like antics of an escaped gorilla. The film also features horror regulars Lionel Atwill and Bela Lugosi in the red herring role of a spooky butler, a part intended for Peter Lorre who wisely avoided the assignment by feigning pneumonia. The plot revolves around a rich man (Atwill) who hires the Ritz Brothers to protect him from a criminal known as The Gorilla; of course, when the previously mentioned gorilla shows up in the mansion, crazy hi-jinx ensue.

The next year, 1940, Monogram studios produced a film called *The Ape*, co-written by Curt Siodmak, who would later move on from "Poverty Row" to write far more notable horror screenplays like *The Wolf Man* (1941), *I Walked with a Zombie* (1943) and *The*

Beast with Five Fingers (1946). Helmed by former silent film director William Nigh, *The Ape* stars Boris Karloff as Dr Bernard Adrian, a scientist who believes that a crippled girl can be cured of paralysis with fluid extracted from a human spine. Alas, the only way that the humanitarian can attain the fluid is by murdering people. Dr Adrian chooses the only natural solution to this dilemma: He kills and skins an ape named Nabu, recently escaped from a carnival, wears its flesh like a costume, and roams about the countryside clawing people to death in the hopes that the simple folk of Red Creek will believe that these murders were perpetrated by the escaped simian. Surprisingly, this clever scheme does not work for very long; however, it does work just long enough for Dr Adrian to attain the necessary amount of fluid to cure the child of her disease. Adrian dies in the gorilla suit, riddled with bullet holes from the rifles of the local sheriff and his ape-hunting posse, his last sight that of the girl rising from her wheelchair. The End.

In the following year, Paramount Studios produced the surprisingly stylish *The Monster and the Girl* (1941) directed by Stuart Heisler. Despite its lurid title, the film takes a sophisticated approach to the base subject matter; its story structure is complex and its cinematography atmospheric. The film, barely over an hour long, is peculiar in its construction. The first act of the film appears to be a straightforward courtroom drama that shifts naturally into a *noir* gangster film in its second act, then somehow in its third act metamorphoses into all-out Gothic horror complete with a mad scientist named Dr Perry portrayed by the always devilish George Zucco. Scot Webster, portrayed by Phillip Terry, attempts to save his sister Susan Webster (Ellen Drew) from a gangster named W.S. Bruhl (Paul Lukas), who has forced her into a life of prostitution. Bruhl and his gang frame Scot for murder. Scot is electrocuted and his body given to Dr Perry for experimentation. Perry transplants Scot's brain into that of an ape. Perry, resurrected in the body of the ape, escapes from the doctor's lab and proceeds to murder the gangsters who corrupted his sister and sent him to the electric chair.

Despite the patchwork nature of this cross-genre melodrama, the various acts all cohere into a seamless whole. The shadow of the Scopes trial rears its head as the link between man and ape are made subtly evident in the form of this B-programmer. Neither Dr Perry nor any other character in the film rhapsodizes quite so eloquently about evolution as Dr Mirakle; nonetheless, the message is made clear. After all, how else could this experimental transplant have come off so successfully if ape and human were not genetically compatible, almost like brothers?

The next year found Universal jumping back onto the simian bandwagon with *The Strange Case of Dr. Rx* (1942), in which a cowled mad scientist known only as Dr Rx threatens to transfer the brain of the protagonist, private eye Jerry Church (Patric Knowles), into that of a caged ape named Inbongo (Ray "Crash" Corrigan, who also played Nabu in *The Ape*). This would mark yet another simian-themed film for director William Nigh, helmsman of *The Ape*, who was no doubt acutely aware of how far he'd fallen since his days at MGM directing Lon Chaney in the 1927 silent classic *Mr. Wu.*

It's worth noting briefly, by the way, that Chaney himself starred in a pre-Scopes-Monkey-trial but explicitly *Balaoo*-indebted "man-into-ape" film called *A Blind Bargain* (1922). It was directed by Wallace Worsley, with whom Chaney would reunite for *The Hunchback of Notre Dame* (1923). In *A Blind Bargain*—a film for which no prints are known to exist—Chaney takes on dual roles: that of the mad scientist Dr Lamb, as well as his experiment-gone-wrong, an apish assistant over whom the doctor loses control. Considering the impossibility of screening it, it's difficult to assess the film's quality or thematic significance, but it's safe to assume that the "blind bargain" in the title refers to a "Faustian bargain" made by Dr Lamb, which would make this yet another in a long line of cautionary tales about the dangers of meddling with science.

Perhaps the best of the 1940s films that used the theory of evolution as a major plot point was Harry Lachman's *Dr. Renault's Secret*, a Fox production of 1942. Though not an official adaptation—it was not included in Jean Rollin's exhaustive Leroux filmography in *Midi Minuit Fantastique* 24 (Winter 1970)—this was the third film version of *Balaoo*. The basic plot of *Dr. Renault's Secret* is similar to that of *Balaoo* in that it's about a mad scientist (Renault here, Coriolis in the Leroux novel) who captures an ape from Karawak, Java, brings him back to civilization, and transforms him gradually into a human being with the help of "glandular injections and brain surgery." Renault is portrayed by none other than George Zucco, fresh from similar experimentations in *The Monster and the Girl*. In the 1940s, for some reason, it seems as if appearing in a film with an ape was almost sure to attract similar roles. Bela Lugosi, for example, will have three more encounters with apes and gorillas before the end of this chapter.

Despite the fact that the Production Code forbade any overt support of Darwinian evolution in a film, *Dr. Renault's Secret* clearly implies that humans evolved from apes and that the reverse was just as possible. It is yet another "Modern Prometheus" story in which a scientist tampers with the natural order of the world and meets a fatal end as a result. Despite all of Renault's science and training, the "demon baboon," here called Noel as in the Leroux novel (and very effectively portrayed by J. Carrol Naish), reverts to his animalistic self during a festival in a nearby village and kills several people who dared to mock him. One of these victims is none other than Dr Renault. Naish is able to convey to the audience that Noel is not in control of his actions. As with Boris Karloff's portrayal of Frankenstein's Monster, Noel is a sympathetic character capable of redemption. In the final act, Renault's daughter, Madelon (Madeleine in the Leroux novel), with whom Noel has fallen in love, is kidnapped by a thug named Rogell (Mike Mazurki) and taken to a windmill on the outskirts of town. Noel kills Rogell and throws his corpse from the top of the windmill, just as the Monster did to Dr Frankenstein in James Whale's film, before dying himself from wounds sustained during his battle with Rogell.

One might conclude that the story is a condemnation of science: "There Are Things Man Was Never Meant To Know." But it's a mistake to assume that the creators of either *Frankenstein* (book or film) or *Dr. Renault's Secret* would be so narrow-minded in their point of view. Both are cautionary tales, true, but it's important to remember that Frankenstein's crime is *not* that he usurped the powers of Nature and created a human being; his real crime, once having done the deed, is turning his back on that creation and treating him as something *less* than human. Rejected and left for dead in a strange world, possessing the emotional maturity of a child but the strength of several full grown adults, the Monster lashes out at his creator as any child would if he or she shared the Monster's physical attributes. Frankenstein's crime is not creating life, but refusing to recognize his creation's innate humanity.

The same is true of Dr Renault. Renault displays a deep knowledge of Darwin's theories. He clearly wishes to prove that the environment makes the man: Once the "demon baboon" has been evolved physically into a reasonable facsimile of a civilized human being, the proper environment will maintain Noel's civilized façade. And this would probably be true, except for the fact that Renault ruins the experiment himself by treating Noel like an animal, forcing him to sleep in a cage when Noel shows the slightest sign of recidivism and whipping him like a dog if he disobeys the doctor's orders. The doctor treats him like a bloodthirsty animal and receives the same treatment in return. Any "civilized" human being would no doubt react the same way to being caged and tortured.

The film also goes a step further to point out that many of the human beings in the film act far less human than Noel. Almost all of Noel's actions are motivated by love for Madelon whereas Renault's sadism is motivated by egotism and a perverse need for fame and success in the scientific community. The cruel mockery indulged in by Noel's victims at the carnival are motivated by xenophobia. Rogell's kidnapping of Madelon is motivated by greed and perhaps lust. The point is clear: that some humans are incapable of humanity, despite their civilized veneers or fancy clothes or professional standings, whereas the only true beast in the story, Noel, is willing to sacrifice himself for love.

The science fiction novelist Philip K. Dick was plagued by the question of "What Is Human?" throughout his entire writing career. He meditated on similar themes in such novels as *Do Androids Dream of Electric Sheep?* (1968, filmed as *Blade Runner*), *We Can Build You* (1972), and *Flow My Tears, the Policeman Said* (1974). Mary Shelley would no doubt have sympathized with these novels and their creator. Eventually, Dick decided to define humanity as "kindness" and perhaps that's the closest anyone will ever get to a precise summation of the term. *Dr. Renault's Secret,* for all its Gothic trappings, shares a similar point of view.

A year after *Dr. Renault's Secret* hit the silver screen, Bela Lugosi was once again reminded of the intimate link between ape and human in William Beaudine's *The Ape Man* (1943), produced by Monogram studios. Lugosi portrays Dr James Brewster, a gland expert experimenting with the spinal fluid of apes for purposes which Barney A. Sarecky, the screenwriter, never bothers to mention. Brewster experiences the unintended side effects of slowly transforming (reverting?) into an ape. When he discovers that only human spinal fluid can reverse the process (the folks at Monogram were clearly stealing from their own previous film, *The Ape*), the inevitable occurs and innocents start dropping dead all over town. A peculiarity of this film is the postmodern, metafictional touch—thrown in for no apparent reason—of the film's screenwriter (portrayed by Ralph Littlefield) appearing repeatedly as a mysterious character who will sometimes pop up out of the shadows and warn various characters away from situations in which they would otherwise have met a fatal end. In fact, the screenwriter is the one who utters the final line of the film: "Screwy idea, wasn't it?" It seems appropriate to mention that the first horror novelist to insert himself into his own stories was none other than Gaston Leroux.

The Ape Man is often cited as a Golden Turkey camp classic in the *Plan 9 from Outer Space* category, but very rarely are such films acknowledged to be "screwy" by the screenwriter *within the movie itself.* This gradual turn toward the absurd might indicate the lessening of disapproval toward the subject of the link between man and ape which, in the early 1940s, was still controversial enough to be considered taboo by the Production Code. And yet despite its taboo nature, it seems every new year would bring along with it at least one new entry in this ever-growing genre. Though the word "evolution" itself was never mentioned in films like *The Ape Man,* the shadow of Darwin hung over every frame.

Three months after *The Ape Man* hit the theaters came Universal's *Captive Wild Woman*, directed by Edward Dmytryk (who would later move on to direct far more famous films such as *The Caine Mutiny* [1954] and *Raintree County* [1957]). Those who had seen *Dr. Renault's Secret* may have experienced some *déjà vu* when they saw it. Here, a mad scientist, Dr Sigmund Walters (John Carradine), captures a female ape named Cheela (again played by Ray "Crash" Corrigan) and, through the intravenous injection of sex hormones, transforms her into a human female whom he christens "Paula Dupree" (Acquanetta). Like Noel, Paula has difficulty maintaining her civilized façade and commits murder, but redeems herself at the end by sacrificing her life in order to save a loved one, in this case animal trainer Fred Mason (Milburn Stone), the man who captured Cheela in the first place.

Captive Wild Woman is rife with peculiar psychological implications and, with a film such as this, it's difficult to know if any of them were intended by the screenwriters, the director, or the actors. We are told at the beginning of the movie that Dr Sigmund Walters is a famous surgeon who has written groundbreaking articles for peer-reviewed scientific journals. At one point, our heroine Beth Colman (Evelyn Ankers) is sitting in Dr Walters' waiting room reading one of his articles and, for a second, we see the title: "Racial Improvement." Later in the film, Walters brags that his ultimate goal is to breed a race of "super men." Keep in mind that the film was made during the middle of America's involvement with World War II. Since the villain's given name is German, it's not unlikely that the screenwriters wished to associate this mad scientist with the far less fictional ones operating at that time out of Nazi Germany, and some of Carradine's dialogue certainly evokes the insanity of real life megalomaniacs like Dr Josef Mengele. Observe this exchange between Dr Walters and his skittish assistant, Ms Strand (Fay Helm):

> STRAND: Look at this girl. Slowly but surely, you're sapping the life out of her. It's murder, doctor. You *can't* do it!
> WALTERS: Why should a single life be considered so important?
> STRAND: Look, Dr Walters, for thirteen years I've worked with you—shared your experiments, watched you gain the highest honors in the field of endocrinology. I've seen you gain control over the physical characteristics of men and change the breed and sex of animals. I've listened to your dreams of breeding a race of super men.
> WALTERS: Isn't that a laudable intent?
> STRAND: But while you've been doing this, you've lost sight of something else.
> WALTERS: And that is?
> STRAND: Yourself. I saw it start. And watched it grow. Watched a brain that once was fine and brilliant begin to warp and tamper with things no man or woman should ever touch.
> WALTERS: Now maybe you'll listen to me. Haven't I proved beyond a doubt that glands can transform physical matter into any size, shape or appearance?
> STRAND: Yes, you have. But, in doing this, when you took the glands from the guinea pig and grafted them into the rabbit, the guinea pig died. When you grafted the frog's glands into a white mouse, the frog died. And now you propose to experiment with an ape and a woman. That woman must eventually die.
> WALTERS: Then she'll die in the advancement of science.

And, by extension, in the advancement of the human race? In the Darwinian world of Dr Walters, the "fittest" survive … even if he has to change the game board once in a while in order to bring about this process of "natural" selection.

It's fascinating to note that Walters' sentiments of "racial improvement" echo statements made over a century earlier by both the Reverend Thomas Robert Malthus (the most important influence on Darwin's theory of evolution) and Charles Darwin himself.

The following passage is from the revised 1826 edition of Malthus' most famous work, *An Essay on the Principle of Population*, the book that set Darwin on the course that would eventually lead him to write *On the Origin of Species*:

> [I]f we dread the too frequent visitation of the horrid form of famine, we should sedulously encourage the other forms of destruction, which we compel nature to use. Instead of recommending cleanliness to the poor, we should encourage contrary habits. In our towns, we should make the streets narrower, crowd more people into the houses, and court the return of the plague. In the country, we should build our villages near stagnant pools, and particularly encourage settlements in all marshy and unwholesome situations. But above all, we should reprobate specific remedies for ravaging diseases: and those benevolent, but much mistaken men, who have thought they were doing a service to mankind by projecting schemes for the total extirpation of particular disorders.[11]

Malthus, far more than any other contemporary scholar, was Darwin's intellectual role model. Darwin couldn't have been clearer about Malthus being the spark that lit the fire of evolutionary theory in his mind when, in his 1876 autobiography, Darwin himself wrote:

> In October 1838 [...] I happened to read for amusement Malthus on Population, and being well prepared to appreciate the struggle for existence which everywhere goes on from long-continued observation of the habits of animals and plants, it at once struck me that, under these circumstances, favourable variations [among humans] would tend to be preserved, and unfavourable ones to be destroyed. [...]. Here then, I had at last got a theory by which to work.[12]

The evolution of the theory itself is clear; so much so, it could be mapped out like a chart, not unlike an illustration of one-celled organisms emerging from the ocean and transforming gradually into human beings. What began as Malthusian Social Theory transformed into the Theory of Evolution, which in turn metamorphosed into social Darwinism. Social Darwinism, the theory that only the most aggressive members of any species can and should survive, has not just dominated the field of biology, but also the field of economics, throughout the nineteenth, twentieth, and twenty-first centuries.

Many Darwin scholars make the claim that the concept of "Social Darwinism" developed without any input by Darwin himself. They claim that political conservatives applied Darwin's theories regarding the "survival of the fittest" to human society not because they had any genuine interest in Darwin's scientific investigations, but merely to justify their own economic theories: in particular, the theory of laissez-faire capitalism. However, based on Darwin's own writings, it's undeniable that the first "Social Darwinist" was Darwin himself. In Vol. I of his 1871 book, *The Descent of Man*, Darwin wrote:

> With savages, the weak in body or mind are soon eliminated; and those that survive commonly exhibit a vigorous state of health. We civilised men, on the other hand, do our utmost to check the process of elimination; we build asylums for the imbecile, the maimed, and the sick; we institute poor-laws; and our medical men exert their utmost skill to save the life of every one to the last moment. There is reason to believe that vaccination has preserved thousands who, from a weak constitution, would formerly have succumbed to small-pox. Thus the weak members of civilised societies propagate their kind. No one who has attended to the breeding of domestic animals will doubt that this must be highly injurious to the race of man. It is surprising how soon a want of care, or care wrongly directed, leads to the degeneration of a domestic race; but excepting in the case of man himself, hardly any one is so ignorant as to allow his worst animals to breed.[13]

On July 3, 1881, Darwin wrote a letter to his friend William Graham, a Professor of Jurisprudence in Belfast, in which he continued to wax lyrical about the supremacy of certain "higher" races: "Looking to the world at no very distant date, what an endless number of the lower races will have been eliminated by the higher civilised races throughout the world."[14]

In the final analysis, given the passages quoted above, it doesn't seem unreasonable to conclude that Charles Darwin would have felt right at home in the laboratory of Dr Sigmund Walters.

Whether or not John Carradine's character is meant to be a satirical or melodramatic representation of the Nazis is rendered moot by the conflicted attitudes of the filmmakers themselves, for any critique of the Germans' racialist views in *Captive Wild Woman* is undercut, and made ineffective, by the subliminal racism and chauvinism which permeate the film. After all, this is a thriller about a "captive wild woman" who, upon transforming into a beautiful human female, falls so madly in love with the man who abducted her that she's willing to kill in order to possess him. She's also willing to sacrifice her life for him, despite the fact that she never would have been in this weird predicament in the first place had he not torn her from her rightful home and tossed her into a cage for the entertainment of the masses at (where else?) a three-ring circus.

Captive Wild Woman emerges as Universal's conservative antithesis to Fox's *Dr. Renault's Secret*. If the ultimate theme of the earlier film is a secular humanist one about the spark of humanity being present in all sentient beings, no matter their race or class or species or place of origin, the Universal film offers its audience the exact opposite thesis: No matter the environment, no matter the way they're treated, animals remain animals. When Paula grows angry (due to simple jealousy), her tan skin darkens by degrees until it literally blackens. After this stage, she "devolves" further into a half-woman/half-ape creature that might be mistaken for a werewolf, at which point she loses all vestige of her "civilized" veneer and must give in to her inherent bloodlust.

It would be worthwhile to discuss the career of Acquanetta, as it ties into the subtle racial themes lurking beneath the surface of *Captive Wild Woman*. Universal was clearly grooming her to be their next great horror attraction, a female version of Lon Chaney, Jr, whom Universal had starred in a string of hit horror films for the studio, beginning with 1940's *Man-Made Monster* and 1941's *The Wolf Man*. By the time *Captive Wild Woman* was released, Acquanetta had already appeared in two films, *Arabian Nights* (1942) and *Rhythm of the Islands* (1943), in admittedly minor roles, but the Universal publicity machine decided to "introduce" her to the public in *Captive Wild Woman*. She had been a John Powers Agency model in New York and possessed such exotic features that her friend William Randolph Hearst proclaimed her to be the "Venezuelan Volcano." But the Cheyenne, Wyoming-born Mildred Davenport wasn't Venezuelan at all.

Acquanetta starred in two other Universal films, both in 1944: *Jungle Woman* (the sequel to *Captive Wild Woman*) and *Dead Man's Eyes* alongside Lon Chaney, Jr. She was set to star in the third Paula the Ape Woman film, *Jungle Captive* (1945), when Universal discovered that their new ingénue's exotic features did not originate anywhere near Venezuela. In their book, *Universal Horrors*, authors Tom Weaver, Michael Brunas, and John Brunas include this excerpt from an interview conducted with director Edward Dmytryk:

> Acquanetta was a little insecure because she hadn't done much.... [Universal] was beginning to find out where she came from—which eventually ruined her career, of course. Acquanetta and her agent had hidden that from Universal. She was called the "Venezuelan Volcano," and then she had to go someplace out of the country, she had to get a passport, and they found out she was born in Philadelphia [*sic*]! After that, rather quickly, they found out she was part-black—which today wouldn't mean a damn thing. But in those days it still did.[15]

As a result, the role of Paula Dupree was given to another actress, Vicky Lane, and Acquanetta abandoned Hollywood after making only a few more minor films such as RKO's *Tarzan and the Leopard Woman* (1946).

This was not a unique situation in the "Golden Age" of Hollywood, particularly at Universal. Around the same time, actress/singer Carol Bruce, featured prominently in Universal comedies such as Abbott & Costello's *Keep 'Em Flying* (1941) and the Ritz Brothers' *Behind the Eight Ball* (1942), was dropped by the studio when it was discovered that she too had African American heritage.

Acquanetta's situation is particularly telling, however, as the real life, behind-the-scenes studio politics that caused her downfall in Hollywood reflect the subtle racism interwoven into the otherwise outlandish plot of *Captive Wild Woman*. Her penultimate film for Universal was the aforementioned *Jungle Woman* (1944), generally considered by fans to be the worst horror film Universal ever made, and it's hard to disagree. Even the horror films being churned out on "Poverty Row" at such studios as Monogram and PRC are generally better produced that this particular entry in the *Ape Woman* series.

It should be noted that *Jungle Woman* starred none other than J. Carrol Naish, who had previously portrayed Noel the Ape in *Dr. Renault's Secret*. Here he has taken the role of the scientist, Dr Carl Fletcher, who resurrects Paula Dupree and kicks off yet another killing spree. At one point in the film, Fred Mason (Milburn Stone reprising his role from the first film) insists to the good doctor that Cheela the Ape (AKA Paula Dupree) was the "most affectionate creature I ever took out of the jungle." He then adds a twist never mentioned in the first film: There was a legend among the jungle natives that Cheela was a human being who had been transformed into an ape by black magic. With a straight face, Fletcher replies, "Yes, there have been many efforts made in that direction." This is a curious, intertextual moment clearly referencing the other man-into-ape films that preceded this latest effort. This line was no doubt intended to be nothing more than an inside joke planted into the script by the screenwriters, yet it carries a kind of metafictional significance. Naish's very presence in the film operates as a not-so-subtle wink to the audience, a veritable breaking of the fourth wall: the filmmakers admitting they're completely aware of the fact that the film is derivative of *Dr. Renault's Secret.*

Before we leave the subject of the *Ape Woman* trilogy, it should be noted that *Captive Wild Woman* is by no means on the same level as its tepid sequels. Except for George Waggner's *The Wolf Man*, Universal produced very few quality horror films throughout the 1940s. Despite *Captive Wild Woman*'s questionable subtext, or perhaps *because* of it, the film possesses a strange, kinetic energy—fueled to a great degree by Carradine's frantic performance—that propels the film along at a relatively fast pace that seems far more modern than many of the other B-pictures Universal was producing in this period of creative decline.

Along with *Jungle Woman*, 1944 brought with it a horror "sequel" of a different kind: Monogram's *The Return of the Ape Man* starring Bela Lugosi, John Carradine and *maybe* George Zucco (more on this conundrum later), again proving the dictum that working alongside an ape even once inevitably brings with it similar roles in the future. Carradine once again plays a scientist, but this time he's allowed to be the "good scientist" (Prof. John Gilmore) for a change while Lugosi plays Prof. Dexter, a mad doctor intent on bringing a frozen 30,000-year-old Neanderthal back to life.

Judging from the title, one might reasonably assume that this film is a sequel to *The Ape Man*, as it was produced by the same studio and also stars Bela Lugosi. Apparently Monogram wished the audience to think this without bothering to actually write a direct sequel; the "Ape Man" in this movie refers to the Neanderthal whom Lugosi and Carradine discover while on a scientific expedition in the Arctic, and the word "return" refers to the Ape Man's release from suspended animation. But, while it has nothing to do with the plot of the 1943 film, it nevertheless shares many similar themes.

The Return of the Ape Man was directed by Philip Rosen, who had previously directed Lugosi in Monogram's East Side Kids comedy, *Spooks Run Wild* (1941), but the only comedy in *The Return of the Ape Man* is unintentional. The scene in which the tuxedoed Prof. Dexter stalks the streets of the city with a very serious expression on his face and a lit blowtorch in hand, intent on corralling the fire-frightened Ape Man back to his lab, has to be seen to be fully appreciated. To the audience's surprise, Dexter's strategy works, but not before the Ape Man breaks the neck of a cop on the beat.

Back at the lab, Dexter kills Gilmore and puts a portion of his brain into the skull of the Neanderthal in order to grant the creature *just enough* intelligence to obey Dexter's orders. Huh? What was that? Yes, it's not quite clear how all that works. Dexter's original intention was to prove that a living being could be revived from suspended animation, so what's all this business about controlling the Ape Man's mind? The audience doesn't know, and neither did the screenwriters.

Like George Zucco's ape in *The Monster and the Girl*, the Ape Man/ Gilmore escapes from Dexter's cage and begins slaughtering people. This particular killing spree seems to have little rhyme or reason attached to it. For example, the Ape Man/Gilmore chokes his wife for no particular reason, then finally gets around to snapping Dexter's spine. Then the Ape Man dies in an electrical fire. The End.

It should be noted that, just as J. Carrol Naish (the ape in *Dr. Renault's Secret*) ended up as the scientist in *Jungle Woman*, George Zucco (the scientist in *Dr. Renault's Secret*), ends up on the opposite end of the evolutionary chain in *The Return of the Ape Man*… sort of. In the credits, *two* actors are listed as playing the Neanderthal: George Zucco (top-billed) and Frank Moran. It would make sense for different actors to play the Ape Man before and after his brain surgery, but this is not the case. In truth, Zucco appears in only a fleeting shot or two, buried under a giant fake nose and a bad wig; for some reason, the younger and burlier Frank Moran took over the role for the rest of the picture. The only explanation is that Zucco—a leading British stage actor back in the 1920s and, by all reports, a proud man of rigid standards in his personal life—realized the depths to which he had sunk and walked out on his contract.

In his 1993 book, *Poverty Row Horrors*, Tom Weaver writes:

> If Zucco feigned sickness in order to avoid becoming associated with the film, all he missed out on was getting paid: Monogram not only

> played him up in all publicity, but also concocted stories that centered around him for their pressbook. According to the pressbook, *Return*'s theater scenes were shot at a vacant theater near the Monogram studios, and passersby were horrified when they saw Zucco (in two-and-a-half hours' worth of Ape Man makeup) emerging from the car which delivered him to the location site.[16]

Of course, more than likely the only person horrified by Zucco's makeup was Zucco himself. The overall ludicrous nature of *The Return of the Ape Man* serves as an appropriate paradigm for the de-evolution of the Darwinian horror movie in the early 1940s.

In the same year as the release of *Jungle Captive* came Harry L. Fraser's *The White Gorilla,* an insane patchwork largely composed of deteriorating clips from a now-lost silent film called *Perils of the Jungle* (1927). The racial subtext of this film, if not intentional, erupted straight from the Id of Harry L. Fraser. Starring Ray Corrigan as both the protagonist (a displaced American hunter named Steve Collins) and the eponymous gorilla, the film is about an ape ostracized from his tribe because of his aberrant white fur. The narrator makes it clear that the gorilla is constantly being tortured by his black brothers due to the fact that he's white. It's an ironic twist on reality that the transparent racial implications of this film cast the white gorilla as the outsider, while at that same time performers like Acquanetta and Carol Bruce were being ostracized from Hollywood due to their Black heritage.

5. The Scopes Monkey Trial and Its Cinematic After Effects: The 1950s

BY THE EARLY 1950s, old style Gothic horror had pretty much died out at the box office. What filled the gap was a series of innovative films that blended Gothic surfaces with modern politics, technologically-induced paranoia and stories that centered on what Dr Carl Jung called "a modern myth of things seen in the sky," i.e., flying saucers. Unlike vampires and werewolves, Unidentified Flying Objects represented a threat new enough to be plausible. In the early 1950s, even mainstream newspapers like the *Los Angeles Times* and *New York Times* carried UFO stories on their front pages almost every single day. Edgar G. Ulmer's *The Man from Planet X*, Christian Nyby's

The Thing from Another World, and Robert Wise's *The Day the Earth Stood Still* all hit theaters in 1951 behind a backdrop of the Korean War, the beginnings of the Cold War with the Soviet Union, rampant experimentation with atomic power, the formation of the United Nations, and a genuine fear of strange specters invading the night skies of Earth. In an uncertain world where whole countries could conceivably be destroyed by the push of a button, the link between ape and human didn't seem so scary anymore. And yet members of the old guard carried on.

Curt Siodmak's *The Bride of the Gorilla* premiered in theaters in October of 1951, by which time its essential plot had been seen many times before. In fact, the film is widely regarded as Siodmak's disguised remake of *The Wolf Man* (which he scripted), though Siodmak always denied this. At first Siodmak had intended *The Wolf Man* to be a psychological thriller whose audience would never know for certain if Lawrence Talbot (Lon Chaney, Jr) was a werewolf or suffering from a mental illness. Universal deemed this ambiguous approach uncommercial and demanded that Siodmak rewrite the film so that the supernatural aspect was more explicit. (Ironically, only a year later, Val Lewton at RKO would produce a major hit with *Cat People*, an elegant horror film that employed the exact same psychological approach Siodmak intended to use.)

Like *The Wolf Man*, *Bride of the Gorilla* is about a man burdened with the curse of transforming into a beast. Both films even include Lon Chaney, Jr in the cast. (In *Bride*, he plays a Police Commissioner named Taro.) Unlike Lawrence Talbot, however, protagonist Barney Chavez (Raymond Burr) is an unsympathetic character whose curse is cast upon him by an old native witch when she sees him murder his elderly employer, Klaas Van Gelder (Paul Cavanagh). The murder is not in any way justified, as Chavez merely wishes to get his hands on the man's young wife, Dina (Barbara Payton).

Again Siodmak wrote the script in order to explore the fine line between sanity and insanity, and again the producers demanded he rewrite it so that the supernatural element was made emphatic. It's difficult to believe this alternate approach would have helped the film rise above its limitations. By 1951 audiences had already seen this more "realistic" approach, not only in *Cat People* but also in *The Beast with Five Fingers* (1947) directed by Robert Florey from a Siodmak script. At the beginning of the 1950s, the American people—consciously or unconsciously—wanted to see ideas that reflected the space age horrors around them, which is why 3-D extravaganzas like *It Came from Outer Space* (1953) and Technicolor interstellar adventures like *This Island Earth* (1955) were soon to steal all the attention away from quaint "chiller-dillers" like *Bride of the Gorilla.*

Our next entry reunites Bela Lugosi with one of his recurring nemeses: a gorilla. Strangely, in another embryonic postmodern moment, Bela Lugosi is *featured* in the title, as if he's an actual character in the story. *Bela Lugosi Meets a Brooklyn Gorilla* (1952) was directed by William Beaudine, who previously directed Lugosi in *The Ape Man, Ghosts on the Loose* (1943) and *Voodoo Man* (1944), all for Monogram.

Bela Lugosi Meets a Brooklyn Gorilla is ostensibly a comedy—the first and only outing for Duke Mitchell and Sammy Petrillo, who up to this point had made a career in Las Vegas mimicking the very popular comedy duo of Dean Martin and Jerry Lewis. In fact, the film was almost not released in theaters at all due to the fact that Martin and Lewis sued the producers of the film on the grounds that Mitchell and Petrillo copied their routine so precisely.

As might be expected, the plot isn't too complicated. After their plane malfunctions, Mitchell and Petrillo parachute onto a remote jungle island and are lucky enough to be saved by Dr Zabor (Bela Lugosi), who has a laboratory on the island where he's performing delicate experiments involving (what else?) evolution. Zabor ends up transforming Mitchell into a gorilla and wacky shenanigans abound. The team of Mitchell & Petrillo broke up soon after the release of the film, but no one noticed.

Our next entry combines two strains of cinematic terror: the simian monster so ubiquitous in the Golden Age of Hollywood with the in vogue invasion-from-space plot, resulting in a film so absurd it borders on avant-garde cinema. Phil Tucker's *Robot Monster* (1953) concerns itself with an invasion from space by aliens who look like gorillas wearing diving helmets. The titular simian, also known as Ro-Man, represents the vanguard of an invading fleet of Ro-Men. Ro-Man successfully kills everyone on Earth with a "calcinatory death ray"—except for eight people. Alas, despite direct orders from his planet's leader, "The Great One" (who looks exactly like Ro-Man), Ro-Man can't bring himself to wipe out the remaining humans when he falls in love with a pretty young thing named Alice. At the end, it turns out the whole adventure was a dream anyway. Or was it?

Robot Monster, a 3-D film populated by *very* un-3-D characters, could easily be interpreted as an unintentional Dadaist prank. It's of-

Murders in the Rue Morgue

ten mentioned in the same breath as *The Ape Man* and *Plan 9 from Outer Space* as one of the worst films ever made. It's hard to disagree with this assessment, and yet at the same time it's also true that many recent major studio productions could learn something about storytelling from schizophrenic films like this.

In his exhaustive study of American science fiction films of 1950s, *Keep Watching the Skies!*, Bill Warren writes:

> The dialogue for *Robot Monster* [...] may be the worst ever written. It displays an astounding ignorance of almost every possible topic: science, logic, human behavior, dreams, robot monsters, children, everything. Every topic mentioned in the film is discussed badly. Ro-Man explains his actions to the Great One: "I meshed my LPI with the view-screen auditor, and picked up a count of five." Ro-Man becomes impassioned when the Great One says he's starting to think like a human being. "Yes!" the invader cries. "To be like the human! To laugh! Feel! Want! Why are these things not in the plan?" He agonizes over his order to destroy the world. "I cannot—yet I must. How do you calculate that? At what point on the graph do *must* and *cannot* meet? Yet I must—but I cannot!" And *he* has the *best* lines.[17]

Though the Robot Monster's appearance being akin to a simian was merely an accident brought about by the low-budget desperation of the production, it's interesting to note that an ape would be Tucker's *default* monster. Once the alien costume had fallen through, it's as if Tucker said to himself, "What else is *left* but an ape?" This indicates how engrained the image of the ape-as-monster had become in filmmakers by the 1950s: If you can't get an alien, get an ape. And thus *Robot Monster* remains peculiarly true to the tendencies of the other ape/evolutionary films made in its era, which expressed fear of technology and the loss of our humanity. Depending on how you look at his costume, Ro-Man's apeness either succumbs to evolution by his exposure to human beings, or his alien side retreats from the futuristic confusion of LPIs and view-screen auditors into something warmer and devolved, like love. Is the glass half full or half empty? If you're confused, you're probably in the right place.

Despite the disaster that was *Robot Monster*, even major Hollywood studios weren't quite done with apes. Roy Del Ruth's *Phantom of the Rue Morgue* (1954) is a remake of Robert Florey's *Murders in the Rue Morgue* that found actor Charles Gemora reprising his role as the ape from twenty-two years before. In this version, however, Karl Malden steps into the Bela Lugosi role of Dr Mirakle, now called Dr Marais. If Dr Mirakle's perverse experiments represented an outgrowth of the general anxiety exhibited in the 1930s regarding recent legal cases involving the teaching of Darwin in public schools, then Dr Marais' experiments are clearly a reflection of what 1950s America feared about behavioral psychologists—perhaps understandable, as behaviorism, by the time the 1950s rolled around, was the prime methodology used by Madison Avenue to sell useless products to the masses. At a subconscious level, Americans may even have been aware of this fact. After all, this was an open secret by the 1950s, and had been so ever since the father of behaviorism, John B. Watson, was fired from his faculty position at Johns Hopkins University due to a sex scandal involving a female student and was forced to align himself with Madison Avenue advertising firms in order to make a living. This is why the Coca-Cola bottle changed its shape after John B. Watson rolled into town.

Unlike Mirakle, Marais is clearly based on famous behaviorists such as Ivan Pavlov, John B. Watson and B.F. Skinner. Marais is an eccentric professor, employed by the local zoo, who has trained mice to respond to the ringing of bells and uses similar methods to train other animals to kill on command. Just as Mirakle predates Darwin, Marais predates the field of behaviorism by many decades. *Murders in the Rue Morgue* takes place in mid-1840s Paris, *Phantom of the Rue Morgue* in mid-1890s Paris. Darwin doesn't publish *On the Origin of Species* until 1859, John B. Watson doesn't publish his Behaviorist Manifesto "Psychology as the Behaviorist Views It" until 1913. Both characters predate their more famous, real world counterparts by about fifteen years. Both men are scientific geniuses so ahead of their times that they've been shunned by mainstream science, forcing them to conduct their experiments covertly.

Like Mirakle, Marais' experiments are intertwined with sexual frustration. He trains his ape, Sultan, to kill only beautiful women who have scorned him. A bell charm on the wrists of the women is the true cause of their deaths, as it leads Sultan to each of them and triggers the instinct to kill, per Marais' training. As with Erik, however, Sultan eventually breaks free of his training and kills the doctor.

Only two months later, Harmon Jones' *Gorilla at Large* was released. Like *Phantom of the Rue Morgue*, it was shot in 3-D and involves a trained ape, this one named Goliath, who has supposedly committed murder. The entire plot of *Gorilla at Large* is a mystery revolving around a single question: Is the killer an ape or a man? In a way, one might say that this sums up the central conundrum in all these films. Perhaps the proper answer, for all of them, is "both."

The film's carnival sequences, with the Long Beach Nu Pike Amusement Park doubling as The Carnival of Evil, were shot in under a week—a shooting schedule not uncommon for an independent film such as this. What is uncommon, however, is for such a film to boast so many famous actors including Anne Bancroft, Lee J. Cobb, Lee Marvin, Cameron Mitchell and *Bride of the Gorilla's* Raymond Burr. The actor portraying Goliath, George Barrows, had played Ro-Man in *Robot Monster* only a year before and was the first actor since Charles Gemora to have built his own ape suit.

Earlier in 1954 came Universal's science fiction/horror blockbuster for that year: Jack Arnold's *Creature from the Black Lagoon* starring Richard Carlson and Julia Adams, which not only featured one of the most realistic-looking monsters of its day but also boasted sophisticated underwater photography and the most advanced 3-D yet devised. Though this crowd pleaser did not feature apes in any shape or form, the film *was* about evolution. In this case, we discover that man bears kinship not with apes, but with prehistoric "gill-men" who represent a formerly undiscovered link between fish and human.

Creature was so popular it spawned two sequels: Jack Arnold's *Revenge of the Creature* (1955) starring John Agar and Lori Nelson, and John Sherwood's *The Creature Walks Among Us* (1956) starring Jeff Morrow and Rex Reason. The latter film amps up the theme of evolution a thousand fold, as the plot (devised by Arthur Ross, screenwriter for the first film) centers around the plans of Dr William Barton (Morrow), a wealthy scientist who decides he wants to quicken the evolutionary process by surgically transforming the "Gill-man" into an air-breather, i.e., a human being. If this surgery is successful, according to Barton, it will serve as proof that mankind can be surgically evolved to withstand the pressures of outer space. Come again?

Clearly, this third entry was a little less thought-out than the first two; however, it's fascinating that Universal would allow Arthur Ross to mutilate its most popular horror creation since the 1940s, then kill it outright in an atypical downbeat ending in which the now "gill-less" Creature unintentionally drowns himself when he returns to the ocean from which he was kidnapped.

As the 1950s continue, the sympathy for such evolutionary outliers such as the Gill-man rises dramatically. By this third film in the *Creature* trilogy, almost *none* of the human characters are likeable at all. The Creature becomes the hero by a process of elimination. Though the Creature causes havoc in the first film, even his murderous acts can be seen as justifiable; in every entry of the trilogy, he's portrayed as equal to the human beings on an emotional and intellectual level, perhaps even more so in this final film. Thus the series becomes somewhat about our own devolution.

A year later, in 1957, comes the apex in sympathetic evolutionary outliers: the title character of *The Abominable Snowman of the Himalayas*, arguably one of the most effective horror films ever produced by England's Hammer Studios. Buoyed by an intelligent screenplay written by Nigel Kneale (based on his teleplay), the film stars Forrest Tucker as a crass American businessman named Tom Friend and Peter Cushing as a humanitarian British scientist named John Rollason, both of whom intend to discover proof for the existence of the Yeti. Tucker's character is no doubt based on real life Texas oilman Tom Slick, whose exploits searching for the Yeti were well-known in the 1950s and have subsequently been documented at length in such books as Loren Coleman's *Tom Slick and the Search for the Yeti* (1989).

Tom Friend's goal involves nothing more than commercial exploitation, *à la* King Kong's captor Carl Denham, while John Rollason's interest is scientific in nature. Kneale portrays the Yeti not only as equal to human beings, but superior in every way. For example, they possess the ability to communicate mind-to-mind; it's implied that human beings do not possess this skill because we have not yet evolved to their level. It's revealed at the conclusion that the Abominable Snow*men* (despite the implication of the film's title, a whole community of Yeti exist in the Himalayas) are an advanced race of human beings who, essentially, are Nature's replacement for *Homo sapiens*. The Yeti have hidden in the remote Himalayas in order to avoid the savagery of mankind and are now waiting in the wings to build a better civilization once humanity has succeeded in wiping itself off the planet. Here the image of the evolutionary outlier has transformed from being an object of fear in *Murders in the Rue Morgue*, to a sympathetic tragedian in *Dr. Renault's Secret*, to an exploited minority in *The Creature Walks Among Us*, to a vastly superior form of humanity in *The Abominable Snowman*. Appropriate to a writer like Kneale, whose character Prof. Bernard Quatermass in *The Quatermass Xperiment* (1955) was on the cutting edge of the space race, there is a dawning awareness that the intelligence we may find outside our species may well be in advance of our own.

American society was changing at a fast clip, and these changes manifested on the silver screen. Back in the early 1930s, for example, it was almost mandatory that the hero save the girl from whatever threat was menacing her, particularly in a horror film. In *Murders in the Rue Morgue*, Pierre saves Camille from being raped by a libidinous ape within the last five minutes of the film. By the late 1950s, as the generation of Bing Crosby and *The Saturday Evening Post* began to give way to the generation of Bob Dylan and *Mad Magazine*, these clichés mutated in unexpected ways. A certain ambivalence about formerly taboo subjects such as the biological sciences and sexual politics crept into popular culture, and this ambivalence was reflected by (some fundamentalists might say "caused by") the subversives toiling away within the limbo of Z-grade cinema.

In Adrian Weiss' *The Bride and the Beast* (1958), the traditional roles of hero and heroine are turned upside down—hardly surprising, given the fact that the screenplay was written by none other than the cross-dressing *auteur* Edward D. Wood, Jr of *Glen or Glenda?* and *Plan 9 from Outer Space* infamy. Newlyweds Dan Fuller (Lance Fuller) and Laura Carson Fuller (*Gorilla at Large*'s Charlotte Austin) experience an unusual wedding night when Mr Fuller, a game hunter, wakes to find his wife in the loving embrace of a gorilla that Dan keeps locked in his basement for no discernible reason. Suggestively, Dan's pet name for the gorilla is "Spanky." When Dan discovers Spanky slipping off Laura's nightgown in his own bedroom, Dan becomes violently territorial—as any true alpha-male would—and shoots Spanky through the chest with his gun. Instead of being relieved at being "rescued," however, Laura seems upset and insists that Spanky's caress was "kind, gentle." She goes to sleep after her ordeal, but instead of dreaming about her handsome new husband she has a series of intense, ecstatic dreams about a massive gorilla striding through the jungle while Laura writhes in bed, uttering moans that sound more passionate than fearful.

Intent on putting a stop to these weird dreams, the next morning Dan asks a doctor friend to pay a house call and examine his bride. Dr Carl Reiner (William Justine) puts Laura under hypnotic regression and discovers she led the existence of a gorilla in a past life. Reiner warns Dan not to take Laura anywhere near the jungle, as the trip might make her nightmares even worse. Inevitably, Dan insists it's their honeymoon, and he's determined not to alter their plans due to a bunch of New Age mumbo-jumbo.

After an endless series of tepid action sequences composed almost entirely of stock footage cobbled together from 1920s serials, Laura is abducted by a whole group of gorillas and taken to their cave. Laura doesn't seem to put up too much of a struggle. When Dan tracks the gorillas to their lair, Laura pushes him away instead of fleeing with him. As a result, the apes knock Dan unconscious, grab their prize, and escape deeper into the jungle.

The final scene in *The Bride and the Beast* consists of Dan admitting to Dr Reiner that he hasn't seen his wife since that disturbing day. Reiner assures his friend that Laura has "gone back where she came from" and implies that Dan's wife is now where she belongs. The last shot of Dan is a close-up in which he looks as confused as ever, as if he still hasn't realized why his wife wanted to be with those dirty, stinking gorillas more than *him*. The closing shot is of Laura, still dressed in her diaphanous nightgown, lounging in the arms of one of the black gorillas as he lovingly transports her through the jungle like a groom carrying his bride over the threshold. The expression on Laura's face is certainly not one of displeasure.

Within twenty-six years, the role of the hero had transformed from that of the unfailing gentleman of derring-do seen in *Murders in the Rue Morgue* to that of an impotent and confused game hunter whose gun jams at all the wrong times and who's ultimately cuckolded by a group of lustful gorillas. With technology now advancing in leaps and bounds, the average person was beginning to explore their inner kinship with so-called lower life forms.

6. The Scopes Monkey Trial and Its Cinematic After Effects: The 1960s and Beyond

IN 1960 COMES the ultimate Darwinian ape-man movie, this one neither horror nor science fiction: Stanley Kramer's *Inherit the Wind*, starring Fredric March and Spencer Tracy, both of whom had played the ape-like Mr Hyde in the two most famous cinematic adaptations of Robert Louis Stevenson's 1886 novella *Strange Case of Dr Jekyll and Mr Hyde*. March won the Academy Award for Best Actor for his portrayal of the title character(s) in Rouben Mamoulian's *Dr. Jekyll and Mr. Hyde* (1931); a decade later, Tracy assumed the role(s) in Victor Fleming's 1941 version. When Stanley Kramer cast these two actors as the main stars in *Inherit the Wind*, the first film version of the 1955 hit play that dramatized the Scopes Monkey Trial, he was either exhibiting a dark sense of humor or acting as an unwitting agent of synchronicity.

This film, by shining a spotlight on a subject that was merely *subtext* in the horror films of the Golden Age, seemed to put an end to the incessant cycle of ape-man movies that preceded it. Once the subject had been addressed in a literal fashion in such a popular medium as film, perhaps there was no reason to cloak the subject in the veneer of metaphor.

The poster for *Inherit the Wind* is worth mentioning. The stars of the film are dwarfed by the comical image of a monkey wearing a man's reading glasses. This exact image could have been used as the poster for one of Bela Lugosi's occasional forays into slapstick comedy without seeming out of place at all. It's as if the people who designed the poster for the film understood that the picture's main draws were neither Spencer Tracy nor Fredric March, but the monkeys from which the human race evolved. Subtext becomes text, metaphor becomes reportage.

Producer Herman Cohen's *Konga* (1961), directed by John Lemont, was released four months after *Inherit the Wind*, so it had already gone into production well before the popular film's release. *Konga* is one of the last hosts for the viral meme known as "evolution-as-cinematic-horror." It was clearly influenced by *King Kong* (1933)—a film noticeably absent from this discussion because Kong is so clearly intended *not* to be an object of horror. Even in films such as *Dr. Renault's Secret*, the ape-man, as sympathetic as he is, still remains a manifestation of the grotesque by the final reel. Kong, on the other hand, is more of a fairy tale figure who's so larger than life that he transcends mere horror and becomes an object of wonder: indeed, he becomes the *eighth* wonder of the world.

Konga, on the other hand, is not an object of wonder at all. Like many other cinematic apes, he is only a tool employed by the main character, Dr Charles Decker (Michael Gough), to attain vengeance against his rivals. By experimenting with plants (much like Dr Coriolis in Gaston Leroux's novel *Balaoo*, who developed the ape man Noel while experimenting with bread-plant), Decker discovers the means to grow animals to tremendous sizes. He experiments on a chimp, Konga, who is soon hypnotized by Decker and sent on a killing spree.

Eventually, Konga grows far larger than intended and destroys half of London. *Konga*, like Erik and Sultan before him, kills his captor just before being slaughtered for his sins.

My own first exposure to Konga was not the film itself, but a Charlton Comics adaptation by the eccentric artist Steve Ditko, co-creator of Marvel Comics' *The Amazing Spider-Man* (another evolutionary hybrid between human and non-human). Charlton's *Konga* was first published in 1960 and continued—despite the fact that he died at the end of the first issue—for another twenty-two issues, the last of which was published in November 1965. Comics fans consider this series far superior to the film, mainly due to the always fascinating art of Ditko, who drew the first fifteen issues. This evolution, too, is telling, for by abandoning one popular medium for another the ape managed to transform himself from monster to hero.

By the late 1950s and early 1960s, the authority of the Motion Picture Production Code had weakened considerably with the release of such films as Billy Wilder's *Some Like It Hot* (1959) and Alfred Hitchcock's *Psycho* (1960), which became blockbusters despite not being approved by the Code. The Code finally gasped its last in 1968, by which time controversial subjects such as civil rights, homosexuality, and drug use had swelled to the forefront of public consciousness, long since pushing evolution off the map of cultural taboos.

Except for the occasional "throwback" such as the *Planet of the Apes* series (1968–73), which is really more about civil rights and the political upheavals of that era than about evolution, the "man-into-ape" film more or less fades away from the cinema as an active and vital subgenre. Of course, the subject of evolution is by no means resolved in modern society. In his 2006 review of *Inherit the Wind*, film critic Roger Ebert wrote:

> Seen 46 years after its release, but only a few months after Darwin was once again on trial in Dover, Penn., *Inherit the Wind* is a film that rebukes the past when it might also have feared the future. Beliefs that seemed like ancient history to [Stanley] Kramer have had a surprising resiliency; two recent polls show that 38 percent of American teenagers believe "God created humans pretty much in their present form within the last 10,000 years or so," and 54 percent of American adults doubt that man evolved from earlier species. There is hardly a politician in the land with courage enough to state that they are wrong.[18]

What is taboo for one generation is accepted wisdom in the next. And what is *not* accepted wisdom can only be discussed in popular forms under the guise of metaphor. What is not accepted wisdom is the unexamined, the unknown.

What is unknown is often the object of fear.

Therefore, what is not accepted wisdom manifests itself in the popular imagination as horror: stories to be feared.

Fear gives birth to taboos and taboos give birth to horror. At their very best, stories of any kind are a means of inoculation against both the present and the future—inoculations that not only help people deal with the uncertainties of the now, but also allow the coming generation to transform the unknown into accepted wisdom. Horror stories, perhaps more so in film than in any other medium, combine both functions into one.

As Dr Mirakle once said, way back in 1845, "Do they still burn men for heresy? Then burn me, Monsieur. Light the fire. Do you think your little candle will outshine the flame of truth? My life is consecrated to great *experiment*."

Charles Darwin, Edgar Allan Poe, Gaston Leroux, H.P. Lovecraft, Robert Florey, and Bela Lugosi might have said the very same thing—except, for them, the great experiment in question would have been that of reflecting the face of humanity back at itself in the form of the grotesque and the arabesque, the horrifying and the fantastic, the unexamined and the unknown.

Chapter 9

Here Among the Dead

The Phantom Carriage and the Cinema of the Occulted Taboo

"It's a spooky place to wait for midnight, here among the dead."
—David Holm, *The Phantom Carriage*, 1921

1. Thy Soul Shall Bear Witness!

AT ITS CONTROVERSIAL best the cinema has always been about breaking taboos, and perhaps the biggest taboo of all is death. Victor Sjöström's 1921 touchstone film, *The Phantom Carriage*, combines both transgressive subjects into a single narrative that flips the binary opposites of the physical and the spiritual upside down. In western civilization, explorations of metaphysical quandaries have always been somewhat frowned upon unless they are conducted in a socially acceptable context, that is, within the constraints of academia or a mainstream religion such as Christianity. As early as 1921, when cinema was just leaving its infancy stage, Sjöström dared to explore the nature of the spiritual and the physical in a context that appears, on the surface, to be socially acceptable, but in fact draws upon the esoteric philosophies of occult organizations that have never existed anywhere except on the fringe. *The Phantom Carriage* is an early example of filmmaking that cleverly camouflages its true intent, a tradition of the occulted taboo that continues to this day.

The main purpose of fiction, particularly the popular brand of fiction so prevalent in cinema, has always been about discussing the taboos of the day in a safe context—safe, that is, for both the audience and the author. The fictional veneer allows the audience to take in vital information without being offended while also allowing the author to hide his true purpose behind the excuse that the proceedings are all in jest. "We're just entertainers, Grand Inquisitor, that's all. Nothing to be too concerned about." A capital jest, indeed.

In the early 1600s a playwright named William Shakespeare knew this very well and employed the technique to masterful effect in one crowd-pleasing production after another. Shakespeare's plays, of course, were never intended to be worshipped from afar by literary scholars as rarified pieces of High Art preserved under glass, but as intense melodramas filled with blood and guts and bawdy humor. Shakespeare's plays were the seventeenth-century version of tent-pole summer blockbusters, complete with incessant, Quentin Tarantino-like violence, improbable plot twists, and soap-opera-like revelations to keep the crowd's attention fixed on the stage. Shakespeare managed to intersperse within these crowd-pleasing spectacles covert messages of occult knowledge and political satire that would have resulted in imprisonment or even death for anyone attempting to utter such egregious pronouncements in an open and forthright manner. As stated earlier, Shakespeare himself, rather puckishly, displays this method for all to see in the middle of *Hamlet* (1600) when the young and vengeful prince stages an ostensibly fictional melodrama, *The Murder of Gonzago*, for the benefit of the King in order to reveal the conspiratorial machinations with which he believes the King assassinated Hamlet's father for the purpose of attaining the throne.

At its core, Shakespeare's *Macbeth* (1606) is an occult allegory displaying the hermetic secrets of the third degree of Freemasonry in a fictional context, thus transmitting to a mass audience what would otherwise have been hidden information to which only Masonic initiates at the time would have been privy.[1] The purpose of popular fiction, the kind that lasts throughout the ages, has always been to transmit sensitive information to the masses in a form they can appreciate. The unconscious mind, that which hums secrets to us when we're asleep, often picks up far more information than the conscious mind, which so often struggles to understand concepts far beyond its grasp. Poetry, fiction, paintings, song—all of these art forms play on the subliminal brain without even trying. A strident reformer barking through a loud speaker on a street corner almost never succeeds in converting anyone to his cause. The conscious mind rejects him and his message merely due to the fact that the average person resents being *talked* at. People want to be seduced. And what seduces better than the gentle caress and the whisper in the ear? Wrap your message in a catchy tune that rhymes and people will listen ... and even pay to hear it again. People paid to hear and see Shakespeare's plays, and they still do when so many run-of-the-mill melodramas produced in the same year as *Macbeth* have long since faded into obscurity. There is a reason that Bram Stoker's 1897 Gothic melodrama, *Dracula*, has survived into the twenty-first century while James Malcolm Rymer's vampire novel, *Varney the Vampire* (1845–47), is rarely read today. Stoker did his research. *Dracula* manages to transmit genuine hermetic knowledge through a page-turning yarn filled with horrific sights and subliminal sexuality. The last two elements, however, are not the elements that have granted *Dracula* immortality. No, it's the genuine hermetic core of Stoker's novel that's the real achievement, that continues to speak to us through the grotesque and arabesque mask of entertainment.

Talents as diverse as Miguel de Cervantes, John Milton, Alexander Pope, Jonathan Swift, William Blake, Mary Shelley, Sir Walter Scott, Johann Wolfgang von Goethe, Edgar Allan Poe, Herman Melville, Lewis Carroll, Jules Verne, Oscar Wilde, L. Frank Baum, Edgar Rice Burroughs, Herman Hesse, H.P. Lovecraft, William S. Burroughs, Richard Matheson, Ian Fleming, Philip K. Dick, Thomas Pynchon, and Alan Moore have all understood this process and employ fiction for this exact purpose: to tell the hidden truth in an acceptable fashion, in a manner that will be embraced by the masses rather than rejected out of hand.

In the 1600s, Shakespeare used the most popular medium that existed in that day to "broadcast" his peculiar messages of transcendence.[2] Throughout the eighteenth and nineteenth centuries, however, the most popular medium became the novel, and thus Mary Shelley's bastard child of ancient black arts and cutting edge scientific breakthroughs, *Frankenstein*, arose from the printed page rather than the stage of the Globe Theatre. Alice's tumble through the astral realms played out across the pages of a seemingly innocent children's book. Dorothy Gale's metaphysical journey similarly emerged from the nascent field of the American fairy tale.

When the Victorian era gave way to the twentieth century, the novel was eclipsed by a brand new art form as strange as the patchwork demon that emerged from Mary Shelley's imagination way back in 1818. Cinema evolved slowly over the first decades of the twentieth century, then began to mature to a drastic and impressive degree in the early 1920s. The more revolutionary-minded stage actors and playwrights saw the possibilities of this new form as a method of transmitting spiritual knowledge to the proletariat in a way that no Catholic priest could ever attain behind a puny pulpit in even the largest urban cathedral. At the forefront of this burgeoning artistic revolution was Victor Sjöström, and his masterpiece in this taboo-breaking medium was his 1921 film, *The Phantom Carriage*, an adaptation of Selma Lagerlöf's 1912 novel titled *Thy Soul Shall Bear Witness!*

What's most sly and impressive about Sjöström's considerable achievement is that he manages to retain Lagerlöf's occult message while disguising it in the form of a quasi-Christian morality play. When one scratches just beneath the surface, however, one can see that *The Phantom Carriage* is in truth a transgressive allegory drawn from the teachings of Theosophy, of which Selma Lagerlöf was a committed student.

Theosophy is a philosophical-religious system adhered to by members of The Theosophical Society, an organization founded in New York in 1875 by Helena Blavatsky, Henry Steel Olcott and others. The purpose of the society, according to Lewis Spence's 1920 book, *An Encyclopedia of Occultism*, is as follows:

> [T]o promote the study of comparative religion and philosophy [...]. It is set forth in the Theosophical system that all the great religions of the world originated from one supreme source and that they are merely expressions of a central "Wisdom Religion" vouchsafed to various races of the earth in such a manner as was best suited to time and geographical circumstances. Underlying these was a secret doctrine or esoteric teaching which, it was stated, had been the possession for ages of certain *Mahatmas*, or adepts in mysticism and occultism. With these Madame Blavatsky claimed to be in direct communication [...].[3]

During his audio commentary on the digitally restored Criterion DVD of *The Phantom Carriage*, released in the fall of 2011, film historian Casper Tybjerg has this to say about Lagerlöf's interest in mysticism: "Lagerlöf was powerfully attracted by Theosophy and Spiritualism, and the influence of these esoteric doctrines is palpable [...].

Lagerlöf believed that Theosophy and Spiritualism held out the promise of bringing together religion and scientific theories, like the Theory of Evolution."[4] Here Tybjerg emphasizes Lagerlöf's intense desire to meld together concepts that many people assume to be polar opposites: religion and science. Significantly, reconciling extreme dualities is a prominent concern throughout Victor Sjöström's *The Phantom Carriage*.

The Phantom Carriage is filled with dualities, and thus reflective of Theosophy and Gnosticism in particular. From its beginning, Theosophy has been interwoven with Gnosticism, a suppressed form of Christianity with roots that extend at least as far back as the second century CE. To understand the dualities in *The Phantom Carriage*, it is important to understand the unique dualities inherent in Gnosticism. According to Dr Stephan Hoeller, the Bishop of the Gnostic Church in Los Angeles:

> The Gnostic position [...] might be called qualified dualism [...]. The Gnostics had their own myth about the origins of good and evil. It begins with a boundless, blissful Fullness—the Pleroma—that is beyond all manifest existence. The Pleroma is both the abode of and the essential nature of the True Ultimate God (*alethes theos*). Before time and before memory, this ineffable Fullness extended itself into the lower regions of being. In the course of this emanation, it manifested itself in a number of intermediate deities, *demiurgoi*, who were rather like great angels, endowed with enormous talents of creativity and organization. Some of these beings, however, became alienated from their supernal source and so took on evil tendencies. They created a physical world long before the creation of humans, and they created it in the likeness of their own imperfect natures.
>
> Thus the will that created the world was tainted with self-will, arrogance, and the hunger for power; through the works performed by these alienated beings, evil came to penetrate creation. Ever since then, as the Gnostic teacher Basilides reportedly said, "Evil adheres to created existence as rust adheres to iron." As part of the creation, human beings also reflect the flawed nature of the creators. The human body is subject to disease, death, and other evils; even the soul (psyche) is not free from imperfection. Only the spirit (pneuma), hidden deep within the human essence, remains free from the evil and tends toward the True God.[5]

The Phantom Carriage, rather like human beings in the Gnostic creation myth, is infused with paradoxes. The film is a strange and elegant mixture of realism and expressionism, Christianity and hermeticism, complexity and simplicity. Lagerlöf (as author) and Sjöström (as screenwriter/actor/director) weave together elements of both social realism and fairy tale-like phantasmagoria into a seamless whole, a style of cinematic storytelling that has not been successfully realized on the screen in recent years, with rare exceptions such as Guillermo del Toro's 2006 film, *Pan's Labyrinth*, which also juxtaposes scenes of brutal realism with images of the transcendent.

Despite a relatively complex story structure composed of flashbacks within flashbacks and stories within stories, the central conceit of *The Phantom Carriage* is not at all dissimilar to that of a traditional fairy tale. Once upon a time, on New Year's Eve, three men (old before their time) sit in a dilapidated cemetery passing a bottle of cheap liquor back and forth while talking about a local legend: that of Death's Driver. According to the prevailing myth, the last person killed on New Year's Eve must take over the reins of a horse-drawn carriage fashioned by Death himself. For the next year, that person must serve Death by collecting the souls of the recently deceased until the following New Year's Eve. Inevitably (at least according to the logic of fairy tales), our protagonist, an alcoholic ne'er-do-well named David Holm (played by Victor Sjöström), is murdered just before the stroke of midnight. Then comes Death's Driver, who just so happens to be a fellow derelict named Georges (Tore Svennberg), the man who first told Holm about the legend. Georges died exactly a year before in Holm's presence under very similar circumstances. As in all fairy tales, coincidence and fate play a crucial role in this film.

Georges removes Holm from his physical body, binds his astral body hand and foot with rope, and leads him on a soul-searing journey through the world of the living, forcing Holm to confront the consequences of his misspent life in a sermonizing manner that might remind one of Charles Dickens' *A Christmas Carol* (1843), but *The Phantom Carriage* lacks all of the sentimentalism so integral to Dickens' far more famous novel. This is what's most admirable about *The Phantom Carriage*. What at first seems to be a somewhat traditional moral fable inspired by typical Christian piety turns out, if one peers beneath the obvious, to be something far more subversive.

2. "Captive, Come Forth from Thy Prison"

A CLUE TO this esoteric subtext lies in the life of its author, the first woman to win the Nobel Prize for Literature, Selma Lagerlöf. As mentioned before, Lagerlöf was a devoted student of Theosophy, in particular the writings of Helena Blavatsky, whose seminal work, *Isis Unveiled,* was first published in 1877 when Lagerlöf was only nineteen.[6] No doubt, *Isis Unveiled* had a major impact on the teenage Lagerlöf, as strong traces of it can be found both in Sjöström's *The Phantom Carriage* and in Lagerlöf's original source material. Sjöström was determined to bring to the screen a faithful adaptation of Lagerlöf's novel and even performed the entire screenplay for her not long after its completion in order to win the author's approval. Except for a few minor criticisms, she did indeed grant him the approval he was seeking.[7]

Lagerlöf's novel is about spiritual evolution, an evolution that can only come about by freeing oneself from the confinements of the flesh. While traditional Christianity celebrates the human form (i.e., God is made manifest in the flesh, in the form of the Son, which is why the followers of Christ eat of His flesh symbolically every Sunday during the Eucharist), Gnosticism is quite different; it rejects the flesh and considers the material plane to be a realm of the unreal, not unlike Plato's view of the world as expressed in his "Allegory of the Caves" (380 BC) in which human beings and their material concerns are likened to shadows flitting about on a cave wall, the "real world" lying in the light beyond the entrance to the cave. In Gnosticism, the flesh, merely a cage that has temporarily trapped the divine spark buried deep in the core of every human being, must be overcome before true knowledge (*gnosis*) can be attained. In Christianity, anyone who accepts Christ into his or her heart has been saved. After that point, he or she knows everything that needs to be known; no further knowledge is required or even encouraged. In Gnosticism there are always much greater Mysteries waiting for those who are willing—or, in David Holm's case, forced—to walk the arduous path toward *gnosis* and the rejection of material concerns. This is the journey taken by David Holm in *The Phantom Carriage.*

A leading Theosophist, C.W. Leadbeater, wrote in his 1926 book, *Glimpses of Masonic History* (later republished under the title *Ancient Mystic Rites*):

> Even to-day it is quite commonly thought that Christianity had no mysteries, and some of its followers boast that in it nothing is hidden. That mistaken idea has been so sedulously impressed upon the world that it leads many people to feel a certain distaste for the wiser faiths which met all needs, and to think of them as unnecessarily hiding part of the truth or grudging it to the world. In the old days there was no such thought as this; it was recognized that only those who came up to a certain standard of life were fit to receive the higher instruction, and those who wished for it set to work to qualify themselves for it. Knowledge is power, and people must prove their fitness before they will be entrusted with power; for the object of the whole scheme is human evolution, and the interests of evolution would not be served by promiscuous publication of occult truth.
>
> Those who maintain the above-mentioned opinion about Christianity are unacquainted with the history of the Church. Though many of the early Christian writers are bitterly hostile to the Mysteries, they indignantly deny the suggestion that in their Church they have nothing worthy of that name, and claim that their Mysteries are in every way as good and deep and far-reaching as those of their "pagan" opponents. S. Clement says: "He who has been purified in baptism and then initiated into the little Mysteries (has acquired, that is to say, the habits of self-control and reflection), becomes ripe for the greater Mysteries, for Epopteia or Gnosis, the scientific knowledge of God." The same writer also said: "It is not lawful to reveal to profane persons the Mysteries of the Logos."[8]

Unless, perhaps, such revelation arrives in the form of cinematic fiction?

When Georges, now Death's Driver, commands David Holm to abandon his body, he utters the sentence, "Captive, come forth from thy prison." This view of the flesh as a jail cell that's holding back the spiritual evolution of mankind is not an attitude one would find in traditional Christianity, while it is indeed an important aspect of Gnosticism. In *Thy Soul Shall Bear Witness!*, when Lagerlöf describes Holm's eventual return to his physical body, the material plane is referred to as "something suffocating and deadly" and Holm is worried that his "soul's fresh development [will] stop if he [becomes] a mortal once more." After his sojourn on the astral plane, Holm is now convinced that "All his happiness was awaiting him in another world."[9]

The evolution of the spirit is the core of Theosophy, which drew heavily from the ancient teachings of Gnosticism. (One need only consult Blavatsky's aforementioned *Isis Unveiled*, arguably the ultimate Theosophical text, to see the truth of that statement.) Perhaps this is why Charles Darwin's relatively new theory of evolution was supported by Blavatsky, no doubt one of the reasons so many intellectuals of the late nineteenth century and early twentieth century, such as Selma Lagerlöf herself, saw Theosophy and Gnosticism as vital alternatives to what they perceived to be the backwards, anti-scientific views of the traditional Christian church.

In Chapter Two of his concise but comprehensive 2002 book, *Gnosticism: New Light on the Ancient Tradition of Inner Knowing*, Dr Hoeller writes:

> Gnosticism holds that human beings are essentially not the product of the material world. The important term in this statement is *essentially*, for Gnosticism focuses on the essence rather than the physical and mental containers that envelop this essence. Though the theory of biological evolution did not exist at the time of the ancient Gnostics, one might guess that unlike their mainstream Christian brethren, they would not have objected to it. For they believed that the human body originates on earth but the human spirit has come from afar, from the realm of the Fullness, where the true Godhead dwells [...].
>
> People are generally ignorant of the divine spark residing within them. This ignorance serves the interests of the archons,[10] who act as cosmic slave masters, keeping the light sparks in bondage. Anything that causes us to remain attached to earthly things, including the mental concepts we hold, keeps us in enslavement to these lesser cosmic rulers. The majority of men and women are like Adam, who was asleep in Paradise. Modern esoteric teachers (notably G. Gurdjieff) have capitalized on this Gnostic theme, representing humanity as a throng of sleepwalkers. Awakening from this sleep is the combined result of our desire for liberation and the supernal help extended to us.[11]

In Lagerlöf's narrative, Holm's "supernal help" takes the form of an etheric being who—thanks to his "cosmic master," Death—can pierce the veil between dimensional planes. Fortunately for Holm, Death's Driver is not enough of a slave that he's unable to exercise his own free will when he wants to, for ultimately it's the Driver's decision to allow Holm a final chance at life once the man's astral body—freed from its cage of flesh—has attained a sufficient amount of gnosis through the metaphysical journey imposed upon it by the phantom carriage and its "supernal" Driver. David Holm has at last evolved, and Death's Driver is able to respond in kind.

From the perspective of Theosophists like Selma Lagerlöf and Helena Blavatsky, Charles Darwin's theory of the origin of the species—though hardly Theosophical in intent—offers sound advice to the unenlightened: evolve or die. This is the dilemma forced upon Holm just before the stroke of midnight when a glass bottle—significantly, a bottle filled with alcohol—wielded by an angered ruffian slams into the back of his skull, evicting his astral body from its physical shell, not unlike a fish pushed out of the ocean by volcanic activity and compelled to breath air for the first time or a hominid forced to create fire from two sticks in order to survive a sudden blizzard.

In Chapter Five of *Isis Unveiled Vol. I: Science*, titled "The Ether, or 'Astral Light'," Blavatsky has this to say about the metaphysical overtones of Darwinism:

> Modern science insists upon the doctrine of evolution; so do human reason and the "secret doctrine," and the idea is corroborated by the ancient legends and myths, and even by the Bible itself when it is read between the lines [...]. The word *evolution* speaks for itself. The germ of the present human race must have preexisted in the parent of this race, as the seed, in which lies hidden the flower of next summer, was developed in the capsule of its parent-flower; the parent may be but *slightly* different, but it still differs from its future progeny. The antediluvian ancestors of the present elephant and lizard were, perhaps, the mammoth and the plesiosaurus; why should not the progenitors of our human race have been the "giants" of the *Vedas*, the *Völuspa*, and the *Book of Genesis*? While it is positively absurd to believe the "transformation of species" to have taken place according to some of the more materialistic views of the evolutionists, it is but natural to think that each genus, beginning with the mollusks and ending with monkey-man, has modified from its own primordial and distinctive form.[12]

This was pretty strong stuff in 1877. Traditional Christianity is still unable to reconcile Darwin's century-old scientific theories with the core of their religion, but only eighteen years after the publication of *On the Origin of Species,* Blavatsky was already incorporating Darwin's work into her metaphysical framework. That Theosophy offered both a complex spiritual framework as well as an acceptance of the cutting edge science of the day was attractive to writers, poets, painters, artists, and intellectuals of all sorts. Lagerlöf was by no means the only intellectual of the late nineteenth and twentieth century drawn into Theosophy's fold. Jean Toomer, for example, author of the breakthrough 1923 novel *Cane*, was associated with Theosophy for most of his life.

Theosophy essentially updated the suppressed teachings of Gnosticism (i.e., the earliest form of Christianity before the tenets of the New Testament were reduced down to the present, legalistic, formalized structure we know today) and resurrected them for a modern intellectual audience that was losing its residual interest in organized religion and grasping for a deeper and more vital spiritual center to take its place. In the aforementioned *Glimpses of Masonic History*, C.W. Leadbeater sums up the entirety of traditional Christianity with this hypothetical commandment: "Thou shalt not think."[13] In contrast, Theosophy and Gnosticism celebrated the pursuit of knowledge, both intellectual and spiritual. But it is David Holm's *spiritual* evolution that most concerns Lagerlöf and Sjöström. Spiritually, at the beginning of the film, Holm hasn't even reached the infant stage. He's still trapped in the womb, Plato's Cave of Shadows.

In *Isis Unveiled Vol. I*, Blavatsky paints a picture of a universe that has emerged from the process of evolution, replacing Darwin's scientific talk with the language of the poet and the mystic:

> [A]t the creation of the *prima materia*, while the grossest portions of it were used for the physical embryo-world, the more divine essence of it pervaded the universe, invisibly permeating and enclosing within its ethereal waves the newly-born infant, developing and stimulating it to activity as it slowly evolved out of the eternal chaos.[14]

That chaos remains embedded in every molecule of our imperfect world, and in Lagerlöf's narrative David Holm becomes a symbol of that chaos. Holm has wasted his life on alcohol and the pleasures of the flesh, neglecting the spiritual bonds between his wife, Anna (Hilda Borgström), and their children. His younger brother, seduced into a life of alcohol by Holm's encouragement, ends up in prison on a murder charge due to Holm's actions. This impediment, however, is not enough to sway Holm from his downward spiraling path, and he's abandoned by his family. Now consumed by anger and resentment, Holm's acts of self-destruction—his alcoholism, in particular—intensify, culminating in an incurable case of tuberculosis.

The prevalence of alcoholism in Lagerlöf's tale is not without Theosophical significance. Many Theosophists believe that alcohol is dangerous not just to the flesh, but to one's astral body as well. In his 1927 book, *Chakras: A Monograph*, C.W. Leadbeater explains that human beings are surrounded by what he calls "the etheric web." The etheric web is "the protection provided by nature to prevent a premature opening up of communication between the planes—a development which could lead to nothing but injury."[15] Leadbeater goes on to say:

> The malpractices which may more gradually injure this protective web are of two classes—use of alcohol or narcotic drugs, and the deliberate endeavour to throw open the doors which nature has kept closed [...]. Certain drugs and drinks—notably alcohol and all the narcotics, including tobacco—contain matter which on breaking up volatizes, and some of it passes from the physical plane to the astral. [...]
>
> When this takes place in the body of man these constituents rush out through the chakras in the opposite direction to that for which they are intended, and in doing this repeatedly they seriously injure and finally destroy the delicate web. This deterioration or destruction may be brought about in two different ways, according to the type of the person concerned and to the proportion of the constituents in his etheric and astral bodies. First, the rush of volatizing matter actually burns away the web, and therefore leaves the door open to all sorts of irregular forces and evil influences.[16]

When Leadbeater uses the phrase "evil influences," he's literally referring to non-physical entities from other dimensions that—according to Theosophists—can possess human beings who have laid themselves open to invasion through continual acts of debauchery and the harboring of various unhealthy obsessions. In both Lagerlöf's novel and Sjöström's film, these "evil influences" are symbolized by an incurable disease, the tuberculosis that ravages Holm's body. Just as possessing entities can pass on their evil influence to those who surround the possessed, Holm's tuberculosis threatens to reach out and destroy even the most pure of heart.

In one of the film's many flashbacks, a Salvation Army sister named Edit (Astrid Holm) chooses to risk her life for David Holm the night he appears on the Salvation Army's doorstep in an inebriated state. While Holm sleeps off his drunkenness in a cot, Edit decides to sew up the numerous holes in his infected clothes, unknowingly picking up his disease. When Holm wakes up the next morning, we are shocked at his violent reaction to Edit's selflessness. He mocks her, laughs, and rips all the new patches off the coat while Edit can only stand and watch, horrified. Holm is so proud and arrogant that he would rather suffer extreme physical discomfort than be indebted to the sister's noble act of kindness. To Holm's disgust, this merely strengthens Edit's desire to save him. Her efforts do indeed pay off, but she doesn't live to see Holm's ultimate transformation (which occurs at the very end of the film). She dies just past the stroke of midnight, on January 1, from the tuberculosis to which David Holm exposed her a year before.

This view of tuberculosis as a corrupting demon continues throughout *The Phantom Carriage*. In one particularly intense scene, David Holm threatens his wife (with whom he has reunited thanks to Edit's efforts) by breathing into the faces of his sleeping children, attempting in his alcohol-induced madness to pass his infection onto them. The chaos in the scene builds and builds, until at last Anne decides to take the children and flee once more. She locks Holm in the kitchen, then tries to wake the children and escape. Sjöström effectively uses crosscutting (still a new technique in 1921) to build the tension as Holm attempts to break through the locked door with an axe, a scene mirrored fifty-nine years later in Stanley Kubrick's 1980 film, *The Shining*, when Jack Torrance (Jack Nicholson) attempts to kill his family by cutting through a locked door with an axe. It's interesting to note that in *The Shining*, Nicholson's character (an alcoholic, like David Holm) isn't just symbolically possessed by demons—he really *is* possessed. One can't help but wonder what Theosophical significance C.W. Leadbeater, or even Selma Lagerlöf, would have seen in *The Shining*.

Just before Edit is about to die due to the infection Holm has spread to her, Death's Driver arrives with Holm's astral body in tow. Before this point Holm has been unable to interact with the material world while in his non-physical state... until the moment Holm expresses genuine sorrow at the pain he has wrought. Only in that second is his astral body capable of penetrating the planes and touching Edit's hand. His spiritual evolution has allowed him to transcend the barriers that separate most people from the higher realms of consciousness. Edit feels the touch and sees him. She is able to recognize the initial spark of transformation in his eyes before passing on.

In Lagerlöf's novel, the Theosophical subtext of this scene is even more obvious. Moments after Edit dies, Death's Driver addresses Holm:

> "Come with me hence at once," he went on; "we two have nothing further to do here. They who have to receive her are come."
>
> He dragged David Holm out with extreme violence. The latter thought that he saw the room suddenly filled with bright figures. He seemed to meet them on the stairs, and in the street—but he was whirled away at such a giddy pace that he could not distinguish them.[17]

Compare Lagerlöf's "bright figures" ascending the stairs with the following passage from Annie Besant's book, well-known to Theosophy's adherents, titled *A Study in Consciousness*. In this excerpt Besant describes a group of supernatural beings whose task is to guide human beings away from spiritual devolution:

> They have received various names in the various religions, but all religions recognize the fact of their existence and of their work. The Sanskrit name Devas—the Shining Ones—is the most general, and aptly describes the most marked characteristics of their appearance, a brilliant luminous radiance. The Hebrew, Christian, and Muhammadan religions call them Archangels and Angels. The Theosophist—to avoid sectarian connotations—names them, after their habitat, Elementals; and this title has the further advantage that it reminds the student of their connection with the five "Elements" of the ancient world: Aether, Air, Fire, Water, and Earth [...]. These beings have bodies formed out of the elemental essence of the kingdom to which they belong, flashing many-hued bodies, changing form at the will of the indwelling entity. They form a vast host, ever actively at work, labouring at the elemental essence to improve its quality, taking it to form their own bodies, throwing it off and taking other portions of it, to render it more responsive; they are also constantly busied in the shaping of forms, in aiding human Egos on the way to reincarnation in building their new bodies, bringing materials of the needed kind and helping in its arrangements. The less advanced the Ego the greater the directive work of the Deva; with animals they do almost all the work, and practically all with vegetables and minerals. They are the active agents in the work of the Logos [the Word of God], carrying out all the details of His world-plan, and aiding the countless evolving lives to find the materials they need for their clothing. All antiquity recognized the indispensable work they do in the worlds, and

> China, Egypt, India, Persia, Greece, Rome, tell the same story. The belief in the higher of them is not only found in all religions, but memories of those of the desire and of the ethereal physical plane linger on in folk-lore, in stories of "Nature-spirits", "Fairies", "Gnomes", "Trolls", and under many other names, memories of days when men were less deeply enwrapped in material interests, and more sensitive to the influences that played upon them from the subtler worlds.[18]

A Study in Consciousness was published in 1904, only eight years before the publication of *Thy Soul Shall Bear Witness!* Lagerlöf undoubtedly read a great deal of Annie Besant's work, as Besant was elected President of the Theosophical Society in 1907.

Besant, as well as many other Theosophists, delved into the ancient rites of Freemasonry due to its numerous Gnostic and Kabbalistic roots. In 1902, Besant was initiated into the International Order of Co-Freemasonry, eventually becoming its Grand Commander. Perhaps it is no surprise, therefore, that Lagerlöf's story—similar to Shakespeare's *Macbeth*—can be viewed as a quasi-Masonic allegory that subtly mirrors the rituals of the third degree of Freemasonry.

The third degree is a ritual in which the initiate is metaphorically killed with a violent blow to the back of the head delivered by fellow Masons acting as ruffians (not unlike the ne'er-do-wells we see lounging about in the cemetery at the beginning of *The Phantom Carriage*, one of whom kills Holm with a similar blow to the back of the head), resurrected by a command from the Master of the Lodge, then granted esoteric wisdom via a symbolism-laden, metaphysical journey enacted within the confines of the Lodge's ritual room. The initiate takes on the role of a poor, blind beggar clothed in rags whose sight is obstructed by a blindfold (representing spiritual desolation) and whose neck is bound with a "cable tow" (or a noose), just as Holm's wrists are bound by Death's Driver at the beginning of his odyssey. Only after he has been "killed" and then resurrected is the initiate's blindfold and cable tow removed, just as Holm must burst free from the ropes binding his wrists before he can slip back through to the physical plane and make contact with Sister Edit in the seconds before she passes on. In *The Phantom Carriage*, Death's Driver acts as a stand-in for the Master of the Lodge. After all, though Death's Driver is the servant of a higher "master," he is at the same time Holm's Master. Such pyramidal relationships mirror the evolutionary scales of the human soul in Theosophical thought.

At the conclusion of *The Phantom Carriage*, the last words spoken by David Holm are: "Lord, please let my soul come to maturity before it is reaped." The casual observer might interpret these words as Christian at base, but when one understands the hermetic overtones that Lagerlöf and Sjöström have layered onto their narrative one begins to realize that this film is structured like an Egyptian pyramid: esoteric secrets are layered, one on top of the other, with even deeper secrets buried within the architecture itself, there to be uncovered for those viewers intuitive enough—or determined enough—to pick up on the hidden meanings. But one can appreciate the architectural wonders of the Great Pyramid without understanding what it means. Lagerlöf and Sjöström knew this, creating a structure that could stand the test of time because its most valuable secrets are those that are revealed to the unconscious. Like ethereal images flickering on a movie screen, the secrets of the mind are often best seen in the dark.

3. Double Exposure (and Other Dualities)

THOUGH DARKNESS PERMEATES *The Phantom Carriage*, this does not occlude the light of *gnosis* that emerges from David Holm's soul in the final reel. These binary opposites, darkness and light, are realized in the film thanks to the breakthrough special effects that Sjöström integrates seamlessly into Lagerlöf's plot.

The technical aspects of the film were a major reason for *The Phantom Carriage's* initial international success and remains one of its most impressive qualities. Needless to say, the wizardry of 1921 cinema pales in comparison to the latest advances in makeup and special effects on display in such twenty-first-century Swedish dark fantasies as Tomas Alfredson's 2008 film, *Let the Right One In* (which owes a considerable debt to the ground first broken in fantastic cinema by *The Phantom Carriage*). Nonetheless, there is something quite endearing about the crude and yet effective in-camera effects used by Sjöström to bring Lagerlöf's parable to life. No matter how sophisticated the graphics, there is something rather cold and unappealing about the computer-generated effects so prevalent in recent films of the *fantastique*; however, there is an ineffable quality about the most basic effects (i.e., those performed in-camera) that lend phantasmagoric films a veneer of authenticity, that tricks the human brain into thinking that the chimerical events unfolding before our eyes are indeed possible. Perhaps our brain knows, subliminally, that a *human hand* was involved in the creation of these effects, thus emphasizing the realistic over the fantastic.

It is appropriate and poetic, thematically, that Sjöström used *double* exposure to bring this dream/nightmare (nightmare/dream) to fruition. The process of double exposure involves filming the background image first, then rewinding the film and shooting the spectral beings and objects (i.e., Death's Driver, his skeletal horse, David Holm's astral body, and the carriage itself) against a black background. This process mirrors the theme of duality found throughout the film. The purgatorial world inhabited by Holm's astral double is similar to the twilight realm in which the film itself dwells. *The Phantom Carriage* hovers gracefully between two worlds, between the extremes of phantasmagoric expressionism and stark realism.

It must be remembered that *The Phantom Carriage* emerged during a period in which the seductive shadow of expressionism hung over the cinema. Two of the most important expressionist films ever made, Robert Wiene's *The Cabinet of Dr. Caligari* and Paul Wegener and Carl Boese's *Der Golem*, had been released only a year earlier. F.W. Murnau's equally iconic film, *Nosferatu*, went into production the same year *The Phantom Carriage* was released. It's unlikely, therefore, that Sjöström did not have to contend with this shadow while conceiving how best to bring *The Phantom Carriage* to life. Lagerlöf's novel could very well have lent itself to a purely expressionist interpretation, similar to *The Cabinet of Dr. Caligari*. Though it's intriguing to imagine what such a film would have been like, Sjöström must have known that this approach would have emphasized the phantasmagoria of Lagerlöf's story over the tangible strains of social realism. In order to represent the theme of Gnostic duality so prevalent in *Thy Soul Shall Bear Witness!*, Sjöström had to balance the darkness with the light, the expressionistic with the realistic.

Having no doubt seen contemporary expressionist films, such as those mentioned above, Sjöström would have recognized expressionism's potential to manifest images of what Sigmund Freud called "the uncanny." In his 1919 essay "The Uncanny," Freud applied his psychoanalytic theories to such fantasy tales as E.T.A. Hoffmann's "The Sand-Man," contending that stories like these are built around emotions and images that are (paradoxically) both strange and familiar at once, unearthing repressed and primal impulses buried deep within us:

> [T]his uncanny is in reality nothing new or alien, but something which is familiar and old-established in the mind and which has become

> alienated from it only through the process of repression. This reference to the factor of repression enables us, furthermore, to understand [the] definition of the uncanny as something which ought to have remained hidden but has come to light.[19]

The most famous works of expressionism of the early 1920s all invoked this transgressive world of the uncanny and the supernatural at a time when, in Hollywood, the prevailing wisdom was that the virgin pure medium of film—a *populist* medium at heart—was not the proper home for such taboo stories. The masses simply would not accept tales of the uncanny in the form of film, so insisted The Powers That Be, which explains why so many American movies of the 1920s featured ostensibly supernatural events that always turned out to be prosaic in the end. The examples are numerous, but the most prominent of these films would include Rupert Julian's *The Phantom of the Opera* (1925), Roland West's *The Bat* (1926), Paul Leni's *The Cat and the Canary* (1927), and Tod Browning's *London after Midnight* (1927). Some critics even insist to this day that *The Phantom Carriage* falls into this category, that the phantasmagoria in the film is a result of David Holm's disordered brain after having been knocked unconscious by the ruffian's bottle in the graveyard; however, I think I have already demonstrated, via Lagerlöf's personal beliefs, that the uncanny elements of the tale are intended to be literal representations of reality—a form of "magic realism," as it were, long before that term was coined in the 1950s. And perhaps "magic realism" is the best term that could be applied to Sjöström's film, for it's clear that Lagerlöf believed a little magic was sometimes the only means by which one could access the inner realms of the soul and thus light oneself up with the quotidian wonders of reality.

Sjöström somehow evokes this world of "magic realism" by emphasizing the real over the magical, choosing to shoot many of the scenes in natural surroundings rather than on a soundstage. As Caspar Tybjerg says during his Criterion commentary, "To fully grasp how atmospheric *The Phantom Carriage* would have seemed to contemporaries, we need to understand that few (if any) previous films had been enveloped in the darkness of night the way this one is." Indeed, almost every scene takes place in the dark with night-for-night shooting that is exquisitely vivid, a feat that required superior technical skills for the time period. The near-permanent darkness not only adds to the spookiness of the naturalistic graveyard scenes at the

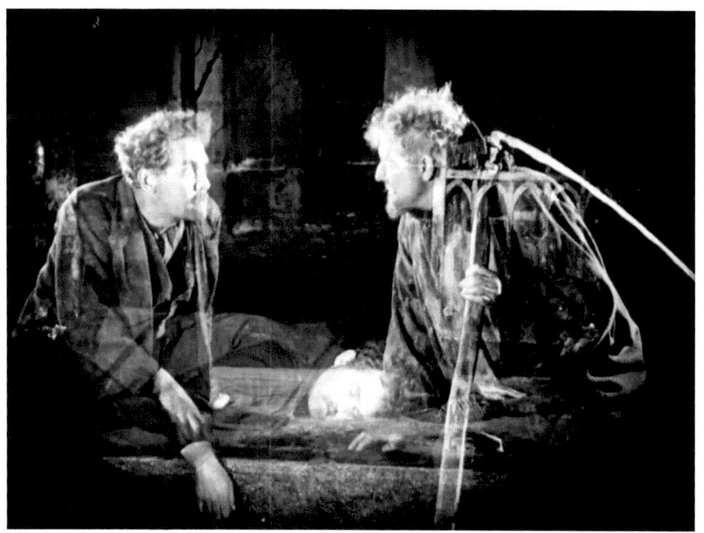

Two images from *The Phantom Carriage*.

beginning of the film, but also acts as a contrast to the light (i.e., the Gnostic illumination) that will swell up within Holm at the end of his spiritual journey. This final illumination would be difficult for the viewer to accept if so much darkness had not preceded it.

This duality, this melding of light and dark, is encapsulated in a single shot that occurs nineteen minutes into the film: a silhouette of Death's Driver creeping over the horizon of a shadowy, desolate hill. Almost the entire screen is filled with the ragged landscape, symbolic of the darkness the carriage has left in its wake. Though our eyes are overwhelmed by this blackness, one cannot help but be drawn toward the band of waning light at the top of the screen, representative of the faint—but very real—light that awaits us all if we heed Lagerlöf's warning and mature our souls before they are reaped.

The overall realism of the film renders the magical moments even more startling when they appear. The most expressionistic sequence in *The Phantom Carriage* is the one that lingers in the mind long after the memory of the final scene has faded away. Almost exactly eighteen minutes into the film, we are introduced to a story within a story within a story—a series of visual vignettes that could stand on their own as an experimental short film about the travails endured by the single human unfortunate enough to be initiated by Death into the dual role of Driver and Soul Collector. The carriage and its ghostly servant are brought to life through meticulous double exposures that must have been grueling for Sjöström and his crew to pull off in the early 1920s. We see Death's Driver forced to collect the soul of a rich but desperate man who has just blown his brains out with a pistol. We next see the Driver and his skeletal horse trundling across the surface of the ocean. The Driver leaves the carriage in order to descend beneath the waves and collect the fresh soul of a drowned sailor lying peacefully on the ocean floor. The sailor almost appears to be sleeping, his battered skull using a large white rock as a final pillow. These are the most famous scenes in the film, and serve to establish not only the depressing horror of the Driver's task, but the fact that no man on Earth (rich or poor), no place on Earth (on land or at sea), is inviolate to Death's touch.

The double exposure technique had been employed before to bring incredible sights to the silver screen (Georges Méliès had used the technique as early as 1898 in his short film *The Four Troublesome Heads*), but never in such an appropriately foreboding context. It was the perfect technique to realize Lagerlöf's uncanny fantasy. Perhaps for the first time in cinema, special effects and emotional content came together to create a unique and harrowing frisson.

4. Cinema of the Occulted Taboo

THE EFFECTS (AND affects) of *The Phantom Carriage* can be seen in the cinema to this day, even among filmmakers who may never have encountered Victor Sjöström's masterpiece, a film that in 1924 Charlie Chaplin hailed as "the best film ever made." Chaplin also referred to Sjöström as "the greatest director in the world."[20] Ingmar Bergman often insisted that his first viewing of *The Phantom Carriage* at the age of fourteen sparked his initial desire to become a filmmaker, no doubt the reason he cast Sjöström in two of his films, including the 1957 classic, *Wild Strawberries*. The influence of *The Phantom Carriage* on Bergman's *The Seventh Seal*—a 1957 film about a medieval knight who challenges Death to a chess game during the Black Plague—is unmistakable.

The Phantom Carriage is part of a long storytelling tradition that appears to be unstoppable. Many esotericists have recognized the immense potential cinema possesses with regard to unobtrusively disseminating occult information to the average man and woman. Consider the example of Manly P. Hall, founder of The Philosophical Research Society in Los Angeles and author of dozens of encyclopedic volumes about the history of the occult. At first, Hall attempted to use periodical fiction for this purpose. In the first two decades of the twentieth century, one couldn't find a better medium for mass communication than the numerous magazines that filled up newsstands all across the country and featured brand new short stories every week. Many of these publications were open to the subject of the supernatural, just as long as it was broached in the context of fiction. Hall presented to the public little gems of esoteric wisdom in the form of elegantly crafted pulp short stories. Some of these pieces Hall later collected in a 1925 book titled *Shadow Forms*, in the introduction to which he writes, "In an erratic moment we conceived the notion of attempting to portray certain great occult truths through the medium of fiction. We believe many people will read stories who would never consider a philosophical dissertation on the subject."[21] One such occult-related project Hall succeeded in bringing to the screen was a mystery titled *When Were You Born?* (1938), directed by

William C. McGann and starring Anna May Wong as a Chinese woman in San Francisco who solves a murder using the techniques of astrology. The film begins with a five-minute-long prologue by Hall in which he briefly explains the history of astrology.

But Hall was not the only esotericist who brought to the cinema his unique insight into the world of the occult. Jean Cocteau, among the most acclaimed directors of the twentieth century, reshaped ancient myth and folklore into powerful visual tone poems such as *Beauty and the Beast* (1946) and *Orpheus* (1950). According to the 1982 bestselling nonfiction book, *Holy Blood, Holy Grail* by Michael Baigent, Richard Leigh and Henry Lincoln, Cocteau was the Grand Master of a centuries-old occult secret society known as the Prieuré de Sion.[22] Whether this tantalizing claim is accurate or not, it is evident from his work that Cocteau did indeed possess a deep and intimate understanding of hermeticism. Kenneth Anger, an acknowledged follower of Aleister Crowley's religion, Thelema, poured his occult knowledge into such avant-garde films as *The Inauguration of the Pleasure Dome* (1954), *Invocation of My Demon Brother* (1969), and *Lucifer Rising* (1972). Anger's contemporary, Alejandro Jodorowsky, is not only a knowledgeable practitioner of alchemy and the Tarot (in fact, he has created his own spiritual system called "psychoshamanism," about which he writes extensively in his 2010 book *Psychomagic: The Transformative Power of Shamanic Psychotherapy*), but he also happens to be one of the most visionary film directors alive today. Since 1970 he has written and directed the most illuminating metaphysical allegories ever committed to celluloid, foremost among them *El Topo* (1970), *The Holy Mountain* (1973) *Santa Sangre* (1989) and *The Dance of Reality* (2013), all of which seethe and overbrim with unbridled *gnosis*.

Hall, Cocteau, Anger, Jodorowsky, Lagerlöf, and Sjöström were neither the first nor the last artists to exploit the power of the cinema for the purpose of disseminating occult knowledge. The examples read like a list of some of the most cutting edge films to emerge from the cinema during the past eleven decades. Some of these films you may have watched but never really *seen*, and some you may never even have heard of, but all are blessed with at least a touch of genuine magic: Giuseppe de Liguoro's *L'Inferno* (1911), Benjamin Christensen's *Häxan* (1922), Rex Ingram's *The Magician* (1926), James Whale's *Frankenstein* (1931) and *Bride of Frankenstein* (1935), Carl Dreyer's *Vampyr* (1932), Karl Freund's *The Mummy* (1932), Walt Disney's *Snow White and the Seven Dwarfs* (1937), *Pinocchio* (1940), *Fantasia* (1940),

Peter Pan (1953), *Sleeping Beauty* (1959) and *Alice in Wonderland* (1951), Victor Fleming's *The Wizard of Oz* (1939), Jacques Tourneur's *I Walked With a Zombie* (1943) and *Night of the Demon* (1957), Julian Roffman's *The Mask* (1961), Luis Buñuel's *The Exterminating Angel* (1962), Orson Welles' *The Trial* (1962), Federico Fellini's *8 ½* (1963), Robert Stevenson's *Mary Poppins* (1964), J. Lee Thompson's *Eye of the Devil* (1966), Michelangelo Antonioni's *Blow-up* (1966), Stanley Kubrick's *2001: A Space Odyssey* (1968) and *Eyes Wide Shut* (1999), Terence Fisher's *The Devil Rides Out* (1968), George Lucas' *THX 1138* (1971) and *Star Wars* (1977), Rene Laloux's *Fantastic Planet* (1973), Robin Hardy's *The Wicker Man* (1973), John Huston's *The Man Who Would Be King* (1975), Hal Ashby's *Being There* (1979), Jeannot Szwarc's *Somewhere in Time* (1980), Ken Russell's *Altered States* (1980), Ridley Scott's *Blade Runner* (1982), David Lynch's *Blue Velvet* (1986), *Twin Peaks: Fire Walk With Me* (1992) and *Mulholland Drive* (2001), Jan Švankmajer's *Alice* (1988) and *Faust* (1994), Brian Yuzna's *Society* (1989), Peter Greenaway's *Prospero's Books* (1991), David Cronenberg's *Naked Lunch* (1991) and *eXistenZ* (1999), Hayao Miyazaki's *Porco Rosso* (1992), *Spirited Away* (2001) and *Ponyo* (2008), Jim Jarmusch's *Dead Man* (1995), Darren Aronofsky's *Pi* (1998) and *The Fountain* (2006), Alex Proyas' *Dark City* (1998), Roman Polanski's *Rosemary's Baby* (1968), *The Tenant* (1976), and *The Ninth Gate* (1999), the Wachowskis' *The Matrix* series (1999–2021), Richard Kelly's *Donnie Darko* (2001), the Hughes Brothers' *From Hell* (2001), Matthew Barney's *The Cremaster Cycle* (2003), Francisco Athie's *Vera* (2003), Christiane Cegavske's *Blood Tea and Red String* (2006), Christopher Nolan's *Inception* (2010), the various *Harry Potter* films (2001–2011), Ari Aster's *Hereditary* (2018) and *Midsommar* (2019), Robert Eggers' *The Lighthouse* (2019), Brandon Cronenberg's *Possessor* (2020), Larry Wade Carrell's *Girl Next* (2021), and Phil Tippett's *Mad God* (2021). These examples could all be placed under a single category that one might call the "Cinema of the Occulted Taboo."

This type of film, which disguises its true purpose behind the seductive veneer of entertainment, pervades the cinema even today: subtle movies that continue to creep across the landscape of the twentieth century and beyond, like an army of phantom carriages steered by implacable drivers intent on fulfilling their sacred tasks, quietly disseminating seeds of ancient wisdom through shadow shows projected on blank screens all across the globe, hopefully paving the way for new paradigms and new dreams and new nightmares … new worlds of gods and monsters.

Afterword

With Heraclitus in a Darkened Room

WE'RE HERE TO go, says William S. Burroughs.

Sometimes to other stars, sometimes to other realities.

In a way, all of the films under discussion here have been about other worlds, other realities. Alternate dimensions. The sometimes disturbing, sometimes wonderful, sometimes absurd, always illuminating obverse worlds that exist on the other side of the looking glass. The other side of the luminous movie screen (silver or otherwise). The other side of the magic door that leads into the secret center of the mind.

Once that hidden chamber is uncovered, it's tempting to get addicted to its alluring comforts. To relax and take up residence there for good. That's what Dominick Cobb and his wife, Mal, end up doing in *Inception* to their everlasting regret. But the purpose of these secret chambers, the purpose of any form of meditation or self-reflection or positive fantasy—whether cinematic or not—is to eventually use that occult knowledge and apply it to the real world. The world from which all dreams emerge in the first place.

Oliver Stone once said that his film, *JFK*, was a key to unlock a doorway into an alternate mythology of US history. Some of Stone's most vociferous, literal-minded critics decried this statement, thinking the director was trying to hedge his bets and avoid committing to the historical veracity of his film. But of course, *all* films—all stories—are doorways into alternate mythologies. Some of these mythologies are "truer" than others. It's up to the listener, the reader, the viewer, to decide which myths are worthwhile totems that may help guide you through the confusing labyrinth of the noumenal world and which ones are merely false idols intended to lead you astray. Dead ends abound in labyrinths, and your basic perception can easily be fooled. But isn't that the joy of entering any maze in the first place?

My first book, *Cryptoscatology: Conspiracy Theory as Art Form*, was all about uncovering the hidden truths lying beneath the unreliable surfaces of modern conspiracy theories. *Hollywood Haunts the World* is about the hidden truths lying beneath the equally unreliable surfaces of debased cinematic genres such as horror, science fiction, fantasy, noir, and conspiracy-theory-laden thrillers and docudramas that combine elements of these disparate genres into one. Ultimately, both books are about labyrinths. About navigating through twisting, disorientating corridors that loop in upon themselves while somehow maintaining one's own balance, one's own private citadel of consciousness that might recognize truth when confronted by the many eccentric disguises in which it often likes to costume itself.

The secret history of the world can be decoded in these mazes. Through film, yes, but through all sorts of jabberwocky as well. Through trash. Through the seemingly transient and the insignificant. Through the peripheral and the hopelessly obscure. Truth, of course, has always hidden itself in the most unlikely of places. The Greek philosopher Heraclitus (535–435 BC) once wrote, "The nature of things is in the habit of concealing itself." Where better to conceal oneself than amidst the discarded, the overlooked, the underestimated? I think if Heraclitus had lived in the twentieth or twenty-first century, he would have been a film reviewer. And a damn good one at that.

And I suspect he would have enjoyed the potpourri of films we've screened here today, uncomfortable truths hermetically sealed within celluloid. Alternate mythologies all.

Now that we've succeeded in reaching the end credits, let's lift an overpriced Styrofoam cup of sugary soda high in the air and make a toast. Here's to lounging in the back row of a downtown theater at midnight accompanied by the ghosts of Heraclitus and Selma Lagerlöf, William Shakespeare and Helena Blavatsky, Edgar Allan Poe and Robert Florey, Charles Darwin and Bela Lugosi, André Breton and Joseph H. Lewis, Sigmund Freud and Edgar G. Ulmer, Carl Jung and all those tragic little aliens (or "bogies," as the villagers of the Orkney Islands might say) who passed away amidst the wreckage of Roswell, Frank Sinatra and José M.R. Delgado, John F. Kennedy and Lee Harvey Oswald, Stanley Kubrick and John A. Keel, and a host of other peculiar phantoms. All of whom are eating buttery popcorn while watching ancient B-films flickering on a tattered screen in the center of a secret labyrinth.

As André Breton once said, "Three cheers for darkened rooms."

See you all at the movies.

Sources

"WHAT'S AT THE End of Main Street?: The Struggle between the Artificial and the Real in Recent Gnostic Cinema" was serialized, in somewhat abbreviated form, in *New Dawn Magazine* #158 (September/October 2016) and *New Dawn Magazine* #159 (November/December 2016) edited by David Jones.

"The Box in the Desert: Budd Boetticher, *Breaking Bad,* and the Twenty-first-century Western" appeared in *ReFocus: The Films of Budd Boetticher* edited by Gary D. Rhodes and Robert Singer (Edinburgh University Press, 2017).

"The Brain(s) that Killed Kennedy: The JFK Assassination as Seen Through Film" appears here for the first time.

"One Chants Out Between Two Worlds: *It Came from Outer Space, Twin Peaks,* and the Legacy of Jack Parsons" appears here for the first time.

"The Man from Planet X: Hollywood's First Invasion from Outer Space" appeared in *The New York Review of Science Fiction* #266 (October 2010) edited by David Hartwell and Kevin J. Maroney.

"Golden the Film Was—Oh! Oh! Oh!: Cinema and the Art of Perception Management" appears here for the first time.

"Invisible Ghosts: The Films of Bela Lugosi as Borderline Surrealism" appeared in *Bela Lugosi and the Monogram Nine* published by Ben Ohmart (BearManor Media, 2019).

"The Suppressed Science of Dr. Mirakle: The Cinematic Ancestors and Descendants of Charles Darwin" originally appeared in *The New York Review of Science Fiction* #260 (April 2010) edited by David Hartwell and Kevin J. Maroney and was reprinted, in greatly expanded form, in *Video Watchdog Magazine* #166 (January/February 2012) edited by Tim and Donna Lucas.

"Here Among the Dead: *The Phantom Carriage* and the Cinema of the Occulted Taboo" appeared in *Expressionism in the Cinema* edited by Olaf Brill and Gary D. Rhodes (Edinburgh University Press, 2016).

Notes

Foreword & Introduction

1 Richard Abel, *The Red Rooster Scare: Making Cinema American, 1900–1910* (Berkeley: University of California Press, 1999).
2 "'Genre' Motion Pictures and an Example," *Moving Picture World*, May 7, 1910, 725.
3 W. Stephen Bush, "Happy Ending," *Moving Picture World*, September 6, 1915, 1107.
4 Gary D. Rhodes, "'Movie': How a Single Word Helped Shape Hollywood History," *Film and History*, Vol. 46, No. 1 (Summer 2016), 43–52
5 Quoted in David Bordwell, Janet Staiger, and Kristin Thompson, *The Classical Hollywood Cinema: Film Style & Mode of Production to 1960* (New York: Columbia University Press, 1985), 4.
6 *McLuhan's Wake* (DVD, The Disinformation Company, 2006).
7 Gary D. Rhodes, *Lugosi* (Jefferson, NC: McFarland, 1997), p. *xiii*.

Chapter 1 What's at the End of Main Street?

1 Stephan A. Hoeller, *Gnosticism: New Light on the Ancient Tradition of Inner Knowing* (Wheaton, IL: Quest Books, 2002), pp. 17–18.
2 Ibid. p. 237.
3 Ibid. p. 18.
4 Ibid. p. 238.
5 Marshall McLuhan and Wilfred Wilson, *From Cliché to Archetype* (New York: Viking Press, 1970), p. 99.
6 Jon Rappoport, *The Secret Behind Secret Societies* (San Diego: Truth Seeker Books, 1998), p. 282.
7 Ibid. pp. 351–52.
8 Ray Villard, "Are We Living Inside a Computer Simulation?," Discovery.com, December 16, 2012 (accessed October 6, 2018).
9 J.B.S. Haldane, *Possible Worlds and Other Essays* (London: Chatto & Windus, 1928), p. 286.
10 Jeffrey Steinberg, "The Creation of the 'Littleton' Culture," *The New Federalist*, August 30, 1999, pp. 5–7.
11 John A. Keel, *The Mothman Prophecies* (New York: Tor Books, 2002 [1975]), p. 272.
12 Robert Keser, "Distribute This!: Francisco Athie's *Vera* (Mexico, 2003)," Brightlightsfilm.com, January 31, 2004 (accessed October 6, 2018).
13 John Lamb Lash, *Not In His Image: Gnostic Vision, Sacred Ecology, and the Future of Belief* (White River Junction, VT: Chelsea Green, 2006), p. 290.
14 Ibid. pp. 290–91.
15 Ibid. p. 292.
16 Steve Ditko, *Mr. A*, No. 21 (Spring 2017), p. 2.
17 Ibid.
18 David E. Worcester, *Genesis of a Music*, Pacifica Radio, KPFK, Los Angeles, 24 July 1993.
19 Zeph E. Daniel, "End Times Programming," Educate-Yourself.org, October 23, 2004 (accessed March 3, 2023).
20 Branko Marcetic, "*Society*, the Cult Horror Film Where the Monster Is Class Conflict," Jacobin.com, October 31, 2021 (accessed March 3, 2023).
21 William Lindsay Gresham, *Nightmare Alley* (New York: Signet, 1949 [1946]), p. 55.

22 Anton Szandor LaVey, *The Satanic Bible* (New York: Avon Books, 1969), p. 116.

23 Michael Aquino, *The Church of Satan* (San Francisco: Independently Published, 2002 [1983]), p. 17. Available at: <https://archive.org/stream/michael-a-aquino-church-of-satan/michael-a-aquino-church-of-satan_djvu.txt>.

24 Ibid.

25 Bruce L. Edwards, *C.S. Lewis: Life, Works, and Legacy Volume 1: An Examined Life* (Westport, CT: Praeger, 2007), p. 283.

26 William S. Burroughs, Preface to Brion Gysin and Terry Wilson's *Here To Go: Planet R-101* (San Francisco: Re/Search Publications, 1982), pp. *x-xi*.

27 William S. Burroughs, *The Place of Dead Roads* (New York: Henry Holt, 1983), p. *xi*.

Chapter 2
The Box in the Desert

1 Karen Herman, "The Writer's Cut: Breaking Bad Creator Vince Gilligan Interview," YouTube.com, October 14, 2013 (accessed April 2, 2014).

2 Emily Brennan, "Albuquerque's Role on 'Breaking Bad,'" NYTimes.com, August 6, 2013 (accessed April 1, 2014).

3 Kimberly Nordyke, "Conan O'Brien Interviews Entire 'Breaking Bad' Cast, Tries to Get Scoop on Series Finale," Hollywoodreporter.com, September 23, 2013 (accessed April 1, 2014).

4 "Taylor Hackford on *Decision at Sundown*," *The Films of Budd Boetticher* (DVD, Sony Pictures, 2008).

5 Nordyke, "Conan O'Brien Interviews Entire 'Breaking Bad' Cast."

6 Alexandra Klausner, "DreamWorks CEO Offered to Pay $75m for Just Three More 'Breaking Bad' Episodes (Before He Found Out How It Ended)," Dailymail.com, October 9, 2013 (accessed April 1, 2014).

7 Brennan, "Albuquerque's Role on 'Breaking Bad.'"

8 Quoted in Bruce Ricker's documentary film *Budd Boetticher: A Man Can Do That* (Rhapsody, 2005).

9 Mike Flaherty, "The Showrunner Transcript: *Breaking Bad's* Vince Gilligan on Season Four and his Experiences on *The X-Files*," Vulture.com, May 16, 2011 (accessed April 2, 2014).

10 Herman, "The Writer's Cut."

Chapter 3
The Brain(s) That Killed Kennedy

1 Curt Siodmak, *Donovan's Brain* (New York: Berkley Medallion, 1969), p. 101.

2 Curt Siodmak, *Wolf Man's Maker: Memoir of a Hollywood Writer* (Lanham, MD: The Scarecrow Press, 2001), pp. 308–09.

3 Lincoln Lawrence, *Were We Controlled?* (New York: University Press, 1967), pp. 25–27.

4 José M. R. Delgado, *Physical Control of the Mind: Toward a Psychocivilized Society* (New York: Harper & Row, 1969), p. 281.

5 Lawrence, *Were We Controlled?* (New York: University Press, 1967), pp. 33–35.

6 Ibid. p. 35.

7 Bill Warren, *Keep Watching the Skies!: American Science Fiction Movies of the Fifties (The 21st Century Edition)* (Jefferson, NC: McFarland, 2010), p. 185.

8 John M. Miller, "*The Gamma People*," TCM.com (accessed October 1, 2018).

9 Tom Weaver, "Re: *Zombies of Mora Tau* and *Gamma People*", Classichorrorfilmboard.com, April 8, 2012 (accessed October 1, 2018).

10 Cary Reich, *The Life of Nelson A. Rockefeller: Worlds to Conquer 1908–1958* (New York: Doubleday, 1996), p. 551.

11 Jon Rappoport, *U.S. Government Mind Control Experiments on Children* (n.p., 1996), p. *vi*.

12 Ibid. p. 9.

13 Ibid. pp. 61–64.
14 Ibid. p. 26.
15 Ibid. p. 102.
16 Ibid. p. 23.
17 Ibid. p. 84.
18 Walter Bowart, *Operation Mind Control* (Ft. Bragg, CA: Flatland Editions, 1994 [1978]), Chp. 28, p. 11.
19 Ibid., Foreword, pp. 20–22.
20 Warren, *Keep Watching the Skies!*, p. 552.
21 Anthony Summers, *Conspiracy* (New York: McGraw-Hill, 1980), p. 288.
22 Warren, *Keep Watching the Skies!*, pp. 556–57.
23 Bowart, *Operation Mind Control*, Chp. 1, p. 2.
24 Ibid. Chp. 1, p. 3.
25 Incidentally, throughout the 1960s, Dr Bryan worked as a technical advisor on other hypnosis-themed horror/science fiction films such as Roger Corman's *Tales of Terror* (1962) and Francis Ford Coppola's *Dementia 13* (1963).
26 Warren, *Keep Watching the Skies!*, p. 5.
27 Ibid. p. 17.
28 Lawrence, *Were We Controlled?*, p. 9.
29 Glenn Erickson, "*The Manchurian Candidate*: Savant Blu-ray Review," DVDTalk.com, May 24, 2011 (accessed October 2, 2018).
30 William Torbitt, *NASA, NAZIS & JFK* (Kempton, IL: Adventures Unlimited Press, 1996), p. 196.
31 Jim Garrison, *On the Trail of the Assassins* (New York: Warner Books, 1988), p. 101.
32 Ibid. p. 137.
33 Ibid. p. 102.
34 Ibid. p. 103.
35 Ibid.
36 Jim Marrs, *Crossfire: The Plot That Killed Kennedy* (New York: Carroll & Graf, 1989), p. 499.
37 Garrison, *On the Trail of the Assassins*, pp. 293–94.
38 Marrs, *Crossfire*, p. 500.
39 Lawrence, *Were We Controlled?*, pp. 69, 72.
40 Ibid. p. 82.
41 Bowart, *Operation Mind Control*, Chp. 28, p. 2.
42 Ibid. Chp. 28, p. 1.
43 Lawrence, *Were We Controlled?*, p. 23.
44 See, for example, Michael C. Ruppert's "Suppressed Details of Criminal Insider Trading Lead Directly into the CIA's Highest Ranks" (the full text of which can be read here: <https://www.hereinreality.com/insidertrading.html#.Yo7sUKjMKUk>).
45 Bowart, *Operation Mind Control*, Chp. 21, p. 10.
46 Ibid. Chp. 22, p. 1.
47 Ibid. Chp. 22, pp. 1–3.
48 Marrs, *Crossfire*, p. 431.
49 John A. Keel, *Our Haunted Planet* (Greenwich, CT: Fawcett Gold Medal, 1971), p. 166.
50 Marrs, *Crossfire*, p. 200.
51 Bowart, *Operation Mind Control*, Chp. 22, p. 6.
52 Epstein interviewed DeMohrenschildt about Oswald and the JFK assassination only two hours before DeMohrenschildt's death.
53 Bowart, *Operation Mind Control*, Chp. 22, p. 7.
54 Garrison, *On the Trail of the Assassins*, p. 64.
55 Michio Kaku and Daniel Axelrod, *To Win a Nuclear War: The Pentagon's Secret War Plans* (Boston, MA: South End Press, 1987), p. 166.
56 Ibid. p. 164.
57 Ibid. p. 166.
58 Seymour Hersh, *The Price of Power: Kissinger in the Nixon White House* (New York: Summit Books, 1983), p. 130.
59 William Grimes, "Loren Singer, 'Parallax View' Author, Dies at 86," NYTimes.com, December 23, 2009 (accessed October 2, 2018).
60 William S. Burroughs, *Dead City Radio* (Island Records, 1990).
61 Marrs, *Crossfire*, p. 233.

62 *Who Killed Winter Kills?*, YouTube.com (accessed October 2, 2018).

63 There are many indications that "Heaven's Gate" was a front for yet another mind control experiment funded by one or more American intelligence agencies. I analyze this story in some detail in Chapter 3 of my book, *Cryptoscatology: Conspiracy Theory as Art Form*.

64 Marrs, *Rule By Secrecy* (New York: HarperCollins, 2000), p. 30.

65 Ray Nelson, "Eight O'clock in the Morning," in Terry Carr (ed.), *The Others* (Greenwich, CT: Fawcett Gold Medal, 1969), pp. 73–79.

66 Charles Fort, *Book of the Damned* in Tiffany Thayer (ed.), *The Books of Charles Fort* (New York: Henry Holt, 1941), p. 156.

67 Jonathan Lethem, *They Live* (Berkeley: Soft Skull Press, 2010), pp. 29–30.

68 Nelson, "Eight O'clock in the Morning," p. 74.

69 John Carpenter, "Foreword," in Russ Cochran (ed.), *Tales from the Crypt* (West Plains, MD: Gemstone Publishing, 2006), p. 7.

70 Stephen King, *Danse Macabre* (New York: Berkley, 1983 [1981]), p. 328.

71 Lethem, *They Live*, p. 123

72 Ibid. p. 61.

73 Ibid. p. 55.

74 Ibid. p. 118.

75 *Tobe Hooper Interview* (DVD, Dark Sky Films, 2008).

76 Albert Pike, *Morals and Dogma* (Richmond, VA: L.H. Jenkins, 1956 [1871]), p. 790.

77 *Philip K. Dick: A Day in the Afterlife* (Videocassette, BBC, 1994).

78 Information about the Kennedys' secret war against Castro can be seen in Episode Six of the multi-part History Channel documentary titled *The Men Who Killed Kennedy*. The last fifteen minutes of Episode Six are dedicated to the subject. The entirety of Episode Six, titled "The Truth Shall Set You Free," can be seen on YouTube: <www.youtube.com/watch?v=zOH1znZH-Mml>. For further information about the US government's various attempts to assassinate Castro, and how these attempts tie in with the JFK assassination, read Warren Hinckle and William Turner's 1993 book *Deadly Secrets: The CIA-Mafia War Against Castro and the Assassination of JFK*.

79 Edward T. Haslam, *Dr. Mary's Monkey* (Walterville, OR: TrineDay, 2007), p. 341.

80 Ibid. p. 345.

81 Lawrence, *Were We Controlled?*, pp. 66–67.

82 Jim Keith, *Mass Control: Engineering Human Consciousness* (Lilburn, GA: IllumiNet Press, 1999), p. 79.

83 Armen Victorian, "Mind Controllers," Wanttoknow.info/mindcontrollers10pg (accessed October 3, 2018).

84 Haslam, *Dr. Mary's Monkey*, pp. 343–44.

85 Steve Erickson, *These Dreams of You* (New York: Europa Editions, 2012), p. 186.

86 *The Mindscape of Alan Moore* (DVD, The Disinformation Company, 2005).

87 Marrs, *Crossfire*, p. 298.

88 Warren, *Keep Watching the Skies!*, p. 559.

89 James Joyce, *Finnegans Wake* (New York: Viking, 1968 [1939]), p. 263.

90 Louis Pauwels and Jacques Bergier, *The Morning of the Magicians* (New York: Avon Books, 1968), p. 73.

91 Ray Bradbury, *A Graveyard for Lunatics* (New York: Alfred A. Knopf, 1990), p. 283.

Chapter 4 One Chants Out Between Two Worlds

1 For those of you with a penchant for tracking dizzying connections among disparate subjects, it's interesting to note that Richard Carlson reportedly

dated a struggling young actress named Elizabeth Short only a few months before she was murdered in January of 1947 by the self-named serial killer, "the Black Dahlia Avenger." According to John Gilmore's 1994 book, *Severed: The True Story of the Black Dahlia Murder*, Carlson claimed he had given Short a charm bracelet while driving her home one night. Lauretta Ruiz, Short's drama coach, said, "I was trying to convince Richard to do [a] play—he was very attractive, and an excellent young actor. We met in a restaurant once, and Elizabeth and another young actor were with me. Richard showed up and said he had met Beth before. He was standing politely as we slipped into the booth, and he had recognized Beth immediately. But he seemed unsettled. Beth asked him if he remembered the bracelet, and she said she still had it. I had no way of knowing that they'd met before, but I sensed something out of the ordinary had gone on between them. To this day I can't imagine what it might've been" (p. 89). This odd connection later inspired Alex Gildze's poem entitled "Richard Carlson Gives Elizabeth Short a Charm Bracelet." On YouTube, you can see a video of Gildzen reading his poem at a soiree in Cleveland, Ohio on May 9, 2009: <https://www.youtube.com/watch?v=wKtM2UdzWvk>.

2 *The Universe According to Universal* (prod. David J. Skal), *It Came from Outer Space* (Blu-ray, Universal Pictures, 2017).

3 George Pendle, *Strange Angel* (New York: Harcourt Books, 2006), pp. 126–27.

4 Mike Bara and Richard C. Hoagland, *Dark Mission: The Secret History of NASA* (Los Angeles: Feral House, 2007), pp. 229–30.

5 *The Universe According to Universal* (prod. David J. Skal), *It Came from Outer Space* (Blu-ray, Universal Pictures, 2017).

6 Jacques Vallee, *Messengers of Deception: UFO Contacts and Cults* (Brisbane, Australia: Daily Grail Publishing, 2008 [1979]), p. 12.

7 George Adamski and Desmond Leslie, *Flying Saucers Have Landed* (New York: The British Book Centre, 1953), p. 177.

8 Ibid. p. 176.

9 Ibid.

10 According to the late James Shelby Downward, the location of Palomar Mountain might very well be a connecting point between the respective avocations of Jack Parsons and George Adamski. In his posthumous book, *Stalking the Great Whore* (written in the 1970s but not published until 2023), Downard writes, "The Mount Palomar Astrophysical Observatory, built by the California Institute of Technology (Cal Tech), operates a 200-inch telescope at Mount Palomar in northern San Diego County. Cal Tech, located in Pasadena, California, was the base of operations of rocket scientist Jack Parsons, who became the High Priest of the California chapter of Aleister Crowley's OTO. Prior to Parsons' involvement with the group, they were guided in their 'illuminism' by one Wilfred T. Smith, who later 'passed the torch' to Parsons. Prior to the installation of the 200-inch telescope, Smith had traveled to the remote woods of Palomar where he and his acolytes erected a stone temple near the future site of the telescope. OTO members believed that Palomar was the sexual chakra of the Earth and Parsons later traveled back and forth between Palomar and his sex magic mansion in Pasadena" (p. 216).

11 *Tim Burton Sits Down With Ray Harryhausen* (prod. John Paul Rosas), *Earth vs. the Flying Saucers* (DVD, Columbia Pictures, 2008).

12 Tom Weaver, *Universal Terrors, 1951–*

1955 (Jefferson, North Carolina: McFarland, 2017), pp. 118–19.

13 Pendle, *Strange Angel*, p. 8.

14 Ibid. p. 10.

15 Ray Bradbury, *It Came from Outer Space* (Colorado Springs, CO: Gauntlet Press, 2004), p. 208.

16 Kenneth Grant, *Hecate's Fountain* (London: Skoob Books, 1992), pp. 21–24.

17 Weaver, *Universal Terrors, 1951–1955*, p. 99.

18 Mark Frost, *The Secret History of Twin Peaks* (New York: Flatiron Books, 2016), pp. 249–50.

19 Ibid. p. 249.

20 George C. Andrews, *Extra-terrestrial Friends and Foes* (Lilburn: IllumiNet Press, 1993), pp. 116–17.

21 Frost, *The Secret History of Twin Peaks*, p. 260.

22 Pendle, *Strange Angel*, pp. 262–63.

23 Spencer Kansa, *Wormwood Star: The Magickal Life of Marjorie Cameron* (Oxford: Mandrake, 2014), p. 77.

24 Ibid. p. 80.

25 Grant, *Hecate's Fountain*, p. 29.

26 According to Kenneth Grant's *Hecate's Fountain*, "Seven is the number of the Goddess, and the Sphere ascribed to Venus on the Sephirotic Tree" (p. 21).

27 Weaver, *Universal Terrors, 1951–1955*, p. 123.

28 John Carter, *Sex and Rockets: The Occult World of Jack Parsons* (Port Townsend, WA: Feral House, 1999), p. 60.

29 George Pendle, "The Occult Rocket Scientist Who Conjured Spirits with L. Ron Hubbard," *Vice*, January 2, 2015 (website accessed January 24, 2020).

30 These connections go far deeper than just Parsons alone. Former NASA consultant and CBS News advisor Richard C. Hoagland, in collaboration with Boeing engineer Mike Bara, explore these little known connections at great length in their aforementioned book, *Dark Mission: The Secret History of NASA*.

Chapter 5
The Man From Planet X

1 Tom Weaver, Michael Brunas, John Brunas, *Universal Horrors: The Studio's Classic Films, 1931–1946* Second Edition (Jefferson, NC: McFarland, 2007), p. 87.

2 Ibid. p. 94.

3 Burl Lampert, Email to Robert Guffey, March 24, 2009.

4 Peter Bogdanovich, *Who the Devil Made It* (New York: Knopf, 1997), p. 558.

5 Charles Berlitz and William Moore, *The Roswell Incident* (New York: Pocket Books, 1997), pp. 65–66.

6 George Adamski, *Flying Saucers Farewell* (New York: Abelard-Schuman, 1961), p. 107.

7 Carl G. Jung, *Flying Saucers: A Modern Myth of Things Seen in the Sky* (New York: Harcourt, Brace and Company, 1959), pp. 162–65.

8 Bill Warren, *Keep Watching the Skies!: American Science Fiction Movies of the Fifties* (Jefferson, NC: McFarland, 1982), p. 44.

9 Col. Philip J. Corso and William J. Birnes, *The Day After Roswell* (New York: Pocket Books, 1997), p. 85.

10 Burl Lampert, Email to Robert Guffey, March 24, 2009.

11 Frank Scully, *Behind the Flying Saucers* (New York: Henry Holt, 1950), p. 22.

12 Ibid.

13 Dept. of "Credit Where Credit Is Due" Dept.: To the best of my knowledge, the poetic metaphor relating the practices of ancient druids to modern Hollywood filmmaking originated with the late conspiracy theorist, Jordan Maxwell, author of *Matrix of Power*.

14 Tom Weaver, *Interviews with B Science Fiction and Horror Movie Makers* (Jefferson, NC: McFarland, 1988), p. 275.

15 Warren, *Keep Watching the Skies!*, pp. 42–44.

16 Weaver, *Interviews with B Science Fiction and Horror Movie Makers*, p. 280.
17 Ibid. p. 274.
18 Burl Lampert, Email to Robert Guffey, March 24, 2009.
19 Ibid.

Chapter 6
Golden the Film Was —Oh! Oh! Oh!

1 Bruce Rux, *Hollywood vs. the Aliens: The Motion Picture Industry's Participation in UFO Disinformation* (Berkeley: Frog Ltd., 1997), p. 309.
2 Ibid. p. 142.
3 David Alexander, *Star Trek Creator: The Authorized Biography of Gene Roddenberry* (New York: Roc, 1994), p. 139.
4 J. Michael Straczynski, *Becoming Superman: My Journey from Poverty to Hollywood* (HarperVoyager, 2019), p. 307.
5 Ibid. p. 313.
6 Ibid. pp. 313–321.
7 Ibid. pp. 321–322.
8 Ibid. p. 322.
9 Tom Weaver, "Audio Commentary," *The Man from Planet X* (Blu-ray, Shout! Factory, 2017).
10 Rux, *Hollywood vs. the Aliens*, pp. 109–10.
11 Robbie Graham, *Silver Screen Saucers* (Hove, U.K.: White Crow Books, 2015), p. 57.
12 Robert Guffey, *Chameleo: A Strange but True Story of Invisible Spies, Heroin Addiction, and Homeland Security* (New York: OR Books, 2015), p. 207.
13 Daniel J. Reab, *Orwell Subverted: The CIA and the Filming of Animal Farm* (University Park, Pennsylvania: The Pennsylvania State University Press, 2007), pp. 11–19.
14 Graham, *Silver Screen Saucers*, p. 39.
15 David L. Robb, *Operation Hollywood: How the Pentagon Shapes and Censors the Movies* (New York: Prometheus Books, 2004), p. 45.
16 Ibid.
17 "John E. Horton, 87; Movies' Longtime Link to Pentagon," *Los Angeles Times*, June 12, 2006 (website accessed January 24, 2020).
18 Rux, *Hollywood vs. the Aliens*, pp. 167–68.
19 Ibid. p. 257.
20 Ibid. pp. 257–58.
21 Tricia Jenkins, *The CIA in Hollywood: How the Agency Shapes Film and Television* (Austin: University of Texas Press, 2012), pp. 67–68.
22 Ibid. p. 69.
23 William E. Kelly, "The Big Con at Dealey Plaza," *JFKcountercoup*, January 4, 2008 (website accessed January 24, 2020).
24 Cordwainer Smith, *The Best of Cordwainer Smith* (Garden City, New York: Nelson Doubleday, 1975), p. 96.
25 Ibid. p. 94.
26 Ibid. p. 96.
27 Jacobsen, Annie. *Area 51: An Uncensored History of America's Top Secret Military Base* (New York: Little, Brown and Company, 2011), p. 385.
28 What follows is an excerpt from Don Berliner and Stanton T. Friedman's *Crash at Corona*: "It wasn't just the U.S government that recognized the [UFO] crash(es) in New Mexico as an important event. In August 1991 it was revealed in *Rabochaya Tribuna (The Workers' Tribune)* published in Moscow, that no less a figure than Soviet dictator Joseph Stalin took the news to heart back in 1947. The nearly full-page interview with Professor Valery Burdakov, of the Scientific Geoinformation Center of the USSR Academy of Sciences, revealed that Stalin had called in several of his top scientists after the 'sensational news generated by the capture of a "saucer" that purportedly had crashed near Roswell.' These scientists included Sergey Korolyev, designer of the first Soviet military rocket in 1947

and of the launchers that put Sputnik I into space in 1957 and Yuri Gagarin up in 1962. It was he who told Professor Burdakov about Stalin's great interest. Other involved scientists reportedly included M. Tikhonravov, who had been experimenting with liquid-fuel rockets since the early 1930s; Mstislav Keldysh, who worked for Korolyev in 1947 and later became president of the USSR Academy of Sciences; and nuclear physicist Alexandr Topchiyev, who became vice president of the academy. According to Burdakov, Stalin had several women assigned to Korolyev as translators to help him with 'a pile of foreign materials and books' related to the UFO phenomenon, and Burdakov was told that the research had to be done in secrecy. 'Several days later, he was invited to come and see Stalin himself,' Burdakov said. 'Stalin asked him for his opinion and Sergey [Korolyev] replied that, in his view, the UFO is not a weapon of a potential enemy and does not represent any serious danger for the country, but evidently the phenomenon is real.' Korolyev advised Stalin that, when the opportunity arose, the phenomenon should be studied further, and Stalin replied that Korolyev's opinion was similar to those of other specialists who had been presented with this problem. The others are thought to have included Keldysh and Topchiyev. It appears that Stalin may have created [a clandestine] group [...] to learn what it could from the crash activity in New Mexico. And it can be surmised (in the understandable absence of detailed information) that the initial lead could have come from Soviet spies, some of whom are known to have been in New Mexico in the early post-World War II period" (39–40).

29 Greg Bishop, *Project Beta: The Story of Paul Bennewitz, National Security, and the Creation of a Modern UFO Myth* (New York: Paraview Pocket Books, 2005), p. 150.

30 Ibid. p. 83.

31 Mark Pilkington, Email to Robert Guffey, June 9, 2021.

32 "Alex Jones Interviews Dean Haglund," Archive.org, December 1, 2005 (website accessed January 24, 2020).

33 George Hunt Williamson, *The Saucers Speak* (London: Neville Spearman, 1963), p. 72.

34 Ibid. p. 57.

35 Ibid. p. 125.

36 Ibid. p. 145.

37 "Blowing the Whistle on the Government's UFO Cover Up," *UFO Universe Magazine*, May 1991, p. 48.

Chapter 7
Invisible Ghosts

1 Those of you familiar with my 2019 book, *Bela Lugosi and the Monogram Nine* (which I co-wrote with Gary D. Rhodes), will no doubt recognize this chapter. A few years ago, when Gary was reading *Hollywood Haunts the World* as a work-in-progress, he suggested we use this essay in a collaborative book analyzing the nine films Bela Lugosi made for Monogram Studios in the early 1940s. I thought this was a great idea, as no one had ever written a book focusing on that particular cycle of underappreciated films. Since "Invisible Ghosts: The Films of Bela Lugosi as Borderline Surrealism" was first conceived as a key chapter in *Hollywood Haunts the World*, I couldn't imagine this book existing without it. This is why the piece appears in both volumes (in case you were wondering).

2 Gary D. Rhodes, *Lugosi* (Jefferson, NC: McFarland, 1997), p. *xv*.

3 Tom Weaver, *Poverty Row Horrors!: Monogram, PRC and Republic Horror*

Films of the Forties (Jefferson: McFarland, 1993), p. 31.
4 André Breton, *Manifestoes of Surrealism* (Ann Arbor: The University of Michigan Press, 1969), p. 125.
5 Ibid. p. 13–14.
6 H.P. Lovecraft, *Supernatural Horror in Literature* (New York: Dover, 1973 [1927]), p. 30.
7 Breton, *Manifestoes of Surrealism*, p. 15.
8 David Kalat, "Audio Commentary" (prod. David Kalat), *The Strange Woman* (DVD, All Day Entertainment, 2005).
9 Franklin Rosemont, "Lovecraft, Surrealism & Revolution," in Franklin Rosemont (ed.), *Surrealism & Its Popular Accomplices* (San Francisco: City Lights, 1980), p. 17.
10 "Daughter of Edgar Ulmer" (prod. David Kalat), *The Daughter of Dr. Jekyll* (DVD, All Day Entertainment, 2005).
11 Pierre Fournier, "Dare You See It?," *Monsterpalooza*, No. 1, 2011, p. 58.
12 "Deanimated: The Invisible Ghost," *Cinema of the World*, Worldscinema.org (accessed June 25, 2012).
13 Nancy Joyce Peters, "Backyard Bombs and Invisible Rays: Horror Movies on Television," in Franklin Rosemont (ed.), *Surrealism & Its Popular Accomplices* (San Francisco: City Lights, 1980), p. 39–42.

Chapter 8 The Suppressed Science of Dr. Mirakle

1 It's worth noting here that another English biologist, Alfred Russel Wallace, arrived independently at a theory of evolution by natural selection around the same time as Darwin.
2 Tom Weaver, Michael Brunas, John Brunas, *Universal Horrors: The Studio's Classic Films, 1931–1946* Second Edition (Jefferson, NC: McFarland, 2007), p. 55.
3 H.P. Lovecraft, *The Lurking Fear* (New York: Del Rey, 1971), p. 49.
4 Anthony Pearsall, *The Lovecraft Lexicon* (Tempe, AZ: New Falcon, 2005), pp. 238–39.
5 S.T. Joshi, *H.P. Lovecraft: A Life* (West Warwick, RI: Necronomicon Press, 1996), p. 236.
6 H.P. Lovecraft, *The Ancient Track: The Complete Poetical Works of H.P. Lovecraft* (San Francisco: Night Shade Books, 2001), p. 509.
7 Ibid. p. 393.
8 Weaver, Brunas, and Brunas, *Universal Horrors*, p. 52.
9 Ibid. p. 53.
10 Bryan Senn, *Golden Horrors: An Illustrated Critical Filmography, 1931–1939* (Jefferson, NC: McFarland, 1996), pp. 50–1.
11 Thomas Robert Malthus, *An Essay on the Principle of Population*, Sixth Edition (London: John Murray, 1826), Book IV, Chapter V, para. 1. The entire text can be read online at: http://www.econlib.org/library/Malthus/malPlong.html.
12 Charles Darwin, *The Autobiography of Charles Darwin* (London: Collins, 1958), p. 120. The entire text can be read online at: http://darwin-online.org.uk/content/frameset?itemID=F1497&viewtype=text&pageseq=1.
13 Charles Darwin, *The Descent of Man Vol. I* (London: John Murray, 1871), p. 168. The entire text can be read online at: http://darwin-online.org.uk/content/frameset?itemID=F937.1&viewtype=text&pageseq=1.
14 Charles Darwin, *The Life and Letters of Charles Darwin Vol. I* (London: John Murray, 1887), p. 316. The entire text can be read online at: http://darwin-online.org.uk/content/frameset?viewtype=text&itemID=F1452.1&pageseq=1.
15 Weaver, Brunas, and Brunas, *Universal Horrors*, p. 343.
16 Tom Weaver, *Poverty Row Horrors!: Monogram, PRC and Republic Horror Films of the Forties* (Jefferson, NC: McFarland, 1993), p. 172.

17 Bill Warren, *Keep Watching the Skies!: American Science Fiction Movies of the Fifties Vol. I and II* (Jefferson, NC: McFarland, 1997), p. 146.

18 Roger Ebert, Review of *Inherit the Wind* directed by Stanley Kramer, Rogerebert.suntimes.com, January 28, 2006 (accessed September 30, 2018).

Chapter 9
Here Among the Dead

1 For an in-depth analysis of *Macbeth's* Masonic overtones, see Chapter 9 of my book, *Cryptoscatology: Conspiracy Theory as Art Form* (Walterville, OR: TrineDay, 2012).

2 For further examples, see *A Midsummer Night's Dream* (1590) and *The Tempest* (1610), two hermetic allegories that would have been banned by the Catholic Church if Shakespeare had chosen instead to write nonfiction essays about the Gnostic themes embedded at the core of both fictions.

3 Lewis Spence, *An Encyclopedia of Occultism* (New York: Citadel, 1993 [1920]), p. 411.

4 Caspar Tybjerg, "Audio Commentary" (prod. Karen Stetler), *The Phantom Carriage* (DVD, The Criterion Collection, 2011).

5 Stephan A. Hoeller, *Gnosticism: New Light on the Ancient Tradition of Inner Knowing* (Wheaton, IL: Quest Books, 2002), pp. 76–7.

6 Helena P. Blavatsky, *Isis Unveiled Vol. I: Science* (Pasadena, CA: Theosophical University Press, 1988 [1877]).

7 Tybjerg, "Audio Commentary."

8 C.W. Leadbeater, *Ancient Mystic Rites* (Wheaton, IL: The Theosophical Publishing House, 1986 [originally published under the title *Glimpse of Masonic History*, 1926], pp. 114.

9 Selma Lagerlöf, *Thy Soul Shall Bear Witness!* (trans. William Frederick Harvey) (London: Odham's, 1921 [1912]), p. 180.

10 According to Dr Hoeller, an archon is an "inferior cosmic being ruling over and imposing limitations on creation" (*Gnosticism*, p. 257).

11 Hoeller, *Gnosticism*, pp. 17–18.

12 Blavatsky, *Isis Unveiled*, pp. 152–3.

13 C.W. Leadbeater, *Ancient Mystic Rites*, p. 115.

14 Blavatsky, *Isis Unveiled*, p. 157.

15 C.W. Leadbeater, *Chakras: A Monograph* (Wheaton, IL: The Theosophical Publishing House, 1969 [1927]), p. 62.

16 Ibid. p. 63.

17 Lagerlöf, *Thy Soul Shall Bear Witness!*, pp. 128–9.

18 Annie Besant, *A Study in Consciousness* (Wheaton, IL: The Theosophical Publishing House, 1967 [1904]), pp. 62–4.

19 Sigmund Freud, *The Complete Psychological Works of Sigmund Freud Vol. XVII* (London: Hogarth, 1955), p. 241.

20 Tybjerg, "Audio Commentary."

21 Manly P. Hall, *Shadow Forms: A Collection of Occult Stories* (Los Angeles, CA: The Philosophical Research Society, 1979 [1925]), p. 5.

22 Michael Baigent, Richard Leigh and Henry Lincoln, *Holy Blood, Holy Grail* (New York: Dell, 1983), p. 131.

Index

Names

Index

Index

Titles

Page numbers in **bold** denote illustrations

Index

About the Author

ROBERT GUFFEY IS a lecturer in the Department of English at California State University, Long Beach. His most recent books include *The Expectant Mother Disinformation Handbook* (Madness Heart Press, 2024), *Cryptopolis & Other Stories* (Lethe Press, 2024), the Rondo Award-nominated novel *Dead Monkey Rum* (Planet Bizarro Press, 2023), which master painter Robert Williams praised as "a mental gymnasium" and award-winning filmmaker Irek Dobrowolski described as "addictive like a heavy drug," the Wonderland Award-nominated collection *Widow of the Amputation and Other Weird Crimes* (Eraserhead Press, 2021), the Rondo Award-nominated novel *Bela Lugosi's Dead* (Crossroad Press, 2021), and *Operation Mindfuck: QAnon & the Cult of Donald Trump* (OR Books, 2022), which Alan Moore described as "jaw-dropping and essential." Guffey's previous books include the darkly satirical, apocalyptic novel *Until the Last Dog Dies* (Night Shade/Skyhorse, 2017), which award-winning novelist Adam-Troy Castro called "one of the great books of the year," the journalistic memoir *Chameleo: A Strange but True Story of Invisible Spies, Heroin Addiction, and Homeland Security* (OR Books, 2015), which *Flavorwire* called, "By many miles, the weirdest and funniest book of [the year]," the novella collection *Spies & Saucers* (PS Publishing, 2014), and *Cryptoscatology: Conspiracy Theory as Art Form* (TrineDay, 2012). A graduate of the famed Clarion Writers Workshop in Seattle, he has written for numerous publications, among them *The Believer, The Evergreen Review, The Los Angeles Review of Books, The Mailer Review, Phantom Drift, Postscripts, Rosebud, Salon,* and *TOR.com*. He lives in Long Beach, California with his wife and daughter. His website is Cryptoscatology.com.

Acknowledgements

Buddy Barnett, Stephen R. Bissette, Larry Blamire, Catherine Bottolfson McCallum, the late Walter Bowart, Olaf Brill, the late Roland Bush, Mario Camantigue, Michael Copner, Chris Doyle, Adam Gorightly, Joe & Karen Guffey, Melissa Guffey, Olivia Guffey, the late David Hartwell, Stephan A. Hoeller, Mitch Horowitz, David Jones, David Kerekes, Randy Koppang, Burl Lampert, the late Donna Lucas, Tim Lucas, Kevin J. Maroney, Roger Navarro, Ben Ohmart, Mark Pilkington, George Porcari, Gary D. Rhodes, the late Richard Schowengerdt, Robert Singer, and Damien Watts